# ELLIPSIS AND NONSENTENTIAL SPEECH

Studies in Linguistics and Philosophy

Volume 81

# ELLIPSIS AND NONSENTENTIAL SPEECH

edited by

REINALDO ELUGARDO

*The University of Oklahoma,*
*Norman, U.S.A.*

and

ROBERT J. STAINTON

*University of Western Ontario,*
*London, Canada*

Springer

A C.I.P. Catalogue record for this book is available from the Library of Congress.

ISBN-10 1-4020-2299-9 (HB) Springer Dordrecht, Berlin, Heidelberg, New York
ISBN-13 978-1-4020-2299-9 (HB) Springer Dordrecht, Berlin, Heidelberg, New York
ISBN-10 1-4020-2301-4 (e-book) Springer Dordrecht, Berlin, Heidelberg, New York
ISBN-13 978-1-4020-2301-9 (e-book) Springer Dordrecht, Berlin, Heidelberg, New York

Published by Springer
P.O. Box 17, 3300 AA Dordrecht, The Netherlands.

*Printed on acid-free paper*



Printed in the Netherlands.

We dedicate our
work on this volume
to our families,
with much love.

RE and RS

# TABLE OF CONTENTS

REINALDO ELUGARDO AND ROBERT J. STAINTON

# INTRODUCTION

The papers in this volume address two main topics:

Q1: What is the nature, and especially the scope, of ellipsis in natural language?
Q2: What are the linguistic/philosophical implications of what one takes the nature/scope of ellipsis to be?

As will emerge below, each of these main topics includes a large sub-part that deals specifically with nonsentential speech. Within the first main topic, Q1, there arises the sub-issue of whether nonsentential speech falls within the scope of ellipsis or not; within the second main topic, Q2, there arises the sub-issue of what linguistic/philosophical implications follow, if nonsentential speech does/does not count as ellipsis.

## I. THE NATURE AND SCOPE OF ELLIPSIS

### *A. General Issue: How Many Natural Kinds?*

There are many things to which the label 'ellipsis' can be readily applied. But it's quite unclear whether all of them belong in a single natural kind.

To explain, consider a view, assumed in Stainton (2000), Stainton (2004a), and elsewhere. It is the view that there are fundamentally (at least) three very different things that readily get called 'ellipsis', each belonging to a distinct kind. First, there is the very broad phenomenon of a speaker omitting information which the hearer is expected to make use of in interpreting an utterance. Included therein, possibly as a special case, is the use of an abbreviated form of speech, when one could have used a more explicit expression. (See Neale (2000) and Sellars (1954) for more on this idea.) To take one example, when Rob says 'Pass the book', he does not explicitly say to whom it should be passed, or when exactly; nor does he specify linguistically precisely which book he wants. Still, the speech act can easily be more specific than what these words taken alone suggest. One might think of this kind of omission as "pragmatic ellipsis".

Second, there is the phenomenon familiar from theoretical syntax, in which certain structures are present at some "deep" level of representation, but are not pronounced. Examples taken to illustrate this include VP ellipsis, gapping and sluicing:



*R. Elugardo and R. J. Stainton (eds.), Ellipsis and Nonsentential Speech*, 1–26.

1. *VP ellipsis*: Ray eats meat but Rob doesn't [$_{VP}$_____]
2. *Gapping*: Ray loves to slice meat and Rob [$_{V}$_____] to chop vegetables
3. *Sluicing*: Rob doesn't eat meat, but no one knows why [$_{S}$_____]

There are two different ways of spelling out this second variety of ellipsis. One idea is that while we pre-theoretically think of (1) itself as "the sentence", in reality a sentence is better thought of as an ordered pair, such as (4):

4. <[$_{S}$Ray eats meat but Rob doesn't eat meat], *Ray eats meat but Rob doesn't*>

The first element of the pair provides the underlying syntax, which is input into the semantics. The second element indicates how this complex structure is actually pronounced. Other theories have it that there are special null elements, which are never pronounced no matter where they appear, in the syntax of elliptical sentences. That is, instead of ordinary linguistic material being present but unheard, there is extraordinary linguistic material present. For instance, rather than sentence (1) being captured by (4), on this approach it would be better captured by (5):

5. [$_{S}$Ray [$_{I'}$[$_{I}$*pres., sing., 3$^{rd}$person*] [$_{VP}$[$_{V}$eat$_{1}$] meat$_{2}$]] but Rob [$_{I'}$doesn't [$_{VP}\Delta_{1}$ [$_{NP}\Delta_{2}$]]]]

The structure in (5) is pronounced as it is, i.e., with only one overt appearance of 'eat meat', because the two deltas are never pronounced. They do, however, contribute to the content of (5), via what they are co-indexed with: 'eat' and 'meat' respectively. Call the phenomenon of hidden syntactic material, however the hidden parts are theorized, "syntactic ellipsis". (An early "deleted ordinary material" account may be found in Sag (1976). An early "empty element" account can be found in Williams (1977).)

Notice how different this second variety of ellipsis is from what was said about 'Pass the book'. In that case, there was no suggestion of hidden linguistic material — there, the speaker merely left unsaid points which were obvious enough not to need mention. It should be evident that someone who claims that (1)–(3) are syntactically elliptical, employing either of the theories just enumerated, is saying much more than that speakers of these expressions will count upon hearers to fill in omitted information from context. Such a theorist intends to say that there is hidden, covert, syntactic structure in the expression produced. Thus syntactic ellipsis, if it works as suggested above, is a very different beast from pragmatic ellipsis.

A third thing called 'ellipsis', but which Stainton (2004b) insists is not the same as either of the former two, is when an ordinary word or phrase takes on a special conventional meaning. For instance, arguably 'out', as shouted by a baseball umpire, simply has a different context-invariant content than the linguistic particle which appears embedded in 'Steven wrung out the clothes'. 'Out' so used is different from pragmatic ellipsis, because the content conveyed is a feature of English, not just something provided contextually. But it is different from syntactic ellipsis too, because it's highly implausible that the linguistic item which umpires produce has unpronounced syntactic structure. The umpire says a mere word. It has no subject, no verb, no inflection. Not even covert ones. A similar phenomenon appears with conventionalized phrases like 'No shirt, no shoes, no service' — its conventional meaning is a conditional proposition, despite its syntactically nonsentential form. Think too of 'Congratulations' or 'Happy Birthday'.[1] Call this third phenomenon "semantic ellipsis".[2]

Stainton's view, which sharply contrasts pragmatic, syntactic and semantic ellipsis, illustrates the point that things which are called 'ellipsis' may be treated as very different phenomena, i.e., as not constituting a single natural kind at all. And it serves as a departure point for our larger question, Q1: which cases *really do* belong to the same kind, and how many wholly different phenomena are there, which may with good reason be called 'ellipsis'?

Mary Dalrymple's contribution to this volume, "Against Reconstruction in Ellipsis", makes progress on this broad issue of the nature/scope of ellipsis, i.e., of what things fall together as genuine kind-instances. In particular, she argues that "syntactic ellipsis" as introduced above, is not a real phenomenon at all. This is not to say, of course, that VP ellipsis doesn't happen: it's a datum that (1) is well-formed, for example. But Dalrymple rejects the theoretically loaded account of what is going on. Sag (1976) thinks of VP ellipsis and such as deletion of syntactic material, and Fiengo & May (1994) treat it as reconstruction of syntactic material within the ellipsis site. But, suggests Dalrymple, their general approach is wrongheaded. There is, she thinks, no hidden/covert syntactic material in sentences like (6). The syntax of (6) and the like, is precisely what appears on the surface.

6. John saw the flying saucer, and Bill did too

Most of her paper counters familiar arguments in favor of covert syntax, and provides new evidence against reconstruction accounts.

To explain the *content* of (6) and the like, Dalrymple proposes that "the interpretation for a sentence containing ellipsis is provided semantically, on the basis of sentence interpretations and not syntactic structures . . . " (Dalrymple, this volume) In particular, the meaning of 'Bill did too' in (6) is arrived at by solving for a *property* — not a bit of hidden structure, mind you, but a content — which is predicated of John, and which can also be predicated of Bill. (See Dalrymple, Shieber & Pereira (1991) for the details.) Crucially, if Dalrymple is right about how such sentences are interpreted, then the examples of VP ellipsis, gapping and sluicing, which were called above "syntactic ellipsis", might not be *so* fundamentally different from pragmatic ellipsis after all. The latter, recall, was exemplified by (7), where non-linguistic context helped to fill in unspecified information — i.e., about who was to receive which book.

7. Pass the book

The difference, if Dalrymple is correct, would seem to be not a matter of covert structure, but rather of where the unspecified information is coming from, since it is never contributed by an element of structure. In (1)–(3), it comes from within the sentence itself — so an agent can assign a meaning to the type, outside any utterance context. In (7), it must come from the discourse context, so one cannot assign anything more to the type 'Pass the book' than what that surface provides. But "figuring out", on the basis of available information, is at play in both kinds of case. Thus on a Dalrymple-type view, there may be fewer varieties than what Stainton (2000) and Stainton (2004a) had supposed: where Stainton assumes syntactic and pragmatic ellipsis to be *wholly* disparate phenomenon, merely having in common that they are called 'ellipsis', Dalrymple's approach suggests that they are actually both examples of information recovery.[3]

Paul Portner and Raffaella Zanuttini's article, "The Semantics of Nominal Exclamations", also bears on the broad issue of the scope of ellipsis. The authors take nominal exclamations to be good examples of what we above labeled semantic ellipsis. According to them, (8) is not clausal *syntactically speaking*.

8. The strange things he says!

Grammatically, (8) is a noun phrase (more exactly, a DP). Nor is it even syntactically elliptical for something clausal. Syntactically, at every level, what appears here is the very DP that appears embedded in (9):

9. [$_{DP}$The strange things he says] surprise me

Nevertheless, Portner and Zanuttini argue that (8) is semantically different from what appears embedded. The meaning of (8) is of the same semantic type as (10).

10. What strange things he says!

A nominal exclamation, then, despite its genuinely nominal syntax, does not have a typical nominal denotation: it is semantically elliptical — just like 'out' said at the baseball game, or 'Congratulations' sent in an e-mail.

In sum, Stainton has supposed that syntactic, semantic and pragmatic ellipsis are all quite distinct. One author in the present volume at least raises a doubt about the supposed difference: Dalrymple proposes, in effect, that paradigm cases of so-called "syntactic ellipsis" aren't so different, in the imagined way, from the things that Stainton has called "pragmatic ellipsis". (This allows Dalrymple to exorcize certain kinds of hidden structure from the grammar.) Portner and Zanuttini, in contrast, provide reasons for thinking that another part of Stainton's tripartite division is on the right track, since there is a distinct sub-variety among the things pre-theoretically labeled 'ellipsis': semantic ellipsis.

*B. The Specific Issue: Which Kind Does Nonsentential Speech Belong In?*

Let's begin with an example. Suppose Corinne lifts up a letter, and says 'From Spain'. It is agreed on all sides that Corinne may thereby say, of the displayed letter, that it is from Spain. Some theorists take this to be merely pragmatic ellipsis: the speaker means a proposition, but what she produces is a perfectly ordinary prepositional phrase. This has been the view of Ellen Barton, and of the present authors. Others maintain that what Corinne produced was syntactically elliptical, either containing special null elements, or containing ordinary syntactic material which somehow goes unpronounced. Jason Stanley (2000) has suggested this — as has, very recently, Jason Merchant (2003). A major theme of the present volume is the question: Which of these views is correct? Put otherwise, does (apparently) sub-sentential speech fall into the scope of pragmatic, or syntactic ellipsis?[4]

Before considering in detail the various stances on how sub-sentential speech relates to the nature/scope of ellipsis, it will be helpful to do a *prima facie* "compare and contrast". Some of what is suggested immediately below will be questioned by various papers in the volume. But it may help to start with some appearances. Let us begin with (apparent) similarities between sub-sentential speech and paradigm cases of syntactic ellipsis.

### *B.1. Some Apparent Similarities Between Sub-Sentential Speech and Paradigm Syntactic Ellipsis*

First, it's clear that speakers in such cases mean rather more than what is pronounced: what (seems to be) pronounced is a phrase, of semantic type <e, t>, yet the speaker conveys a proposition. Second, what is conveyed is not merely conversationally implicated. Just as a speaker of (1) would *assert* that Rob doesn't eat meat, Corinne asserts of the displayed letter that it is from Spain.

1. Ray eats meat but Rob doesn't

In both cases, it is hard to cancel the proposition meant: to hold up a pen and say 'Purchased in Germany', and then to continue by saying 'Not to say that this thing in my hand was purchased in Germany' would be odd in a way that canceling an implicature is not. And one could not, if it turned out that the pen was known to be purchased in Japan, respond that no lie was committed since nothing was actually said. Thus the speech acts are similar: in both elliptical sentence and sub-sentence use, we have a proposition asserted, despite a phonologically reduced form.

Both paradigm elliptical sentences and sub-sentences have complex meaning properties as well. Both can be ambiguous, stand in entailment relations, admit of subtle semantic contrasts, etc., as the following examples attest:

11. Two packs of cigarettes and a case of beer from Brazil [Can be used to issue an ambiguous order: Do the cigarettes need to be from Brazil to satisfy it?]
12. A case of beer from Brazil [Can be used to issue an order logically entailed by that made using (11)]
13. A case of gin from Brazil [Subtle semantic contrast with the order that would be made with (12), introduced systematically by changing just one word]

Beyond these speech act and semantic similarities, there are grammatical similarities too. Sub-sentences are subject to grammatical constraints, just as syntactically elliptical sentences are. If Rob points at a small dog and says (14), this is grammatically ill-formed in Spanish — because of the gender mismatch between the masculine nominal 'perro' ("dog") and the feminine indefinite article ('una') and modifier ('chica'). The phrase in (14) is ungrammatical just as the full sentence 'Hay una perro chica' ("There is a small dog") is.

14. * Una perro chica<br>A-*fem* dog small-*fem*<br>"A small dog"

In sum, just as syntactic ellipsis is not some kind of speech error, neither is sub-sentential speech. Both reflect linguistic competence. Indeed, the grammar of sub-sentences recursively generates an unlimited number of in principle useable expressions — just as there exists a potential infinity of syntactically elliptical sentences.

Finally, because both sub-sentential speech and syntactically elliptical speech derive from the specifically linguistic syntactic-semantic competence, it is unsurprising that this shared competence can be damaged by trauma, illness, or what have you, producing damage to both kinds of speech. If, as in a well-attested aphasia, a speaker loses the ability to produce vegetable words, say, she won't be able to make an assertion either with 'That is an awfully ripe tomato' or with 'An awfully ripe tomato'.

This cluster of similarities — pragmatic, semantic, syntactic and psychological — is part of what motivates some theorists to assimilate (apparently) sub-sentential speech to syntactic ellipsis. The idea, applied to an example, is that 'Purchased in Germany' has hidden syntactic material in just the way 'Ray eats meat but Rob doesn't' (supposedly) contains an unpronounced verbal element. In particular, such theorists are wont to deny that 'Purchased in Germany' actually *is* sub-sentential. It is, say such theorists, only apparently so — the appearances coming from the sound heard. What is really produced is either (15) or (16), depending upon how one treats paradigm cases of syntactic ellipsis. Both of these, notice, are syntactically sentences.[5]

15. <[$_{S}$[This [was [purchased in Germany]]]], *purchased in Germany*>
16. [$_{S}$[Δ [Δ[purchased in Germany]]]]

Whether such an assimilation is the right approach is precisely one of the key issues of this volume: it is Q1, applied to the special case of nonsentential speech versus VP ellipsis and the like. Before we try to answer Q1 directly, however, let us continue with the "compare and contrast", highlighting some seeming differences between (apparently) sub-sentential speech and paradigm cases of syntactic ellipsis, like VP ellipsis and sluicing.

### *B.2 Some Apparent Differences Between Sub-Sentential Speech and Paradigm Syntactic Ellipsis*

Starting with pragmatic differences, the discourse contexts in which VP ellipsis and sluicing may occur freely and without awkwardness are far more restrictive. Subject to some important caveats, the details of which are discussed in Stainton (2004b), VP ellipsis and the like (generally) need to be licensed by appropriately similar prior linguistic material. In contrast, sub-sentences (or what appear to be sub-sentences) seem to be far more easily licensed by features of the world. To draw an analogy familiar at least since Hankamer & Sag (1976), VP ellipsis is like anaphora of the kind one finds with 'himself' and 'each other', which must be controlled by an element of structure; whereas sub-sentence use is more like the use of deictic pronouns such as 'it', 'that' or 'she', easily controlled by some non-linguistic entity. Sub-sentence use, like the use of a deictic, is odd when it is unclear what object or property is being spoken about. For example, both (17) and (18) would be equally odd where no dress (or anything that could be taken as being a dress) is salient in the discourse context, and both would be equally false if said of something that is mistakenly taken to be a dress, e.g., a kilt.

17. Nice dress!
18. That is a nice dress

However, either kind of expression can occur *without appropriate prior discourse*. In contrast, (19) sounds awkward, and occurs less easily if there's no appropriate linguistic antecedent, even when a nice dress is salient:

19. Mary's is too

This isn't to say that (19) can never be spoken without a linguistic antecedent. As numerous authors have stressed — most recently, Stanley (2000) and Merchant (2003) — there are ways of rendering (19) felicitous without prior talk. But there remains a difference in pragmatic markedness, of a piece with the use of anaphoric 'so', or 'each other' or 'herself' without prior appropriate discourse. To use the jargon of Hankamer and Sag (1976), it is harder, though not impossible, to "pragmatically control" VP ellipsis and sluicing. In contrast, pragmatic control of sub-sentences is perfectly straightforward.

Another pragmatic difference concerns the various non-communicative uses of sub-sentences versus paradigm cases of sentential ellipsis. Ordinary words and phrases can be used in isolation in quite different ways than sentences (typically) can. Words and phrases appear unembedded on labels and business cards, in shopping lists and dictionaries, as book titles, and so on. And, so occurring, they are not used to state anything. Indeed, they don't encode propositions at all. To take an example, the very phrase 'Ripe bananas' can be uttered while pointing at some fruit, possibly to teach someone what bananas look like when ripe. This is a propositional use. But this phrase could also be the title of a book, or it could appear on a shopping list, where it would not encode any proposition. (Granted, it may be that a proposition can be gleaned from this phrase, say, appearing on a shopping list; but this is not to say that 'Ripe bananas' on the list *itself* expresses a proposition. That token doesn't express a proposition.) So, unlike VP ellipsis constructions and the like, the locutionary content of a sub-sentence token — even in isolation — is not inevitably propositional. There is a further semantic difference as well.[6] It is typically thought that full sentences are marked with illocutionary force: declaratives are marked as being "used to assert", interrogatives are marked as being "used to ask", and so forth. We take this to be a difference in content between sentence categories. But there is a still sharper difference in content between (most) nonsentences and sentences: the former are not marked with illocutionary force at all (with the exception of special conventionalized ones such as 'Out!', 'No shirt, no shoes, no service', and such). To take one example, the bare phrase 'Both hands' is not itself marked, in its overt syntax, as being order-prone or assertion-prone, though it can be used to perform either kind of speech act, given the right conversational situation.[7]

This last point about pragmatic differences leads to some reflections about the syntax and semantics of sub-sentences. In paradigm cases of ellipsis, there is something in the structure itself which "calls out" for contextual completion; that is, there is an (unpronounced) element of the structure, or anyway an aspect of the expression's semantics, which linguistically drives the search for "saturation" to full propositionality. (See Recanati (2002) for illuminating discussion of the different ways that a linguistic item can drive this search.) For example, it's a context-invariant, speaker-independent feature of 'does too' that it triggers the need for a structure or content to fill in — just as it is a context-invariant, speaker-independent feature of 'that' that it triggers the need for contextual slot-filling. In the case of 'does too', either there is hidden ordinary material that needs to get copied in, or there is an unpronounced anaphoric "delta" that needs to be linked to prior material. At the very least, if one follows Dalrymple, the *content* of 'does too' requires completion. But in any case, structure/content drives the search for missing material. Something *in* the syntactic structure, some item in it, or some meaning feature of it, does the work. In contrast, if 'Ripe bananas', that very phrase, is what is used in sub-sentential assertion, then it cannot be the content or the form of that phrase which triggers the hearer to seek out a proposition-meant,[8] since this same structure and content occurs in grocery lists, where no such search is triggered. Indeed, that very structure appears embedded in sentences, and it surely does not there "call out for" completion. (Put another way, genuine sub-sentences do not express propositional characters, functions from context to propositions — for if they did, then barring an implausible lexicalized ambiguity, a proposition is presumably what they would always express in context, whether used in isolation or embedded. In which case, what drives the search cannot be the propositional character of the expression, but instead must be something about the speaker's aims.)

This semantic feature brings with it a psychological difference, at least according to some authors, which has to do with how much of the message conveyed is "decoded", using the language faculty itself. If sub-sentences do not mean propositions, even once all grammatically-driven saturation has taken place, then the computation of the proposition-meant must be performed outside the language faculty. This is precisely the view of Ellen Barton (1990) and of the present authors. Understanding a sub-sentence is as much a pragmatic affair as understanding conversational implicature or sarcasm: neither is carried out by the language faculty itself.

One final difference, again psychological, derives from the kind of structure being processed. Nonsentences are not headed by INFL — this is precisely what makes them nonsentential — and they do not in general even contain inflectional markers (i.e., tense, agreement).[9] As a result, one would predict that language users who have deficits specific to INFL should have trouble with sentence processing, including the processing of elliptical sentences, but should have little or no trouble with nonsentences. This differential pattern is indeed attested in aphasia, whether congenital or induced. (See Elugardo & Stainton (2003) for discussion and references.)

### *B.3. On The Reality of Sub-Sentential Speech*

This completes our survey of *prima facie* similarities and differences. The question now is, are the differences real and deep? In particular, are they real, and deep enough, that we have two kinds of phenomenon here, merely sharing the label 'ellipsis'? Two papers in this volume address directly the issue of whether (apparently) sub-sentential speech really belongs in the same kind as VP ellipsis and such. Peter Ludlow's paper "A

Note on Alleged Cases of Nonsentential Assertion" defends the more traditional take, which treats what we call 'sub-sentences' as sentence fragments. He does this partly by noting "fragments" which seem only to be generable inside sentences. He draws attention to apparently transformed examples like the passive (20), the 'tough'-moved (21), the Q-floated (22), and the idiom-chunk containing (23).

20. Hood sunk
21. Tough watch
22. All in the garden
23. Close tabs

Since these transformations only apply to sentences, it seems that (20)–(23) must be sentential after all, at some level. Ludlow also notes cases which contain elements that need to be licensed by something "above", like (24), which contains an anaphor which, it is said, must be bound by a c-commanding antecedent.

24. From myself

Since no c-commanding licenser is present on the surface, and since the structure is well-formed nonetheless, Ludlow suggests that the licensing item must be covert, as in paradigm ellipsis cases. That is, it's well-known that (24) is well-formed as an answer to 'Where did you get those presents?' The usual explanation given is that the thing produced, in response, is actually, at the level of syntax, either (25) or (26), depending upon one's theory of syntactic ellipsis:

25. $[_{S}\ [_{NP}\ \text{I}]_{1}\ [_{I'}\ \textit{agr}\ [_{VP}\ \text{got those presents}\ [_{PP}\ \text{from myself}_{1}\ ]]]]$
26. $[_{S}\ [_{NP}\Delta]_{1}\ [_{I'}\ \textit{agr}\ [_{VP}\Delta\Delta\Delta\ [_{PP}\ \text{from myself}_{1}\ ]]]]$

Ludlow suggests that something of the same kind must be going on when things like (24) appear to be used on their own. Hence, here again, supposed sub-sentential speech collapses into syntactic ellipsis.

Ludlow also argues, on theory-internal grounds, that Minimalism in syntactic theory simply cannot countenance the base generation of words and phrases. He worries, in his Section 8, that if a grammar were allowed to generate (20) through (24), then it would generate anything at all, so that we would lose our grip on what "crashing" (very roughly, not yielding a grammatical structure) would come to. Ludlow writes:

> As the theory is currently constructed, the derivation crashes if it does not at a minimum yield something that is sentential in structure; if that constraint is yanked out of the theory then the theory collapses like a house of cards. Crucially, the theory requires that grammatical elements must be combined and moved (under economy constraints) until a successful derivation is computed. If success could be won for any arbitrary subsentential element, then the theory would be incapable of blocking anything (105)

This is the second part of Ludlow's attack.

In sharp contrast, Barton and Progovac suggest, in "Nonsententials and Minimalism", that Minimalism actually predicts, in a way that other frameworks do not, that sub-sentences *will* be generated. That is because, in Minimalism, structures are built "from the bottom up", and they must not contain superfluous unmotivated structure.

As a result, adding sentential structure to a phrase created from the bottom up, without necessity, is predicted not to happen. Barton and Progovac write:

> Interestingly, the distinction between sentences and phrases is not a significant theoretical problem in the framework we are adopting in this paper, Chomsky's (1989, 1995) Minimalist Program. Given Minimalism, a clause is simply a phrase whose head is I (short for Inflection). Moreover, the derivation of a structure is built bottom up, by merging words and phrases in a binary function . . . Since both phrases and clauses are derived bottom-up through merger, to say that generation must start with a sentence would be problematic in this framework for two reasons. First, it would be contrary to the minimalist considerations of structure building. Second, it would be pure stipulation, given that there is nothing special about sentence/clause in this framework (74).

The authors also deal at length with several concerns about base-generating sub-sentences. Here is one example. In Minimalism, as in prior frameworks, Case features on NPs — or anyway, on NPs that serve as arguments — must be licensed by other elements of structure. Yet such Case marked NPs occur in isolation, according to those who would base generate them. For example, the Korean (27) is fine as an answer to the unspoken question of who bought the book:

27. Yongsu-ka
    Yongsu NOM

So used, it would mean that Yongsu bought the book. If we are to avoid the conclusion that some *hidden* element of structure is licensing Case marking in such cases — which would support a syntactic ellipsis analysis of (27) and related cases –some account must be given of why bare NPs, unembedded, are exceptions to the need for Case checking. Barton and Progovac propose a single principle which accounts for examples like this, their Case Feature Corollary, and they discuss its application to complex cross-linguistic contrasts.

*B.4. A General Overview: Four Stances*

Having introduced some of the key features of both paradigm ellipsis constructions (e.g., VP ellipsis, sluicing) and (apparent) sub-sentences, and having described two competing takes on whether these belong in the same kind or not, we can now identify four stances towards sub-sentences, arising from two distinct poles of opposition. First, there is the pole of opposition between (a) those who think sub-sentence use belongs in the same natural kind as elliptical speech and (b) those who think they do not belong to the same kind. This, of course, bears directly on Q1: it is the issue of the scope of ellipsis when applied to sub-sentences. Second, within groups (a) and (b), there is also a division between those who think sub-sentential speech is worrisome in some way (i.e., it carries some undesirable theoretical consequences), and those who disagree. This, of course, is the issue of implications, Q2. These oppositions actually cross-cut, yielding the four mentioned stances:

A. Elliptical and sub-sentential speech belong to the same kind, hence the latter is not worrisome.
B. Elliptical and sub-sentential speech belong to the same kind, hence the latter is worrisome.

C. Elliptical and sub-sentential speech do not belong to the same kind, hence the latter is not worrisome.
D. Elliptical and sub-sentential speech do not belong to the same kind, hence the latter is worrisome.

Stance A, exemplified by Ludlow's article in this volume, focuses on the similarities canvassed above, and either downplays or outright denies the (supposed) differences. Finding the similarities to be so important, and being antecedently convinced that paradigm elliptical constructions do not introduce theoretical worries about, for instance, the pragmatic determinants of what is asserted or the centrality of truth conditions to semantics (about which more below), the proponent of stance A shrugs off sub-sentential speech as unthreatening. Stance B, whose spirit can be found in Dalrymple's contribution to this volume, shares the focus on similarities. However, the proponent of stance B sees the direction of similarity as going rather in the other direction, as it were: paradigm ellipsis constructions end up being in certain respects more like the use of ordinary words and phrases to assert, ask, order, etc. Thus any worries which sub-sentence use seems to raise — whether in syntax, semantics, pragmatics, or philosophy of language — are raised already by VP ellipsis and the like.

Stance C draws attention to some key difference(s) between sub-sentence use and paradigm ellipsis cases, and goes on to say that because of this difference, or differences, such-and-such worrisome consequences don't actually follow from the genuineness of sub-sentential speech. Tim Kenyon's paper, "Nonsentences, Implicature, and Success in Communication", provides a nice example of this stance. He urges that sub-sentential speech is subject to indeterminacy of propositional content to a far greater extent than fully sentential speech. According to Kenyon nonsentence use is, in this respect, more like conversational implicature, in which it is often difficult or even impossible to identify "the" proposition which the speaker meant. (For instance, what unique and precise proposition did the letter writer mean when, as in Grice's (1975) delightful case, she wrote 'Mr. X's command of English is excellent, and his attendance at tutorials has been regular'? Surely this is a bad question: there is no one proposition meant.) Roughly speaking, Kenyon then goes on to argue that, given this very substantial difference, sub-sentential speech does not in the end pose worries for those who want propositions to get their logical forms from natural language sentences — for, arguably, there aren't propositions at play in sub-sentential speech. (More on this below.) Jason Stanley (2000) makes a similar move, at least with respect to some cases of sub-sentential speech: he says that many examples do not result in genuine speech acts being performed, and this difference with sentential speech makes such uses of sub-sentences unthreatening. That's another example of Stance C.

Lenny Clapp's "On the Interpretation and Performance of Nonsentential Assertion" resists precisely this move. Clapp raises two key concerns. First, Clapp argues, Stanley's criterion for genuinely having truth conditions — i.e., having a "determinate content" — would rule out far too much. Indeterminacy of the kind that Stanley objects to in sub-sentence cases, Clapp argues, is rampant. Great swaths of ordinary talk, never treated as peculiar by ordinary speakers/hearers, would be treated as lacking genuine truth conditions. It would thus turn out that speakers/hearers are very commonly mistaken about whether an utterance had truth conditions, and about what they were. Related to this, Clapp notes that Stanley and others have sought a compositional semantics that applies to *utterances*, not just to expression types: a theory of semantic performance, not just semantic competence. This, thinks Clapp, is a hallmark of Davidson-style truth conditional semantics: the truth theory is intended to interpret not abstract linguistic items, but speakers. But to utilize Stanley's pragmatic strategy of setting aside much sub-sentential talk as not really propositional after all, is precisely to argue that, "despite appearances", occurrences of sub-sentences do not actually express truth conditions. The problem is, the theory is supposed to account for the appearances. Being a performance theory, it is intended to explain how hearers in fact interpret utterances, on-line as it were. Put otherwise, unlike generative syntax, truth conditional semantics is by design not insulated from what speakers and hearers actually do. Clapp sums up the difficulty as follows:

> . . . to the extent that the defender of truth-conditional semantics claims that competent speakers make incorrect judgments concerning the truth conditions of utterances, he raises counterexamples to truth-conditional semantics (124).
>
> This model is a theory of *performance*; it alleges to describe, albeit in very general terms, the process whereby speaker-hearers actually determine the truth conditions of utterances. If this model predicts that speaker-hearers are often, perhaps usually, mistaken in their interpretations, then the model, truth-conditional semantics generally, must be rejected (126).

Finally, Stance D is represented by Barton and Progovac, who think that sub-sentences are syntactically quite different from paradigm cases of syntactic ellipsis, and would add that this poses worries for traditional sentence-only grammars. (See also Botterell's contribution, for another example of this stance.)

We can sum up this section on whether sub-sentence use belongs in the same class as familiar cases of syntactic ellipsis as follows. The pattern which emerges is this: if sub-sentence use is to be worrisome, it must be similar enough to elliptical speech in many respects, to be worth paying attention to; yet also different enough that it cannot simply be assimilated to (otherwise non-worrisome) syntactically elliptical speech. To establish whether this is the case, various authors in this volume argue for the reality of, or hotly dispute, the surface appearances.

Talk of being "worrisome" and "being worth paying attention to" leads naturally to the next theme: implications. We turn to that now.

## II. IMPLICATIONS OF THE SCOPE OF ELLIPSIS

### *A. The General Issue*

As noted at the outset, this volume has two questions as its foci:

- Q1: What is the nature, and especially the scope, of ellipsis in natural language?
- Q2: What are the linguistic/philosophical implications of what one takes the nature/scope of ellipsis to be?

The focal point of the volume in terms of Q2, implications, is very much on the implications of sub-sentential speech. However, there are some implications that arise with respect to the issue of the scope and nature of ellipsis more broadly.

The paper by Dalrymple carries implications for syntax, and for the syntax-semantics interface. If there is no "hidden structure" in paradigm ellipsis constructions, as Dalrymple suggests, then the usual syntax for these is incorrect. That is implication enough. In addition, however, it cannot be the case, on a Dalrymple-type view, that the interpretive possibilities of elliptical sentences is accounted for by "hidden syntax", there being none. So, semantics must do more in these cases than has previously been imagined. For instance, the usual explanation for why sentence (1) means, in part, that Rob doesn't eat meat, is that the second clause either contains the words 'eat meat' at some level, or that this second clause contains an empty element that is anaphoric to the first occurrence of 'eat meat'.

1. Ray eats meat but Rob doesn't

Given what 'eat meat' means, and what anaphoric linking means — viz. sameness of content — either story explains why the second clause has this meaning. But, obviously, this explanation of the meaning of (1) is not available, if Dalrymple is correct.[10] For there is no element of structure at all in the second clause, ordinary or null, which expresses EAT MEAT. Since syntax cannot carry this burden, semantics proper must do so. This is precisely what Dalrymple proposes about paradigm ellipsis constructions: there is a semantic rule, which solves higher order equations ranging over *properties* (rather than natural language syntax), which does the work of assigning to (1) the meaning that *Ray eats meat but Rob doesn't eat meat*. Thus the resulting shift in where to draw the syntax/semantics boundary.

Dalrymple's view also has implications for an on-going debate about the semantics/pragmatics boundary. Since this issue crops up in several papers in this volume, and is the focus of Emma Borg's contribution ("Saying What You Mean"), we will discuss it at some length here. An unarticulated constituent is a constituent of the proposition expressed by an utterance, for which there is no corresponding constituent of the expression uttered, neither at the surface nor at any deeper level. The now classic example of this phenomenon is John Perry's (1986) 'It's raining', in which the proposition (often) expressed by the utterer contains a place, though (so it seems) there is no "slot" for location (at any level) in the sentence. Other familiar examples include responding 'I've had breakfast' to 'Are you hungry?', in which the proposition asserted makes reference to the day of speaking, though the sentence contains no "slot" for this, or Robyn Carston's (1988) 'Jane didn't get enough credits and can't continue', where the proposition expressed is that *Jane cannot continue university study*, though there is no element of the sentence that contributes this. (See Emma Borg and Lenny Clapp's papers, and Recanati (2002), for still more cases.)

It has been controversial whether there really are unarticulated constituents. Some theorists have denied that there are, by urging that there is more "hidden material" in the syntax than what has been supposed. Stanley (2000) and Stanley and Szabo (2000) take this approach. Others have denied that the proposition expressed does actually go beyond what the surface form suggests, so that there is no need for such hidden syntax. This can be done by simultaneously appealing to a more liberal notion of what the "proposition expressed" can be (so that, for instance, *that it is raining* or *that Jane can't continue* tout court can count as such), and by stressing the contrast between what is conveyed and what is strictly and literally expressed by the utterance. Herman Cappelen and Ernie Lepore, in series of papers (Cappelen & Lepore (2002), Cappelen and Lepore (2003)), have explored just this two-pronged strategy. Emma Borg pursues it further in her contribution to this volume. Crucially, however, if Dalrymple is right, then unarticulated constituents are absolutely ubiquitous because every utterance of a VP ellipsis construction will provide an example. On her sort of view, though the proposition expressed by an utterance of (6), 'John saw the flying saucer and Bill did too', contains two occurrences of the relational property *see the flying saucer*, the sentence produced contains only one occurrence of a syntactic constituent corresponding to this content. At every level. (And, one feels, "the proposition expressed" by the second clause can't be *that Bill did too*, on pain of utterly trivializing that notion.)

To illustrate the point, consider the usual take on paradigm syntactic ellipsis constructions, VP ellipsis or otherwise. It is exemplified, as Borg notes, by the standard treatment of (28) and (29):

28. A: Has Bill gone? B: Yes, he has.
29. A: Whose dog is that? B: It's Bill's.

As Borg writes: "In both of these cases, B's utterance appears to express a proposition containing a constituent not found at the vocalised, surface form level. However, because the additional material *is* present in the immediate linguistic environment of the utterance, and can be simply recovered from here, it is often assumed that the unvocalised material can be treated as a genuine constituent of the sentence B produces. The material is present at the syntactic level, it is suggested, but elided at the surface level" (239). But it is just this last step that Dalrymple's work calls into question; and if (28) and (29) *are* cases of unarticulated constituents, then the aim of avoiding them is pretty much doomed from the start: if Darlymple is on the right track, attempts to avoid unarticulated constituents in 'It's raining' and 'Jane can't continue' seem like courageous battles in a war already lost. On the other hand, if the Sag or Williams account of ellipsis is correct after all, then there are no unarticulated constituents in such cases — every element of the proposition expressed will correspond to either an ordinary (but possibly unpronounced) bit of syntax, or it will correspond to an (always unpronounced) "empty element".

In addition, Marga Reimer's paper, "The Ellipsis Account of Fiction-Talk", highlights the importance of Q1, and in particular of contrasting the various notions of 'ellipsis'. As she explains, both David Lewis (1978) and Michael Devitt (1981) have urged that sentences like (30) are actually elliptical. What such a sentence really means, they both suggest, is explicitly captured only by the paraphrase (31) — because the corresponding pre-clausal material is elided in (30):

30. Sherlock Holmes lives at 221B Baker Street
31. According to the Conan Doyle stories, Sherlock Holmes lives at 221B Baker Street

The advantage of taking (30) to be elliptical is that we can understand how that sentence can be true, even though 'Sherlock Holmes' does not refer to any actual person: sentence (30) can be true in just the way that (31) can be, namely, if the relevant fiction contains or implies the (matrix) sentences in question. Now, several authors — including especially Bach (1987) and Bertolet (1984) — have criticized this means of explaining how this kind of sentence can be true, on the grounds that it is not plausible that the sentence in (30) is itself elliptical. What might be plausible, goes this critique, is merely that *users* of (30) "speak elliptically", such that *they* assert something whose content is close to

(31). But, if that's what is going on, then the *expression* these users produce does not itself express this content, even in the context of a discourse about a fictional story. Undoubtedly, the speaker may convey something true, in uttering (30); but the sentence itself does not thereby become true.

Put in terms of the contrasts drawn at the outset, Lewis and Devitt may be criticized on the grounds that, while it might be plausible that "pragmatic ellipsis" is going on in fiction-talk, it's not especially plausible that either semantic or syntactic ellipsis has occurred. And, it seems, for the sentence in (30) to itself be true, it is not enough that pragmatic ellipsis occurs during discussions of Holmes: sentence (30) must, as a matter of context-invariant semantics, have just the same meaning as (31). It seems, then, that Lewis and Devitt cannot get the result that they want, if uses of (30) don't belong either to the same kind as uses of the syntactically elliptical (1), or to the semantically elliptical (8).

1. Ray eats meat, but Rob doesn't
8. The strange things he says!

Thus does the debate about the nature and scope of ellipsis intersect with issues about fiction-talk.

Reimer's idea, put in present terms, is that fiction sentences themselves, of the sort in question, can be true, when interpreted relative to the appropriate context — even if these unrestricted character-describing sentences are neither syntactically nor semantically elliptical. In particular, she argues that sentence (30), the type that is, does not have to be synonymous with (31) in order for (30) itself to be true. Thus one can grant that uses of (30) do not belong in the same kind as either syntactic or semantic ellipsis, and yet still obtain the desired result that the sentence itself — and not just the proposition which the speaker means — can be true.

### *B. The Specific Issue: Implications of Nonsentential Speech*

Numerous implications have been argued for on the basis of nonsentential speech. Some of these implications will be described at length in this volume: what must be base-generated by syntax, the province of logical form, whether quantifier phrases are meaningful in isolation, what the evidence-base should be for lexical semantics, whether there are unarticulated constituents which pragmatically add to what is asserted, etc. We also note here some implications that are less directly addressed in the papers included in this volume, to further motivate interest in the question of whether that phenomenon is genuine or not. (Moreover, it will be useful to have a wider array of implications in mind, when we revisit the issue of what "genuineness" amounts to at the end. As will emerge, what counts as "genuine" nonsentential speech actually may depend upon what implication one has in mind.)

Numerous implications arise, or seem to, because the supposed "primacy of the sentence" seems to conflict with sub-sentence use. The relevant slogan here is Frege's "context principle": that words only have meaning in the context of a sentence. (Though it's very unclear whether Frege himself is committed to the various ways of implementing his dictum.) In semantics, taking the sentence to be primary has led some to maintain that the sentence is the minimal unit of meaning. This shows up especially clearly in truth-theoretic semantics, in which the meaning-giving theorems are exhausted by statements of the truth conditions of whole sentences. In meta-semantics, the sentence is often taken to be the minimal unit from which meaning flows: sentences are primary because they have meaning fundamentally, goes the idea; words have meaning only in terms of meaning patterns that emerge within sentences. Put in truth-theoretic terms, the idea is that the theorems entailed make the reference axioms (and other base axioms) true, not vice versa: the source of the axioms' correctness is that they generate the right truth theorems. (Semantic holism is sometimes held to follow.) Even assuming that these Frege-inspired doctrines are not *falsified* by the use of sub-sentences, at a minimum it calls for a careful examination of what exactly is being claimed by proponents of sentence primacy, in the guise of the just-presented semantic and meta-semantic doctrines. For, if words and phrases can be used and understood on their own, why think that they do not genuinely have meaning? And why suppose that they must "get" all of their meaning from sentences? It's agreed on all sides that lexical axioms will need to be consistent with the meanings of whole sentences. Equally, it would be a serious methodological mistake to ignore the contribution of words/phrases to complete sentences — which, it seems to us, is the only point Frege himself needs to insist upon. Granting these two points, however, if sub-sentential speech is genuine, shouldn't the axioms also have to be consistent with the unembedded use of words and phrases?

Even more directly, the use of sub-sentences calls into question doctrines about the primacy of the sentence in speech acts. For example, Michael Dummett (1973) once analyzed assertion as, roughly, the production of a declarative sentence in conventionally specified circumstances. This analysis has been challenged, in Stainton (1997), on the grounds that assertions can be made without employing sentences: given the right speech context, and the right speaker's intentions, an assertion can be made with a mere word, or lexically-headed phrase. Thus it may be, if the phenomenon in question is genuine, that sentences are less central both in context-invariant semantics/meta-semantics and in communication.

Andrew Carstairs-McCarthy's contribution to this volume, "The Link Between Sentences and 'Assertion': An Evolutionary Accident?" raises further questions about the hypothesis of the centrality of the sentence. He maintains that "the primacy of the sentence is illusory" (149). In defense of this view, he presents two hypothetical languages wholly lacking the sentence/noun phrase contrast. He argues that users of such languages could still make assertions, despite not having any sentences at all. (Carstairs-McCarthy is at pains to defend against the complaint that his invented languages smuggle in such a syntactico-semantic contrast implicitly.) His radical alternative to taking sentences to be primary to, say, noun phrases, is that the fundamental contrast for semantics is simply that between fitting and failing to fit the world. The sentence/noun phrase distinction actually exists, he thinks, not because of any communicative imperative — or because of any deep ontological divide between events versus facts, or deep epistemological divide between knowledge by description versus by acquaintance — but simply because of an evolutionary accident. (See Carstairs-McCarthy (1999) for a detailed defense of his view.)

A second important implication of sub-sentential speech has to do with the relationship between language and thought. There are at least three related ways of coming at issues in this domain.

First, if a hearer can understand a sub-sentence as conveying a thought, without having to recover any natural language sentence that encodes that thought, then one can, a fortiori, grasp occurrent thoughts that outstrip the linguistic vehicle employed in grasping them. This suggests, in turn, that there can be a gap between the "inner speech" processed by the hearer, and the propositional content she grasps. (This is, in a way, a lesson already taught by externalism about speech act content: if externalists are correct, then frequently it is the speaker/hearer's environmental situation, and not just the linguistic items passing through their heads, which partially determines the thought to be grasped. But the nonsententialist view takes externalism about speech act content one step further, since in sub-sentences cases, there is *nothing whatever* in the linguistic item tokened — no indexical, demonstrative nor even any unpronounced structure — which stands for the environmentally-determined element.)

A second, cognitive-science oriented, way of making the point about language-thought relations and sub-sentence use is to reflect upon informational integration in speech processing. Somehow information from memory, inference, vision, olfaction, and so forth gets integrated with information from the language faculty, in speech comprehension: it is seldom the case that the content decoded just is the content expressed, and the gap between the two generally gets filled by information from these and other such non-linguistic sources. But how exactly does this happen? One model has all of the information being built into the uttered natural language representation somehow — integration happens *in* natural language, e.g. by assigning perceived items as contextualized referents for elements of natural language syntax. Arriving at an interpretation, on this view, is a matter of adding more material/content to the signal spoken, until that enriched signal takes into account all that is necessary to yield the proposition expressed.[11] This first pictures comports well with the idea that thoughts are grasped via contextualized natural language expressions. But defending it typically involves saying that, frequently, there are unheard elements in the linguistic structure produced: if this is your preferred model of information integration, you will be prone to deny the genuineness of nonsentential speech. Thus, the story would go, a hearer who has 'In Italy' consciously run through her mind, as a reply to 'Where does the Pope live?', can still be said to have the occurrent thought THE POPE LIVES IN ITALY via a natural language sentence — namely, via the elliptical (32) or (33).

32. <$[_{S}\ [_{DP}$The Pope$][_{I'}$ *agr* $[_{V}$live$]\ [_{PP}$ in Italy$]]]$, *in Italy*>

33. $[_{S}\ [_{DP}\Delta][_{I'}\ [_{V}\Delta]\ [_{PP}$ in Italy$]]]$

(Recall that italics, in (32), indicates the part which is actually pronounced.) A wholly different model has the linguistic input converted into a not-specific-to-language format, with the same occurring with information from all other sources, so that integration takes place in these non-natural language representations. Integration happens after translation into Mentalese, say. It is the latter picture that seems to fit better with sub-sentence use and comprehension, taken as a genuine phenomenon, since, if genuine, there is often no proposition-expressing natural language representation arrived at. (For extended discussion of these sorts of implications of sub-sentential speech — i.e., about language and thought, and about informational integration — see Elugardo and Stainton (2003).)

Third, the overarching issue of language-thought relations arises with regard to what sub-sentence use entails for the province of logical form. Some theorists are tempted by the idea that only items of natural language even have logical form. Mental states, and "propositions", do not have form *of the right kind*: goes the idea, such things have ideational content but not the kind of syntactic structure necessary for having logical form. (Think of theories which take propositions to be sets of worlds; and theories which consider mental states to be neural nets, or holistic properties of whole agents.) Others hold the less radical view that (a) things other than natural language expressions can have logical forms, but (b) these non-linguistic things can have logical form only derivatively, from the logical forms of natural language expressions: a belief/desire, or a proposition, stands in formal/structural entailment relations only because, say, it is expressed by a natural language sentence which stands in just these relations. Roughly, this "derivative logical form" idea is what Elugardo and Stainton (2001) label 'vernacularism', a view which they object to precisely on the grounds that in sub-sentential speech propositions having logical forms are grasped without access to any natural language sentence which encodes them. Steven Davis, in his paper "Quinean Interpretation and Anti-Vernacularism", considers very carefully what vernacularism amounts to. Specifically, taking Elugardo and Stainton (2001) as his point of departure, Davis clarifies at length what "logical form" and "derivative" might be, and he canvasses different ways of spelling out the idea of "derivative logical form": psychologically/descriptively, but also logically/normatively. Having clarified the general terrain, Davis goes on to take issue with the form of argument presented against vernacularism in Elugardo and Stainton (2001): he finds the evidence presented there to be of the wrong kind. Tim Kenyon, in "Nonsentences, Implicature and Success in Communication", also takes issue with Elugardo and Stainton's arguments against vernacularism. Specifically, he takes our claim that premises can be put forward with sub-sentences — a claim crucial to establishing that something with *logical form* is in fact at play — to assume incorrectly that successful communication entails a single "thing-meant". Put otherwise, Kenyon suggests that our arguments, if they worked, would equally entail the propositional determinacy of conversational implicatures — successful communication, surely. Indeed, it would seem that our (implicit) premises would equally entail, quite incorrectly, that a smirk must express a specific proposition, if it is to be successful communication. But, Kenyon argues, it just isn't the case that implicatures, let alone smirks, involve determinate propositions meant.[12] (Lenny Clapp's paper also discusses the issue of content determinacy at length. See especially his Section 4.) Thus Davis and Kenyon both resist this argument for distancing thought from language.

Speaking of kinds of evidence, and of determinacy, consider a third possible implication of sub-sentential speech. It has to do with the evidence-base for linguistics, and for indeterminacy in attribution of tacit knowledge. It has seemed to many philosophers that lexical meaning must be underdetermined by the utterance of whole sentences. That is because, as emphasized especially by Quine and Putnam in various places, it is possible to hold all whole sentence meanings constant, while assigning quite different contents to their lexical parts. Assuming that the linguist's evidence-base must be restricted to what can be manifested in ordinary speech behavior, however, this threatens not just underdetermination but indeterminacy — given the added premise that sentential speech, including the use of syntactically elliptical sentences and semantic ("one-word") sentences, *exhausts* ordinary speech behavior. But the use of genuine sub-sentences to perform speech acts affords (albeit inconclusive) evidence for choosing between otherwise co-extensive theories. See Stainton (2000) for discussion.

So far, in looking at Q2 as applied specifically to nonsentential speech, we have considered three broadly philosophical implications: the primacy of the sentence, language-thought relations, and the evidence-base for linguistics. We turn now to implications for linguistics proper.

A quite obvious implication, addressed from opposing sides by Peter Ludlow's "A Note on Alleged Cases of Nonsentential Assertion" and Ellen Barton and Ljiljana Progovac's "Nonsententials in Minimalism", has to do with the generative power of the human linguistic competence. If nonsententials are simply "sentence fragments", remnants of full sentences somehow reduced, then natural language grammars do not need to generate them — at least not as underived structures. A grammar for a language can still fundamentally be, as traditionally assumed, a description of the well-formed *sentences* of that language, possibly supplemented by some rules for deleting material from sentences. Since we have addressed this above, we won't say more about it here.

A second, related, implication for linguistics concerns what elements of structure must be assigned a meaning by semantics. If you will, it's the issue of what the semantic theory must generate, not what the syntax must generate. In particular, Andrew Botterell and Alex Barber both consider at length the issue of whether definite descriptions need to be assigned a meaning "in isolation" — that is, whether it is enough to assign meaning to sentences containing definite descriptions, by a syncategorematic rule for 'the F', or whether a meaning must also be generated for 'the F' itself. (Syncategoremata are linguistic items that do not have a meaning relatum, but which nevertheless impact in a regular way upon the meaning of larger expressions. Obvious examples include those prepositions whose semantic impact varies radically according to what complement it takes, as with 'à' in French. Also the logical connectives, like 'if-then'.)

Noting that definite descriptions are sub-sentences, which seem to be usable in isolation in just the way that other sub-sentences can be, Botterell, in his "Knowledge by Acquaintance and Meaning in Isolation", argues that definite descriptions do have "meaning relata", as he puts it. The meaning entry for 'the F', associated with his idea, would look something like this:

34. An expression of the form "the F" stands for a function *h* from the set F and a set G, such that *h* outputs a true proposition for input set G iff F contains exactly one object and every object in F is in G.

Botterell reaches this conclusion as follows: if anyone can grasp or deploy a thing, then that thing must exist; but speakers and hearers can grasp and deploy the meaning in isolation of definite descriptions, since they can assert propositions by uttering definite descriptions unembedded; therefore, the meaning in isolation of the latter must exist. Botterell then considers numerous maneuvers for avoiding this argument — foremost among them, appeal to ellipsis, and denial that a genuine speech act is performed with unembedded definite descriptions.

The implications for linguistics of using definite descriptions unembedded are also discussed at length by Alex Barber, in his "Co-extensive Theories and Unembedded Definite Descriptions". Barber initially takes up two questions: First, what are the implications of this kind of sub-sentential speech for the syntax of definite descriptions? Second, what are the implications for the semantics of definite descriptions? We take these questions in turn.

Barber argues that, despite initial appearances, the unembedded use of definite descriptions actually does not adequately support a restricted quantifier syntax over a binary syntax for quantifier phrases. Put crudely, the contrasting views of syntax are:

35. Binary syntax: $[_S$ The $[_S$ F is G]]
36. Restricted quantifier syntax: $[_S$ $[_{DP}$ The F]$[_{VP}$ is G]]

The problem which Barber identifies is this: arguments for the structure in (36), from the use of things like 'The halibut next to the mackerel' in isolation, make implicit appeal to the generalization that only constituents may be used in isolation. But that generalization, Barber argues, is far too strong. And without it, the use of definite descriptions unembedded cannot be used to argue for (36) over (35). Moreover, Barber notes, theorists who have favored the binary syntax have been interested in syntax in the sense of logical form. Hence it is open to them to maintain that even if the generalization about constituency and use in isolation held, it would at best tell us about surface constituency. Whereas their concern is whether 'the F' is a constituent at the level of logical form. Barber concludes that sub-sentential speech yields inconclusive results, vis-à-vis debates about the syntax of definite descriptions.

Turning to Barber's second question, he considers the idea that a generalized quantifier semantics may be supported by sub-sentential speech of this kind. (As Barber notes, this semantic issue ties back into the syntactic one as well: if 'the F' stands for a generalized quantifier, then this semantics might, in turn, support taking 'the F' to be a syntactic constituent, especially at the level of logical form — roughly on the grounds that the content of 'the F' would be a constituent at the semantic level.) The alternative to the generalized quantifier view, the semantic alternative favored in Russell (1911), is to treat 'the F' syncategorematically, as follows:

37. A sentence of the form, 'The F is G' is true iff there is exactly one F and all Fs are Gs.

In contrast with (34), the generalized quantifier semantics favored by Botterell, this rule does not assign a referent to 'the F'. Indeed, it doesn't provide any semantic rule for this sub-part of the sentence. For precisely this reason, it may seem that (37) can provide no clue as to what the meaning of definite descriptions would be if they were not embedded within a sentence. One might thus infer that (34) is a more adequate semantic clause for definite descriptions because (34) does, but (37) does not, assign a meaning to 'the F' as used in isolation. Hence, it seems (34) is, but (37) is not, compatible with Botterell's datum that we can grasp and deploy the meaning in isolation of definite descriptions. But Barber finds this argument put forward by Stainton as well as by Botterell unpersuasive. According to Barber, it is sufficient for 'the F' to have a denotation — that thing which, as it happens, makes true/false the quantified claim — in order for 'the F' to be used and understood on its own. For instance, 'the halibut next to the mackerel' need only denote, rather than semantically refer to, the intended fish, in order for the hearer to pragmatically search for the proposition meant. (Those unfamiliar with the refer/denote contrast, compare: 'Someone stole my shoes', if true, is made-true by some individual. That person is the denotation of 'someone', in the situation in question. But 'someone' does not semantically refer to said person. Indeed, it does not refer to any individual at all, because it's a quantifier.) Crucially, however, the syncategorematic semantics allows 'the F' to have a denotation.

In sum, with respect to the semantic question, Botterell thinks that the genuineness of sub-sentential speech, including in particular the unembedded use of definite descriptions, demands an addition to linguistic semantics. Phrases of the form 'the F' must, Botterell thinks, be themselves assigned a meaning. It is not enough to syncategorematically assign meanings to all sentences containing descriptions. Barber disagrees. He grants the genuineness of the usage, but thinks that the strictly Russellian syncategorematic semantics can be left untouched regardless, because definite descriptions have denotations that can serve as the departure point for pragmatically arriving at the proposition asserted. If Barber is right, there is no need for one's semantic theory to generate meanings for definite descriptions, in addition to generating meanings for sentences containing definite descriptions.

Before leaving the issue of meaning for definite descriptions, we should highlight yet another apparent implication — for the relationship between semantics and epistemology. Having concluded that definite descriptions do have meaning in isolation, Andrew Botterell turns to the larger philosophical issue of whether Russell himself could have endorsed something like (34) as the meaning rule for 'the F'. That is, as it happens Russell denied that definite descriptions are meaning units — as Botterell nicely puts it, for Russell they no more have meaning-relata than 'and Mary met on' does in (38). But might this have been a minor oversight, easily fixed?

38. Jane and Mary met on Friday

In particular, could Russell have simply agreed that definite descriptions refer to generalized quantifiers, (roughly) functions from sets to propositions, if only this option had occurred to him? Botterell suggests not. Though the generalized quantifier view and Russell's own syncategorematic treatment of 'the F' assign the same truth conditions to whole sentences containing definite descriptions — hence both are acceptable to Russell as far as that goes — the former has the second-order function (from sets to propositions) being a *constituent* of the proposition expressed. The thing is, for Russell, every such constituent must be knowable by acquaintance: "Every proposition which we can understand must be composed wholly of constituents with which we are acquainted" (Russell 1911, 23). Botterell argues that this epistemic constraint on what things can be "part meanings" will not let Russell adopt a generalized quantifier semantics for 'the F', since (as Botterell argues at length) Russell could not, given his foundationalist and empiricist epistemology, have allowed that we can be acquainted with generalized quantifiers. Barber maintains that, as far as sub-sentential speech is concerned, the syncategorematic theory and the generalized quantifier theory are equally viable. Indeed, if anything, the former is pragmatically superior, for reasons explained by Barber. In that case, Russell's "knowledge-by-acquaintance" constraint on the meaning-constituents of sentences of the form, 'The F is G', will not be violated. Russell can therefore avoid Botterell's problem by accepting the syncategorematic view of definite descriptions.

### *C. An Epilogue On Genuineness and Implications*

In the foregoing, we have essentially been discussing, in mutual isolation, the premises of the following simple argument:

*Premise 1*: If nonsentential speech is genuine, then philosophical/linguistic thesis $\Phi$ is true (false).
*Premise 2*: Nonsentential speech is genuine.

For example, Botterell's paper argues for P1, where the $\Phi$s in question are that (a) definite descriptions have meaning in isolation, so that (b) there can be constituents of propositions (namely, generalized quantifiers) that agents can fail to be acquainted with. Barber disagrees about P1, as applied to these cases. He grants that nonsentential speech is genuine, including in particular the unembedded use of definite descriptions. But he remains unconvinced that (a) and (b) follow from this. And, so it seems, Barton and Progovac's paper defends P2, while Ludlow's paper argues against it. In fact, however, treating these premises as mutually independent is actually a simplification. The reason is that what counts as "genuine" varies. We end with this complication.

For some implications, it is enough if words/phrases can be used and understood in isolation: it doesn't actually matter, for those purposes, whether they can be used to communicate propositions. For instance, as far as the scope of syntax goes, even if phrases like (11) and (24) cannot be used assertorically, if they are grammatical at all, and are not derived by simple deletion, then one's grammar surely must account for them.

11. Two packs of cigarettes and a case of beer from Brazil
24. From myself

That we can distinguish between the grammaticality of (11), and the ungrammaticality of 'Cigarettes beer a and', without embedding either in a sentence, already seems to have implications for syntax. Similarly for the scope of semantics. It seems clear that agents can understand words and phrases in isolation: in grocery lists, in dictionaries, on business cards, on posters, and so on. (In particular, they can do this with quantifier phrases and definite descriptions.) This alone seems to suggest that our semantic competence can do more than assign contents to complete sentences.

In contrast, the implications about language-thought relations would seem to require more than the bare grammaticality and interpretability of sub-sentences. For the cases of interest are precisely ones in which a proposition is meant, and understood, even though the linguistic items produced do not encode propositions. What these language-versus-thought implications do *not* require is that the proposition be asserted. It is enough that it be meant or grasped. On the other hand, the thesis of the primacy of the sentence in speech acts requires more than conveying propositions. One can, given the right circumstances, convey a proposition by waving a handkerchief, or by purposely vomiting on someone's expensive fur coat. But this is neither here nor there, with respect to the thesis that genuine full-blown speech acts must be sentential, since one cannot strictly speaking *assert* by either of those means. To falsify the primacy thesis, one does need it to be the case that sub-sentences can be used to make assertions (or to ask questions, issue orders, etc.) And insofar as the primacy of the sentence in semantic and metasemantics is held to derive from the primacy of the sentence in speech acts — a view endorsed by Dummett, for instance — these latter theses too can only be falsified by cases of nonsentential assertion.

So, is the idea that the anti-primacy implications set a higher standard of genuineness than the language-versus-thought implications, which in turn set a higher "genuineness" standard than implying changes for syntax and semantics? Actually, no. The anti-primacy implications are arguably established even if, in making an assertion sub-sententially, speakers have a sentence in mind, and hearers do too. To say that assertions must be sentential is not to say merely that sentences are involved somehow; it's to say that one must *utter* a sentence to make a genuine assertion. In contrast, the language-thought implications — about grasping thoughts, about integrating information, and about non-derivative logical forms for mental states — all require that no sentence was used at all. Stranger still, it's unclear whether problems for sentence primacy and language-thought relations even require that words and phrases be base-generated: it's not how words and phrases get generated, but that they do, and that they are used assertorically or communicatively, which would seem to matter for these two debates. For instance, even if it's the case that the bare phrase 'All in the garden' is generated in a process that at some stage involves a sentential frame, if what speakers produce, and hearers understand, is this very phrase *without any accompanying sentential frame*, then more is grasped in thought than what is encoded linguistically, and assertions are really being made sub-sententially.

In reality, then, there are various aspects of "genuineness" vis-à-vis sub-sentence use:

- Being generated and used at all;
- Being generated directly, not via transformation;
- Being used and understood in isolation, not embedded in any sentential frame;
- Being used unembedded to communicate something propositional;
- Being used unembedded to perform a genuine speech act;
- Being used unembedded, to either convey or even assert a proposition, when no complete sentence can be accessed by the speaker/hearer.

In light of this, one might suppose that the argument form should really be:

*Premise 1**: If nonsentential speech is genuine in respects R, then philosophical/linguistic thesis Φ is true (false).
*Premise 2**: Nonsentential speech is genuine in respects R.

Strictly speaking, that's right. And some authors have taken this to heart. What many authors choose to do instead, however, is to stick with the original P2 — 'Nonsentential speech is genuine' — with 'genuine' interpreted so that it implicitly includes *all* of the aspects noted just above. If that very strong reading of P2 can be established, then that would, of course, be enough for any of the implications. Alternatively, authors who wish to avoid the implications have attempted to argue that the original P2 is false even on the weakest reading of 'genuine'. So that none of the implications follow.[13]

## NOTES

[1] Ray Jackendoff makes a similar point in his discussion of 'Hello', 'Abacadabra', and the like. See Jackendoff (2000), pp. 239–240.

[2] To be sure, all expressions, including sentences, can acquire special conventional meanings. Thus, it might seem that our label, "semantic ellipsis", is just another name for the category of idioms. In which case, one might well wonder if we are making the true but uninteresting point that sentences and sub-sentential expressions can have idiomatic uses. By "semantic ellipsis", we mean something more than just idioms — we also mean to include the idea of one expression being a conventional *abbreviation* for a longer, more

complex, expression. We mention this third category of ellipsis because some have suggested that a case in which a speaker performs a sub-sentential speech-act that has a definite propositional content and a definite illocutionary force, but where the speaker is not using a syntactically elliptical sentence, is really a case in which the speaker is using a sub-sentential expression as "shorthand" for a sentence, cf. Stanley (2000). In Elugardo and Stainton (2004), we argue that those cases are not semantic ellipses in any plausible sense. See also Portner and Zannutini's novel extension of the notion.

3 This isn't to say that Dalrymple must conclude that VP ellipsis is *exactly* like inferring information omitted by the speaker as obvious. To find an unnoticed similarity between two things is not necessarily to reduce one to the other. Indeed, a seeming difference remains: for Dalrymple, there is a special-purpose semantic rule for finding the content of "ellipsis sites"; whereas "obvious information" from context, being thoroughly pragmatic, is presumably not found and deployed by a dedicated language-internal algorithm.

4 A third option, not yet endorsed in print so far as we know, is that 'From Spain' and the like have a special content, despite having ordinary syntax: that is, that 'From Spain' is semantically elliptical in the way that Portner & Zanuttini take 'The strange things he says!' to be. We ignore this option here. See Stainton (1995), however, for critical discussion of this approach.

5 It will be noticed that what goes unpronounced in (15) is not a syntactic constituent. This is a problem, since most theories of ellipsis assume that only constituents may be elided. Jason Merchant (2003) has cogently argued for an alternative underlying structure, within this general framework, which allows the derivation of the sound pattern via the omission of a syntactic constituent. He proposes that the pronounced part, 'Purchased in Germany', is first moved into a focus position, and then the whole clause out of which it was moved goes unpronounced. The source structure is thus something like [[Purchased in Germany]$_1$ [$_s$This was $t_1$]], with the embedded sentence being elided.

6 We don't want to overstate this difference. In particular, we're happy to grant that sentences can be used as names for bands or pubs, or as titles of books. Our point, rather, is about how central and unmarked the non-propositional use of sub-sentences is, as compared to non-propositional uses of complete sentences.

7 One could argue that some sentences do not have their illocutionary force marked either. For instance, 'I will be there' is not marked as promise-prone or prediction-prone. We contend, however, that many simple declarative sentences, e.g., 'Rob was born in 1964', are marked as assertion-prone, whereas very few sub-sentences are so marked. (The exceptions are precisely those cases that are plausibly treated as semantically elliptical, e.g., 'Congratulations'.)

8 Alternatively, if a search is triggered, then the trigger is some contextual feature of the utterance or a use of the bare phrase. For example, suppose you find a slip of paper on your desk with the words 'ripe bananas' written on it, and you then ask the author of those words what she meant by them. Notice that your inquiry is not triggered by some formal or semantic feature of 'ripe bananas' that calls out for some completion, as in the case of 'does too', since there is no such feature: you know, implicitly, that it is a phrase and that it means *ripe bananas*. What you don't know, and what prompts your inquiry, is the author's intended meaning of 'ripe bananas' on that occasion, e.g., whether the author meant to remind you to buy some ripe bananas, to tell you that the bananas you bought yesterday were too ripe, to ask you to add to the list of fruit to buy, etc.

9 The exception, of course, is when a lexically headed phrase contains a sentence as a sub-part, as in 'The book which John bought at auction'. This is a nonsentence, but it contains INFL.

10 A related implication of Dalrymple's take on VP ellipsis is that (1) does not structurally entail that *Rob does not eat meat*. Instead, the whole sentence (1) has this entailment as a matter of lexical semantics, because of what 'does' means in English. That is, (1) entails that *Rob fails to eat meat* in a way not traceable to logical structure, in the same fashion that 'Rob knows that Ray eats meat' entails that *Ray eats meat* by virtue of the lexically marked meaning of 'know'.

11 Though they do not explicitly embrace it, it seems to us that the "integration in natural language" picture fits quite well with recent work by Jeff King & Jason Stanley (forthcoming). Theorists who would link grasping occurrent thoughts quite closely to grasping natural language vehicles for them include Carruthers (1996) and Ludlow (1999).

12 In several papers in this volume, work by one or both of the editors is specifically addressed. As editors, we have not insisted that authors respond to "what we had in mind" in writing, but only to what we actually wrote. We therefore issue the following reminder: a description that appears in this volume labeled as "Elugardo & Stainton's" view should not be taken to imply that it captures what we believed then or believe now.

13 We would like to thank our contributors for their patience and for their comments. We especially would like to acknowledge Alex Barber and Steven Davis for their detailed comments. Thanks also to Catherine Wearing for her corrections and valuable suggestions. The research and writing that went into producing

this project was conducted with the generous funding of our joint Social Sciences and Humanities Research Council Grant. We are grateful to the Council for its continued support. Finally, thanks to Danielle Tennenhouse for proof reading assistance.

## REFERENCES

Bach, K., *Thought and Reference*. Oxford: Clarendon Press. 1987.

Barton, E., *Nonsentential Constituents*. Amsterdam: John Benjamins. 1990.

Bertolet, R., "On A Fictional Ellipsis." *Erkenntnis* 21 (1984): 189–194.

Cappelen, H., and Lepore, E., "Unarticulated Constituents and Hidden Indexicals: An Abuse of Context in Semantics." Forthcoming in M. O'Rourke and C. Washington (eds.), *Essays in Honor of John Perry*. Cambridge, MA: The MIT Press. 2003.

Cappelen, H., and Lepore, E., "Indexicality, Binding, Anaphora and *A Priori* Truth." *Analysis* 62(11) (2002): 271–281.

Carstairs-McCarthy, A., *The Origins of Complex Language: An Inquiry into the Evolutionary Beginnings of Sentences, Syllables, and Truth*. Oxford: Oxford University Press. 1999.

Carston, R., "Implicature, Explicature and Truth-Theoretic Semantics." In R. Kempson (ed.) *Mental Representations*. Cambridge: Cambridge University Press. 1988: 155–181.

Carruthers, P., *Language, Thought and Consciousness*. Cambridge: Cambridge University Press. 1996.

Chomsky, N., *The Minimalist Program*. Cambridge, MA: The MIT Press. 1995.

Chomsky, N., "Some notes on economy of derivation and representation." *MIT Working Papers in Linguistics* 10 (1989): 43–74.

Dalrymple, M., Shieber, S.M., and Pereira, F.C.N., "Ellipsis and higher-order unification." *Linguistics & Philosophy* 14(4) (1991): 399–452.

Devitt, M., *Designation*. Cambridge, MA: The MIT Press. 1981.

Dummett, M., *Frege: Philosophy of Language*. Oxford: Duckworth. 1973.

Elugardo, R., and Stainton, R.J., "Shorthand, Syntactic Ellipsis, and the Pragmatic Determinants of What is Said." *Mind & Language* 19(4) (2004): 442–471.

Elugardo, R., and Stainton, R.J., "Grasping Objects and Contents." In A. Barber (ed.) *The Epistemology of Language*. Oxford: Oxford University Press. 2003: 257–302.

Elugardo, R., and Stainton, R.J., "Logical Form and the Vernacular." *Mind and Language* 16(4) (2001): 393–424.

Fiengo, R., and May, R., *Indices and Identity*. Cambridge, MA: The MIT Press. 1994.

Grice, H.P., "Logic and Conversation." In P. Cole and J. Morgan (eds.) *Syntax and Semantics 3: Speech-Acts*. New York: Academic Press. 1975: 41–58.

Hankamer, J., and Sag, I., "Deep and Surface Anaphora". *Linguistic Inquiry* 7(3) (1976): 391–428.

Jackendoff, R., *Foundations of Language*. Oxford: Oxford University Press. 2000.

King, J., and Stanley, J., "Semantics, Pragmatics, and the Role of Semantic Content." In Z. Szabo (ed.) *Semantics versus Pragmatics*. Oxford: Oxford University Press. 2004: 111–164.

Kripke, S., "Semantic Reference and Speaker Reference." In P.A. French, T.E. Uehling, Jr. and H.K. Wettstein (eds.) *Contemporary Perspectives in the Philosophy of Language*. Minneapolis: University of Minnesota Press. 1977: 6–27.

Lewis, D., "Truth in Fiction." *American Philosophical Quarterly* 15(1) (1978): 37–46.

Ludlow, P., *Semantics, Tense and Time*. Cambridge, MA: The MIT Press. 1999.

Merchant, J., "Fragments and Ellipsis." University of Chicago Manuscript, 2003. Forthcoming in *Linguistics and Philosophy*.

Neale, S., "On Being Explicit: Comments on Stanley and Szabo, and on Bach." *Mind & Language* 15 (2000): 284–294.

Perry, J., "Thought Without Representation." *Proceedings of the Aristotelian Society.* Supplemental Volume LX (1986): 263–283.

Recanati, F., "Unarticulated Constituents." *Linguistics & Philosophy* 25 (2002): 299–345.
Russell, B., "Knowledge by Acquaintance and Knowledge by Description." *Proceedings of the Aristotelian Society* 11. Reprinted in N. Salmon & S. Soames (eds.) (1988) *Propositions and Attitudes*. Oxford: Oxford University Press. 1911.
Sag, I., *Deletion and Logical Form*. Ph.D. Thesis. Massachusetts Institute of Technology, 1976.
Sellars, W., "Presupposing." *The Philosophical Review* 63 (1954): 197–215.
Stainton, R.J., "The Pragmatics of Nonsentences." In L. Horn & G. Ward (eds.) *Handbook of Pragmatics*. Oxford: Blackwell. 2004a: 266–287.
Stainton, R.J., "In Defense of Nonsentential Assertion." In Z. Szabo (ed.) *Semantics vs. Pragmatics*. Oxford: Oxford University Press. 2004b: 383–457.
Stainton, R.J., "The Meaning of 'Sentences'." *Nous* 34 (2000): 441–454.
Stainton, R.J., "Quantifier Phrases, Meaningfulness 'in Isolation', and Ellipsis." *Linguistics & Philosophy* 21 (1998): 311–340.
Stainton, R.J., "What assertion is not." *Philosophical Studies* 85(1) (1997): 57–73.
Stainton, R.J., "Non-Sentential Assertions and Semantic Ellipsis." *Linguistics and Philosophy* 18(3) (1995): 281–296.
Stanley, J., "Context and Logical Form." *Linguistics & Philosophy* 23 (2000): 391–434.
Stanley, J., and Szabo, Z., "On Quantifier Domain Restriction." *Mind & Language* 15 (2000): 219–261.
Williams, E., "Discourse and Logical Form." *Linguistic Inquiry* 8(1) (1977): 101–139.

# PART I

# THE NATURE AND SCOPE OF ELLIPSIS

# A

# HOW MANY VARIETIES?

MARY DALRYMPLE

# AGAINST RECONSTRUCTION IN ELLIPSIS

## PREFACE

This paper was originally written in 1991, and a version was presented at the Annual Meeting of the Linguistic Society of America, Philadelphia, in January 1992. This version of the paper is substantially the same as the original version, although it has been updated to take into account revisions to work that was cited in prepublication form in the original paper as well as to respond to subsequent work that referred to or commented on the original version.

I am grateful to Ash Asudeh, Andy Kehler, and Tracy Holloway King for help with the current version of this paper and to Joan Bresnan, Bob Frank, Mark Gawron, Aaron Halpern, Dan Hardt, Polly Jacobson, Ken Kahn, Lauri Karttunen, Yo Matsumoto, Fernando Pereira, Ivan Sag, Stuart Shieber, Bonnie Webber, and Steve Wechsler for helpful discussion and assistance with earlier versions.

## INTRODUCTION

Analyses of elliptical constructions fall into two general types. According to the first type of analysis, covert syntactic structure is present in the ellipsis site at some level or stage of derivation. For example, the analysis of Sag, 1976 involves deletion of syntactic material in the ellipsis site; other analyses, such as Fiengo and May, 1994, involve reconstruction of syntactic material within the ellipsis site. According to the second type of analysis, in contrast, the interpretation for a sentence containing ellipsis is provided semantically, on the basis of sentence interpretations and not syntactic structures; this view does not rely on the presence of covert syntactic structure in the elided sentence. According to the analysis of Dalrymple et al., 1991, for example, the interpretation of elided material is provided by means of solving a semantic equality.

Certain phenomena seem to indicate that reconstruction analyses — analyses involving the presence of covert syntactic material — are correct; these phenomena involve constraints that are usually taken to be syntactic but that hold even in sentences with ellipsis. We will see that syntactic reconstruction does not, in fact, constitute a viable account of ellipsis, since in some cases there is no syntactic antecedent that provides the appropriate syntactic material for reconstruction in the ellipsis site, while in other cases a reconstruction analysis would require grammatical instances of ellipsis to contain reconstructed syntactic material that is not syntactically well-formed. These facts argue against positing deleted or reconstructed syntactic material in the ellipsis site; instead, the syntactic structure of a sentence containing ellipsis is exactly what appears on the surface.



*R. Elugardo and R. J. Stainton (eds.), Ellipsis and Nonsentential Speech*, 31–55.

The semantic analysis accounts easily for many of the problems encountered by a reconstruction analysis: many examples whose grammaticality is unexpected on a syntactic reconstruction analysis are analyzed correctly and unproblematically on the semantic analysis. The challenge for the semantic analysis is to provide a satisfactory account of certain ungrammatical examples, those which are analyzed on a reconstruction account as binding theory violations. We observe a correlation between the availability or unavailability of a strict reading and the presence of such 'reconstruction' effects, and propose an analysis of the recalcitrant cases by appeal to the meanings of the predicates involved in ellipsis resolution.

## 1. THE PROBLEM

Many analyses of elliptical constructions assume the presence of syntactic structure at some level in the ellipsis site. Consider, for example, the following sentence:

(1) John saw the flying saucer, and Bill did too.

Following the terminology of Dalrymple et al., 1991, we will refer to the phrase containing elided material as the *target* and to the phrase which provides the interpretation for the target as the *source*. Here, the source is the first conjunct, *John saw the flying saucer*; the target is the second conjunct, *Bill did too*.

According to the analysis of Sag, 1976, sentence (1) is transformationally derived from (2):

(2) John saw the flying saucer, and Bill saw the flying saucer too.

The Verb Phrase Deletion transformation deletes the verb phrase of the target on the condition that the interpretation of the target verb phrase is identical (up to alphabetic variance) to the interpretation of the source verb phrase.

Under other analyses, the target contains a fully specified yet unpronounced verb phrase; this is the analysis of Williams, 1977. Under such analyses, the syntactic structure of sentence (1) is:

(3) John [saw [the flying saucer]], and Bill did [Δ [ΔΔΔ]] too.

where Δ represents an unpronounced element. Analyses of this sort differ minimally from deletion analyses: under one analysis, phonological material is present at an early stage of the derivation and is later deleted, while under the other, unpronounced material is present throughout the derivation.

Other analyses also involve copying or reconstruction of syntactic material. For example, Lappin and McCord, 1990 propose an operation which copies syntactic material from the source to the target; the interpretation for the target is provided when the syntactic material copied from the source is reinterpreted in the target.

May, 1985 and Haïk, 1987 propose to copy the syntactic representation of the relevant portion of the source into the elided portion of the target at the level of Logical Form (LF). The analysis of Fiengo and May, 1994 is similar, also involving reconstruction at the level of LF. As May, 1985 notes, LF "represents whatever properties of syntactic form are relevant to semantic interpretation — those aspects of semantic structure that are expressed syntactically." Thus, analyses positing reconstruction at LF also involve the presence of syntactic material in the ellipsis site. At LF, then, the representation of sentence (1) will contain two copies of the (interpretation of the) source VP:

(4) [John [saw the flying saucer]] and [Bill [saw the flying saucer]]

In contrast to analyses of this nature, Dalrymple et al., 1991 provide an analysis of ellipsis according to which the interpretation of an elided constituent depends on a particular relation between the meanings of the source and target clauses; the analysis will be described in Section 5. This analysis provides an interpretation for the elided portion of the target without appealing to the presence of covert syntactic material in the ellipsis site.

Given an analysis such as this one, there is no *a priori* motivation for syntactic copying or reconstruction from the source to the target. That is, if it is possible to provide the interpretation for the target sentence without copying or reconstructing syntactic material from the source to the target, then the null hypothesis would be that no syntactic copying or reconstruction occurs — that the syntax of the elided constituent is exactly what appears on the surface.

However, some facts seem at first glance to indicate that syntactic information from the source does play a role in the target. In particular, certain dependencies involving the ellipsis site and other elements in the target sentence seem to provide evidence that reconstruction in the target of some portion of the syntax of the source is necessary: (1) anaphoric dependencies and (2) long-distance dependencies such as those found in wh-questions and relative clauses. Some constraints on these relations are generally held to be syntactic in nature; if these constraints hold even in target sentences in ellipsis, there would seem to be a need for a covert syntactic representation of the elided portion of the target over which the constraints can hold. In terms of reconstruction theories, the appearance of constraints on long-distance and anaphoric dependencies involving the ellipsis site of elided sentences is taken to indicate that the constraints hold at the level of Logical Form.

In the following, we examine evidence of this sort, showing that reconstruction analyses do not in fact make the correct predictions. We will concentrate for the most part on apparent evidence for reconstruction which comes from anaphoric dependencies. The question of how the phenomena of ellipsis and long-distance dependencies interact syntactically — in particular, whether a syntactically visible trace appears in the ellipsis site — is an important and interesting one, but one which we will not address here; see Haïk 1985; 1987 for a detailed discussion of the interaction of long-distance dependencies and ellipsis, with particular attention to antecedent-contained ellipsis. Haïk provides examples of apparent subjacency violations such as:

(5) Haïk, 1987, p. 511:
*John met everyone that Peter wondered when he could.

We will refer to analyses in which covert syntactic structure is present in the ellipsis site, whether at some level of a transformational derivation or at the level of Logical Form, as *(syntactic) reconstruction analyses*. Section 2 presents evidence involving anaphoric dependencies which seems to support syntactic reconstruction; Section 3 shows that syntactic reconstruction analyses face a number of difficulties in accounting for the full range of ellipsis data and in making predictions as to the grammaticality and ungrammaticality of many examples. Section 4 examines several proposals for ellipsis resolution involving reconstruction, showing that each faces difficulties in addition to the general problems for reconstruction analyses noted in Section 3. Finally, Section 5 discusses the evidence that seems to argue for a syntactic reconstruction analysis, noting a semantic correlation in the data: examples which appear to involve reconstruction effects are exactly those that disallow a strict reading and give rise only to a sloppy reading under ellipsis. We provide a reanalysis and explanation of these cases in terms of the interpretations of the constructions involved.

## 2. EVIDENCE FOR SYNTACTIC RECONSTRUCTION: ANAPHORIC DEPENDENCIES

Sentences like the following are generally taken to be ill-formed because a particular syntactic relation holds between the pronominal and the name *Sue*:

(6) *She$_i$ talked to Sue$_i$.

In this light, consider examples such as the following:

(7) *I talked to Sue$_i$, and she$_i$ did too.

On a reconstruction analysis, the syntactic structure of this sentence would be (at some level):

(8) I talked to Sue$_i$, and she$_i$ talked to Sue$_i$.

If binding constraints are taken to hold at this level, the reason for the ungrammaticality of sentence (7) is clear; in the target, the pronominal and the name *Sue* stand in a relation which is not syntactically permitted. Note that the relation between the overt occurrence of *Sue* in the source and the pronominal *she* in the target could not be the cause of the ungrammaticality of sentence (7); the following sentence is perfectly grammatical:

(9) I talked to Sue$_i$, and she$_i$ talked to Bill.

It is the elided VP in the second conjunct of sentence (7) that is responsible for its ungrammaticality.

## 3. EVIDENCE AGAINST SYNTACTIC RECONSTRUCTION

Although the facts cited above seem to provide clear evidence for syntactic reconstruction analyses, other facts show that the situation is not so clear; there are many cases in which a syntactic reconstruction analysis provides results that are clearly incorrect.

The counterexamples to reconstruction analyses to be presented in this section are varied, each requiring a different sort of modification to a syntactic reconstruction analysis in order to conform with the facts to be presented. These counterexamples seem unconnected, however, only when ellipsis resolution is seen as a syntactic process;

Section 5 shows that when it is seen instead as a semantic process, these cases fail to be problematic, and a unified view is possible.

### *3.1. Lack of a Reconstruction Source*

As pointed out by Sag, 1976, Dalrymple et al., 1991, Kehler, 1995, and others, there is not always a clear syntactic source for the reconstructed VP in cases of ellipsis. Consider the following example:

(10) A lot of this material can be presented in a fairly informal and accessible fashion, and often I do. (from text of Chomsky, 1982, page 41)

Here there is no constituent in the source clause that can serve as the interpretation for the elided VP in the target; what is required is a VP such as [*present this material in a fairly informal and accessible fashion*], which is not a constituent that occurs in the source clause. Example (11), taken from the Associated Press Newswire, is similar:

(11) In March, four fireworks manufacturers asked that the decision be reversed, and on Monday the ICC did. (from text of Rosenthal, 1988)

Fiengo and May, 1994 propose to account for such active/passive examples under a reconstruction analysis by assuming that the presence of a trace of the passivized object in the source verb phrase allows for reconstruction of an active target verb phrase with a full object phrase. However, examples not involving passivization can also be found; example (12) is from instructions on a bottle of Agree shampoo:

(12) Avoid getting shampoo in eyes — if it does, flush thoroughly with water.

Here, the target verb phrase that is required on a syntactic reconstruction analysis is *get in eyes*; again, this is not a constituent that appears in the source sentence. Kehler, 1995 provides example (13), citing Gregory Ward (p.c.):

(13) This letter deserves a response, but before you do . . .

Here, the required target verb phrase is *respond*, which does not appear in the source sentence. Further examples are provided by Dalrymple et al., 1991 and Kehler, 1995; see also Lappin, 1996 for discussion of similar examples.

### *3.2. Deep Anaphora*

Hankamer and Sag, 1976 demonstrate a dichotomy of anaphoric processes: *deep anaphora* permits nonlinguistic antecedents and does not involve deletion or reconstruction of syntactic material, while *surface anaphora* permits only linguistically expressed antecedents and requires deletion or reconstruction of syntactic material in the target clause.

According to Hankamer and Sag, sluicing, stripping, gapping, and VP deletion are all instances of surface anaphora. Hankamer and Sag provide evidence bearing on all of these cases; some of their evidence (for Sluicing and Gapping) follows:[1]

(14) Sluicing (Hankamer and Sag, 1976, page 408)
  a. Syntactically controlled:
     Hankamer: Someone's just been shot.
     Sag: Yeah, I wonder who.
  b. Pragmatically controlled:
     [Hankamer produces a gun, points it offstage and fires, whereupon a scream is heard]
     Sag: #Jesus, I wonder who.

(15) Gapping (Hankamer and Sag, 1976, page 410)
  a. Syntactically controlled:
     Hankamer: Ivan is now going to peel an apple.
     Sag: And Jorge, an orange.
  b. Pragmatically controlled:
     [Hankamer produces an orange, proceeds to peel it, and just as Sag produces an apple, says:]
     #And Ivan, an apple.

However, 'do it' anaphora is, by the criteria of Hankamer and Sag, deep anaphora, since nonlinguistic antecedents are acceptable:

(16) 'Do it' Anaphora
  a. Syntactically controlled (Hankamer and Sag, 1976, page 392)
     Sag: Why don't you stuff that ball through that hoop?
     Hankamer: I'm trying to do it.
  b. Pragmatically controlled:
     [Hankamer attempts to stuff 12″ ball through 6″ hoop:]
     Sag: It's not clear that you'll be able to do it.

Either a linguistic or a nonlinguistic antecedent is acceptable as an antecedent for 'do it' anaphora.

It is even possible to produce a strict/sloppy ambiguity by nonlinguistic means using 'do it' anaphora:

(17) [John touches his finger to his nose. John says to Bill:]
     Now you do it.
  a. sloppy: Bill touches his own nose.
  b. strict: Bill touches John's nose.

The existence of examples such as this indicates that the basis of the strict/sloppy ambiguity is semantic and does not rely on a difference in the syntactic representation of the source clause.

Since no linguistic antecedent is necessary for 'do it' anaphora, syntactic reconstruction would not be expected to occur, since there is not always a syntactic source to reconstruct from. Notably, though, ungrammatical examples of exactly the sort that prompt an appeal to reconstruction occur with 'do it' anaphora:

(18) *I hit Bill$_i$, and then he$_i$ did it.

Moreover, some reconstruction analyses assume that reconstruction is only applicable in cases of VP deletion, not in cases of 'so' anaphora. On those analyses, the ungrammaticality of example (19) is equally mysterious:

(19) *I hit Bill$_i$, and then he$_i$ did so.

However, if the ungrammaticality of examples (18) and (19) is not explained by syntactic reconstruction, they can be accounted for on a par with examples like (20), obviating the need for an appeal to reconstruction in these cases:

(20) *I hit Bill$_i$, and then he$_i$ did.

*3.3. Unexpected Grammaticality*

The evidence for syntactic reconstruction that was presented above appeals to putative violations of binding conditions within the reconstructed target clause. However, some sentences that seem to have the same syntactic properties as sentence (7) above are, unexpectedly, grammatical.

Haïk, 1987, page 524, citing Cormack, 1984, judges sentence (21) to be grammatical, claiming that it provides evidence that 'condition C does not hold at LF':

(21) I shaved Bill$_i$ because he$_i$ wouldn't.

The reconstructed form of sentence (21) is ungrammatical, however:

(22) *I shaved Bill$_i$ because he$_i$ wouldn't shave Bill$_i$.

Section 5 demonstrates that there is, in fact, a definable class of such systematic counterexamples to the predictions of a reconstruction analysis.

There are a number of other examples of sentences which, contrary to the predictions of a syntactic reconstruction analysis, are fully grammatical. The sentences in (23–24) illustrate one type of counterexample to a syntactic reconstruction analysis: the elided portion of the target sentence appears in an embedded clause, and a reconstruction analysis predicts an anaphoric violation involving an element in the matrix clause containing the target clause and an element in the reconstructed ellipsis site in the target.

(23) VP Deletion:
  a. John voted for Sue$_i$ because she$_i$ told him to (*vote for Sue$_i$).
  b. I didn't vote for Sue$_i$, even though she$_i$ asked me to (*vote for Sue$_i$).
  c. John likes Sue$_i$, but she$_i$ doesn't know that he does (*likes Sue$_i$).
  d. John took several pictures of Sue$_i$, and she$_i$ said that George did too (*took several pictures of Sue$_i$).

(24) Sluicing (examples from Levin, 1982):
  a. John told Sue$_i$ something, but she$_i$ doesn't know what (*John told Sue$_i$).
  b. Someone likes Janet$_i$ but only she$_i$ knows who (*likes Janet$_i$).

If reconstruction involves copying syntactic material from the source to the target, then the presence of a referring expression in the copied material and a c-commanding coreferent element in a higher clause should result in ungrammaticality; contrary to the predictions of a reconstruction analysis, however, these examples are fully grammatical.

In example (25), a binding violation is also predicted by a reconstruction analysis. In these cases, the violation predicted by a reconstruction analysis involves coreference between an embedded occurrence of a referring expression and a less embedded element in the same clause in the target sentence. Again, if reconstruction consists of making a copy of syntactic material in the ellipsis site of the target, the grammaticality of these examples is unexplained.

(25) VP Deletion:
a. John got to $\text{Sue}_i$'s apartment before $\text{she}_i$ did (*got to $\text{Sue}_i$'s apartment).
b. I like $\text{Sue}_i$'s apartment, but $\text{she}_i$ doesn't (*like $\text{Sue}_i$'s apartment).

## 4. RECONSTRUCTION SOLUTIONS

We now turn to a more detailed examination of several specific reconstruction proposals, showing that the facts discussed in the previous section present difficulties for these approaches. Besides these difficulties, we also discuss additional problems faced by each of these reconstruction analyses.

### *4.1. Proposal: Copying before Indexation*

One type of account of the unacceptability of examples such as (7) above has been proposed by, *inter alia*, Hellan, 1988, Lappin and McCord, 1990, and Kitagawa, 1991. On this approach, constraints on anaphoric binding can (or must) hold of the reconstructed representation, and coindexing of arguments can (or must) occur after reconstruction.

For example, Kitagawa, 1991 presents the following example:

(26) $\text{John}_i$ blamed $\text{himself}_i$ and Bill did too.

At LF, the reconstructed representation is:

(27) $\text{John}_i$ blamed $\text{himself}_i$ and $\text{Bill}_j$ did [blame $\text{himself}_j$] too.

Under the assumption that constraints on reflexive binding hold at LF, a sloppy reading is correctly predicted to be possible for this sentence.

Consider, then, the following sentence and its reconstructed representation:

(28) a. *John talked to $\text{Mary}_i$, and $\text{she}_i$ did too.
b. *John talked to $\text{Mary}_i$, and $\text{she}_i$ did [talk to $\text{Mary}_i$] too.

The ungrammaticality of example (28a) is exactly parallel to the ungrammaticality of example (28b), and on these analyses is explainable on exactly the same basis.

There are several problems for the claim that anaphoric elements can be provided with indices after reconstruction has taken place. Among these problems are those discussed in Section 3: not all cases of ellipsis involve syntactic material in the source that is suitable for reconstruction in the target, and when suitable material is present, the wrong predictions for grammaticality often result. Further, seemingly similar violations hold even in examples involving deep anaphora such as 'do it', where no linguistic antecedent is required.

Other problems for these analyses are also found. In particular, an analysis in which indexing can follow reconstruction predicts that if a pronominal appears in the source, the target can have an interpretation in which the pronominal is indexed differently.[2] Consider, for example, the following sentence:

(29) Sue saw him, and Jane did too.

The reconstructed representation for this sentence is:

(30) Sue saw him, and Jane saw him.

This representation may be indexed in the following way, without violating any binding condition:

(31) Sue saw $him_i$, and Jane saw $him_j$.

The binding theory does not preclude indexing the pronominal differently in the source and the target, although this is not a possible interpretation for example (29).[3]

Kitagawa, 1991 offers a potential explanation for these facts. He proposes that some pronominals, those which are not c-commanded by their antecedents, have what he calls 'inherent indices'; these, he says, are indexed at D-structure and thus cannot be reindexed after reconstruction has taken place. His proposal builds on work by Reinhart, 1983, who claims that sloppy readings are only possible for pronominals that are c-commanded by their antecedents.

Wescoat, 1989 provides a number of counterexamples to Reinhart's claim and, by extension, to Kitagawa's. He shows that sloppy readings are often possible even in cases where the antecedent of a pronoun does not c-command it:

(32) a. The policeman who arrested John failed to read him his rights, and so did the one who arrested Bill.
b. The person who introduced Mary to John would not give her his phone number, nor would the person who introduced Sue to Bill.

Wescoat notes that these sentences can be paraphrased in the following way:

(33) a. The policeman who arrested John failed to read John John's rights, and the one who arrested Bill failed to read Bill Bill's rights.
b. The person who introduced Mary to John would not give Mary John's phone number, and the person who introduced Sue to Bill would not give Sue Bill's phone number.

Wescoat's findings demonstrate the existence of pronouns that are not c-commanded by their antecedents but that are nevertheless not 'inherently indexed' in Kitagawa's sense. Hirschberg and Ward, 1991 also provide experimental evidence that sloppy readings are possible for pronouns that are not c-commanded by their antecedents.

There appears, then, to be no ready syntactic characterization of 'inherent indexing' that explains the lack of a reading such as (31) for sentences such as example (29) while still allowing for both strict and sloppy readings in cases of pronominal anaphora.

Finally, an approach that requires binding constraints to hold of a reconstructed representation does not predict the existence of strict readings for reflexives. Kitagawa, 1991 discusses the following example:

(34) John considers himself to be intelligent, and Bill does too.

For many speakers, the following interpretation of this sentence is available:

(35) $John_i$ considers $himself_i$ to be intelligent, and Bill considers $him_i$ to be intelligent too.

Kitagawa's reconstructed representation for example (34) is:

(36) $John_i$ considers $himself_i$ to be intelligent, and
$Bill_j$ does [consider $himself_i$ to be intelligent] too.

The availability of this interpretation is unexpected, since this is not an indexing for this structure that is permitted by the binding conditions.

To account for the possibility of strict readings for reflexives, Kitagawa proposes that reflexives are specified with the feature '+Anaphor', and that under reconstruction this feature need not be copied. When it is not copied, the strict reading for the reflexive is available. Given the other assumptions made by Kitagawa (in particular, the assumption that indexing of anaphoric elements is done at LF), this analysis suffers from the reindexing problem alluded to above: if the reflexive may be indexed at LF without regard to the feature '+Anaphor', then coindexing the reflexive with any discourse antecedent should be possible. That is, the following indexation should be well-formed when the feature '+Anaphor' is not copied:

(37) $John_i$ considers $himself_i$ to be intelligent, and
$Bill_j$ does [consider $himself_k$ to be intelligent] too.

An appeal to inherent indexing would not seem to be applicable here, since reflexives cannot in general take discourse antecedents and should not 'have referential indices already at the level of D-Structure' (Kitagawa, 1991, page 25).

We have seen that the solution of indexing anaphors at LF, either optionally or obligatorily, suffers from a number of problems. We now turn to another analysis of these facts: an analysis under which NP's can be differentially realized during reconstruction.

### *4.2. Proposal: Vehicle Change*

Fiengo and May, 1994 propose a process called 'vehicle change' which can occur in the course of reconstructing the target. They propose that a referring expression or a variable in a reconstructed phrase can be realized as the *pronominal correlate* of the expression (Fiengo and May, 1994, page 221). They provide the following illustrative example:

(38) Mary loves John$_i$, and he$_i$ thinks that Sally does too.

Their representation for the logical form of this sentence is:

(39) Mary loves John$_i$, and he$_i$ thinks that Sally loves $^P$John$_i$ too.

The notation $^P$*John* stands for the pronominal correlate of *John*; this sentence, then, is predicted to have the same status as:

(40) Mary loves John$_i$, and he$_i$ thinks that Sally loves him$_i$ too.

In essence, Fiengo and May's position is that a referring expression can have the syntactic behavior of a pronoun or reflexive in the reconstructed target sentence.

An approach such as this one can account for the grammaticality of examples such as (23)–(24), discussed in Section 3.3. The reconstructed representations of those examples contain a referring expression which can be reconstructed as its pronominal correlate:

(41) a. John likes Sue$_i$, but she$_i$ doesn't know that he does.
b. John likes Sue$_i$, but she$_i$ doesn't know that he likes $^P$Sue$_i$.

(42) a. John told us the truth about Sue$_i$, but she$_i$ would never have done so.
b. John told us the truth about Sue$_i$, but she$_i$ would never have told us the truth about $^P$Sue$_i$.

These sentences have the same status as unelided sentences with the pronominal correlates of the referring expressions:

(43) a. John likes Sue$_i$, but she$_i$ doesn't know that he likes her$_i$.
b. John told us the truth about Sue$_i$, but she$_i$ would never have told us the truth about her$_i$.

Fiengo and May also claim that sentences such as the following are grammatical with a restricted class of verbs such as *vote (for)*:

(44) John voted for Sue$_i$, and she$_i$ did too.

This is because the object *Sue* in the source sentence can be reconstructed as its pronominal correlate *her(self)* in the target, producing a well-formed binding configuration.

However, Kehler, 1995 points out that Fiengo and May's approach has an undesirable consequence: their classification of verbs predicts that a strict reading is easily available for example (45a), but impossible for (45b). With Kehler, we find that a sloppy reading is preferred to an equal degree for these two examples:

(45) a. John voted for himself and Bill did too.
b. John shaved himself and Bill did too.

Other objections to Fiengo and May's analysis can also be raised: examples in which there is no clear source for reconstruction, such as those given in Section 3.1, are unexplained, and the facts presented in Section 3.2, showing that similar violations hold in the case of deep anaphora such as 'do it', remain mysterious.

## 5. A SEMANTIC SOLUTION

A semantic analysis of ellipsis such as the one presented in Dalrymple et al., 1991 does not suffer from the shortcomings described in Section 3, since it makes correct predictions as to the acceptability or unacceptability of the examples discussed in that section. Further, a semantic analysis allows for an explanation of examples that appear to motivate a syntactic reconstruction analysis. In the following section, the analysis presented in Dalrymple et al., 1991 will be briefly sketched.

### *5.1. Ellipsis Resolution as Semantic Equality*

Dalrymple et al., 1991 propose that the problem of ellipsis resolution is statable equationally; solutions to these equations are provided by means of higher-order unification. Consider sentence (1), repeated here:

(46) John saw the flying saucer, and Bill did too.

The interpretation of the target sentence, *Bill did too*, is that some property $P$ holds of *Bill*:[4]

(47) $P(\mathit{Bill})$

Resolving the ellipsis consists in determining what this property is.

Sentence (46) also tells us that Bill and John have something in common: they play the same role in some type of situation. In other words, there is a parallelism (here, syntactically determined) between elements in the source and target;[5] in sentence (46), the parallel elements are the subjects, *Bill* in the target clause and *John* in the source clause.

Property $P$, then, is the property that holds of each of the parallel elements: it represents what Bill and John have in common. This property is determined by the interpretation of the source clause. In particular, when $P$ is applied to *John*, the element in the source clause that is parallel to *Bill*, the result is the interpretation of the source clause:[6]

(48) $P(\mathit{John}) = \mathit{saw}(\mathit{John}, \mathit{the\ flying\ saucer})$

In other words, the property that holds of *Bill* is the property that, when applied to *John*, gives the interpretation of the source clause.

An equation such as the one in (48) can be solved by means of higher-order unification (Huet, 1975), with the result that $P$ is instantiated to the following property:

(49) $P \mapsto \lambda X.\mathit{saw}(X, \mathit{the\ flying\ saucer})$

As a result, the interpretation of the target clause ($P$ applied to *Bill*) is:

(50) $\mathit{saw}(\mathit{Bill}, \mathit{the\ flying\ saucer})$

A prime advantage of the analysis is its treatment of strict/sloppy ambiguities, which proceeds straightforwardly and without appeal to syntactic or semantic ambiguity in the source clause. Indeed, this is one of the strengths of the analysis; as Dalrymple et al. point out, analyses in which strict-sloppy ambiguities are attributed to a putative ambiguity in the source clause face a number of difficulties. The examples in (51) allow both a strict and a sloppy reading:

(51) a. Sue$_i$ got to her$_i$ apartment before Jane did.
b. Bill$_i$ defended himself$_i$ against the accusations better than his$_i$ lawyer did.

For example (51b), let us assume the following semantic representation for the source clause *Bill defended himself*:

(52) $\mathit{defend}(\mathit{Bill}, \mathit{Bill})$

The parallel elements are *Bill* in the source clause and *his lawyer* in the target clause. The interpretation of the target clause *his lawyer did* is:

(53) $P(\mathit{lawyer})$

where predicating $P$ of the parallel element in the source clause gives the meaning of the source:

(54) $P(\mathit{Bill}) = \mathit{defend}(\mathit{Bill}, \mathit{Bill})$

There are two solutions to this equation, the first corresponding to the sloppy reading for the target and the second to the strict reading:[7]

(55) a. $P \mapsto \lambda X.\mathit{defend}(X, X)$
b. $P \mapsto \lambda X.\mathit{defend}(X, \mathit{Bill})$

Either solution for $P$ is appropriate and can be applied to *lawyer* to yield an interpretation for the target. The first solution, $\lambda X.\mathit{defend}(X, X)$ requires coreference between the two argument positions of *defend* and produces a sloppy interpretation for the target clause when applied to *lawyer*:

(56) $\mathit{defend}(\mathit{lawyer}, \mathit{lawyer})$

The second solution, $\lambda X.\mathit{defend}(X, \mathit{Bill})$, produces a strict interpretation for the target:

(57) $\mathit{defend}(\mathit{lawyer}, \mathit{Bill})$

In this setting, the general ellipsis resolution problem can be thought of as:

- determining the parallel elements in the source and target;
- solving an equation involving the meaning of the source and a relation over the parallel elements in the source;
- applying this relation to the parallel elements in the target.

The equations to be solved are all of the following form:

(58) $P(s_1, s_2, \ldots s_n) = s$

where $s_1$ through $s_n$ are the interpretations of the parallel elements of the source, and $s$ is the interpretation of the source itself. The interpretation of the target is, then:

(59) $P(t_1, t_2, \ldots t_n)$

where $t_1$ through $t_n$ are the interpretations of the corresponding parallel elements of the target. Dalrymple et al., 1991 and Shieber et al., 1996 provide details of this analysis and its interaction with other phenomena.

For present purposes, the important feature of this analysis is that ellipsis resolution depends on a semantic equality between the source and target clause: some relation $P$ is obtainable given the meaning of the source clause and is then used in the interpretation of the target. We will refer to this analysis as the *semantic equality analysis*.

### *5.2. A Reformulation of the Problem*

Section 3 discussed a range of cases in which incorrect predictions are made by a syntactic reconstruction analyses. The problems discussed were:

- lack of a syntactic reconstruction source
- appearance of reconstruction effects in examples not involving reconstruction, such as 'do it' anaphora
- the existence of sentences incorrectly predicted to be ungrammatical by a reconstruction analysis

On a syntactic reconstruction analysis, these counterexamples appear to be unrelated; each case requires a different sort of modification to the reconstruction theory, and some cases do not seem to admit of a solution at all on that approach. However, when the same phenomena are looked at on a semantic approach, these problems disappear; on a semantic equality analysis, the acceptability and unacceptability of the examples discussed in Section 3 is as expected.

Section 3.1 discussed examples such as the following:

(60) A lot of this material can be presented in a fairly informal and accessible fashion, and often I do.

This example is problematic on a syntactic reconstruction analysis because there is no apparent syntactic source for the reconstructed VP. For a semantic analysis, however, such examples are unproblematic; there is no requirement for parallelism between source and target to be determined by purely syntactic means. In example (60), the parallelism between the source and target is determined semantically, and the parallel elements are the 'logical' subjects of the source and target clause. Other examples of nonsyntactic parallelism are discussed by Dalrymple et al., 1991; on an analysis that does not require the resolution of ellipsis by purely syntactic means, such examples are expected.

Section 3.2 discussed cases not involving reconstruction — in particular, cases of deep anaphora — in which apparent reconstruction effects are found:

(61) *I hit $\text{Bill}_i$, and then $\text{he}_i$ did it.

If the unacceptability of such examples is due to semantic rather than syntactic factors, there is no reason to expect judgments to differ for cases of deep and surface anaphora; the unacceptability of examples (61) and (62) is due to exactly the same (semantic) factors:

(62) *I hit $\text{Bill}_i$, and then $\text{he}_i$ did.

Section 3.3 noted two sorts of examples that are incorrectly predicted to be ungrammatical on a reconstruction analysis. The first sort is illustrated by example (63):

(63) $\text{John}_i$ likes $\text{Sue}_j$, but $\text{she}_j$ doesn't know that $\text{he}_i$ does (*likes $\text{Sue}_j$).

On a semantic equality analysis, there is no reason to expect that sentences such as these would be ungrammatical. Assuming for simplicity that the interpretation for the pronoun $he_i$ is *John*, the result of resolving the ellipsis in example (63) is that the property $\lambda X.\mathit{like}(X, \mathit{Sue})$ is predicated of *John*; no ungrammaticality or semantic anomaly is predicted to result.

The second sort of example that is incorrectly predicted to be ungrammatical on a reconstruction analysis is illustrated by (64):

(64) John got to $\text{Sue}_i$'s apartment before $\text{she}_i$ did (*got to $\text{Sue}_i$'s apartment).

In contrast, consider an unacceptable example:

(65) *John hit $\text{Sue}_i$, and $\text{she}_i$ did too.

The phenomenon to be explained on a semantic equality analysis is, then, the contrast between example (64) and example (65): why apparent 'reconstruction' effects are found in one case but not in the other. In the following, we will see that this contrast correlates with a contrast in possibilities for strict and sloppy readings for sentences such as these.

### *5.3. Strict and Sloppy Possibilities*

It is sometimes claimed that only sloppy readings are available for reflexives in English. As we have seen, this claim is too strong; cases of strict readings involving reflexives are found and will be discussed below. To be sure, there are many cases where strict readings are difficult or impossible to produce:

(66) a. John was talking to himself, but Bill wasn't.
b. John locks himself in the bathroom when bad news arrives, but Bill would never do so.

c. John prepared himself for the worst, and so did Bill.
d. John rewarded himself with a piece of cake because Bill did.
e. John seated himself at the head of the table before Bill could.
f. John always surrounds himself with admirers. Bill doesn't, although he could.
g. John worked himself to a frazzle even when it was obvious that Bill wasn't going to.

Only a sloppy reading is available for these sentences: that is, example (66a) can only mean that Bill was talking to himself, not that Bill was talking to John. We will refer to cases such as these as *sloppy-only* cases.

There are other cases, however, in which strict readings are available for reflexives. Among these cases are the following:

(67) a. Bill defended himself against the accusations better than his lawyer did.
b. Bill described himself to Sue because I couldn't do it.
c. Bill didn't expect himself to win, but I did.
d. John voted for himself even though no one else did.

We will refer to these cases as *strict-sloppy* cases: cases in which either a strict or a sloppy reading is available.[8]

Now let us turn to an examination of reconstruction effects in each of these cases. In the sloppy-only type, the predictions made by a reconstruction analysis are borne out; the following sentences are unacceptable on the indicated indexing:

(68) a. *John was talking to $\text{Bill}_i$, but $\text{he}_i$ wasn't.
b. *John locks $\text{Bill}_i$ in the bathroom when bad news arrives, but $\text{he}_i$ would never do so.
c. *John prepared $\text{Bill}_i$ for the worst, and so did $\text{he}_i$.
d. *John rewarded $\text{Bill}_i$ with a piece of cake because $\text{he}_i$ did.
e. *John seated $\text{Bill}_i$ at the head of the table before $\text{he}_i$ could.
f. *John always surrounds $\text{Bill}_i$ with admirers. $\text{He}_i$ doesn't, although $\text{he}_i$ could.
g. *John worked $\text{Bill}_i$ to a frazzle even when it was obvious that $\text{he}_i$ wasn't going to.

The facts differ, however, for the strict-sloppy type. Here, the predictions made by a reconstruction analysis are not borne out; the acceptability of the examples in (69) contrasts sharply with the unacceptability of the examples in (68):

(69) a. The lawyer defended $\text{Bill}_i$ against the accusations better than $\text{he}_i$ could have.
b. I described $\text{Bill}_i$ to Sue because $\text{he}_i$ couldn't do it.
c. I expected $\text{Bill}_i$ to win even when $\text{he}_i$ didn't.
d. I voted for $\text{John}_i$, even though $\text{he}_i$ didn't.

These examples are incorrectly predicted by a reconstruction analysis to have the same status as their unelided counterparts:[9]

(70) a. *He$_i$ can defend Bill$_i$ against the accusations.
b. *He$_i$ couldn't describe Bill$_i$ to Sue.
c. *He$_i$ didn't expect Bill$_i$ to win.
d. *He$_i$ didn't vote for John$_i$.

Apparent 'binding violations' are, then, found only in sloppy-only cases. Such violations are not found in strict-sloppy cases.

Actually, the claim that strict readings are unavailable for sentences such as example (71) (=66a) is not quite accurate.

(71) John was talking to himself, and Bill was too.

It is possible to construct a situation in which a strict reading is available. Consider a situation in which John is conversing with a pre-recorded video image of himself, and Bill is also conversing with this image; at least for some speakers, sentence (71) can be used to describe this situation. Crucially, in this situation the anomaly of sentences such as (72) also disappears:

(72) I was talking to John$_i$ (on the television screen), and he$_i$ was too.

Situations can be constructed in which strict readings are available for the other 'sloppy-only' cases given in (66); apparent reconstruction effects also disappear in these situations. Again, then, the possibility of a strict reading correlates with the lack of apparent reconstruction effects. Cases in which a strict reading is available are those in which such effects are not found.

Interestingly, sloppy-only examples need not always involve reflexives; sloppy-only examples with pronominals are also found:

(73) John$_i$ broke his$_i$ arm, and Bill did too.

On the most natural reading of the source sentence *John broke his arm*, in which John broke his arm accidentally (perhaps by falling down), a strict reading is impossible to produce. A strict reading for example (73) may be forced, but the implication then is that John broke his arm deliberately, or in the same way as he would break another person's arm.

Consider, then, the following example:

(74) #The mafia hit man broke John's$_i$ arm, and he$_i$ did too.

This sentence is deviant in the same way as examples such as (68), characterized as binding violations in a reconstruction analysis; the only interpretation available is analogous to the forced strict reading of example (73), in which John broke his arm deliberately. Examples such as (73) contrast with structurally similar examples such as (75), in which both a strict and a sloppy reading are available:

(75) Sue$_i$ got to her$_i$ apartment before Jane did.

As noted above, in examples of this type no reconstruction effects are found; sentences such as the following are perfectly felicitous:

(76) John$_j$ got to Sue$_i$'s apartment before she$_i$ did.

These examples show that the appearance of 'reconstruction' effects does not correlate with the syntactic distribution of reflexives and pronominals in sentences not involving ellipsis. In cases in which the reconstructed target would contain a reflexive, apparent reconstruction effects are found in some cases but not in others; the same is true in cases in which the reconstructed target would contain a pronominal. Instead, the appearance of 'reconstruction' effects correlates precisely with the unavailabity of strict readings: sloppy-only cases give rise to reconstruction effects, whereas strict-sloppy cases do not.

### *5.4. Predicate Types and Semantic Equality*

We have seen that apparent 'binding violations' involving ellipsis are not found in every case, but instead pattern according to the availability of a strict reading: sloppy-only examples give rise to apparent binding violations, while strict-sloppy examples do not give rise to such violations. The analysis of Dalrymple et al., 1991 provides an explanation for the facts noted above.

**Strict-sloppy examples** Both a strict and a sloppy reading are available for example (77):

(77) Bill$_i$ defended himself$_i$ against the accusations better than his$_i$ lawyer did.

As shown in Section 5.1, the equational statement of ellipsis resolution produces two interpretations for the elided VP in the target. The first interpretation, $\lambda X.\mathit{defend}(X, X)$, produces a sloppy interpretation when applied to the parallel element in the target clause, *lawyer*:

(78) $\mathit{defend}(\mathit{lawyer}, \mathit{lawyer})$

The second solution, $\lambda X.\mathit{defend}(X, \mathit{Bill})$, produces a strict interpretation:

(79) $\mathit{defend}(\mathit{lawyer}, \mathit{Bill})$

Given this, the lack of an apparent 'anaphoric violation' is predicted for sentences such as (80):

(80) The lawyer defended Bill$_i$ against the accusations better than he$_i$ could have.

Ellipsis resolution for example (80) proceeds as follows:

(81) source interpretation: $\mathit{defend}(\mathit{lawyer}, \mathit{Bill})$
target interpretation: $P(\mathit{Bill})$
parallel elements: *lawyer*, *Bill*

$P(\mathsf{lawyer}) = \mathsf{defend}(\mathsf{lawyer}, \mathsf{Bill})$
$P \mapsto \lambda X.\mathsf{defend}(X, \mathsf{Bill})$

Property $P$ may be applied to the parallel element in the target, *Bill*, to yield the interpretation for the target:

(82) *defend(Bill, Bill)*

No problem arises in predicating the property $\lambda X.\mathsf{defend}(X, \mathsf{Bill})$ of *Bill*, since no special coreference or disjointness requirements are imposed by the predicate *defend*. If such requirements were imposed, it would not be possible to obtain both a strict and a sloppy reading for example (77).

In some cases, though, individual predicates may impose requirements of disjointness or coreference on their arguments; in these cases, the number of available interpretations for the target may be reduced. In the next section, some such predicates will be examined.

**Disjoint Predicates** Some predicates require their arguments to be disjoint in reference. For example, the following examples are anomalous, at least on a literal reading:

(83) a. #Sue murdered herself.
b. #Sue can't find herself.
c. #Sue tried to avoid herself.
d. #Sue beat herself in the hundred-yard dash.
e. #Sue borrowed five dollars from herself.
f. #Sue chased herself.

The relation *murder* requires that a different individual fill its first and second argument positions, and likewise for the other examples given above. It is the meanings of these individual predicates rather than any fact about their syntax that imposes this requirement, since many grammatical sentences have similar syntactic structure to these.

Not surprisingly, then, the following example is also unacceptable:

(84) #I murdered $\text{Sue}_i$ before $\text{she}_i$ could.

No appeal to syntactic constraints is necessary to rule out this sentence; resolving the ellipsis involves predicating the property $\lambda X.\mathsf{murder}(X, \mathsf{Sue})$ of *Sue*. If this were possible, sentence (83a) would be acceptable — but it is not.

Examples corresponding to the remaining sentences in (83) are anomalous in a similar way:

(85) a. #I can't find $\text{Sue}_i$, and $\text{she}_i$ can't either.
b. #I tried to avoid $\text{Sue}_i$, but $\text{she}_i$ didn't.
c. #I beat $\text{Sue}_i$ in the hundred yard dash, even though $\text{she}_i$ didn't.
d. #I borrowed five dollars from $\text{Sue}_i$ before $\text{she}_i$ did.
e. #I chased $\text{Sue}_i$, but $\text{she}_i$ didn't.

Again, the anomaly of these examples is due to requirements imposed by the predicates involved: predicates such as *find* and *avoid* require noncoreference between their subject and object. On the indicated indexing of the pronoun in the target clause, resolving the ellipsis necessarily involves a violation of this requirement.

Not all cases of required noncoreference involve arguments of the same syntactic predicate. Idiomatic examples involving pronominals can also impose such requirements, as the following examples illustrate:

(86) a. #John$_i$ isn't his$_i$ cup of tea.
b. #With this job, John$_i$ is following in his$_i$ footsteps.
c. #John$_i$ wouldn't harm a hair of his$_i$ head.

Corresponding examples involving ellipsis are, similarly, unacceptable:

(87) a. #I guess I'm not John$_i$'s cup of tea, but he$_i$ is.
b. #With this job, I am following in John$_i$'s footsteps, just as he$_i$ is.
c. #I wouldn't harm a hair of John$_i$'s head, and neither would he$_i$.

Predicates of various syntactic forms can, then, impose requirements of noncoreference on their arguments. We will refer to these predicates as *disjoint* predicates.

*5.5. Sloppy-Only Cases and Coreference Requirements*

Now let us consider a sloppy-only case:

(88) John was talking to himself, and Bill was too.

Only a sloppy reading is available for this sentence. Ellipsis resolution proceeds as follows in this case:

(89) source interpretation: $\mathit{talk\text{-}to}(\mathit{John}, \mathit{John})$
target interpretation: $P(\mathit{Bill})$
parallel elements: *John, Bill*
$P(\mathit{John}) = \mathit{talk\text{-}to}(\mathit{John}, \mathit{John})$

We would expect higher-order unification to produce the following two solutions for $P$:

(90) a. $P \mapsto \lambda X.\mathit{talk\text{-}to}(X, X)$
b. $P \mapsto \lambda X.\mathit{talk\text{-}to}(X, \mathit{John})$

When applied to *Bill*, solution (90a) correctly yields the sloppy reading for the target:

(91) $\mathit{talk\text{-}to}(\mathit{Bill}, \mathit{Bill})$

Recall, however, that the strict reading for the target in (88) is missing; solution (90b) incorrectly yields the unavailable strict reading:

(92) $\mathit{talk\text{-}to}(\mathit{Bill}, \mathit{John})$

This solution should be ruled out, since this reading is not available for the target clause of example (88). The evidence presented thus far indicates that the predicate *talk-to* with a reflexive object is special: it imposes a requirement of coreference between its first and second argument, disallowing the second of the two solutions for $P$ given in (90) and making unavailable the strict reading of the sentence given in (92).

However, it is quite clear that there are other examples in which coreference between the first and second arguments of *talk-to* is not obligatory. The following example is perfectly grammatical:

(93) Bill talked to John.

When this sentence appears as a source for ellipsis resolution, no problems of interpretation arise:

(94) Bill talked to John, and Sue did too.

The ellipsis is resolved in the following way:

(95) source interpretation: *talk-to*(*Bill*, *John*)
target interpretation: $P$(*Sue*)
parallel elements: *Bill*, *Sue*
$P$(*Bill*) = *talk-to*(*Bill*, *John*)
$P \mapsto \lambda X$.*talk-to*($X$, *John*)

Applying $P$ to *Sue* produces the expected interpretation for the target:

(96) *talk-to*(*Sue*, *John*)

It is evident that in this case the first and second arguments of *talk-to* need not be coreferent.

The two cases we have just examined differ in whether or not the first and second arguments of *talk-to* are coreferent or disjoint in reference:

- coreference between these two arguments in the source requires corresponding coreference in the target, while
- disjoint reference in the source requires disjoint reference in the target.

The lack of a strict reading for sentences such as example (88) is diagnostic of this situation.

Let us refer to a predicate like $\lambda X$.*talk-to*($X$, $X$), the interpretation of *talking to himself*, as a *reflexive predicate*. A reflexive predicate requires coreference between its two arguments. A predicate like $\lambda X$. *talk-to*($X$,*John*), the interpretation of *talking to John*, is the corresponding *disjoint predicate* involving the individual John. A disjoint predicate requires noncoreference between its two arguments. To make this difference clear, we will use the subscript *refl* for reflexive predicates and the subscript *disj* for disjoint predicates. On the semantic equality analysis, the facts discussed above are as predicted for cases in which a distinction exists between reflexive and disjoint predicates; if the reflexive predicate is used in the source, it must be used in the target, and similarly for the disjoint predicate. This formal distinction corresponds to the intuitive difference between the noncommunicative activity of talking to oneself and the communative, social activity of talking to someone else.

Note also that the disjoint predicate $\textit{talk-to}_{disj}$ is similar to predicates such as *murder*, discussed above, since the disjoint predicate holds in cases where the arguments of a predicate are necessarily disjoint in reference. Recall that the presence of 'anaphoric violations' is expected in cases such as these; the ungrammaticality of examples (97a) and (97b) are due to the same factor:

(97) a. #Sue murdered herself.
b. #I murdered $\text{Sue}_i$ before $\text{she}_i$ could.

In both cases, requirements imposed by the disjoint predicate *murder* are violated; the property $\lambda X.\textit{murder}(X, \textit{Sue})$ may not be predicated of *Sue*.

In example (88), then, ellipsis resolution proceeds in the following way:

(98) John was talking to himself, and Bill was too.
source interpretation: $\textit{talk-to}_{refl}(\textit{John}, \textit{John})$
target interpretation: $P(\textit{Bill})$
parallel elements: *John*, *Bill*
$P(\textit{John}) = \textit{talk-to}_{refl}(\textit{John}, \textit{John})$

The expected solutions for $P$ are:

(99) a. $P \mapsto \lambda X.\textit{talk-to}_{refl}(X, X)$
b. $P \mapsto \lambda X.\textit{talk-to}_{refl}(X, \textit{John})$

Of the two solutions for $P$, however, only one produces a well-formed interpretation for the target. Applying the predicate $\lambda X.\ \textit{talk-to}_{refl}(X, \textit{John})$ to *Bill* induces a violation of the requirements imposed by the predicate $\textit{talk-to}_{refl}$:

(100) $\textit{talk-to}_{refl}(\textit{Bill}, \textit{John})$

Assuming a difference between the reflexive and disjoint predicates for *talk-to* allows an explanation of the lack of a strict reading for examples such as (88) on a semantic equality analysis.

Now let us turn to an examination of apparent reconstruction effects in examples involving the disjoint predicate $\textit{talk-to}_{disj}$:

(101) #John was talking to $\text{Bill}_i$, and $\text{he}_i$ was too.

Ellipsis resolution proceeds as follows:

(102) source interpretation: $\textit{talk-to}_{disj}(\textit{John}, \textit{Bill})$
target interpretation: $P(\textit{Bill})$
parallel elements: *John*, *Bill*
$P(\textit{John}) = \textit{talk-to}_{disj}(\textit{John}, \textit{Bill})$
$P \mapsto \lambda X.\textit{talk-to}_{disj}(X, \textit{Bill})$

Applying *P* to *Bill* yields the following interpretation for the target clause:

(103) $talk\text{-}to_{disj}(Bill, Bill)$

However, this representation is ill-formed, since, like predicates such as *murder*, disjoint *talk-to* requires noncoreference between its first and second argument.

It was noted above that cases where only sloppy readings are available tend to be those in which the anaphoric violation predicated on a reconstruction analysis is local, most often where coarguments of the same predicate are involved. Encoding a special requirement of coreference or disjoint reference involving two argument positions is possible for lexical predicates such as verbs, but impossible when the two positions to be related in this special way are arguments of different predicates.

## 6. CONCLUSION

Cases in which syntactic constraints apparently hold of elements within an ellipsis site have been cited as motivation for reconstruction analyses of ellipsis. However, reconstruction accounts cannot account for the fact that there are cases in which no syntactic material is available for reconstructing into the target phrase in ellipsis; further, in cases where such material is available, reconstruction analyses make incorrect predictions as to the interpretations and grammaticality of sentences involving ellipsis. We have shown that apparent reconstruction effects are in fact semantic rather than syntactic; they are due to requirements placed by predicates on possible coreference between their arguments and are signaled by the inability of these predicates to exhibit strict readings in ellipsis.

## NOTES

1 The symbol '#' indicates semantic ill-formedness.

2 This problem has been independently noted by Robert May (p.c.).

3 Lauri Karttunen notes that such an indexing may be allowed in some special cases, as in the following example:

> John and Bill were staying in different cities. They didn't know it, but they were each being chased by an FBI agent. The agent that was chasing John was staying in the same hotel, and the agent that was chasing Bill was posing as an employee of the restaurant where Bill ate. John's agent passed him in the hall every day, and Bill's agent usually served him breakfast. However, John didn't realize he was an FBI agent, and Bill didn't either.

The intended interpretation for the last sentence in the discourse is that John didn't realize that John's agent worked for the FBI, and Bill didn't realize that Bill's agent worked for the FBI. The reconstructed representation would have the kind of indexing represented in (31), since the reconstructed occurrence of *he* would refer to a different person from the overt occurrence of *he*. Cases of this kind are not felt by all speakers to be completely felicitous. For speakers who find them acceptable, the pronoun seems to be interpreted as a function from individuals to FBI agents chasing those individuals, and it is the fact that the individuals acting as arguments to those functions are parallel elements in the ellipsis construction that makes this interpretation possible. In cases where such an interpretation for the pronoun is not available, the pronoun may not refer to different individuals in the source and the target.

4 For the sake of simplicity, issues of possible tense and aspect differences between the source and target have been ignored. Such differences are also handled by the mechanism described in this section.

5 Parallelism between elements in the source and target need not always be syntactically determined; Section 3.1 discusses cases of nonsyntactic parallelism.

[6] The representation of the meaning of the phrase *the flying saucer* as **the flying saucer** is not intended as a serious proposal for the semantic analysis of definite noun phrases; in the following, semantic representations will be simplified to the greatest extent possible for ease of explication.

[7] The process of higher-order unification actually produces four solutions to this equation:

(a) $P \mapsto \lambda X.\mathit{defend}(X, X)$
(b) $P \mapsto \lambda X.\mathit{defend}(X, \mathit{Bill})$
(c) $P \mapsto \lambda X.\mathit{defend}(\mathit{Bill}, X)$
(d) $P \mapsto \lambda X.\mathit{defend}(\mathit{Bill}, \mathit{Bill})$

Solutions (c) and (d) are eliminated on the basis of what Dalrymple et al., 1991 call the *primary occurrence constraint*, requiring abstraction on the semantic argument position corresponding to the parallel element in the source. This requirement ensures that the parallel element in the target plays the primary role in the interpretation of the target clause. In the case at hand, parallelism obtains between the subjects of the source and target clauses, and the semantic argument position corresponding to the subject of the source is the first argument position of *defend*. Any other occurrences of the semantic representation of the parallel element in the source are referred to as *secondary* occurrences: here, the position corresponding to the object of *defend* is a secondary occurrence. There are no constraints requiring or prohibiting abstraction on secondary occurrences.

[8] Fiengo and May, 1994 and Hestvik, 1995 point out a structural difference between sloppy-only and strict-sloppy cases: examples with coordination tend to permit only a sloppy reading, while examples with subordination tend to allow a strict as well as a sloppy reading. That is, example (a) permits a strict reading more easily than example (b):

(a) Bill defended himself against the accusations better than his lawyer did.
(b) Bill defended himself against the accusations, and his lawyer did too.

Fiengo and May, 1994 and Hestvik, 1995 propose a syntactic account of this difference, appealing to movement of reflexives or to a more fine-grained typology of reflexives. However, Kehler, 1995; 2000 demonstrates conclusively that *coherence relations* between clauses are the crucial factor: in sloppy-only cases, the relation between the source and target is one of Resemblance, which tends to involve coordination, whereas in strict-sloppy cases, the relation between the source and target is often one of Cause-Effect, which tends to involve subordination. Cases involving coordination but a Cause-Effect relation are strict-sloppy, not sloppy-only, as predicted by Kehler's account but not by the syntactic accounts of Hestvik or Fiengo and May. In the following, we will attempt to abstract away from this difference, limiting our attention to the sloppy-only vs. strict-sloppy distinction in similar constructions.

[9] Lappin, 1992 and Hestvik, 1995 propose that the target sentences in (69) have the same syntactic structure as nonelided examples with heavily accented pronouns, as discussed by Evans, 1980: *I expected Bill$_i$ to win even when HE$_i$ didn't expect Bill$_i$ to win.* However, Kehler, 1995 points out that such examples are stylistically quite marked and sound more stilted than those in (69), requiring much heavier accent on the pronoun to be acceptable. The two sorts of cases do not in fact seem to be comparable.

## REFERENCES


Chomsky, N., *Noam Chomsky on the Generative Enterprise.* Dordrecht: Foris Publications. 1982.

Cormack, A., "VP-Anaphor: Variables and scope." MS, University College, London, 1984. Cited in Haïk, 1987.

Dalrymple, M., Shieber, S.M., and Pereira, F.C.N., "Ellipsis and higher-order unification." *Linguistics and Philosophy* 14(4) (1991): 399–452.

Evans, G., "Pronouns." *Linguistic Inquiry* 11(2) (1980): 337–362.

Fiengo, R., and May, R., *Indices and Identity*. Linguistic Inquiry Monographs. Cambridge, MA: The MIT Press. 1994.

Grolier, *Academic American Encyclopedia*. Danbury, CT: Grolier Electronic Publishing. 1989.

Haïk, I. *The Syntax of Operators*. PhD thesis, MIT. 1985.

Haïk, I., "Bound VPs that need to be." *Linguistics and Philosophy* 10 (1987): 503–530.

Hankamer, J., and Sag, I.A., "Deep and surface anaphora." *Linguistic Inquiry* 7(3) (1976): 391–428.

Hellan, L., *Anaphora in Norwegian and the Theory of Grammar*. Dordrecht: Foris Publications. 1988.
Hestvik, A., "Reflexives and ellipsis." *Natural Language Semantics* 3 (1995): 211–237.
Hirschberg, J., and Ward, G., "Accent and bound anaphora." *Cognitive Linguistics* 2(2) (1991): 101–121.
Huet, G., "A unification algorithm for typed $\bar{\lambda}$-calculus." *Theoretical Computer Science* 1 (1975): 27–57.
Kehler, A., *Interpreting Cohesive Forms in the Context of Discourse Influence*. PhD thesis, Harvard University. 1995.
Kehler, A., "Coherence and the resolution of ellipsis." *Linguistics and Philosophy* 23(6) (2000): 533–575.
Kitagawa, Y., "Copying identity." *Natural Language and Linguistics Theory* 9(3) (1991): 497–536.
Lappin, S., "The syntactic basis of ellipsis resolution." In *Proceedings of the Stuttgart Ellipsis Workshop*, Stuttgart: University of Stuttgart. 1992.
Lappin, S., "The interpretation of ellipsis." In Lappin, S. (ed.) *Handbook of Contemporary Semantic Theory*. Oxford: Blackwell Publishers. 1996: 145–175.
Lappin, S. and Benmamoun, E., *Fragments: Studies in Ellipsis and Gapping*. Oxford: Oxford University Press. 1999.
Lappin, S. and McCord, M., "Anaphora resolution in slot grammar." *Computational Linguistics* 16(4) (1990): 197–212.
Levin, L.S., "Sluicing." In Bresnan, J. (ed.) *The Mental Representation of Grammatical Relations* Cambridge, MA: The MIT Press. 1982: 590–654.
May, R., *Logical Form: Its Structure and Derivation*. Cambridge, MA: The MIT Press. 1985.
Reinhart, T., *Anaphora and Semantic Interpretation*. Chicago: The University of Chicago Press. 1983.
Sag, I.A., *Deletion and Logical Form*. PhD thesis, MIT, 1976.
Shieber, S.M., Pereira, F.C.N., and Dalrymple, M., "Interactions of scope and ellipsis." *Linguistics and Philosophy* 19(5) (1996): 527–552. Reprinted in Lappin and Benmamoun, 1999.
Wescoat, M., "Sloppy readings with embedded antecedents." MS, Stanford University. 1989.
Williams, E., "Discourse and logical form." *Linguistic Inquiry* 8(1) (1977): 101–139.

PAUL PORTNER AND RAFFAELLA ZANUTTINI

# THE SEMANTICS OF NOMINAL EXCLAMATIVES

## 1. INTRODUCTION

In this contribution we consider a type of exclamative construction in English which shows an unusual pairing between syntactic form and semantic/pragmatic function. This is the nominal exclamative, illustrated in (1):

(1) The strange things that he says!
(2) What strange things he says!

(1) is a noun phrase, and thus contrasts syntactically with (2), which is a clause. Yet the two seem to be synonymous. We will argue that the noun phrase is not embedded in an elliptical structure; rather, the phrase we see is all there is. And furthermore we will argue that (1) is not just pragmatically equivalent to (2); the two are in fact semantically equivalent as well. This raises the question, of central concern to this volume, of how a noun phrase achieves such a clause-like function.

More specifically, we will argue that certain noun phrases containing a relative clause can have either "clause-like" or "noun phrase-like" meanings. When the meaning is clause-like, it is parallel to that of the clausal exclamative in (2); that is, the noun phrase has the type of meaning of an interrogative clause (a set of propositions, as in Karttunen 1977). We refer to such cases with the term *nominal exclamative.* When the meaning is noun phrase like, it is that of an ordinary definite NP. The syntactic distribution of nominal exclamatives with a clausal meaning is intricate, and shows that an attempt to account for the two meanings in terms of ellipsis or pragmatic inference is inadequate. This leads us to address the question of how the clause-like meaning is compositionally derived. We note that only noun phrases that contain a relative clause may have the clause-like meaning, and based on this we propose an account of (1) which crucially builds on the fact that it contains a relative clause, in this case *that he says.* More precisely, we propose that the noun phrases with a clause-like meaning share an abstract morpheme, present in the relative clause, with the true clausal exclamatives like (2). In contrast, the noun phrase like meaning is not associated with such a morpheme.

## 2. THE CATEGORY OF EXCLAMATIVES

Natural language categorizes sentences into a small number of clause types (Sadock & Zwicky 1985). Clause types constitute a grammatically determined pairing between form and meaning. One of these is the "minor type" of exclamatives, and in labelling examples like (1) as nominal exclamatives we intend to include them within



*R. Elugardo and R. J. Stainton (eds.), Ellipsis and Nonsentential Speech*, 57–67.

this class. Because the fact that they are exclamatives will become relevant at various points in our discussion, we begin by making precise our reasons for considering them to be members of this type.

It is not always a straighforward matter to determine which sentences are to be classified as members of a given clause type. This is so because sentences may be used with a variety of illocutionary forces beyond that conventionally associated with their form. For example, a declarative like *It's cold in here* can be used, in the right context, with the illocutionary force conventionally associated with imperatives, i.e. command. Nevertheless, the notion of clause type takes it that a declarative is basically associated with asserting, and other illocutionary forces that it would receive are pragmatically determined, for example by implicature. When it comes to exclamatives, their conventional force is that of exclaiming. Certainly (1), like (2), can be used to exclaim. Our question is whether (1) is conventionally associated with exclaiming, or whether it is usable in this way through some indirect pragmatic mechanism.

In previous work (Zanuttini & Portner 2000, 2003, Portner & Zanuttini 2000), we have shown that exclamatives are associated with certain semantic and pragmatic properties that can be used to test for membership in the clause type of exclamatives. Here we will pick out a few of these which make the case that (1) is truly an exclamative in this sense; please see the works cited for more details.

All exclamatives are factive, and this leads to contrasts like the following:[1]

(3) a. I know what strange things he says.
b. *I don't know what strange things he says.

While (3)a is fine, with an exclamative clause embedded under the factive predicate *know*, (3)b is ungrammatical because negating *I know* conflicts with the exclamative's presupposition of factivity. We see the same pattern with nominal exclamatives:[2]

(4) a. I certainly know the strange things he says.
b. *I don't know the strange things he says.

Thus nominal exclamatives pass the first test for exclamative status.

The second major property of exclamatives is that they generate a characteristic conventional scalar implicature to the effect that certain elements are at the extreme end of some contextually determined scale.[3] This leads to contrasts like the following:

(5) a. It's amazing what strange things he says.
b. *It isn't amazing what strange things he says.
c. *Is it amazing what strange things he says?

Although an exclamative can be embedded under the predicate *amazing*, negating or questioning this predicate gives rise to ungrammaticality. This is because negation denies the "amazingness", or extreme scalar quality, of the proposition; similarly, interrogative form casts into doubt its truth. Since conventional implicatures are non-defeasible, the result is unacceptable. We find the same pattern with nominal exclamatives:[4]

(6) a. It's amazing the strange things he says.
b. *It isn't amazing the strange things he says.
c. *Is it amazing the strange things he says?

Based on these tests, we conclude that the examples we are focusing on share the defining semantic and pragmatic properties of the exclamative clause type.

## 3. PROPERTIES OF NOMINAL EXCLAMATIVES

The goal of this section is to go back to example (1) to show that it is indeed (a) a noun phrase and (b) an exclamative with the same type of meaning as a clausal exclamative like (2). Demonstrating the first point is straightforward: we will show that both the internal structure and the distribution of these phrases is that of an NP. As for the second point, subject agreement allows us to distinguish subjects which have a clause-like meaning from those which have a noun phrase like meaning. Thus in this section we argue that nominal exclamatives pattern with noun phrases in terms of their structure and with clausal exclamatives in terms of their semantic type. In the next section we will investigate how this unorthodox pairing of form and meaning can be compositionally derived.

A superficial inspection of (1) certainly suggests that it is a noun phrase: it contains a definite determiner, an adjective, a head noun and a relative clause. This string can certainly function as a noun phrase in examples like (7):

(7) We discussed the strange things that he says.

However, one can imagine other analyses of (1) in its exclamatory function; perhaps *the strange things* has been topicalized from the object position of *says.* That is, it derives from a structure like *that he says the strange things* by fronting of the definite NP. In this case the presence of the complementizer would be unusual for English, but maybe this construction is different from other root clauses in the licensing of overt complementizers. We see a case roughly of this sort in embedded contexts in Italian. In the following, a hanging topic precedes an overt complementizer (Benincà & Poletto 2004):

(8) Mi dispiace [questo libro [che non ne abbia parlato nessuno]].
to-me displeases this book that neg of-it has spoken nobody
'It bothers me that, as for this book, nobody has said anything about it.'

The embedded clause *questo libro che* . . . bears a passing similarity to example (1), and yet it is undoubtedly a clause, and so we should consider whether (1) might be clausal also.

One piece of evidence that (1) is nominal rather than clausal comes from the parallelism it shows with undisputed relative clauses:[5]

(9) a. It's amazing the strange things that/which/*who/∅ he says!
b. Two nice houses that/which/*who/∅ he would like to buy are on sale.
(10) a. It's amazing the strange people that/which/who/∅ he invited!
b. Two cute girls that/which/who/∅ he met stole the cookies.

(11) a. It's amazing the unbelievable trees that/which/*who/*∅ grow there!
b. Two of the small palms that/which/*who/*∅ grow there came from Australia.
(12) a. It's amazing the wierd friends that/?which/who/*∅ visit him all the time!
b. Two British friends that/?which/who/*∅ teach at Oxford asked questions.

In (9), we see that the nominal exclamative containing an inanimate head noun and an object gap allows *that, which*, and ∅; these possibilities are exactly the same as those in the clear relative clause. Similar patterns can be seen with the animate noun/object gap, an inanimate noun/object gap, and animate noun/object gap cases in (10)–(12).

The possibility of wh words in examples like (10)a poses a significant problem for the view that this is actually a clausal structure. If *the strange people* has been moved from the object position, there is no source site for *which* or *who.* If, however, we take the wh word to have been moved from object position, this requires that we treat *the strange people* as an unmoved left-dislocated element. Since left-dislocation in English always requires the presence of a resumptive pronoun, this analysis is ruled out.[6] Thus, the obvious conclusion from the data in (9)–(12) is the right one: nominal exclamatives are simply noun phrases containing a relative clause.

This conclusion is further supported by examining the external distribution of nominal exclamatives. We must restrict our attention to those predicates which support the exclamative interpretation, but if we do we see that nominal exclamatives only occur as the complements of predicates which subcategorize for a noun phrase. Grimshaw shows that, among those predicates that embed exclamatives, some subcategorize for both noun phrases and clauses, whereas others only take clauses (data from Grimshaw 1979, section 4.1):

(13) a. John couldn't believe what a height the building was. (clausal complement)
b. John couldn't believe the incredible height of the building. (nominal complement)
(14) a. I don't give a damn what an outrageous size his salary is. (clausal complement)
b. *I don't give a damn the outrageous size of his salary. (nominal complement)

Both *couldn't believe* and *give a damn* support the exclamative interpretation; that is, they 's-select' exclamatives in Grimshaw's terms. However, whereas *couldn't believe* subcategorizes for both clauses and noun phrases ('c-selects' these categories, in Grimshaw's terminology), *give a damn* only takes clauses. As would be predicted if they are noun phrases, nominal exclamatives are only possible with predicates of the first type:

(15) John couldn't believe [the strange things she said].
(16) *I don't give a damn [the strange things she said].

A potential problem with our view is the fact that the complement of (15) is very similar to what Grimshaw calls 'concealed exclamatives', following Elliott (1971) and ultimately Baker (1968). A concealed exclamative is a noun phrase which fulfills the s-selection requirements of a predicate that takes an exclamative complement (likewise there exist concealed questions, examples from Grimshaw 1979:299):

(17) John asked the height of the building. (concealed question)
(18) John couldn't believe the height of the building. (concealed exclamative)

Notice that these examples are synonymous with *John asked how high the building was* and *John couldn't believe how very high the building was*, respectively. Thus one might wonder whether we are justified in treating examples like (1) as a distinct class of 'nominal exclamatives' separate from concealed exclamatives.[7] There is a crucial difference between the two constructions. The examples which are the focus of this paper, i.e. (1) and (15), can stand alone with exclamative sentential force, whereas the concealed exclamative in (18) cannot. So, although # *The height of the building!* can be used to exclaim, it is elliptical, in the sense that it feels like a sentence fragment. It refers to something to which we attribute a contextually provided property. In contrast, examples likes *The strange things he says!* are not perceived as elliptical in the same way. As we will see in the discussion below, the nominal exclamatives have a full exclamative meaning on their own, and in this way contrast with ordinary noun phrases used as concealed exclamatives or with the indirect illocutionary force of exclaiming.

We have just shown that nominal exclamatives really are nominal: they have the syntax of noun phrases. The other side of our claim is that they have the sort of meaning which is typically associated with a clause, and are essentially synonymous with clausal exclamatives. Intuitively, as already mentioned, this way of looking at nominal exclamatives is supported by the fact that they do not feel elliptical when uttered out of the blue. In this respect, they contrast with ordinary noun phrases used with the function of exclaiming:[8]

(19) The silly questions these students ask!
(20) Those silly questions!

One might wonder if the reason the noun phrase in (20) feels elliptical is that it lacks sufficient informational content. However, there are cases in which an ordinary noun phrase (lacking a relative clause) has the same content as a nominal exclamative, but it still feels incomplete:[9]

(21) The strange people who come from Italy!
(22) The/those strange Italians!

Data of the kind above suggest that only definite NPs which contain a relative clause can be true nominal exclamatives; that is, only they can have exclamative sentential force. But while it is certainly important that speakers' semantic intuitions support a difference of this sort, we would like to have some corroborating grammatical data. We find such data in agreement facts with predicates like *be amazing*. To begin, ordinary noun phrases trigger agreement with *be amazing* when they are in subject position. When they are in post-predicate position, they act as right-dislocated arguments, and agree with the predicate via a pronoun in subject position:

(23) Those Italians are amazing.
(24) a. They're amazing, those Italians.
b. *It's amazing, those Italians.

Nominal exclamatives behave like ordinary noun phrases when in subject position, but in post-predicate position, they are pronominalized by *it* and do not trigger agreement:

(25) The strange people who come from Italy are amazing.
(26) It's amazing the strange people who come from Italy.

It is possible to have an agreeing pronoun and copula with *the strange people who come from Italy* in post-predicate position, but the meaning is different from (26):

(27) They're amazing, the strange people who come from Italy.

(27) says that the people themselves are amazing. In contrast, (26) does not imply that the people themselves are amazing. Rather, it is some aspect of the information that there are such people who come from Italy which is amazing; for example, one might be amazed that they are strange to such a high degree or that so many of them are strange. As these paraphrases make clear, the contribution of *the strange people who come from Italy* is a group of individuals in (27) and some sort of propositional meaning in (26). That is, (27) (like (25)) contains an ordinary noun phrase followed by a relative clause whereas (26) contains a nominal exclamative.

The lack of agreement in (26) is reminiscent of the behavior of clauses linked to the subject argument:

(28) a. It's amazing what strange things he says.
b. *They are amazing what strange things he says.
(29) It's surprising that they won.
(30) It's a good question whether they came to the party.

We attribute the fact that clauses do not trigger agreement to the fact that their meaning is propositional rather than noun phrase-like (referential or quantificational). More specifically, when in subject position they cannot trigger agreement because they lack agreement features (person and number); in post-predicate position, they are pronominalized by *it* and therefore are associated with a third person singular verbal form. Based on this, we can provide an explanation of the data in (25)–(27). On our view, the string *the strange people who come from Italy* has a single structural analysis, but can have either a propositional or a nominal-type interpretation. In example (26) the phrase in post-predicate position has a clause-like meaning, and hence does not trigger agreement. More specifically, we assume that because it is propositional, it is pronominalized by *it* and hence is associated with the third singular form of *be.* In (27) it has a nominal meaning, and so is pronominalized by *they*, yielding plural agreement.

In contrast to the post-predicate cases, as seen in (25) the preverbal NP always triggers agreement. This is simply because it has person and number features and is in the right syntactic configuration for agreement to occur. Note that, in the presence of agreement, the clausal interpretation is ruled out; this leaves us with only the nominal one. The question is why there should be such a connection between agreement and interpretation. Of course this question goes beyond the present case. It involves asking why in general constituents which have a propositional interpretation (canonically, clauses) always co-occur with third person singular verb and pronoun forms, plausibly the default forms. We do not seek to address this question here.

Note that the pattern just described cannot be accounted for under an analysis which treats *the strange people who come from Italy* as syntactically ambiguous between an agreement-triggering phrase (that is, a noun phrase) and a non-agreement-triggering one (e.g. a clause). Under such a proposal, one could not explain why agreement is required in (25), since we would have the option of having the non-agreement-triggering form in subject position. This point also argues against an ellipsis account of nominal exclamatives. One would have to propose that ellipsis is impossible in subject position, given that we always get agreement and a non-propositional interpretation, but as far as we can see this restriction would have to be simply stipulated. Of course the present approach is incomplete as well, since we don't fully understand the connection between agreement and semantic type, but at least the generalizations we appeal to are independently motivated. In general, a noun phrase in subject position triggers agreement, while phrases with propositional meaning never trigger agreement. These requirements cannot both be met in a sentence containing a nominal exclamative in subject position, and so the grammar rules out this possibility.

## 4. COMPOSITIONAL INTERPRETATION OF NOMINAL EXCLAMATIVES

Having shown that nominal exclamatives are structurally noun phrases but semantically clause-like, we now turn to the question of how this unusual pairing of form and meaning can arise. Given their syntactic parallelism with interrogatives, we assume that exclamatives have meanings of the same type as questions (cf. Portner & Zanuttini 2000, Section 5). That is, they denote sets of propositions (Hamblin 1973, Karttunen 1977, etc.) Of course there are differences between interrogative and exclamative denotations, but this won't be our focus here. These differences are of a pragmatic nature; in particular, exclamatives and interrogatives have different sentential forces.

The simplest option is perhaps to postulate an empty operator of some sort which converts an ordinary definite NP meaning into the appropriate question-like meaning. A traditional syntactic analysis of (31)a would be something like (31)b:

(31) a. The things that are in this bag!
b. [$_{DP}$ the [$_{NP}$ things [$_{CP}$ which$_i$ C [$_{IP}$ t$_i$ are in this bag]]]]

Assuming that this noun phrase is referential, an operator with the meaning in (32)a would convert this into the appropriate set of propositions in (32)b:[10]

(32) a. $[\lambda f. \{p : w_0 \in p \ \& \ \exists y[p = \{w : y \leq f(w)\}]\}]$
b. {p : ∃y[p is true and p = 'y is one of the things in this bag']}

However, such an analysis does not explain why the relative clause is required in true nominal exclamatives. A better strategy would be to build the semantic analysis somehow on the presence of the relative clause.

We will pursue an alternative based on Kayne's (1994) analysis of relative clauses. Kayne's approach is promising because it takes noun+relative clause sequences to actually be full clauses (CPs) which are the complement of the determiner. A wh phrase containing the "head noun" begins within the IP and raises to the specifier of CP. The key difference from the traditional account is the idea that the noun which the relative clause modifies originates internal to it.[11]

(33) [$_{DP}$ the [$_{CP}$ [things which]$_i$ C [$_{IP}$ t$_i$ are in this bag]]]

We would like to exploit the basically clausal nature of this analysis to derive the propositional meaning of nominal exclamatives. This would also allow us to explain why nominal exclamatives must contain a relative clause, since noun phrases lacking relative clauses don't have this kind of structure.

Before tackling the exclamative interpretation of (33), perhaps it would be helpful to consider how an ordinary referential interpretation could be derived for such a structure. Within the CP, we have two set-denoting expressions: *things* and $t_i$ *are in the bag.*[12] These two sets are intersected, either by virtue of the meaning of *which*, which would then simply be predicate conjunction, or through a default rule of predicate conjunction (cf. for example, Heim & Kratzer 1998). In the latter case, *which* would be treated as semantically vacuous. The whole CP would then denote a set of individuals, here the things which are in the bag, and the determiner would take this set as argument in the ordinary fashion.

The interpretation of nominal exclamatives can be attributed to an additional morpheme E somewhere in the structure. Though various possibilities are conceivable (E in D, adjoined to CP, or adjoined to DP, among others), we will pursue the idea that E is part of the wh phrase. The motivation for this is the fact that wh phrases in clausal exclamatives often have a unique form, different from their interrogative counterparts. For instance, the *a* in *what a dog* and *very* in *how very tall* are markers of exclamative status and could be identified with a similar E morpheme. A wh word with the following interpretation achieves the correct result:

(34) a. $[\![\text{which}_{EXCL}]\!] = [\lambda P \lambda Q.\ \{p : w_0 \in p\ \&\ \exists x[p = \{w : P(w)(x) = 1 \text{ and } Q(w)(x) = 1\}]\}]$

b. $\{p : w_0 \in p\ \&\ \exists x[p = \{w : x \text{ is a thing in w and x is in the bag in w}\}]\}$

If we take the wh words in ordinary relative clauses to be meaningless, (34)a would simply be the interpretation of E. If, on the other hand, they contribute predicate conjunction, we can still give a compositional interpretation, though E's meaning would be slightly more abstract.[13] In either case, the wh word denotes a function which combines with two properties: that denoted by the noun (represented by P) and that denoted by the IP (represented by Q). The value of this function is then the set of true propositions of the form '*x* is a P and *x* is a Q'.

The analysis that we have given provides a clausal meaning to the nominal exclamative. Moreover, by adopting Kayne's view of relative clauses, the mapping between syntactic categories and semantic types is better motivated than under the alternative. The relative clause CP denotes a set of propositions, and the wh word denotes a function from common noun meanings and predicates to such a set of propositions. These are completely normal meanings for CPs and wh words to have. In particular, we provide the relative wh word with the type of meaning normally associated with interrogative wh words in this case, and this explains the synonymy between clausal and nominal exclamatives. In contrast, a traditional structural analysis of relative clauses could make use of an operator like that in (34)a. However, this would result in the relative clause CP denoting a function from common noun meanings to sets of propositions—an unprecedented semantic type for CPs.

One issue that comes up at this point is the role of the determiner *the* in nominal exclamatives. Given what we have said, the sister of *the* denotes a set of propositions, and this is not the ordinary type to be the argument of a determiner. We would like to suggest that an answer to this puzzle resides in a point that we made earlier, that exclamatives are always factive. We propose that *the* in this case marks factivity. This idea is pretty natural from the perspective of a theory of definiteness which makes the sole function of *the* to be that of marking a familiarity presupposition (Heim 1982, for example). Factivity has a clear intuitive relation to familiarity, and so it's plausible that the function of *the* could be extended to marking factivity.[14] Moreover this idea lets us explain why no other determiner is possible in nominal exclamatives.

There are other possible ideas for how factivity is marked in nominal exclamatives. In other work, we have proposed that factivity is marked in clausal exclamatives by a null operator in the CP domain. Such an operator could exist in nominal exclamatives as well, presumably in the relative clause which is obligatorily present. We are not aware at this point of empirical evidence that would let us decide between these alternatives.

## 5. CONCLUSION

Our central contribution has been to argue that nominal exclamatives like *The strange things that he says!* are noun phrases but have a semantic content of the kind more typical of clauses. In particular, we hypothesize that they have the semantic type of wh clauses, i.e. denoting a set of propositions. They are not derived by ellipsis from full clauses, nor is their similarity to clausal exclamatives to be explained by a pragmatic process like implicature. This combination of properties may be at first glance surprising, since it shows that grammar is not constrained by simple correlations between syntactic category and semantic type like *noun phrase* → *entity/predicate/quantifier* and *sentence* → *proposition/set of propositions.* This raises the question of whether this mapping is irregular and arbitrary.

Towards answering this question, we have argued that Kayne's (1994) syntactic analysis of relative clauses provides a better foundation than more traditional views for explaining the pattern of nominal exclamatives found in English. In particular, the fact that, according to Kayne's view, a noun phrase with a relative clause ultimately consists of a determiner taking a clausal complement helps us see why nominal exclamatives always contain relative clauses. Hence, the fact that nominal exclamatives constitute an exception to the typical relationship between syntactic category and semantic type is not as surprising as it seems at first. The interpretation of these forms derives from the presence of clausal structure in combination with a hypothesized exclamative morpheme. This leads to a view of the syntax/semantic interface which takes the category/type mapping to be derived compositionally from the internal makeup of the syntactic forms. The mapping is not arbitrary; it is motivated "from the bottom up". Regularities exist in the mapping because the internal structure of categories shows consistency, but exceptions can arise when some aspect of the structure is unique. Nominal exclamatives provide such a case.

## NOTES

1 (3)b is acceptable on an irrelevant reading where the complement of *know* is a free relative. We can rule out the free relative interpretation by adding a modifier to the wh phrase: *I (*don't) know what incredibly strange things he says.*

2 As we noted in the introduction, the noun phrases which can function as a nominal exclamative can typically also be used as an ordinary referential definite. In our examples, the referential reading is difficult to get,

and so they seem ungrammatical, but similar examples will be acceptable on the (irrelevant) referential reading: *I don't know the strange things he lectures about.*

3 The implicature is conventional, rather than conversational, because it does not arise due to reasoning based on any sort of Gricean Cooperative Assumption. Rather, it is associated with this particular linguistic form. Note that one could not explain the pattern we see with embedded exclamatives by appealing to the conversational use of the corresponding non-embedded forms. When embedded, they do not have a conversational use of their own. Similarly, as pointed out by Rob Stainton, *Big guy!* can be used as an exclamative, but when it's part of a larger sentence, it has no such conversational use of its own: *I have met that big guy before.*

4 Example (6)c is similar to the grammatical example *Are they amazing, the strange things he says?* However, in this case we have subject verb agreement, and this corresponds to the referential interpretation of the noun phrase; see section 3 for discussion.

5 We embed the (a) examples under *it's amazing* to make sure they are read as exclamatives rather than ordinary definite NPs. Other exclamative-embedding contexts, like *I am amazed at*, allow both exclamative and ordinary NP complements. Thus, *I am amazed at the strange people that he invited* could have an embedded-exclamative meaning (= 'I am amazed at what strange people he invited') and a referential complement meaning (= 'I am amazed at certain people, namely the strange people that he invited'; i.e., I'm amazed at some aspect of these people, though not necessarily at the fact that he invited them).

6 One might consider the possibility that the wh word acts as the resumptive pronoun, but there would be no other instances of such a use in English. Moreover, the cases which lack a wh word would have no overt resumptive pronoun. This means we'd have to say that the initial material is a topic when there is no wh word and a left-dislocated element when there is, a complicated possibility for which there is no evidence.

7 In fact, Elliott (1971) calls examples like (15) concealed exclamatives. Against this, we are arguing that the two kinds of examples need to be distinguished, even though they are both syntactically noun phrases.

8 Bare wh phrases like *What silly questions!* are more able to stand on their own than definites lacking a relative clause. Perhaps they are elliptical for clausal wh exclamatives (which, in that case, would be seen as tolerating ellipsis better than nominal exclamatives and declarative clauses).

9 It's interesting to note that (22) is much worse with *the* than with *those*. We are not sure why this would be the case, but it does show that there is something special about the nominal exclamative. Moreover, *those strange people who come from Italy* seems incomplete, and no longer has the feel of a nominal exclamative.

10 This operator gives the set of true propositions of the appropriate form. Alternative meanings for questions could be handled with appropriate changes to our operator. What we have to say could work as well if definite NPs are quantificational, though we will consider only the referential analysis for simplicity. Note that we assume that the operator combines with the intension of the NP meaning, corresponding to the variable f.

11 Assuming that we start out with *which things* as a constituent, Kayne derives the order *things which* by moving *things* from the complement to the specifier position of a QP headed by *which*: $[_{QP}$ things$_i$ $[_{Q}$ which $t_i$]]. We omit this detail for simplicity. An unresolved issue is how the precise form of the wh phrase is chosen, though this is a problem that afflicts traditional accounts of relative clauses as well. For instance, why is a null operator available in object relatives but not object interrogatives?

12 Various techniques could be used to create a set out of the IP $t_i$ *are in the bag*. In terms of Heim & Kratzer's system, the index i from the wh phrase would be adjoined to C', and this would trigger a rule of Predicate Abstraction.

13 This proposal raises the question of why nominal exclamatives cannot have the clausal exclamative-type of wh phrase: *what a* and *how very*. Presumably this reduces to the broader question of why the wh phrases in relative clauses differ in form from their interrogative counterparts (cf. footnote 11).

14 On other approaches to the definite article, where *the* would have some semantic function in addition to marking a definiteness presupposition, we could still see its use in marking factivity as an extension of its usual function, though the shift would be greater.

## REFERENCES

Baker, C.L., *Indirect Questions in English.* PhD thesis, University of Illinois. 1968.

Benincà, P., and Poletto, C., "Topic, focus, and V2: Defining the CP sublayers." In L. Rizzi (ed.) *The Structure of CP and IP: The Cartography of Syntactic Structures*. New York and Oxford: Oxford University Press. 2004: 52–75.

Elliott, D.E., *The Grammar of Emotive and Exclamatory Sentences in English.* PhD thesis, The Ohio State University. 1971.

Grimshaw, J., "Complement selection and the lexicon." *Linguistic Inquiry* 10(2) (1979): 279–326.

Hamblin, C.L., "Questions in Montague English." *Foundations of Language* 10 (1973): 41–53.

Heim, I., *The Semantics of Definite and Indefinite Noun Phrases.* Amherst: GLSA. 1982.

Heim, I., and Kratzer, A., *Semantics in Generative Grammar.* Malden, MA, and Oxford: Blackwell. 1998.

Karttunen, L., "Syntax and semantics of questions." *Linguistics and Philosophy* 1 (1977): 3–44.

Kayne, R.S., *The Antisymmetry of Syntax.* Vol. 25 of *Linguistic Inquiry Monographs.* Cambridge, Mass.: MIT Press. 1994.

Portner, P., and Zanuttini, R., "The force of negation in Wh exclamatives and interrogatives." In L. Horn and Y. Kato (eds.) *Studies in Negation and Polarity: Syntactic and Semantic Perspectives.* New York and Oxford: Oxford University Press. 2000: 201–39.

Sadock, J.M., and Zwicky, A., "Speech act distinctions in syntax." In Timothy Shopen (ed.) *Language Typology and Syntactic Description.* Cambridge: Cambridge University Press. 1985: 155–196.

Zanuttini, R., and Portner, P., "The characterization of exclamative clauses in Paduan." *Language* 76(1) (2000): 123–32.

Zanuttini, R., and Portner, P., "Exclamative clauses: At the syntax-semantics interface." *Language* 79(3) (2003): 39–81.

# B

# ELLIPSIS AND NONSENTENTIAL SPEECH: THE GENUINENESS ISSUE

ELLEN BARTON AND LJILJANA PROGOVAC

# NONSENTENTIALS IN MINIMALISM

## 0. INTRODUCTION

The grammatical status of nonsententials — utterances smaller than a sentence — has long intrigued grammarians. Historical and descriptive grammarians have mostly assumed that nonsententials are simply sentence fragments, remnants of full sentences somehow reduced by straightforward deletion (Sweet, 1900; Follet, 1966; Quirk et al., 1972). Generative grammarians have sometimes assumed this analysis (Morgan, 1973), but more recent work has investigated the complexity of the structure of nonsententials as well as the implications of the analysis of nonsententials for theories of grammar, discourse, and pragmatics (Haegemann, 1987; Morgan, 1989; Barton, 1990, 1991, 1998). In this introduction, we review the competing theories of deletion and derivation for nonsententials (§0.1). In the rest of the chapter, we first update the grammatical analysis of nonsententials, describing their derivation within the Minimalist program (§1.0); we then consider NP nonsententials (§1.1) and VP nonsententials (§1.2) in detail. We propose a unified analysis of NP and VP nonsententials that centers upon the variability of nonsententials with respect to feature-checking as a defining characteristic; specifically, we propose a Case Feature Corollary which states that nonsententials are not required to check Case features. We use this analysis to provide a unified analysis for a number of previously puzzling cases within the derivation of nonsententials, including missing subjects (§2.1), auxiliaries (§2.2), determiners (§2.3), prepositions (§2.4), and complementizers (§2.5). In the Conclusion (§3), we consider the implications of this analysis of nonsententials for the Minimalist program.

### *0.1. Deletion and Derivation Accounts of Nonsententials*

Two competing theories of the derivation of nonsententials have focused either on deletion from full sentence structures (Morgan, 1973, 1989) or derivation straight from major categories as initial nodes (Barton, 1990, 1991, 1998).[1] Recently, both Morgan (1989) and Barton (1998) have agreed that the full story of nonsententials seems to require both deletion and derivation analyses. Morgan (1989) argues that most nonsententials derive from complete sentence representations, but he acknowledges a very restricted set of base-generated nonsententials, just those that can be interpreted pragmatically without recourse to any linguistic context (e.g., *Fire!* or *One ticket*), following Yanofsky (1978). Barton (1998) argues for a larger set of base-generated nonsententials, specifically all those major categories that show no overt evidence of sentential derivation (e.g., utterances in telegraphese like *Sudden flu attack* or *At Newbury, Vermont border*). Barton argues for a deletion analysis only of nonsententials



*R. Elugardo and R. J. Stainton (eds.), Ellipsis and Nonsentential Speech*, 71–93.

that show overt evidence of sentential derivation (e.g., *am ill* or *car broken down* in telegraphese).

To account for base-generated nonsententials, Barton (1991) proposed the $X^{max}$ Generalization in (1):

(1) $X^{max}$ Generalization
The initial node of a generative grammar is $X^{max}$.

The $X^{max}$ Generalization, which generalizes the principles of X-bar theory to eliminate the stipulation that the initial node of a grammar is S, accounts for nonsentential NPs, VPs, AdjPs, AdvPs, and PPs. Barton (1998) showed that the $X^{max}$ Generalization accounts straightforwardly for independent major category utterances like the following examples from a corpus of telegraphese:[2]

(2a) Sudden car problem
(2b) My regrets
(2c) In trouble
(2d) Still at JFK
(2e) At Newbury, Vermont border
(2f) Urgent
(2g) Maybe tomorrow
(2h) Immediately

The independent NPs in (2a)–(2b), PPs in (2c)–(2e), the AdjP in (2f), and the AdvPs in (2g)–(2h) are base-generated under their phrasal categories as initial nodes.

To account for nonsententials with overt evidence of sentential properties in the corpus of telegraphese, Barton (1998) proposed the two deletion rules in (3) to account for nonsententials that showed evidence of sentential origins and derivations:

(3a) (Generalized) Deletion Rule 1
Optionally delete subjects up to recoverability.
(3b) Deletion Rule 2
Optionally delete functional categories up to recoverability.

The deletion rule in (3a) accounts for nonsententials with evidence of deleted subjects, particularly the first-person singular I, as in the examples in (4):

(4a) Am ill
(4b) Am at border in Newbury, Vermont

The generalization of the rule accounts for nonsententials with tensed forms and modals, like those in (5):

(5a) Was to present a paper
(5b) Have been detained
(5c) Had wanted to participate in conference and defend paper
(5d) Can't make conference
(5e) Will arrive one day late

This Generalized Deletion Rule is similar in nature to the syntactic rules that allow deleted subjects in pro-drop languages like Italian and Spanish, although there was no firm evidence in the corpus that any subjects other than first person singulars were deleted.

The deletion rule in (3b) accounts for nonsententials with missing functional categories like those in (6):

(6a) Get lawyer
(6b) Car dead
(6c) Problems arisen
(6d) Flight canceled
(6e) Detained JFK Airport New York
(6f) Arrested alleged drug smuggling Newport, Vermont
(6g) Regret I will be unable to present my paper at the conference

The nonsententials in (6a) and (6b) have missing determiners within NPs (*get (a/the) lawyer* and *(the) car*). The nonsententials in (6c)–(6d) have missing auxiliaries (*problems (have) arisen* and *flight (was) canceled*). The VPs in (6e) and (6f) have missing prepositions (*detained (at) JFK Airport*, *arrested (for) alleged drug smuggling*). The VP with an embedded clause in (6g) has a missing complementizer (*regret (that)*).

This analysis is not without significant theoretical problems, however. First is the rather suspicious need for deletion rules in the first place: as generative grammar has developed, specific deletion rules like those in (3) have become more difficult to motivate. Second is the question of the asymmetry inherent in rule (3a): a deletion rule that specifically deletes subjects establishes an unmotivated subject-object asymmetry — why do subjects delete, but not objects? Third is the question of overlap across rules (3a) and (3b): since subjects are (arguably) functional categories in sentential projections, rule (3b) should be able to subsume rule (3a). Fourth is the question of overgeneration from these rules, especially (3b): some functional categories, like infinitive *to* do not delete, and not all pronouns delete (under the assumption that pronouns are functional categories; cf. §1.1 and §2.1). Finally, the analysis is not well-situated within the current theoretical framework of generative grammar, an update we undertake in the following section.

## 1. NONSENTENTIALS — BASIC ANALYSIS

### *1.0. Introductory Note*

In this section, we provide both theoretical and empirical reasons for permitting the grammar to generate $X^{max}$ nonsententials, that is, independent phrases below the sentential level. Theoretically, this analysis is in keeping with the minimalist considerations of Economy. We first take up the issue of Economy and provide an overview of major phrases that can act as nonsententials with minimal derivations (§1.0). Empirically, there are numerous patterns (not just examples) which follow from a nonsentential analysis, but cannot be derived by a sentential analysis, as we show in §1.1 for NP nonsententials and in §1.2 for VP nonsententials. We note the striking parallelism between the two types of nonsententials, and propose a unified analysis.

Interestingly, the distinction between sentences and phrases is not a significant theoretical problem in the framework we are adopting in this paper, Chomsky's (1989, 1995) Minimalist Program. Given Minimalism, a clause is simply a phrase whose head is I (short for Inflection). Moreover, the derivation of a structure is built bottom-up, by merging words and phrases in a binary fashion, but only as long as there is evidence for further merger. Superfluous structure is prohibited by the Economy Principle as formulated by Chomsky (1989: 69): "Derivations and representations . . . are required to be minimal . . . with no superfluous steps in derivations and no superfluous symbols in representations." A constituent thus is considered to be a maximal projection if it projects no further, allowing a head, which projects no further, to be at the same time a maximal projection. Such a head can be a N projecting to NP, a V projecting to VP, a P projecting to PP, an I projecting to IP, and so on. Since both phrases and clauses are derived bottom-up through merger, to say that generation must start with a sentence would be problematic in this framework for two reasons. First, it would be contrary to the minimalist considerations of structure building. Second, it would be a pure stipulation, given that there is nothing special about sentence/clause in this framework. Indeed, given bottom-up merger, there is even no need for the $X^{max}$ generalization as stated in (1), although the central idea that categories project to independent maximal categories remains, though the details of derivation in Minimalism are different.

Consistent with Minimalism, then, the following major category phrases will be considered $X^{max}$ nonsententials, generated not as sentences, but as maximal projections of nonsentential phrases:

(7a) sudden flu attack (NP)
(7b) car problem (NP)
(7c) the nearest bar (DP)
(7d) in trouble (PP)
(7e) fond of animals (AP)
(7f) most unfortunately (AdvP)
(7g) play baseball (VP)

The Minimalist framework allows, actually requires, generation of phrases below sentential level in these cases because there is no evidence for their sentential status. Thus, in his textbook on Minimalism, Radford (1997: 86–97) analyzes a series of answers to questions as maximal projections of phrases:

(8a) What are the rebel ministers unhappy about?
Plans to privatize hospitals. (NP)
(8b) Which way is [he] going to vote?
Against government plans to privatize hospitals. (PP)
(8c) What will the rebel ministers do?
Vote against government plans to privatize hospitals. (VP)

Like Barton (1998), Radford maintains that only maximal projections can act as nonsentential answers to questions, which is in accordance with the intuition of the $X^{max}$ Generalization.

Given the bottom up structure building strategy in Minimalism, (7a) is derived by first merging the noun *attack* with the specifier *flu*, creating an NP. Next, the NP merges with the adjective *sudden*, which is adjoined to the NP, as illustrated in (9)

(9)

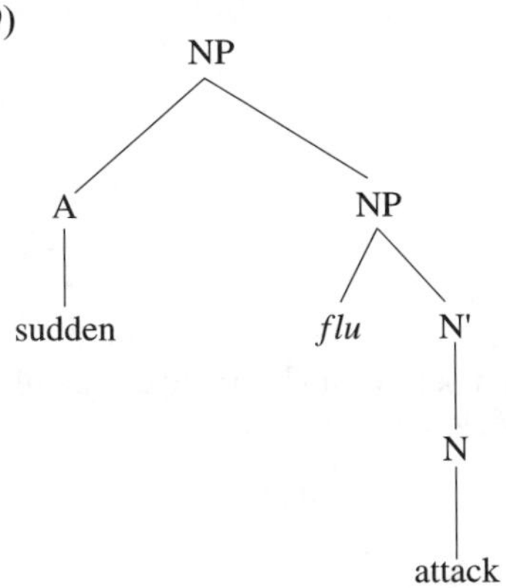


In (7b), the noun *problem* merges with the noun *car* to form an NP. There is no evidence for any further merger, and therefore no evidence of any other category on top of these NPs. According to Minimalism, it would thus be not only arbitrary, but also inaccurate, to posit any extra structure in (7a) or (7b).

In a similar fashion, (7c) is analyzed as a DP, in which the NP *nearest bar* merges with the determiner *the*. (7d) is analyzed as a PP, in which the preposition *in* merges with the noun *trouble*. In (7e), the adjective *fond* is analyzed as merging with the prepositional complement *of animals* into an AP. In (7f), the adverb *unfortunately* merges with *most* into an AdvP. In (7g), the verb *play* merges with the noun *baseball* into a VP. Just as was the case with the NPs, there is no evidence for any higher projection on top of these maximal projections. Projecting a sentential category on top of these NPs would not only be arbitrary, but also contrary to the minimalist principles of structure building.

Thus our analysis of nonsententials as $X^{max}$ projections via merger is supported and reinforced within the framework of Minimalism by two of its basic properties: (i) the bottom-up strategy of phrase creation based on merger of words, rather than a top-down strategy which would start with an arbitrary top category, such as sentence; and (ii) by the general requirement in Minimalism for economy, which prohibits any superfluous and unmotivated pieces of structure. In addition, our analysis would predict that nonsentential NPs will be able to occur without determiners (§1.1). Parallel to this, our analysis would also predict that VPs can occur without tense or agreement (§1.2). Both scenarios occur, and both follow straightforwardly from our analysis, as we will show.

### *1.1. NP Nonsententials*

This section describes NPs as nonsententials, arguing in more detail that they are correctly generated as NP maximal projections, without any sentential structure on top of them, and proposing an analysis that Case feature checking does not hold in nonsententials.

The fact that nonsentential NPs frequently occur without determiners is consistent with the DP analysis (Abney, 1987; Longobardi, 1994), which we adopt. According to the DP analysis, D takes NP as its complement, as in (10) below:

(10)

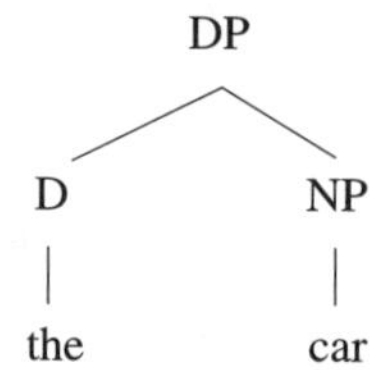


Under the DP analysis, both (7a) and (7b), repeated below, can be analyzed as full NPs, as shown in (9), without a need to postulate any deleted or null determiners.

(7a) sudden flu attack (NP)
(7b) car problem (NP)

Any sentential analysis of (7a) and (7b) would face the difficult question of why the determiner is deleted here, while it would otherwise be obligatory in a full sentence, as demonstrated by the examples in (11):

(11a) He was struck by a sudden flu attack.
*He was struck by sudden flu attack.
(11b) We are having a car problem.
*We are having car problem.

Longobardi (1994) argues that NPs are obligatorily headed by Ds if they are arguments, but not otherwise. This explains the grammaticality and ungrammaticality of the examples in (11): *a sudden flu attack* and *a car problem* are grammatical as full DP arguments, while *sudden flu attack* and *car problem* are ungrammatical as arguments because they are not full DP projections. This analysis follows from the general assumption that arguments can only be visible (i.e. interpretable) in LF (Logical Form) if they are assigned structural Case. The assignment of structural Case is assumed to require the projection of DP, in which D assigns Case to the NP, which would explain why a DP is required with arguments. But when NPs are not functioning as arguments, there is no need for a DP projection to assign structural Case. The examples in (12a) and (12b) illustrate felicitous uses of bare NPs as vocatives and complements. In contrast, (12c) and (12d) again illustrate that singular common nouns in argument positions, such as subjects or objects, require a determiner.

(12a) *Teacher*, can I please answer the question?
(12b) They elected her *president*.
(12c) I saw the teacher/the president.
*I saw teacher/president.
(12d) The teacher/the president gave a lecture.
*Teacher/President gave a lecture.

In sum, the frequent appearance of bare NPs as nonsententials suggests that such NPs are not to be analyzed as arguments of clauses, whose other constituents have been deleted, but rather as independent nonsentential NPs.

In the Minimalist Program, Case assignment is achieved through feature checking. The basic principles of feature checking are described in Radford (1997, Ch. 5) and summarized briefly here. Consider the example in (13) and its structural representation in (14):

(13) The teacher will understand her.

(14)

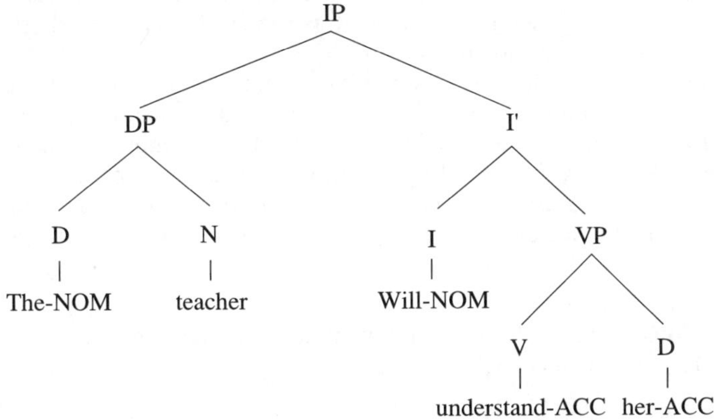


The Nominative feature of the determiner *the*, and its projection DP, is checked against the Nominative feature of the finite modal verb *will*, in the spec-head configuration of IP. Similarly, the Accusative feature of the pronoun *her* is checked against the accusative feature of the transitive verb. (It is irrelevant for our discussion that the accusative feature checking is commonly believed to take place in an Agreement phrase, into which both the verb and the object move.) According to Postal (1969), Longobardi (1994), and much of the current literature, pronouns are associated with D, either by base-generation in D, or by movement (overt or covert) into D. This is a natural assumption not only because pronouns are the locus of Case features, but also because they are a functional category. (For empirical arguments in various languages, see Longobardi, 1994.)

Thus, if NP nonsententials are not analyzed as clausal arguments, derived by deletion from full sentences, then they will not require a D or a projection to DP. Thus NP nonsententials can occur straightforwardly without determiners, as they do in (7a) and (7b). In fact, there are data in English and other languages that suggest not only that NP nonsententials do not have to occur with determiners, but also that they need not be assigned Case either. This reinforces the previously noted assumption that Case is assigned only to DPs. Consider the following English pattern discussed in Morgan (1973, 1989) and Barton (1990):

(15a) Who can eat another piece of cake?
(15b) ?*I/?*We/?*He/?*She
(15c) Me/?Us/Him/Her
(15d) I/We/He/She can eat another piece of cake.
(15e) I can/We can/He can/She can
(15f) *Me can/*Us can/*Him can/*Her can

Rather unexpectedly, the pronouns that would be subjects in full-fledged clauses cannot appear naturally in the Nominative Case as nonsententials, as shown in (15b); instead, nonsentential pronouns most often appear in the Accusative Case, as shown in (15c). The Nominative pronoun seems grammatical only when it appears in a full sentence, as in (15d) or in a minimal sentence with a modal, as in (15e), both clauses in which an Accusative Case pronoun would be ungrammatical, as shown in (15f). Nominative Case is straightforward in (15d) and (15e) because the modal verb would force a projection of a clause, or an IP, since modals are analyzed as heads of IPs. But the pattern in (15b) and (15c) poses an insurmountable problem for a sentential analysis because a sentential analysis cannot generate Accustaive Case nonsententials, like those in (15c), from a sentential analysis, as shown in (15f).

Within a nonsentential analysis, however, the grammaticality of independent nonsententials in the Accusative Case, as in (15c), suggests that Case feature checking does not need to take place in nonsententials, under the assumption that Accusative Case is the unmarked Case form for English. In fact, the absence of feature checking for Case features may indeed be the defining property of nonsentential constituents. We therefore explore the following strong hypothesis in the rest of this paper:

(16) Case Feature Corollary (CFC)
Nonsententials differ from sententials in one basic property: they are not required to check Case features.

On the assumption that D is formally required only for Case feature checking, the claim in (16) that feature checking need not take place in nonsententials would explain both sets of data: (i) the frequency of bare NPs among nonsententials, as shown in (7a) and (7b), and (ii) the intriguing data of Case distribution, as shown in (15b) and (15c).

It remains to explain why the pronouns in (15c) are in accusative form. It may simply be that the accusative forms are the default Case in English, explaining why the accusative pronouns would be used for what would correspond to both subject and object nonsententials. The assumption that Accusative Case is the default Case for English is consistent with the evidence from child language: accusative case is often used for both subjects and objects in child speech. In discussing a child's utterance like *Me want to see outside*, Radford (1997: 357) specifically suggests that the case of *me* may not be checked at all and that "objective case is the default case form in English," an explanation that he notes extends to answers to questions. Radford's example of a question-answer sequence (*Who failed syntax? Me.*) is exactly parallel to our data in (15).

This analysis of nonsentential NPs in English finds striking support in Korean. As reported in Morgan (1989), in some constructions, Korean nouns must appear without Case when the NP is in a non-argument position, as in the complement NP in (17a); Case for this NP would be ungrammatical in Korean, as shown in (17b):

| | | | |
|---|---|---|---|
| (17a) | I kos-I | chaek | ita |
| | this-NOM | book-NO-CASE | is |
| (17b) | *I kos-I | chaek-i | ita |
| | this-NOM | book-NOM | is |
| | 'This is a book.' | | |

Of note here is the tendency in colloquial English also to use the default Accusative Case in complement positions, as in (18a), even though prescriptively only Nominative is permitted, as in (18b). Nominative, however, sounds rather unnatural:

(18a) This is me/him/us.
It's me/him/us.
(18b) ?This is I/he/we.
?It's I/he/we.

These data lend further credence to the idea that Accusative is default Case in English. If a language has a default Case, then it would allow it only in non-argument positions, as is the case with English. Likewise, if a language has case-less nouns, like Korean, they would only appear in non-argument positions.

Furthermore, in Korean, nonsentential answers to questions such as (19a) can take two different forms: the appropriately case-marked noun form, as in (19b), or the case-less noun form, as in (19c), reinforcing the conclusion that nonsententials can indeed be case-less, even if they correspond to an argument in a question. In Korean, however, the Accusative form is ungrammatical, as shown in (19d), which would follow if Accusative is not the default Case in Korean, the way it is in English.

(19a) Nu-ka ku chaek-ul sa-ass-ni?
'Who bought the book?'
(19b) Yongsu-ka-NOM
(19c) Yongsu-NO-CASE
(19d) *Yongsu-rul-ACC

In nonsententials that have no sentential connection, and are not answers to questions, only case-less forms of nouns are acceptable in Korean, as expected:

(20a) phyo han-cang
ticket one-NO-CASE
(20b) *phyo han-cang-I
ticket one-NOM
(20c) *phyo han-cang-ul
ticket one-ACC
'One ticket'

Thus, for both English and Korean it holds that nonsententials are not required to check Case features, even if they are answers to questions in which they would correspond to an argument. In Korean, this is clearly demonstrated by the use of case-less noun forms, while in English it is demonstrated by the use of default Accusative Case forms. The Case Feature Corollary in (16), then, accounts for the distribution and properties of nonsentential NPs.

It is still unclear, though, why Korean also allows Nominative/Accusative distinctions in answers, as shown in (19), while English permits only default Accusative answers, as shown in (15). Pending further research on this topic, we make the following tentative assumptions. English pronouns have weak Case features, the property which allows them as nonsententials to stay in N and project to NP only, that is, to not raise to D within a DP projection. Thus, a default-marked Accusative pronoun stays in N and projects to NP, and a DP is never projected, since the pronoun does not require it. Likewise, the case-less nouns in Korean are NPs, with no Case features, and they project no DP. On the other hand, the case-marked nouns in Korean, on the assumption that their Case features are strong, necessarily project a DP. One way of interpreting strong features on lexical items is to see them as inseparable from the phonetic form of the lexical items that support them (cf. Radford 1997: 226–30). For Korean Case marked nouns this would mean that their strong Case feature cannot be realized or pronounced without the projection of both NP and DP, since the features of the lexical item itself straddle both projections. Since English pronouns only have weak Case features, the projection of DP with nonsententials will not be forced in English. In other words, Economy would prohibit an analysis of (15c) in which a DP would be generated with an empty D position, because the NP analysis is more economical, and nothing requires a DP. Also, one would have to say that the use of non-default Case in Korean, and with it the DP, is suggestive of the role the argument would play in a clause, and that for that reason Accusative cannot be used interchangeably with Nominative. In other words, a DP, whose sole purpose is to make an argument visible, would necessarily enforce a matching of Case to appropriate arguments. A precise formulation of this proposal, however, requires further research.

Although tentative, this line of analysis is nevertheless consistent with the data in Serbian, a language in which, as we argue, nouns and pronouns carry strong Case features that require a D and projection to DP (see Progovac (1998) for a discussion of Serbian pronouns in D). Serbian differs from both English and Korean in that it does not seem to have either default Case or case-less forms. If our discussion of strong Case is on the right track, in Serbian, a pronoun would necessarily have to be in D to realize the strong Case features, and a nonsentential would have to carry an appropriate Case feature. Thus, in Serbian, data like (15) work the opposite way from English, and instead work the same way as the Korean Case-marked nouns in (19b) and (19d):

(21a) a Ko bi pojeo jos jedno parče torte?
Who would eat another piece of cake?
(21b) Ja/Mi/On/Ona
I/We/He/She
(21c) *Mene/*Nas/*Njega/*Nju
Me/Us/Him/Her
(21d) Ja (Mi/On/Ona) bih pojela jos jedno parče torte.
I/We/He/She would eat another piece of cake.

Since there are no case-less nouns/pronouns in Serbian, and since there is no default Case, there are no other options.

Given the Korean data in (19), Morgan (1989) suggests that utterances smaller than a sentence can receive a dual analysis. He suggests (19b) be analyzed as a sentential, with a subsequent deletion, while (19c) be analyzed as an $X^{max}$, with nothing deleted. In contrast, our conclusion is that only one system is in place, the $X^{max}$ system. Following the principles of merger and economy, this system assumes that a minimal $X^{max}$ category will be projected, depending on the need, whether it is a phrase or a sentence. Thus, in (7a) and (7b), the minimal $X^{max}$ needed is an NP, in (7c) it is a DP, in (15c) it is an NP with the pronoun in the default Accustaive Case, and in (15d) and (15e), it is an IP.

The $X^{max}$ analysis thus predicts both the sentential and the non-sentential data, while the sentential analysis wrongly excludes the nonsentential data, particularly the NPs without determiners, as in (7a) and (7b), and the pronouns in the Accusative Case, as in (15c). We thereby conclude that the $X^{max}$ analysis is superior to the sentential analysis, precisely because it offers a unified analysis of the entire range of data.

In sum, we have provided both empirical and theoretical evidence for analyzing NP nonsententials as $X^{max}$ constituents, rather than as sententials. In an attempt to explain the properties of NP nonsententials, we have also proposed that the sentential requirement on Case feature checking does not hold in nonsententials, proposing the Case Feature Corollay in (16). This explains two basic enigmas of NP nonsententials: (i) their frequent appearance without determiners (which are assumed to be the locus of Case features), and (ii) their ability to appear in the default Case form. VP nonsententials raise remarkably similar considerations as NP nonsententials, and will be discussed in the next section.

### *1.2. VP Nonsententials*

Barton (1990, 1998) has proposed that the following data involve a contrast between the nonsentential in (22b) and the truncated sentential with a deleted subject in (22c). Notice that either is a possible answer to the question in (22a).

(22a) What does John do all summer?
(22b) Play baseball.
(22c) Plays baseball.

In (22b), there is no agreement with the subject, and no tense. The minimal analysis is that it constitutes a VP. Within the nonsentential analysis proposed here, the representation of (22b) would be a maximal projection of VP straightforwardly:

(23) [VP play [NP baseball]]

In fact, the occurrence of (22b) provides a strong argument against always projecting a full sentence, or IP. With the "wrong" agreement, (22b) would never have been a constituent of a grammatical sentential in response to (22a), as shown in (24):

(24) *John play baseball all summer.

As such, (22b) and its representation in (23) provide strong empirical support for the $X^{max}$ analysis. The $X^{max}$ analysis for structures like (22b) seems to be a standard one within the Minimalist Program: recall that Radford (1997: 93) analyzes bare VP answers to questions as maximal projection VPs (cf. (8c)).

On the other hand, the presence of agreement and tense marking in (22c) may suggest a sentential (IP) analysis, with the subsequent deletion of the subject, as in (25):

(25) [IP he [I' Pres/3SG [VP plays [NP baseball]]]]

Even this case would be consistent with our $X^{max}$ analysis. As pointed out in the case of NPs discussed in the previous section, the $X^{max}$ analysis generates both phrases and clauses, depending on the need. With tense/agreement features and a subject, (25) would be generated non-problematically as an IP. But the analysis of the truncated sentence in (22c) as derived from (25), though, would require some kind of deletion rule, like the ones proposed in (3), and adopting such specific deletion rules is theoretically undesirable (and, as will be shown in §2, empirically inadequate as well).

However, there may be no need to assume a full sentential analysis or a deletion analysis even in the case of (22c). It is worth exploring two other, more economical, representations for (22c). First, and most minimalist, one can say that (22c), just like (22b), projects to a VP only, although with different choices of inflection on the verb for (22c). This analysis of (22c) would have the representation in (26):

(26) [VP plays [NP baseball]]

This analysis follows from the assumption in Minimalism that lexical verbs are selected from the lexicon randomly, with any configuration of agreement and tense features. Thus the VP *play* in (22b), as represented in (23), is selected in its base form without any tense/agreement features, while the VP *plays* in (22c), as represented in (26), is selected with third person present tense/agreement features. The particular features of a verb become relevant, though, only if percolation to I and feature checking take place, which we argue does not hold in nonsententials. So our analysis predicts that nonsentential VPs can occur either as (23) or (26), accounting for the dual data in (22b) and (22c).

Alternatively, one can argue that (22c) involves an IP with no projected specifier, where the tense/agreement features of the verb have percolated to I, as illustrated in (27):

(27) Plays baseball.
[IP Pres/3SG [VP plays [NP baseball]]]

This would be parallel to many attested examples with auxiliary or modal verbs, such as (28):

(28) Can't make conference.
[IP Can't [VP make [NP conference]]]

It is an assumption of Minimalism that the projection which projects no further is the maximal projection, or XP. Thus, each of the examples in (27) and (28) would be considered an IP, rather than an I', and would thus not be contrary to the $X^{max}$ analysis.

There is a potential complication with (27) and (28), though, given the widely held assumption that subjects are generated VP internally (Kitagawa 1986, Sportiche 1988). A recent version of this hypothesis is that the subject is generated as a specifier of vP, which is a projection higher than VP (see Chomsky 1995; Larson, 1988). This would not be a problem in the VP analysis for (23) and (26), since subjects are not involved in these derivations. However, the IP analysis in (27) and (28) raises the question of whether or not a subject has been merged in the specifier of vP, given that in (27) and

(28) we do build IPs. It is possible that a null PRO subject can merge in the specifier of vP in (27), and in comparable nonsententials, given that no Nominative Case checking will take place in IP. Such a representation would look like (29):

(29) [IP Pres/3S [vP PRO [VP plays [NP baseball]]]]

For a structure like (28) with a modal, a representation would look like (30):

(30) [IP Can't [vP PRO [VP make [NP conference]]]]

Originally, PRO was analyzed as a pronoun which can only appear in case-less positions (see Chomsky 1981). Given the hypothesis in (16), no Case feature checking is required to take place in (29) or (30), thus making it possible for PRO to merge and remain in vP. Presumably, the reference for the empty PRO would be determined from discourse.

Theoretically, however, the minimal analysis for (22c) would project to a maximal VP, but (26) raises the question of feature checking. It is generally assumed that a finite verb has Nominative specifier features, which are uninterpretable, and thus in need of checking and eliminating (Chomsky, 1995; see Radford, 1997, Ch. 5). In a full sentence like (25), these features would be checked in a specifier/head configuration with the Nominative pronoun *he*, which has such features, on the common assumption that the features of the verb raise covertly to I. On the other hand, if we assume a VP analysis for (22c), as in (26), the Nominative specifier features of the verb *plays* cannot be checked. However, as we argued for English nonsentential NPs in §1.1, the requirement for Case checking may be generally relaxed in nonsententials, as per (16), repeated below.

(16) Case Feature Corollary (CFC)
Nonsententials differ from sententials in one basic property: they are not required to check Case features.

With no requirement for Case feature checking, (26) can be grammatical as is. This follows from the fact that Agreement on the verb is considered to be weak in English, so the verb would not raise overtly to an Agreement projection (or I), even in a full sentence (cf. Pollock, 1989). This allows the weak verb to remain in the VP projection, just as it allows the weak pronouns to remain in N. Thus, the case-marked pronouns in (15c) were argued to be in the N position, and that a DP need not project given that its head would be null, and given that the features of the pronoun would not raise to D overtly. No case checking would take place. In the case of the VP in (26), similar considerations hold. The agreement features on the verb in English are weak, and so the verb can remain in VP. Without feature percolation and/or verb movement, if an I projected, I would be null. But a null I and IP projection are not motivated, given Economy. Pending further research in this area, then, we tentatively adopt the minimal VP analysis for both (22b), as represented in (23) and for (22c), as represented in (26), although the analysis in (29) is also a possibility for (22c) as well.

Notice, however, that there is one difference between agreement on verbs and Case on pronouns, even though they have both been argued to involve weak features in English. For the pronouns, we argued that they have a default Case, Accusative, and that pronouns would necessarily surface in the Accusative Case if no feature checking takes place. One cannot say the same thing for agreement, given that both agreement forms are attested, as in (22b) and (22c). If we want to keep the VP analysis of (22b) and (22c), we would have to say that the relevant property with both pronouns and verbs is weak features, rather than the existence of a default form. If weak features can stay put in the lexical projection of their host (agreement in V, and Case in N), as is generally assumed, and if, in addition, Case feature checking need not take place in nonsententials, as per our proposal in (16), then we can say that indeed both (22b) and (22c) are VPs, as represented in (23) and (26). While pronouns are required to appear in their default Case if no feature checking is to take place, the verb can appear with either agreement, because the verb has no default form.

Notice in contrast that in a language with strong verbal agreement, such as Serbian, there is only one option with the VPs — they have to be inflected for appropriate agreement:

| | | | | |
|---|---|---|---|---|
| (31a) | Šta | ti | radi-š? | |
| | what | you | do-2SG | |
| | 'What are you doing?' | | | |
| (31b) | Pere-m | | sudove. | |
| | wash-1SG | | dishes | |
| | 'I am washing dishes.' | | | |
| (31c) | *Pere | | | sudove |
| | wash-UNINFLECTED | | | dishes |

The only legitimate answer to the question in (31a) is one which shows agreement, as is the case with (31b). The uninflected base form in Serbian (31c) is only used for the 3rd person singular, never for the first person singular. In this respect, the third person singular form in Serbian may be comparable to the bare English form *play* in (22b), which is likewise uninflected, at least overtly. (31c) is, however, not a possible answer to the question in (31a). Thus in Serbian, but not in English, an IP must be projected in order to accommodate strong Agreement features on verbs. This is parallel to the situation with NPs, where strong Case features forced a projection of DP in both Korean and Serbian. Since Serbian uses pro-drop, it would be impossible to determine if the subject is there in the form of a pro, or if the specifier projection of I has not merged. The Serbian example would then receive either the full IP analysis, as per (25), or the analysis with no merged specifier, similar to (29).

In sum, we have provided both empirical and theoretical arguments for the $X^{max}$ analysis of VP nonsententials. More specifically, we have argued for a unified VP analysis of (22b) and (22c) as maximal VP projections as represented in (23) and (26), while leaving open the possibility of a vP analysis with an unmerged PRO subject, as represented in (29). In general, this analysis of VP nonsententials is parallel to the analysis of NP nonsententials, which likewise can stop short of merging the D position. It is argued that these properties of VP and NP nonsententials are related, and that they both follow from the Case Feature Corollary in (16), which proposes that Case feature checking requirement in nonsententials is relaxed. Indeed, this analysis suggests that relaxed feature checking may be the defining property of nonsententials.

## 2. MISSING CATEGORIES: FUNCTIONAL DELETION OR MINIMAL MERGER?

### *2.0. Introductory Note*

The basic argument of §1. is that Case feature checking requirement is relaxed in nonsententials, as per (16), repeated below:

(16) Case Feature Corollary (CFC)
Nonsententials differ from sententials in one basic property: they are not required to check Case features.

If this is true, much of what seems to be missing structure in nonsententials can be accounted for without invoking deletion. For example, missing determiners can be accounted for by NP maximal projections failing to merge Ds. Also, missing subjects can be accounted for by failing to merge anything beyond VP or vP'. Case checking involves a relationship between the verbal and nominal projections. In a full clause, the verb is dominated by Agreement/Tense Phrases in which Accusative and Nominative Case are to be checked. Likewise, nouns are dominated by DPs, which host the Case features. These DPs then raise to the appropriate agreement projections to check their Case features. If it is true that nonsententials are not required to check Case features, we predict that neither VPs nor NPs will require the corresponding accompanying functional projections in nonsententials. In this section we explore further this basic analysis, and compare it to Barton's (1998) proposal that missing categories in telegraphese are due to a functional deletion rule, as formulated in (3b), repeated below:

(3b) Deletion Rule 2
Optionally delete functional categories up to recoverability.

In this section we look at the following data, and provide a unified analysis for all: missing subjects (§2.1); missing auxiliaries (§2.2); missing determiners (§2.3); missing prepositions (§2.4); and missing complementizers (§2.5). We conclude that the analysis in (16) fares better empirically as well as theoretically. Theoretically, the analysis in (16) is more economical, and therefore to be preferred, all other things being equal. It is more economical because it does not merge/generate elements that will be deleted later. Empirically, the Functional Deletion analysis overgenerates, a problem not faced by the analysis of minimal merger proposed in this paper.

### *2.1. Missing Subjects*

In §1.2, we analyzed the examples in (22c) and (28), repeated below, as nonsententials in which (overt) subjects were never merged. In (22c), which we analyzed as a VP as in (26), there was no motivation for a subject to be merged. On the other hand, in (28), given the VP-internal Subject Hypothesis, reinterpreted as vP-Subject Hypothesis, there was an opportunity to merge a subject, namely in the specifier of vP, a projection between

IP and VP, as in (30). We argued in §1.2 that subjects in this case may be merged as empty PROs.

(22c) Plays baseball.
(26) [VP plays [NP baseball]]
(28) Can't make conference.
(30) [IP Can't [vP PRO [VP make [NP conference]]]]

Thus, the lack of an overt subject in nonsententials such as (22c) and (28) can be accounted for by appealing to the rules of Merger, which can stop merging at VP, as in (26), or which can merge a PRO subject, as in (30). As pointed out in Baltin (1995) and Radford (1997), a PRO subject will not raise out of its underlying (Spec-VP) position, the way overt subjects normally do.

On the other hand, Barton (1998) argued for a full-fledged sentential analysis of the examples comparable to (22c) and (28). She proposed a general principle of Functional Deletion, which allows deletion of all and only those functional categories which are recoverable from context. In the case of subjects in (22c) and (28), one can argue that they involve pronouns, which are functional categories, and which are, moreover, recoverable from discourse or pragmatic context: the pronoun *he* in (22c), and the pronoun *I* in (28).

However, the Functional Deletion analysis overgenerates. For example, object pronouns are not deleted even when fully recoverable from context. Consider the following examples:

(32a) Grandma coming for dinner.
Doesn't care for pasta. (subject omission)
(32b) Grandma ill.
Saw her last night in the hospital. (subject omission)
(32c) Grandma ill.
* (I) Saw last night. (*object omission)
(Grandma is ill. I saw her last night.)

Even though the subject pronouns can be omitted in (32a) and (32b), the equally recoverable object pronoun in (32c) cannot. We are hence dealing with a Subject/Object asymmetry in omission possibilities:

(33) Recoverable subject pronouns, but not object pronouns, can be deleted in nonsententials.

The generalization in (33) would have to be an exception under the Functional Deletion approach in (3b).

On the other hand, this Subject/Object asymmetry would follow straightforwardly from the minimal Merger analysis of $X^{max}$ nonsententials explored in this paper, coupled with the independent facts about PROs in subject, but not object, positions. (32a) and (32b), which are parallel to (22c) in that the verbs carry overt tense and agreement features, can be analyzed either as maximal projections of VP, as in (26), or as projections of IP with an unmerged PRO subject, as in (30). In either analysis, the object argument/pronoun is required by the selection properties of the transitive verb *saw* within the VP. In the latter analysis, it is independently established that PROs can only be subjects, so PRO would never appear in object position in an analysis of a construction like (32c). Thus our analysis makes no prediction that (32c) is possible or grammatical, and there is no need either for deletion rules like (3) or for an independent principle like (33) which would allow deletion of subject pronouns only while prohibiting deletion of object pronouns. The nonsentential analysis proposed here, then, explains the Subject/Object asymmetry straightforwardly.

*2.2. Missing Auxiliaries*

Examples of nonsententials with missing auxiliaries come in two sets: (i) those that are also missing the subjects, and (ii) those that include the subjects. The former can easily be accounted for by saying that they involve VP nonsententials, where Merger stops with VP and therefore affords no opportunity or necessity for any subjects to merge. This analysis straightforwardly accounts for the examples with missing subjects and auxiliaries in (34):

(34a) [VP Unable to attend.]
(34b) [VP Explain later.]
(34c) [VP Scheduled to present paper at conference.]

In fact, a similar story can be told for the examples with overt subjects, such as (35):

(35) Car broken down.

Recall the vP-Subject Hypothesis introduced in §1.2. The argument is that the subjects, as external arguments of the verb, are generated in the specifier position of the projection immediately dominating VP, that is, vP. In full sentences, the overt subjects raise to the specifier of IP in order to check the Nominative Case features of the finite verb. If the features of the finite verb need not be checked at all, as we claim to be the case in these nonsententials per (16), then it is reasonable to assume that the subject can remain in situ, as in (36):

(36) [vP car [VP broken down]]

Thus the example in (35) can be analyzed as a vP nonsentential.

Notice, moreover, that the subject in (35) is a bare NP, and therefore has no Case features, given that D is the locus of such features (cf. §1.1). This implies that even arguments can fail to be Case-marked in nonsententials (as we will also see with object NPs in §2.3 below). It is generally assumed that in full sentences arguments must receive Case for LF visibility, and that the locus of Case features is D, enforcing a DP projection with arguments. Given that the need for an argument to have Case is related to the need of the finite verb to check Nominative Case, one would expect the corresponding examples with determiners to ring unnatural. This expectation is met, as the example in (37) illustrates.

(37) *The car broken down.

Indeed, since there is no finite (auxiliary) verb in (35), the definite article has no role to play, and is thus barred by Economy.[3]

While the Functional Deletion analysis can account for optional deletion of subjects, and while it can account for optional deletion of determiners, it is not clear how such an analysis would capture the ungrammatical examples of the type illustrated in (37), where the two functional deletions are interdependent. On the other hand, this interdependence follows directly from our analysis. Since Case checking involves a relationship between DPs and finite verbs, we predict that omission of finite verbs would correlate with the omission of recoverable determiners.

### *2.3. Missing Determiners*

Missing determiners in NP nonsententials can be accounted for straightforwardly without deletion, by projecting a bare NP as a maximal category, as argued in §1.1 for the analysis of (7a) and (7b), repeated here:

(7a) Sudden flu attack
(7b) Car problem

Since non-arguments are not required to be DPs, each nonsentential NP can be analyzed as a non-argument, and thus as a bare NP projection. But other examples, like those in (38), seem to pose a problem for this analysis:

(38a) Get lawyer
(38b) Scheduled to present paper at conference

In (38a), the NP *lawyer* seems to be an argument of the verb *get*, and in (38b), the noun *paper* an argument of the verb *present*. If the generalization in (16), that the Case features in nonsententials need not be checked, holds, though, then there is no requirement to project a DP with object argument NPs either (as noted for subject argument NPs in §2.2). In this scenario, the reference of bare NPs is necessarily established pragmatically. For example, the NP *lawyer* in (38a) can either refer to any lawyer, corresponding to the indefinite article *a*, or to a specific, say, family lawyer, corresponding to the definite article *the*.

This analysis of missing determiners is more minimal, and more economical, than any analysis that would first generate DPs, and then delete Ds. In addition, as pointed out in §2.2, missing determiners tend to correlate with missing finite verbs. This correlation follows from our analysis incorporating the Case Feature Corollary, but not from the Functional Deletion analysis.

### *2.4. Missing Prepositions*

The following examples of missing prepositions have been attested in Barton's (1998) corpus of telegraphese:

(39a) Am detained (at) JFK Airport New York
(39b) Please pick me up (at) Summerside Motel.
(39c) Please come (to) U.S. border Newport, Vermont
(39d) Arrested (for) alleged drug smuggling Newport Vermont

The exact role of prepositions in theta-role assignment is still not well understood, but it is uncontroversial that prepositions are involved in Case assignment. If so, and if Case feature checking is relaxed in nonsententials, as per (16), then one would expect to find nonsententials without prepositions, provided that they are recoverable from the verb and the rest of the clause. In the examples above, the place adverbials in (39a) and (39b) may be responsible for the recoverability of the locative preposition *at*. Similarly, the directionality of the verb *come* would recover the meaning of *to* in (39c), and *for* will be recoverable from the meaning of the whole utterance in (39d). Given the proposal in (16) that Case features on NPs can remain unchecked, we would expect to find oblique NPs without prepositions, as is the case with the examples in (39). Such an analysis is in keeping with the Economy Principle for two reasons: (i) the meaning of the preposition is predictable from the verb, and (ii) with no Case feature checking, a merger with a preposition is unnecessary and therefore uneconomical.

Notice that the appearance of accusative pronouns, but not nominative pronouns, in PPs is not problematic for this claim, given the assumption that Accusative is the default Case in English:

(40a) Detained with her JFK Airport New York
(40b) *Detained with she Airport New York

The Case Feature Corollary predicts the correct Accusative Case form within PPs.

In this regard, it is instructive to look again at Serbian, a language with strong Case features on the nouns. As pointed out in §1.1, such features on the noun are inseparable from the phonetic form of the noun; thus, in Serbian NPs always appear within a DP projection. The case is somewhat similar for PPs. Each preposition in Serbian governs a particular Case, such as Accusative, Genitive, Instrumental, or Locative. The preposition cannot delete in Serbian if the noun still has the case which would be governed by the preposition, as shown in (41):

| | | | | | |
|---|---|---|---|---|---|
| (41) | Vidimo | se | *(na) | JFK | aerodrom-u. |
| | See-1PL | Reflexive | (on) | JFK | airport-LOC |
| | 'See you (at) JFK Airport.' | | | | |

However, if the locative NP appears in its citation form, which is Nominative Case form, the utterance is possible as a nonsentential:

| | | | | |
|---|---|---|---|---|
| (42) | Vidimo | se, | JFK | aerodrom. |
| | See-1PL | Reflexive | JFK | airport-NOM |
| | 'See you, JFK Airport.' | | | |

We conclude that prepositions cannot delete if they govern Case, that is, participate in feature checking. This implies that the English examples in (39) are more like the Serbian example in (42), in which there was no preposition in the first place, and in which the locative noun phrase expresses the location by itself, and appears in the citation Case in Serbian or as a bare oblique NP in English. This conclusion is consistent with our analysis of minimal merger, but is not consistent with the Functional Deletion analysis. Given the Functional Deletion analysis, one would expect the NP to keep the Case which had presumably been assigned to it by the preposition.

### *2.5. Complementizers and the Infinitive* To

The following examples with missing complementizers are attested in telegraphese:

(43a) Regret I will not be able to present my paper at the conference
(43b) Regret cannot attend.
(43c) Regret unable to give paper as scheduled due to illness.

The complementizer *that* is also often omitted in full sentences, and it is reasonable to assume, all other things being equal, that the clause without the complementizer is an IP, rather than a CP, given minimalist considerations. So far, this is consistent both with Functional Deletion analysis, and with our analysis of minimal merger.

But a Functional Deletion analysis overgenerates here, too, because it predicts that all complementizers, as functional categories, can delete. But a complementizer such as *if/whether* cannot be omitted either in full clauses or in nonsententials:

(44a) I wonder if/whether you will be at the conference.
(44b) *I wonder you will be at the conference
(44c) *Wonder you will be at conference

This is surprising for the Functional Deletion analysis, since the complementizers *if/whether* are functional categories and so subject to deletion according to that analysis.

It is even more surprising that the infinitival particle *to* cannot be omitted, even though it is a functional category with arguably no meaning. The Functional Deletion analysis predicts that infinitive *to* should delete unproblematically. But deleting infitinitive *to* is typically ungrammatical. The following constructed examples reflect the graduated judgments of the dialectologist Dennis Preston (personal communication with Ellen Barton), although most speakers consider all of the examples in (45) ungrammatical:

(45a) ?*Unable continue trip as car is not working
cf. Unable to continue trip as car is not working
(45b) ?*Scheduled present paper at conference
cf. Scheduled to present paper at conference
(45c) *Stopped look at scenery.
cf. Stopped to look at scenery.
(45d) *Too ill travel.
cf. Too ill to travel.

Even though we have no good explanation for these data, our analysis does not directly predict the grammaticality of any of the examples in (45) because infinitive *to* is not involved in feature checking. For us, it is sufficient to say that whatever selection requirements are responsible for the obligatory appearance of *if/whether* in interrogative clauses, and *to* in infinitive clauses, they are not predicted to be relaxed in nonsententials via the Case Feature Corollary in (16). On the other hand, these examples are a counterexample for the Functional Deletion rule in (3b).

### 2.6. Summary

In this section, we have offered empirical and theoretical analyses favoring a minimal merger analysis of $X^{max}$ nonsententials over a functional deletion analysis. Some of the cases of putative functional deletion were shown to be problematic: deleting subjects as functional categories, for instance, sets up an unmotivated Subject/Object asymmetry which is avoided in our current analysis; not deleting complementizers like *if/whether* and infinitive *to* is hard to achieve within functional deletion. Other cases were shown to be more straightforwardly handled in a minimalist analysis, such as missing determiners, auxiliaries, and prepositions. We conclude that the analysis of nonsententials within minimalism is empirically and theoretically preferred.

## 3. Conclusion

In this paper, we have updated Barton's (1990, 1991, 1998) analysis of nonsententials within the Minimalist Program (Chomsky, 1989, 1995). We argued that nonsententials are projected as independent $X^{max}$ projections, consistent with the $X^{max}$ Generalization in (1), although the details of derivation are now described in terms of minimal merger. We further argued that a nonsentential analysis is preferable to a sentential analysis, particularly in its ability to explain NPs without determiners and VPs with various configurations of tense/agreement features. The central generalization within the analysis proposed here is the Case Feature Corollary in (16), which suggests that Case features in nonsententials do not require checking, as they do in full sentences. Empirically, this Corollary was shown to account for a number of patterns of nonsententials, including the aforementioned NPs without determiners and VPs with and without tense/agreement features. The Case Feature Corollary also suggested further investigation of intriguing differences between languages that have strong Case features, like Serbian and Korean, and languages that have weak Case features, like English. Theoretically, proposing a specific Case Feature Corollary may at first seem contrary to the spirit of minimalism. Yet this proposal may have wider significance than the explanation of nonsententials alone: Radford (1997: 182–83) notes that a number of varieties and registers, such as child language and Creoles, are characteristic in their simplification of complex grammatical processes such as feature checking of uninterpretable features, particularly Case. In our description of nonsententials, we have formalized this observation into a specific corollary which may provide a unified analysis for a number of varieties, including nonsententials in such registers as telegraphese as well as child language and Creoles. Further research may find that the Case Feature Corollary is one of the specific ways in which the grammars of varieties and registers differ.

## NOTES

[1] Morgan (1989) uses the term deletion, which we will use here, in part to make a distinction between deletion and ellipsis. Ellipsis involves the generation and licensing of empty categories within sentence structures (e.g., VP Ellipsis, Ellipsis in NP, and Sluicing), as described by Lobeck (1995) and Chao (1988).

[2] Barton (1998) analyzed a corpus of telegraphic utterances from the European Telegram Project (ETP). The ETP defined the unit of analysis as T-phrases–utterances of one or more words indicated to be wholes through the use of various marks of end punctuation such as a period or question mark, a STOP, or a line change. In the corpus of 994 T-phrases, 134 were full sentences, 692 were sentential T-phrases with deletion (e.g., deletion of functional categories, as in *Car broken down*), and 138 were nonsentential T-phrases (e.g., NPs like *Sudden car problem* or PPs like *In trouble*). For details about the ETP and the analysis of telegraphic utterances, see Barton (1998).

[3] We also find similar contrasts with passive nonsententials, which also seem to involve a bare NP subject, and a bare VP/vP.

(i) Flight cancelled.

(ii) *The flight cancelled (by airport authorities).

The complication with Passive, however, is that the subject precedes the verb, even though the passive subject is supposed to be generated as the complement (object) of the verb. This suggests that the subject has moved into a functional projection higher than VP, possibly vP, although it is not clear why. The analysis of passive nonsententials is beyond the scope of this paper, but poses interesting questions for future research.

## REFERENCES

Abney, S., *The English Noun Phrase in its Sentential Aspect*. Ph.D. Dissertation, MIT. 1987.

Baltin, M., "Floating quantifiers, PRO and predication." *Linguistic Inquiry* 26 (1995): 199–248.

Barton, E., *Nonsentential Constituents: A Theory of Grammatical Structure and Pragmatic Interpretation*. Amsterdam: John Benjamins. 1990.

Barton, E., "Nonsentential Constituents and Theories of Phrase Structure." In *Views on Phrase Structure*, ed. Katherine Leffel and Denis Bouchard. Dordrecht: Kluwer. 1991: 193–214.

Barton, E., "The Grammar of Telegraphic Structures: Sentential and Nonsentential Derivation." *Journal of English Linguistics* 26.1 (1998): 37–67.

Chao, W., *On Ellipsis*. NY: Garland. 1988.

Chomsky, N., *Lectures on Government and Binding*. Dordrecht: Foris. 1981.

Chomsky, N., "Some notes on economy of derivation and representation." *MIT Working Papers in Linguistics* 10 (1989): 43–74.

Chomsky, N., *The Minimalist Program*. Cambridge, Mass.: MIT Press. 1995.

Follett, W., *Modern American Usage*. NY: Hill and Wang. 1966.

Haegeman, L., "Register Variation in English: Some Theoretical Observations." *Journal of English Linguistics* 20 (1987): 230–48.

Kitagawa, Y., *Subjects in English and Japanese*. Ph.D. Dissertation, University of Massachusetts. 1986.

Larson, R., "On the Double Object Construction." *Linguistic Inquiry* 18 (1988): 335–91.

Lobeck, A., *Ellipsis: functional heads, Licensing, and Identification*. NY: Oxford University Press. 1995.

Longobardi, G., "Reference and Proper Names: A Theory of N-Movement in Syntax and Logical Form." *Linguistic Inquiry* 25.4 (1994): 609–665.

Morgan, J., "Sentence Fragments and the Notion 'Sentence'." In *Issues in Linguistics: Papers in Honor of Henry and Renee Kahane*, ed. Braj Kachru et al. Urbana: University of Illinois Press. 1973: 719–51.

Morgan, J., "Sentence Fragments Revisited." In *CLS Parasession on Language in Context*. Chicago: Chicago Linguistic Society. 1989: 228–41.

Postal, P., "On So-called "Pronouns" in English." In *Modern Studies in English*, ed. David Reibel and Sanford Schane. Englewood Cliffs, NJ.: Prentice Hall. 1969: 201–224.

Progovac, L., "Determiner Phrase in a language without determiners." *Journal of Linguistics* 34.1 (1998): 165–179.

Quirk, R., Greenbaum, S., Leech, G., Svartvik, J., *A Grammar of Contemporary English*. London: Longman. 1972.
Radford, A., *Syntactic Theory and the Structure of English: A Minimalist Approach*. Cambridge University Press. 1997.
Sportiche, D., "A theory of floating quantifiers and its corollaries for constituent structure." *Linguistic Inquiry* 19 (1988): 425–49.
Sweet, H., *New English Grammar*. Oxford: Clarendon Press. 1900.
Yanofsky, N. "NP Utterances." *Chicago Linguistic Society* 14 (1978): 491–502.

PETER LUDLOW

# A NOTE ON ALLEGED CASES OF NONSENTENTIAL ASSERTION[*]

## 0. INTRODUCTION

It is nearly taken as a given that many of our meaningful assertions are not utterances of sentences per se, but are rather utterances of portions of sentences — words, for example, as in the Wittgensteinian example of the worker who simply utters "slab" when he needs another slab. One widely held view is that one can utter something having non-sentential form and thereby communicate something with propositional content to one's interlocutor.[1] On one formulation, persons use a process of "free enrichment" to flesh out the intended meaning of a non-sentential utterance. As compelling as this idea may seem, in this paper I will argue that many apparent cases of non-sentential speech clearly cannot be non-sentential in point of fact.[2] I will maintain that genuine cases of non-sentential speech are much more rare than commonly supposed (and will hint that interesting cases may not exist at all).

Let's begin with some terminology. Following work in generative grammar over the past forty years, I suppose that a "sentence" is not the simple structure that one sees written on paper or which one hears uttered. Rather, a sentence is an n-tuple of representations <R1, R2,... Rn>, each of which must meet certain well-formedness constraints if the sentence as a whole is to be well formed. For example, in Chomsky (1981) a sentence of natural language was taken to be a 4-tuple of representations <PF, DS, SS, LF> corresponding roughly to "phonetic form, D-structure, S-structure, and logical form". Rules (or at least one rule) would map between these levels of representation (obeying constraints on movement), and additional well-formedness constraints would hold at each level of representation. More recent work (e.g. Chomsky 1995) holds that there are only two levels of representation, LF and PF, so that a sentence is ordered pair <PF, LF>, with certain constraints holding at each level of representation and constraints on the derivation of these representations (more on this theory below). On both models, there is much more to a sentence than meets the eye.

Given this robust notion of sentence, what do we mean when we say that something is a bit of "non-sentential speech"? As I use the expression, it means that there is an utterance that is both well-formed and meaningful, even though *none* of the levels of representation consist of fully inflected clauses, having subject-predicate form. In linguistic terminology, no level of representation would consist of a full IP (inflection phrase), with a DP (determiner phrase — roughly, a noun phrase) and a VP (verb phrase) as constituents. The view that I am defending is that in more cases than not



*R. Elugardo and R. J. Stainton (eds.), Ellipsis and Nonsentential Speech*, 95–108.

(and perhaps all cases) if we utter something that it is well-formed and meaningful then at least one level of representation is a fully inflected clause.

Pretty clearly there are utterances that *appear* to be non-clausal (a number of cases are discussed below), but the question is whether they are in fact non-clausal at *every* level of representation. All sides can agree that at the level of phonetic form (PF) these utterances are not fully clausal. The interesting question is whether or not they are clausal at some other level of representation (for example, LF, or, in earlier incarnations of generative grammar, at D-structure).

Finally, there are two questions that we might want to distinguish.[3]

Q1: Does the grammar generate non-sentential structures?

Q2: Can one utter non-sentential structures and thereby perform a genuine speech act in which propositional content is communicated?

My best guess is that the answer to the first question is "no," although at present I can only argue that it does so less often than we imagine. As for the second question, can one utter something that is non-sentential, intending to communicate some proposition to an audience? There clearly are cases where you can — for example when we establish a code in which a single word — say 'apple' — means that someone in the crowd has a gun. But these codes need to be explicitly established for the cases in question and do not speak to the issue of ordinary linguistic practice; in my view the cases where you have to stipulate the propositional meaning of a non-sentential utterance are not very interesting.[4] My answer to the second question is thus that if the goal is to express propositional content and one is engaged in ordinary linguistic practice without the aid of prior stipulation of meanings, then the answer is no.

I've tried to make my claims somewhat modest, but for all that they seem to fly in the face of the received wisdom, which is that non-sentential speech is ubiquitous. Alleged examples of non-sentential speech are certainly abundant. For example, Stainton (2001) gives the case of someone who holds up a letter and says "from Spain," but other similar cases are possible. Consider the following canonical cases:

a. Found guilty! (Newspaper headline.)
b. Hood sunk. (Famous message sent upon sinking of the battleship Hood.)[5]
c. All in the garden. (Uttered when asked where the children are.)
d. All were. (Said when asked if any colleagues were party members.)
e. Close tabs. (Said with the intention that the hearer keep close tabs on someone.)
f. Wanna? (Said as an invitation to try bungee jumping.)

Clearly in these cases one does not appear to be uttering a fully inflected clause, but here is where we need to exercise caution. Linguistic theory tells us that there is much clausal structure that is inaudible. So, for example, in subordinate clauses we may find the tense inaudible (as in (1)), the subject NP may be inaudible (as in (2)), or, as Larson, den Dikken and Ludlow (forthcoming) have proposed, the verb itself may be inaudible (as in (3)). (Items in all caps and parentheses are inaudible syntactic elements.)

(1) I asked [Bill to leave]
(2) I wanted [PRO to leave]
(3) I wanted [PRO (have) a unicorn]

Likewise objects may go unpronounced as well, as in (4–5).

(4) What did [Bill see OBJ]
(5) I promised [PRO (give) OBJ a unicorn]

In each of the above cases there is a rich linguistic theory which is integrated with these analyses and, right or wrong, the analyses cannot be dismissed out of hand without careful argument that quickly takes us to the core empirical claims of generative grammar (I don't think any party to the debate disputes this much).

These cases are not limited to clauses that are in the scope of a verb, but may be found in many other cases as well, for example in (6).

(6) [PRO (having) an apple a day] keeps the doctor away

Clearly there can be phonologically reduced clauses, but can there be stand-alone clauses with the same properties? That is, do we find phonologically reduced clauses of the following form?

(7) [PRO (give) OBJ [DET slab]]

In this paper I contend that not only are such structures possible but that they are predicted to exist within current linguistic theory. More, there is no established way of accounting for the grammaticality of sub-clausal elements in isolation. Accordingly, I argue that the alleged cases of non-sentential speech are in fact sentential structures having at least one level of representation of this form.

The initial round of arguments will appeal to the fact that often the sub-clausal fragment that is actually pronounced could not be generated unless it was the product of clause-level operations. I'll organize this argument around the operations themselves and show how each of the clause-level operations give rise to what some authors have mistaken for non-sentential or non-clausal speech. I'll then turn to some objections raised by Stainton (forthcoming) concerning the nature of ellipsis within generative linguistics, and will conclude with some remarks about the problem of embedding non-sentential assertion within the most recent versions of generative linguistics.

The first round of arguments are couched within a 1970's version of generative linguistics. This has the virtue of illuminating the arguments in a relatively less abstract and (for philosophers) more familiar way. It also suffices to secure the basic idea that sentence-level processes are at work — processes that have analogues in more recent versions of Generative linguistics. In part 8 I will take up the issue of accounting for non-sentential assertions with the minimalist program of Chomsky (1995).

If we are working within a 1970's model of the grammar then the basic idea is that there are at least two levels of representation (DS and SS) and that there are rules that map between the two levels. For example, there will be a passive formation rule, and also certain deletion rules. In each case I'll be arguing that the DS representations had to have had fully clausal structure in order to yield the SS representations that they do.

## 1. PASSIVES

One of the central problems for theories of non-sentential speech is the fact that many apparently sub-sentential phrases can be shown to be the products of sentence-level syntactic processes. Consider, for example, that many examples of non-sentential speech involve passive forms, as for example in the following newspaper headline:

(1) Found guilty!

The problem is that in a number of standard grammatical theories passive forms are derived from sentence-level processes. So, speculating, a plausible derivation for the sententialist would proceed as follows:

(1a) The jury found the prisoner guilty (underlying D-structure representation)
(1b) The prisoner was found guilty by the jury (passivization)
(1c) The prisoner (aux) found guilty by the jury (aux ellipsis)
(1d) (NP) (aux) found guilty (PP) (argument elipsis)

The crucial step is the step from (1a) to (1b), since it involves a sentence-level passive transformation. For the non-sententialist, there is no obvious way to explain the derivation of the passive form.

It is of course open to the non-sententialist to argue that this passive form is adjectival and not the product of derivational processes, but a related example shows that this suggestion is fallacious. In World War II, when the Bismark sank the Hood, another British ship transmitted a message that simply said the following.

(2) Hood sunk.

Notice that this is a passive form of 'sink', and at least within standard theories of generative grammar the thought would be that (2) undergoes passivization and then deletion as in the following two steps.

(2a) The Germans sank the Hood (underlying D-structure representation)
(2b) The Hood was sunk by the Germans (by passivization)
(2c) (det) Hood was sunk by the Germans (by determiner elipsis)
(2d) (det) Hood (aux) sunk by the Germans (by aux elipsis)
(2e) (det) Hood (aux) sunk (PP) (by argument elipsis)

This case is particularly interesting since there is also a non-derivational form of the passive form of 'sink' ('sunken' — as in 'sunken treasure') which is an adjectival passive. But notice that this adjectival passive cannot appear in cases like the above:

(3) *Hood sunken

The upshot is that we *know* 'sunk' is not adjectival and is rather the product of clause-level operations. The derivation of the passive form remains inexplicable for the non-sententialist.

## 2. Q-FLOAT

Consider a case where we are at a family reunion and a niece asks where the other children are. We utter (4).

(4) All in the garden.

Prima facie, this appears to be a canonical example of non-sentential speech. But closer study shows that even a canonical case like (4) is the product of sentence-level processes — in this case the operation known as Q-float. That is, (4) is derived from a form in which 'All' occurs in a noun phrase and then 'floats' to another position. So, in this case, we begin with the following structure,

(4a) [All the children] are in the garden.

This undergoes Q-float, yielding (4b).

(4b) [the children] are all in the garden.

Then the NP argument and the aux undergo deletion as in the above cases, yielding (4c).

(4c) (NP) (aux) all in the garden

Clearly the non-sententialist is in a bind here. 'all' has to be pulled out of a noun phrase (determiner phrase), but for the non-sententialist there is simply no noun phrase to draw upon. The possibility of the structure in (4) remains mysterious.[6]

## 3. AUX INVERSION AND ELIPISIS

The cases we have considered so far have involved aux deletion, but it is interesting to note that cases where the aux remains also help illuminate the sentential nature of these utterances. Sag (1978) discusses the case of aux inversion and ellipsis, where he notes that we cannot have an ellipsed VP following an inverted auxiliary. An example of an inverted auxiliary would be the following, where the ordering of 'all' and 'were' can be swapped.

(5a) They all were socialists.
(5b) They were all socialists.

As Sag observed, the inverted case cannot appear in the following ellipsis construction.

(6a) Most of them were socialists and perhaps they all were.
(6b) *Most of them were socialists and perhaps they were all.

Now consider the case where several of our friends sit before a congressional committee accused of being socialists. As we watch the proceedings on television, you look at us and raise an eyebrow as if to ask how many of them were in fact socialists. We utter (7).

(7) All were.

Note that we could not have uttered (8).

(8) *Were all.

But why not? For the non-sententialist there is no explanation for why one order should be possible and the other not, but for the sententialist there is a straightforward explanation: (7) *can* be the product of sentence level syntactic operations involving deletion and (8) cannot.

## 4. IDIOM CHUNKS

Idiom chunks are idioms that must appear in concert with certain verbs. A classic example would be the idiom chunk 'keep close tabs'. One can keep close tabs, but one cannot "give close tabs", "make close tabs" etc. This particular idiom requires the presence of the verb 'keep'. It is not licensed with other verbs and it is not licensed by the absence of a verb as the following cases show.

(9) *Close tabs won't affect me.

On the other hand, we can do without the verb 'keep' in certain cases of ellipsis, for example:

(10) I know you want me to keep close tabs on him, but how close tabs?
(11) Fred kept close tabs on Biff, and Mary close tabs on Muffin.

We can also imagine a case where a tricky character has arrived in town and we suspect that he is up to no good. He comes to our office for a meeting. As he leaves our office we turn to our friend and private detective Rocky and say, "close tabs," intending to inform Rocky that we want him to keep close tabs on this fellow. Why can we do this? Well, one natural explanation for the sententialist is simply that the verb 'keep' was originally available in the now-deleted material. What is the non-sententialist to say? How can this element appear without 'keep'? It is entirely unclear what sort of explanation could be offered.

## 5. WANNA CONTRACTION

Suppose that we are watching some friends bungee jumping from a suspension bridge over a river gorge. They try to get various spectators to join in. While they are unsuccessfully attempting to get our friend Biff to try it, we turn to Muffin and utter (13).

(13) Wanna?

Now clearly this cannot mean that we are asking Muffin if she wants Biff to jump. That is, it cannot mean that we are asking something that under free enrichment would be understood as follows.

(13a) (Do you) want (him) to (jump)?

But why not? For the sententialist there is a natural explanation for this fact which stems from the basic rules for wanna contraction. That is, one cannot contract 'want' and 'to' over an NP trace, but you can contract over PRO. Thus we have the following.

(14) Who do you wanna visit?

which has only the meaning that corresponds to (14a) and cannot have the meaning in (14b).

(14a) $\text{Who}_i$ do you want [PRO to visit $e_i$]
(14b) *$\text{Who}_i$ do you want [$e_i$ to visit]

Similarly when someone simply utters 'wanna?', the contraction cannot take place across an argument as in (14b), but can only take place across a PRO argument as in (13b) below.

(13b) (Do you) want PRO to (jump)?

Yet again there is no obvious way for the non-sententialist to account for these facts.[7]

## 6. BARE PREPOSITIONAL PHRASES AND BARE NPs

Now it is certainly possible for the non-sententialist to attempt a tactical retreat, ceding each of these particular examples as being syntactically legit, but decrying all other cases, but this strikes me as a dubious methodological strategy. It effectively amounts to assuming that there is no systematic syntactic explanation for these facts. But why not suppose that there *is* a syntactic explanation, and, if the explanation is not obvious, actually try looking for the explanation? Since in nearly every case involving any structure at all there is some sentence-level syntactic process involved, it seems to me that the default position should be that there is such a process at work.

This is certainly clear in Stainton's own example: 'From Spain'. If we study the construction closely it is hard to see how it could possibly be a stand-alone element. For example, consider a case where I simply hold up the letter, saying nothing, and you ask:

(15) Where from?

The problem here is that to derive such a structure the Wh- can only move to a "COMP" position — in other words, a clause-initial position. Under ordinary circumstances the WH-element would never attach to a prepositional phrase, as the following example shows.

(16) *The letter is where from?

On a full clausal story, we have a ready explanation: the WH-element has moved into a clause initial position, yielding the following structure.

(16′) Where$_i$ [ (is the letter) from e$_i$]

If the questioned version requires a full clausal context it is hard to see how the unquestioned version can be supposed to be non-clausal. But matters are even worse for the non-sententialist.

It is a basic fact about binding theory that reflexives ('himself', 'myself') must be bound in their governing categories. For current purposes, we can say that they must be bound by an antecedent within their clause. Hence we have the following contrast.[8]

(17) I saw myself
(18) *John saw myself (meaning that John saw me)
(19) *I believe that [John saw myself] (meaning that I believe John saw me)

But now suppose that I have taken up writing letters to myself and show you one of these self-addressed letters, saying

(20) From myself

Now clearly this is much more acceptable than the cases where there was no possible antecedent in the clause. Why? A simple answer would be that there is an implicit antecedent available, as in (21).

(21) [(I received this letter) from myself]

Again it is hard to see what account a non-sententialist can give for this construction.

So far we have been considering constructions that involve some structure (even if only on the order of 'from myself'), but won't we reach a stalemate in cases involving only noun phrases? Or, for that matter, consider the following apparent sub-noun phrase discussed by Stainton.

(22) Nice dress.

Won't it be impossible to show a role for syntactic processes in these cases? And if it is impossible to show a role for syntactic processes, then can't the non-sententialist stalemate us at least on these cases of these very minimal utterances? I don't think so.

Noun phrases also have rich syntactic structures that interact in interesting ways with the surrounding sentential context. To see this, consider the case where a friend wonders if I have time for a cup of coffee and pokes into my office, uttering (23).

(23) Quick cup of coffee?

On the face of it this is a fragment of a noun phrase. But as Haik (1983) has observed, 'quick' is not an adjectival element modifying 'coffee' (the coffee itself is not quick), but is in fact an adverbial element. In this particular case it would be plausible to suppose that the adverb is modifying some implicit verb like 'have'.

These cases appear to be completely productive, and at times involve more complex syntactic processes than in the example just discussed. For example, recently on WFAN (a New York sports talk radio station), one of the announcers (Chris "Mad Dog" Russo) commented on an impending game between two inept teams, uttering (24).

(24) Tough watch.

This appears to be a post-deletion fragment of what linguists call a "tough construction," a canonical example of which would be (25).

(25) Chuck is tough to talk to.

(25) is in turn derived from a structure like (26), via what is often called "tough movement."

(26) It is tough to talk to Chuck.

(24) appears to be derived via this process and some others. Speculating, the following sort of derivation may be in play.

(24a) It will be tough to watch that game (base representation)
(24b) That game will be tough to watch (via movement)
(24c) That game will be a tough watch (nominalization)
(24d) Tough watch (Subj, aux, and determiner deletion)

Now it might be objected that speakers given only (24d) are capable of using pragmatics to infer that what Mad Dog intended to say, but this misses two points. First, it was not an accident that Mad Dog chose to express himself in this way. He could not have made the same point by uttering 'Watch tough' or 'To watch tough' or 'watch will be tough' or simply 'watch toughly' or any number of other possibilities. He chose an expression that was the product of sentence-level processes, and no doubt we use those same processes in reverse to form a representation of what he was saying and ultimately to interpret what he was saying. But second, the syntactic story actually provides us a theory of how the interpretation is derived by the hearer. The pragmatic story, on the other hand, offers us all the virtues of theft over honest toil. According to a pragmatic story, anything can be relevant and we use whatever we deem relevant to interpret the utterance. But this is not a theory; it is hand waving on the grandest scale. Can an explicit pragmatic story be told that would actually explain how we come to understand (24) and all other syntactically similar but pragmatically dissimilar cases? Well, as Mad Dog might say, "very tough nut."

## 7. SOME CONCERNS ABOUT ELLIPSIS

Stainton (2001) argues that the kinds of cases discussed above cannot be considered genuine cases of ellipsis, since they are not "properly syntactic."

> If reconstruction of the elided material is to be properly syntactic, then there must be sufficient *linguistic* material for the reconstruction rules to operate on. This will allow the hearer, on linguistic grounds alone, to reconstruct the unique and precise sentence uttered

> by the speaker. Call this the Constraint of Syntactic Recoverability. Ellipsis, given this constraint, cannot happen freely: an entry condition for the rule's application is that the Constraint of Syntactic Recoverability be met.
>
> ... in most instances of less-than-sentential speech, is there a syntactic controller, so described? Absolutely not.

Stainton's point is that in the cases of ellipsis usually discussed by linguists, the ellipsed material is reflected elsewhere in the sentence (as in a case like 'John read the book and I did too'). Of course this objection is unfair for the simple reason that earlier accounts of ellipsis were not considering sub-sentential speech and hence had no reason to integrate the phenomena.

Now of course it is important that the relevant information be recoverable from what is actually pronounced, but the mechanism of syntactic controllers is not the only way by which this may be accomplished. One natural alternative that is an extension of the proposal by Larson, den Dikken, and Ludlow, is that the lexicon contains a number of basic level, phonologically unrealized predicates: 'give', 'have', and 'be', for example. These can be inserted freely into a structure if doing so will satisfy certain grammatical constraints. Likewise, the lexicon might contain phonologically unrealized pronominal elements as well (PRO, for example). In this case it is just a red herring to talk about ellipsis, for the idea is that certain unpronounced lexical items really are in place. The exact mechanisms by which this takes place will be discussed in section 8.

## 8. NON-SENTENTIAL ASSERTIONS AND THE MINIMALIST PROGRAM

In the examples discussed in sections 1–6 I gave a somewhat "retro" analysis, involving the notion of base generated representations and transformations such as passivization, aux deletion, etc. More recent work in linguistic theory — in particular within the "minimalist program" of Chomsky (1995) — puts a different spin on the organization of the grammar. Nevertheless, the recent modifications to the theory merely make it less plausible that sub-sentential assertions are possible. (I will not attempt to embed the analyses in sections 1–6 into the minimalist program — that would be too daunting a task — and some might take the following discussion to be de facto evidence against minimalism. My only point here is that the notion of sub-sentential speech does not appear consistent with minimalism — whether you want to believe in minimalism is another question. However, if one does reject minimalism, then one is presumably working with a model of grammar in which the objections in sections 1–6 can be couched and will have to be answered.)

Here is the basic idea behind the minimalist program. First, there are two levels of linguistic representation, PF and LF, and a well-formed sentence (or linguistic *structure*) must be an ordered pair $<\pi, \lambda>$ of these representations. PF is taken to be the level of representation that is the input to the performance system (e.g. speech generation). LF is, in Chomsky's terminology, the input to the conceptual/intensional system (I would prefer to think of it as the level of representation that is visible to the semantics). Neither of these levels of representation corresponds to the portion of the sentence that is actually spoken or written. During the computation of the LF and PF representations there is a process called "spellout," which yields what we pronounce or write down.

We can already see that there are going to be difficulties for theories of sub-sentential assertion here. Spellout is basically epiphenomenal within the minimalist program; it is not itself a level of linguistic representation and it plays no interesting causal role in the theory. This suggests that subsententialists are setting off in the wrong direction from the outset by mistaking something that is epiphenomenal for something that is a real object of analysis. Even worse, subsententialists often appear to hold that what is pronounced is all that there literally is — for example, that 'all in the garden' is not part of some larger hidden clausal structure and indeed is a fundamental object of analysis. Not only does this turn the basic assumptions of linguistic theory on their head, but it also makes a hash of the basic organizing principle of the grammar. What sense does it make to talk of a computation that yields an LF representation if, by the lights of the subsententialist, the LF representation can be no more structured than the spellout can? For that matter, what does a semantics look like for these subsentential LFs? This is not a trivial problem, given that all extant developed semantical theories since Frege have assumed the sentence (or something larger) to be the fundamental unit of meaning. As we shall see, however, matters soon get worse for the subsententialist.

In the minimalist program it is assumed that each sentence (or better, *structure* $\Sigma$) is constructed out of an *array* or *numeration* N of lexical items. Some of the items in the numeration will be part of the pronounced (written) sentence, and others will be part of a universal inventory of lexical items that are freely inserted into all numerations. Given the numeration N, the computational system ($C_{HL}$) attempts to derive (compute) well-formed PF and LF representations, converging on the pair $<\pi, \lambda>$. The derivation is said to *converge* at a certain level if it yields a representation that is well formed at that level. If it fails to yield a well-formed representation the derivation *crashes*.

Not all converging derivations yield structures that belong to a given language L. Derivations must also meet certain economy conditions — they must be *optimal*. In effect, more economical derivations (following certain articulated economy principles) take precedence over less economical derivations. (Or perhaps only the most economical derivation is possible — all others are ruled out.[9]) Two basic operations govern the derivation of phrase markers and hence all LF representations: *merge*, and *move-α*. Merge governs the combination of smaller grammatical elements into larger ones. When two elements merge, the category of one of the elements is projected to the new higher node. This would be an example of a more general process of *feature projection*. The process of feature projection determines the *label* of the new object. We can represent this idea in the following way. The result of applying merge to $\alpha$ and $\beta$ is $\{\alpha, \beta\}$. The independent process of feature projection determines the label, $\delta$, of this new object. $\delta$ is in turn a set of features that is constructed from features of the two constituents $\alpha$ and $\beta$. Hence the product of merge and project is a complex object $\gamma = \{\delta, \{\alpha, \beta\}\}$.

More problems for the subsententialist: First, merge is not an arbitrary operation that can be applied willy-nilly to any two grammatical elements. For example, one simply cannot merge 'all' and 'in the garden' or, for that matter, 'tough' with 'watch'. If merge were really that prolific a process, the grammar would overgenerate massively. But second, what would it mean for the derivation of a subsentential object to crash? As the theory is currently constructed, the derivation crashes if does not at a minimum yield something that is sentential in structure; if that constraint is yanked out of the theory then the theory collapses like a house of cards. Crucially, the theory requires that grammatical elements must be combined and moved (under economy constraints) until a successful derivation is computed. If success could be won for any arbitrary subsentential element, then the theory would be incapable of blocking anything.

Returning to our discussion of the minimalist program, I assume that the structures resulting from the merge operation will reflect basic X-bar theory principles. Each head X will project to a maximal projection XP, yielding a structure like the following,

(27)

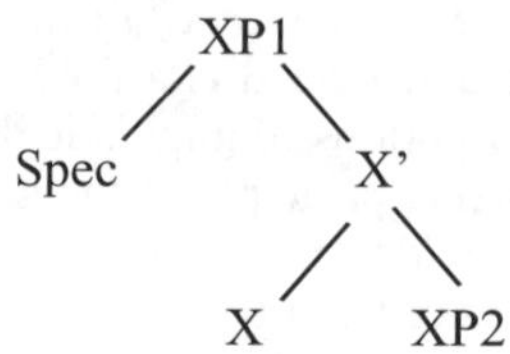


where Spec is the *specifier* of XP1 and XP2 is the *complement* of XP1.[10]

The features of a lexical item will obviously play an important role in this theory. Following Chomsky (1995) we can take a lexical item $l$ to be $\{\alpha, \{F_1, F_2, \ldots, F_n\}\}$, where $\alpha$ is a morphological complex and $F_1, \ldots, F_n$ are inflectional features plus all the relevant semantic, syntactic, and phonological properties of $l$.

The move operation is driven by feature-checking operations. A number of the features of $l$ are interpretable features (and hence will remain in the final LF representation) but a number of other features are not interpretable and rather are features that need to be checked and subsequently erased. A grammatical element may move in order to satisfy certain feature checking operations. So, to take a standard example, an element may have a case feature which needs to be checked, and the element must then move to a case-checking position.

Again, this spells disaster for the subsententialist. Lexical items carry features with them (case features, for example) and if those features are not checked, then the derivation crashes. But what are we to do with subsentential fragments that bear case features or other features? If there is nothing for those features to be checked against then any derivation in which they appear — even the derivation of a subsentential structure — must crash. But if we lift the constraints on feature checking to permit subsentential objects then we have opened the floodgates once again. If items don't need to have their features checked then virtually everything is permissible.

The upshot is that current linguistic theory contains a system of tightly interconnected operations and principles that cannot be relaxed without catastrophic consequences for the grammar as a whole. But this is just what the subsententialist needs — she needs to relax the constraints of standard linguistic theory in an effort to admit objects that she supposes to be grammatical stand-alone entities. But this supposition is without foundation. Such objects simply are not grammatical in isolation. They are only permissible when embedded within a larger sentential context.

## 9. CONCLUSION

In this paper I have attempted to raise some technical concerns about nonsentential assertion. Although, prima facie, it may seem intuitive to talk about using subsentential grammatical forms to make assertions, closer study shows that this conclusion is hasty. Indeed, as we have seen, the current structure of linguistic theory makes it very difficult to make sense of subsentential grammaticality. Furthermore, when studied on a case-by-case basis, it becomes very clear that a broad range of apparent nonsentential assertions are in fact the product of specific sentence-level operations. This raises the question of whether nonsententialist claims about the nature of language are consistent with the preponderance of empirical data and, indeed, whether they are consistent with the theoretical superstructure of linguistic theory that has, for the past fifty years, evolved in response to empirical demands. It would be too strong to say that the notion of nonsentential speech is absurd or even philosophically suspect when considered in isolation. When considered in the context of empirical studies of language, however, nonsentential speech raises a number of serious concerns that urgently need to be addressed. In this paper I have raised a few of these concerns and have observed that to date they have not been addressed in an adequate manner.

## NOTES

* Earlier versions of this paper were presented at the University of Cincinatti workshop on context dependence in semantics, organized by Chris Gauker, and to my graduate seminar at Syracuse University. I am indebted to the participants of those events for helpful questions, and to Tom McKay and Rob Stainton for comments on an earlier draft of the paper. Finally, thanks go to Jason Stanley for encouraging me to write this paper.

1 See Bach (1994, 2000), Barton (1990), Carston (1988, 1991, 2000), Clapp (forthcoming), Recanati (1993, 2002), Sperber and Wilson (1986), and Stainton (2004).

2 On this score I will be in accord with Stanley (2000).

3 Thanks to Rob Stainton for this distinction.

4 Of course it is also possible to argue that one can utter something that is non-sentential with the goal of expressing something that is non-propositional — for example, one might hold that an utterance of 'slab' just means slab and nothing more. So far as I know, no participants in the debate hold this view, and in any case I have trouble seeing that a relevant utterance of 'slab' can't mean "bring me a slab."

5 I take this example to be apparently non-sentential because it is not an inflected clause (it has no tense).

6 Rob Stainton (p.c.) has suggested to me that this case may stem from another construction — one in which 'all' occurs as a stylistic substitute for 'everyone' or 'everything'. In effect, it would be in the same family of constructions as 'All were lost'. I'm not sure what to say about this proposal except that 'All in the garden' doesn't have the same stylistic pomposity that 'All are in the garden' or 'All was lost' do.

7 Stainton (p.c.) notes that the same phenomenon holds for the uncontracted form 'want to?' — it cannot mean "want him to?" The point is fair enough, but presumably the answer lies in the relative ordering of these operations. For example, if the verb must be deleted before the NP (it is more natural to say "him?" than to say "want?" meaning "want him to?") then 'want to' would not be naturally derived from 'want him to?'.

8 Rob Stainton first drew these binding cases to my attention, though neither he nor I can remember exactly when or where he did so. I won't elaborate on the reasons for this memory deficit on our part.

9 See Chomsky (1995).

10 There is currently some question about the status of the X' projection. I pass over that controversy here. Following Kayne (1984, 1994) and much recent work in generative linguistics I will assume that all phrase makers are binary branching and (initially) branch exclusively downward and to the right (movement will allow us to derive more complex structures).

## REFERENCES

Bach, K., "Semantic Slack: What is said and more." In S.L. Tsohatzidis (ed.) *Foundations of Speech Act Theory*. London: Routledge. 1994: 267–291.

Bach, K., "Quantification, Qualification and Context: A Reply to Stanley and Szabo." *Mind and Language* 15 (2000): 562–283.

Barton, E., *Nonsentential Constituents*. Philadelphia: John Benjamins. 1990.

Bobaljik, J., *Morphosyntax: The Syntax of Verbal Inflection*. PhD thesis, Dept. of Linguistics, MIT. 1995.

Bobaljik, J., and Thrainsson, H., "Two Heads aren't Always Better than One." Msc. Harvard University and the University of Iceland. 1997.
Carston, R., "Implicature, Explicature, and Truth-Theoretic Semantics." In R.M. Kempson (ed.) *Mental Representations*. Cambridge: Cambridge University Press. 1988. Reprinted in Davis, 1991.
Carston, R., "Implicature, Explicature and Truth-Theoretic Semantics." In S. Davis (ed.), *Pragmatics: A Reader*. Oxford: Oxford University Press. 1991: 33–51.
Carston, R., "Explicature and Semantics." *UCLA Working Papers in Linguistics* 12 (2000): 1–44. Forthcoming in S. Davis and B. Gillon (eds.), *Semantics: A Reader*. Oxford: Oxford University Press. 2004.
Chomsky, N., *The Minimalist Program*. Cambridge: MIT Press. 1995.
Cinque, G., *Adverbs and Functional Heads: A Cross-Linguistic Perspective*. Oxford: Oxford University Press. 1998.
Clapp, L. "What Unarticulated Constituents Could Not Be." In J. Campbell, M. O'Rourke and D. Shier (eds.) *Meaning and Truth*. New York: Seven Bridges Press. 2002: 231–256.
Kayne, R., *The Antisymmetry of Syntax*. Cambridge: MIT Press. 1994.
Pollock, J.Y., "Verb Movements, Universal Grammar and the Structure of IP." *Linguistic Inquiry* 20 (1989): 365–424.
Poole, G., "Optional Movement in the Minimalist Program." In W. Abraham et. al. (eds.), *Minimal Ideas: Syntactic Studies in the Minimalist Framework*. Amsterdam: John Benjamins. 1996: 199–216.
Recanati, F., *Direct Reference: From Language to Thought*. Oxford: Blackwell. 1993.
Recanati, F., "Unarticulated Constituents." *Linguistics and Philosophy* 25 (2002): 299–345.
Sperber, D., and Wilson, D., *Relevance: Communication and Cognition*. Oxford: Blackwell. 1986.
Stainton, R., "In Defense of Non-Sentential Assertion." In Z. Szabo (ed.), *Semantics vs. Pragmatics*. Oxford: Oxford University Press. 2004: 383–457.
Stanley, J., "Context and Logical Form." *Linguistics and Philosophy* 23 (2000): 391–434.

LENNY CLAPP

# ON THE INTERPRETATION AND PERFORMANCE OF NON-SENTENTIAL ASSERTIONS*

> What is it that we call a sentence? A series of sounds, but only if it has a sense (this is not meant to convey that *any* series of sounds that has a sense is a sentence). And when we call a sentence true we really mean that its sense is true. And hence the only thing that raises the question of truth at all is the sense of sentences.
>
> Gottlob Frege, "Thoughts"

## 1. INTRODUCTION

The issue that is the focus of this anthology can be characterized in terms of the above citation from Frege. Some, whom I will call *sententialists*, maintain that the view espoused by Frege in the above passage is basically correct; sententialists agree with Frege that utterances of *only* complete declarative sentences can be true (or false), though they would reject Frege's Platonist conception of *sense*. Others, whom I will call *non-sententialists*, maintain that Frege's view is fundamentally flawed, and not merely because he assumes an implausible Platonism regarding sense; against Frege, they maintain that utterances of non-sentential words or phrases can also be true (or false).

It is noteworthy that contemporary sententialists and non-sententialists alike reject Frege's Platonism and claim to be pursuing a much different project than Frege claimed to be pursuing. In the pages preceding the above citation, Frege took pains to distinguish his project from any sort of psychological investigation; Frege very much desired to distinguish the "laws of psychology" and the "laws of logic," and his project was to discover the laws of logic. Thus Frege's attitude is in stark contrast with that shared by both the contemporary sententialists and non-sententialists, who are working within a tradition of empirical linguistics — a discipline proudly defined as a branch of psychology or cognitive science. As a consequence, sententialists and non-sententialists alike must be concerned with sorts of natural language phenomena that Frege could, perhaps with justification, disregard as being mere psychological glitches, or deficiencies of natural language. In particular, if confronted with the at least apparent phenomenon of non-sentential assertion, Frege could say that regardless of whether or not the laws of psychology allow for non-sentential assertions, the laws of logic do not. The contemporary sententialist, however, cannot avail himself of this sort of response. How, then, is the contemporary sententialist, who works within the empirical framework established by Chomsky, to account for the apparent phenomenon of non-sentential assertion? As Stainton and Elugardo note in the introduction to this volume, there are two general strategies of response available to the sententialist, both of which involve denying that



*R. Elugardo and R. J. Stainton (eds.), Ellipsis and Nonsentential Speech*, 109–129.

non-sentential assertion is a genuine phenomenon:

> *The Syntactic Strategy*: The sententialist can claim that cases of what appear to be non-sentential utterances expressing truth conditions actually involve some sort of *ellipsis*, and thus what is uttered is really a full sentence — the LF for the utterance has IP as its initial node. This strategy thus grants that the utterances in question express truth conditions, but it denies that they involve sub-sentential syntactic structures.[1]

> *The Pragmatic Strategy*: The sententialist can claim that cases of what appear to be non-sentential utterances expressing truth conditions actually do not express truth conditions at all. This strategy thus grants that the utterances in question involve sub-sentential syntactic structures, but it denies that such utterances really express truth conditions.

As Stanley (2000, 403–4) has pointed out, the sententialist need not commit to only one of these strategies: it is open to him to utilize the syntactic strategy to account for some non-sentential utterances, and to utilize the pragmatic strategy to account for others.[2] My purpose here, however, is to argue that the pragmatic strategy is not a live option for the sententialist. Thus if the sententialist is to succeed in explaining away apparent instances of non-sentential assertions, he must utilize the syntactic strategy, which faces significant difficulties of its own.[3]

The paper proceeds as follows. In section II I describe the general perspective of *truth-conditional semantics* which motivates sententialism, and I distinguish it from *truth-conditional pragmatics*, the general perspective that underlies non-sententialism. I also explicate the model of interpretation that is inherent in truth-conditional semantics.[4] In section III, I illustrate that there are many sorts of *prima facie* counterexamples to truth-conditional semantics in addition to those involving non-sentential utterances. It is important to keep these other sorts of *prima facie* counterexamples in mind because, given the similarities between the various sorts of *prima facie* counterexamples, a sententialist's response to one sort will commit him to a similar response to another sort. And this wider commitment to a strategy of response might have significant consequences. Indeed, this is precisely what I will argue to be the case regarding the pragmatic strategy of response. Thus, in section IV, I explicate Stanley's (2000) utilization of the pragmatic strategy, and I argue that if the sententialist utilizes anything like Stanley's response to account for problematic non-sentential utterances, then he must also utilize this response to account for other sorts of *prima facie* counterexamples. But this wider commitment to the pragmatic strategy is incompatible with the model of interpretation inherent in truth-conditional semantics. In section V, I consider and reject Stanley's appeal to a semantic competence/performance distinction to support his utilization the pragmatic strategy. And finally, in section VI, I briefly consider the consequences of the failure of the pragmatic strategy for the issue of whether or not there are genuine non-sentential assertions, and for the more general debate between truth-conditional semantics and truth-conditional pragmatics.

## 2. TRUTH-CONDITIONAL SEMANTICS, TRUTH-CONDITIONAL PRAGMATICS, COMPETENCE, PERFORMANCE AND INTERPRETATION

The sententialist claims that only utterances of complete sentences can be assigned truth conditions. Or slightly more precisely, the sententialist claims that only declarative utterances whose LFs are fully sentential — whose initial node is an IP — have truth conditions, and thus only such full sentences (at LF) can legitimately be used to make assertions. What is the motivation for the sententialist's claim?

The sententialist's claim is a consequence of the general principle that "all truth-conditional effects of extra-linguistic context can be traced to logical form" (Stanley, 2000, 391). This general principle is more precisely rendered as follows:

> *Utterance Compositionality*: The truth conditions of an utterance are a *function* of (i) the structure of the LF of the utterance, and (ii) the *semantic values* of the terminal nodes of the LF of the utterance (as determined by the context of utterance).

Genuine non-sentential assertions would constitute counterexamples to this principle. Consider two typical non-sentential utterances, each of which involves an articulation of the adjectival phrase, 'totally useless': (i) Suppose I am giving you an assessment of the computer equipment in my department. Pointing at a particular printer I utter, 'totally useless'. In this context my utterance of this adjectival phrase seems to constitute an assertion and thus seems to express truth conditions — my utterance is true if and only if, roughly, the indicated printer is totally useless. (ii) Suppose I am in a meeting, and all the participants are voicing their opinions about a certain policy that has just been proposed. When it is my turn, I utter 'totally useless'. Again, my utterance seems to constitute an assertion and thus seems to express truth conditions — in this context my utterance is true if and only if, roughly, the recently proposed policy would be totally useless. That two utterances of the very same phrase express distinct truth conditions is problematic for the principle of utterance compositionality. For it at least *seems* that my utterances have the same LF, and, given that my utterances involve the very same (non-context-sensitive) lexical items, my utterances must invoke the very same semantic values. Yet, contrary to what would be predicted by utterance compositionality together with these apparent facts, my utterances express distinct truth conditions. Consequently, the defender of utterance compositionality must claim either that, despite phonological and syntactic appearances, my utterances are associated with distinct LFs, or he must claim that, despite semantic and pragmatic appearances, my utterances do not express truth conditions. That is, the defender of utterance compositionality must utilize close cousins of either the syntactic or the pragmatic strategy.[5]

The above examples illustrate why non-sentential utterances pose a threat to utterance compositionality, but they do not quite make explicit why one who endorses utterance compositionality is also committed to sententialism. The above examples illustrate that if utterance compositionality is to be preserved, then either, despite appearances, my two utterances of 'totally useless' do not have the same LF, or they do not express the truth conditions they seem to express. But *this much* does not commit the defender of utterance compositionality to the sententialist claim that only utterances whose LFs are fully sentential express truth conditions. Why does utterance compositionality imply this additional, stronger, claim?

The reason is that sub-sentential words and phrases often appear within the larger syntactic environment of a full sentence. That is, the adjectival phrase 'totally useless' appears phonetically realized in sentences such as 'Software written before 1990 is now totally useless'. And when it occurs embedded in this broader syntactic environment, the adjectival phrase does not express truth conditions; within this sentential (IP dominated) syntactic environment, the adjectival phrase 'totally useless' is not assigned truth conditions as its semantic value. Rather, as it occurs within this larger fully sentential syntactic environment, the semantic import of the phrase 'totally useless' is merely to contribute to the determination of the truth conditions of the full sentence of which it is a proper part. Moreover, it is typically required that the semantic value assigned to a syntactic structure remain constant regardless of any broader syntactic environment in which the structure might appear. Following Davidson (1968) this requirement is sometimes referred to as "semantic innocence."[6] Consequently, if 'totally useless' (or its LF) is not assigned truth conditions when it occurs embedded in a sentence (i.e., in an LF whose initial node is IP), then it cannot be assigned truth conditions when it occurs as a non-sentential utterance. To summarize, semantic innocence requires that if *some* occurrences of the adjectival phrase 'totally useless' do not express truth conditions, then (assuming that the phrase is not radically context sensitive) *all* occurrences of the phrase do not express truth conditions. Moreover, the general compositionality requirements of traditional truth-conditional semantic theories dictate that the adjectival phrase 'totally useless' does not express truth conditions when it appears in a sentential (IP dominated) syntactic environment. And hence the commitment to utterance compositionality together with semantic innocence imply the sententialist's claim that only utterances whose LFs are fully sentential express truth conditions.

The sententialist's claim is thus a consequence of utterance compositionality, together with other plausible constraints on an adequate semantic theory. But what is the motivation for utterance compositionality itself? The commitment to this principle derives from a particular construal of the role of compositionality in the process of *interpretation* — the process whereby speaker-hearers actually come to understand one another's utterances. It is now a familiar idea that our interpretative abilities result, at *least in part*, from our implicit knowledge of semantic rules and principles. Some of these rules and principles, the lexical rules, dictate what the meanings (or *semantic values*) of individual words or morphemes, relative to a context of utterance, are. Others, the combinatorial rules, dictate how the meanings of words and morphemes combine, as directed by the LF of the sentence, to determine the meaning, or truth conditions, of an entire sentence. According to this general compositional conception of semantics then, a semantic theory for a language is a specification of implicitly known compositional rules and principles that in combination assign appropriate truth conditions to every sentence of the language. Larson and Segal (1995, 11–12) summarize the attractions of this general compositional conception:

> The hypothesis that we know a set of compositional semantic rules and principles is a highly attractive one having a great deal of explanatory power. In particular, it accounts for three notable and closely related features of linguistic competence. First, it explains why *our understanding of sentences is systematic* — why there are definite, predictable patterns among the sentences we understand.... Second, the hypothesis accounts for the obvious but important fact that *we can understand new sentences*, sentences that we have never come across before.... Third, the hypothesis accounts for the slightly less obvious but equally important fact that *we have the capacity to understand each of an indefinitely large number of sentences*.

The Frege-inspired truth-theoretic semantic programs defended and developed by Davidson, Montague and their followers are motivated by considerations such as those stated above. It is important to realize, however, that these familiar arguments in support of some sort of semantic compositionality do not entail *utterance compositionality*. The above cited familiar motivations for some sort of compositional semantic theory support utterance compositionality *only if* such a compositional semantic theory is construed as a theory of linguistic *performance*, as opposed to a theory of linguistic *competence*. That is, one might maintain that though implicit knowledge of compositional semantic rules and principles is *necessary* for interpretation, it is nowhere near *sufficient*. One might maintain that implicit knowledge of such compositional semantic rules and principles is just one part of the knowledge and abilities speakers utilize in making judgments concerning the truth conditions of utterances, and that other — more *pragmatic* — knowledge and abilities are also utilized. Moreover, if one regarded such a compositional semantic theory as a theory of only semantic *competence*, as opposed to semantic *performance*, one could adopt something akin to Frege's attitude toward "aberrant" linguistic phenomena; one could maintain that certain linguistic phenomena are beyond the scope of a theory of semantic competence. In particular one could maintain that our purely *semantic* knowledge, processes, and systems do not allow for non-sentential utterances, and thus to explain how we use non-sentential utterances one would have to invoke *pragmatic* knowledge, processes, and systems. Hence, there is an important distinction between those who regard compositional semantic theories of the sort proposed by Davidson and Montague as theories of *semantic performance*, and those who regard them as theories of *semantic competence*.

*Truth-conditional semantics* is the view that such traditional compositional semantic theories ought to be regarded as theories of *performance* — as theories explaining how speaker-hearers actually manage to interpret one another's *utterances*. Thus, those who endorse truth-conditional semantics endorse *utterance compositionality*: they maintain that the truth condition of utterances are determined by *semantics* alone, where *semantics* is limited to determination of LFs, the processes of assigning semantic values to terminal nodes of LFs, and finally the computation of the truth conditions thereby determined.[7] In contrast, those who regard traditional semantic theories as theories of only *semantic competence* deny that such theories suffice as theories of *interpretation*. Following Stanley (2000) I will call such theorists *truth-conditional pragmatists*. These theorists maintain that purely *semantic* (where this term is understood as described above) factors do not suffice to determine the truth conditions of utterances, and that additional *pragmatic* factors are also required to determine truth conditions. Hence truth-conditional pragmatists reject utterance compositionality, and therefore they can maintain something akin to Frege's attitude toward "aberrant" linguistic phenomena; in particular, truth-conditional pragmatists can maintain that the "aberrant" phenomenon of non-sentential assertion is accounted for by pragmatic knowledge, processes and systems that go beyond the knowledge, processes and systems described by traditional compositional semantic theories. In summary, both truth-conditional semanticists and truth-conditional pragmatists accept the recently rehearsed reasons supporting a traditional compositional semantic theory, though they disagree as to whether such a semantic theory is to be understood as only a theory of *semantic competence*, or as a more comprehensive theory of *semantic performance*: truth-conditional semantics understands such a compositional semantic theory to be a theory of semantic performance, while truth conditional pragmatics understands it to be only a theory of semantic competence. Sententialism is supported by the broader perspective of *truth-conditional semantics*, while non-sententialism is supported, or at least allowed for, by the contrasting broader perspective of *truth-conditional pragmatics*.

Because truth-conditional semantics is proposing a theory of semantic performance, it entails a particular model of *interpretation* — the process whereby speaker-hearers actually come to understand one another's utterances. This model of interpretation is explicitly described by Stanley and Gendler-Szabo (2000, 11). According to this model, interpretation of "typical assertions" is a two-step process whereby a hearer identifies the proposition the speaker intends to communicate, or equivalently determines the truth conditions of an assertion. In the first step the hearer uses her syntactic and phonological knowledge, together with whatever clues she can garner from the context of utterance, to determine the LF of the assertion. Stanley and Gendler Szabo (2000, 13) use the equation, "what is articulated + context = what is uttered" to describe this first step, where "what is articulated" is a "phonological sentence," and "what is uttered" is a "grammatical sentence," i.e., an LF. Thus if an interpreter correctly completes the first step, she will have determined the LF of an utterance. In the second step the hearer uses her knowledge of the LF of the utterance, together with her knowledge of the semantic theory for her language and knowledge of the context of utterance, to determine the proposition expressed, or equivalently the truth conditions of the utterance. Stanley and Gendler Szabo (2000, 15) use the equation "what is uttered + linguistic meaning + context = what is said" to describe the second step, where "what is said" is the proposition expressed, or equivalently the truth conditions expressed. I think it is more perspicuous to conceive of this second step as itself proceeding in two sub-steps: In the first sub-step, the interpreter uses her recently acquired knowledge of what is uttered (the LF), and her knowledge of the lexical semantic rules for her language and her knowledge concerning relevant the context of utterance, to determine the semantic values of the semantically significant features of what is uttered (the lowermost nodes of the LF). And in the second sub-step the interpreter uses her knowledge of the thus determined semantic values, together with her knowledge of the combinatorial semantic rules of her language and her knowledge of what is uttered (the LF), to determine "what is said," i.e., the truth conditions of the utterance. In keeping with the principle of utterance compositionality, this two-step model of interpretation requires that the truth conditions interpreters assign to "typical assertions" must be "traced to logical form."

## 3. OTHER SORTS OF *PRIMA FACIE* COUNTEREXAMPLES TO UTTERANCE COMPOSITIONALITY

An adequate understanding and treatment of the problem non-sentential utterances pose for truth-conditional semantics requires consideration of other similar problems. It is not difficult to generalize from the phenomenon of non-sentential utterances to formulate a general description of *prima facie* counterexamples to utterance compositionality. Let an *expression* be a phonological type — a sound-type constituting a linguistic entity; hence some expressions correspond to complete sentences, others to mere words or phrases. (This is hardly precise, but it will serve my purposes.) Suppose an expression S *at least seemed* to have the following four properties:

(a) Some occurrences of S express truth conditions.
(b) S is context sensitive so that the truth conditions it expresses vary from context to context, or perhaps in some contexts S does not express truth conditions at all.
(c) S is neither lexically nor structurally ambiguous.
(d) S contains no context-sensitive words and/or features that account for its context sensitivity.

Such an expression would constitute a *prima facie* counterexample to utterance compositionality. For if S possessed (c), every occurrence of S would have the same LF. And if

S possessed (c) and (d), every occurrence of S would invoke the same semantic values. Hence, utterance compositionality would imply that either no occurrence of S expresses truth conditions, or that every occurrence expresses the same truth conditions. For this principle entails that the truth conditions of *every occurrence* of S are a function of (i) the structure of S's LF, and (ii) the *semantic values* of the terminal nodes of S's LF. So if S also possesses (a) and (b), S constitutes a *prima facie* counterexample to utterance compositionality. If utterance compositionality is to be preserved, the defender of truth-conditional semantics must demonstrate that the *prima facie* counterexample does not, despite appearances, actually possess at least one of (a)–(d).

In section I the *pragmatic* and *syntactic* strategies were defined relative to *prima facie* counterexamples involving non-sentential utterances. It is now apparent, however, that non-sentential utterances are just one instance of a general problem for truth-conditional semantics. Consequently, the syntactic and pragmatic strategies generalize in a straightforward way so that they apply to all sorts of *prima facie* counterexamples:

> *The Syntactic Strategy*: Faced with a *prima facie* counterexample S, the defender of truth-conditional semantics claims that the LFs corresponding to occurrences of S contain phonetically unrealized structure, and thus the LFs corresponding to utterances of S are richer than is suggested by the phonological features of S. (In terms of the definition of a *prima facie* counterexample stated above, despite appearances the *prima facie* counterexample does not actually possess property (c) or (d).)[8]

> *The Pragmatic Strategy*: Faced with a *prima facie* counterexample S, the defender of truth-conditional semantics claims that occurrences of S do not actually express the truth conditions they seem to express, or do not actually express truth conditions at all. (Again, in terms of the definition stated above, despite appearances the *prima facie* counterexample does not actually possess property (a) or (b).)

The *prima facie* counterexamples to utterance compositionality are by no means limited to cases of non-sentential utterances. As Travis (1985), Sperber and Wilson (1986), Carston (1991), Bach (1994), Recanati (1996) and other proponents of *truth-conditional pragmatics* have demonstrated, there are many expressions that at least seem to have properties (a)–(d). The list of *prima facie* counterexamples includes almost all quantified sentences, sentences containing comparative adjectives, propositional attitude ascriptions, sentences containing definite descriptions, modal sentences, counterfactuals, and others. The focus of this paper is non-sentential utterances, and thus I will not review all of these sorts of *prima facie* counterexamples. But my argument against the pragmatic strategy does require the premise that if the defender of utterance compositionality utilizes the pragmatic strategy to explain away the *prima facie* counterexamples involving non-sentential utterances, then he must utilize this strategy with regard to other sorts of *prima facie* counterexamples as well. And making a case for this premise requires me to explicate at least some of the other sorts of *prima facie* counterexamples, and to illustrate how the syntactic strategy can be utilized in an attempt to explain them away. So in the remainder of this section I first discuss the general phenomenon of utterances that require, in the terminology of Bach (1994), "completion" or "expansion" — all such utterances constitute *prima facie* counterexamples to utterance compositionality. I also consider a particular sort of utterance that requires "expansion" — quantified sentences — and I briefly explicate Stanley and Gendler Szabo's (2000) utilization of the *syntactic strategy* in an attempt to explain away *prima facie* counterexamples involving quantified sentences.

Bach (1994) introduces the general notions of "completion" and "expansion" in terms of different sorts of *prima facie* counterexamples to utterance compositionality. Consider typical utterances of the following sentences:

(1) John left (the party/graduate school)
(2) Spike and Butch got in a fight (with Bruno/with each other)

Interpreters of typical utterances of (1) and (2) must work through a process of *enrichment* to arrive at the intended truth conditions of the utterance. (In the above, I have indicated possible enrichments in parentheses.) Bach (1994) suggests that with regard to utterances of sentences such as (1) interpreters must work through a process of *completion* to arrive at truth conditions. The terminology is meant to reflect that, though (1) is *grammatically* a complete sentence, the phonologically realized elements of (1) are insufficient to determine truth conditions. The idea is that one cannot evaluate the thought that John left *simpliciter* for truth or falsity — one must know what it is that John is being alleged to have left. And what it is that an utterer of (1) is alleging John to have left will vary across contexts. Moreover, (1) contains no relevant, phonologically realized, context-sensitive words or features. Thus sentences such as (1) that require completion constitute *prima facie* counterexamples to utterance compositionality. (Or more precisely, *expressions* corresponding to sentences such as (1) constitute *prima facie* counterexamples.)

According to Bach sentences such as (2) are not in need of semantic completion, because the phonologically realized material is itself sufficient to express a "minimal proposition." The minimal proposition expressed by occurrences of (2) is simply that Spike got in a fight, and Butch got in a fight. This minimal proposition, however, is not what speakers typically express in uttering (2). Usually, but not always, when speakers utter (2) they express the proposition that Spike and Butch got in a fight *with each other*. So though the phonetically realized material in (2) is sufficient to determine a minimal proposition, the truth conditions typically expressed by an occurrence of (2) are more discriminating than this minimal proposition, and thus interpreters must work through a process of *expansion* in order to determine the expressed truth conditions. Consequently expressions corresponding to sentences such as (2) also seem to possess properties (a)–(d): These expressions are used to make assertions, and they are context-sensitive, but they contain no relevant context-sensitive features and involve neither lexical nor structural ambiguity. Consequently such expressions constitute *prima facie* counterexamples to utterance compositionality.[9]

Quantified sentences are one sort of sentence whose corresponding expressions typically require completion, and Stanley and Gendler Szabo (2000) have utilized the syntactic strategy in an attempt to explain away such *prima facie* counterexamples. Consider the quantified sentence discussed by Stanley and Gendler Szabo:

(3) Every bottle is empty.

A typical utterance of (3) is in need of expansion. For a typical utterance of (3) does not express the minimal proposition that every bottle in the universe is empty; rather a typical utterance of (3) states a weaker, richer, proposition to the effect that every bottle relevant to the people engaged in the discourse is, to some relevant degree, empty of some relevant substance. Thus the domain of quantification does not include *all* bottles, but is restricted to a proper subset of relevant bottles. But the proper subset of bottles that serves as the restriction varies from context to context. For example, one utterance of (3) is true, roughly, if and only if every wine-bottle on my dinner table at a particular time is empty of wine. But a different utterance of (3) is true if and only if, roughly, every baby-bottle within easy reach of a desperate parent is empty of baby formula. Thus (1) clearly has properties (a) and (b), and it seems to have properties (c) and (d): (3) is neither structurally nor lexically ambiguous. And though (3) contains at least one overt context-sensitive feature, viz. the tensed form of the verb, there is no overt context-sensitive feature that would plausibly account for the variance in the quantifier restriction. Thus sentence (3) seems to possess all of (a)–(d), and consequently it constitutes a *prima facie* counterexample to utterance compositionality.

A closely related phenomenon concerns "incomplete" definite descriptions. Consider the following sentence:

(4) The bottle is empty.

Assuming that definite descriptions presuppose uniqueness, it seems that an utterance of (4) can express truth conditions only if there exists just one bottle in the universe.[10] But typical utterances of (4) do not seem to presuppose that there exists only one bottle in the universe, thus utterances of (4) also require interpreters to work through a process of expansion. Thus (4) also seems to possess properties (a)–(d) and constitutes a *prima facie* counterexample to utterance compositionality. Clearly (4) can be used to express truth conditions, and moreover, different truth conditions in different contexts: In some contexts (4) is true if and only if, roughly, a particular wine-bottle is empty, while in other contexts (4) is true if and only if, roughly, a particular baby-bottle is empty. But again (4) contains on relevant context-sensitive words or features, and it is neither lexically nor structurally ambiguous. So sentences with "incomplete" definite descriptions, or rather their corresponding expressions, also possess properties (a)–(d), and thus also constitute *prima facie* counterexamples to utterance compositionality.

Stanley and Gendler Szabo (2000) utilize a version of the syntactic strategy in an attempt to explain away the *prima facie* counterexamples of the sort exemplified by (3) and (4). Stanley and Gendler Szabo propose that an expression such as (3) be analyzed as containing at the level of LF a "hidden indexical" which takes on different semantic values in different contexts. More specifically, they propose the LF of an utterance of (3) is something like this

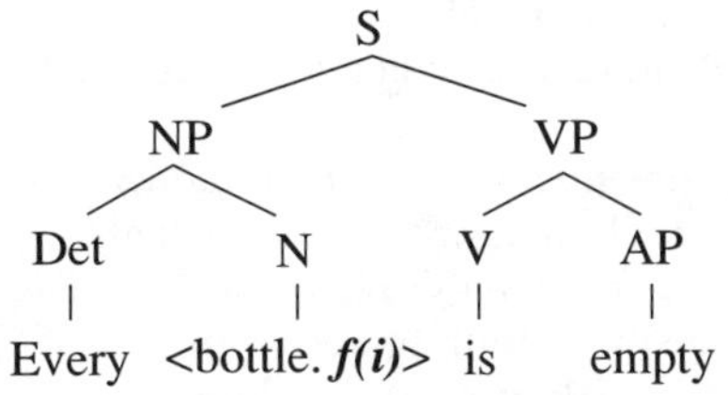


According to Stanley and Gendler Szabo's analysis, the terminal node corresponding to the phonetically realized noun 'bottle' is syntactically complex: It is an ordered pair, the first member of which is the phonetically realized familiar lexical item 'bottle' and the second member of which is a new sort of phonetically unrealized context-sensitive element ***f(i)***. This phonetically unrealized element consists of two parts: ***f()*** is a context-sensitive element that has as its semantic value, relative to a context, a function from individuals to sets (or properties), while ***i*** is a context sensitive element that has as its semantic value, relative to a context, an individual. The set that is determined by applying the function "provided by context" to the individual provided by context serves to further restrict the domain of quantification: the restricted domain is the intersection of the extension of 'bottle' and the set determined by applying the function "provided by context" to the argument "provided by context." (Stanley and Gendler Szabo, not surprisingly, provide no explanation whatsoever as to how the semantic values of ***f()*** and ***i*** are "provided by context.") Thus there is a semantic value invoked by an utterance of (3) which — though not the semantic value of any phonetically realized, or articulated, word or feature in (3) — is nonetheless the semantic value of an element of the utterance's LF. Moreover, since ***f(i)*** is a context-sensitive element, it is assigned different semantic values in different contexts. In terms of the previous example involving different utterances of (3), in some contexts ***f(i)*** is assigned as its semantic value the set of all wine bottles on my dinner table, while in other contexts ***f(i)*** is assigned as its semantic value the set of all baby-bottles within reach of a certain desperate parent. Hence on Stanley and Gendler Szabo's utilization of the syntactic strategy, (3) does not actually possess property (d), for on their analysis, despite appearances, occurrences of (3) really do contain relevant context-sensitive features. A similar sort of explanation of course applies to sentences such as (4) containing "incomplete" definite descriptions. In this way Stanley and Gendler Szabo utilize the syntactic strategy to explain away *prima facie* counterexamples involving quantified sentences.

## 4. THE PRAGMATIC STRATEGY OF RESPONSE AND ITS APPLICATION TO ALL OF THE *PRIMA FACIE* COUNTEREXAMPLES

To utilize the pragmatic strategy in response to a *prima facie* counterexample is to argue that, despite appearances, occurrences of the problematic expression do not actually express truth conditions, or at least not the truth conditions they seem to express. In this section I will argue that the pragmatic strategy is not a live option for the defender of utterance compositionality. My comments will focus on Stanley (2000), because Stanley is the only theorist I am aware of who utilizes the pragmatic strategy with regard to some *prima facie* counterexamples involving non-sentential utterances. It will become apparent, however, that the problems I raise with regard to Stanley's utilization of the pragmatic strategy undermine *any* attempt to utilize the pragmatic strategy to defend utterance compositionality from *prima facie* counterexamples.

Stanley (2000) maintains that, despite the judgments of ordinary speaker-hearers, occurrences of non-sentential utterances do not actually express truth conditions. He presents two arguments in support of this claim. He first suggests that "linguistic speech acts must determinately be made with the relevant sort of force. That is, for an act to count as a speech act of kind *k*, it must determinately be performed with the force appropriate to acts of kind *k*" (407). Stanley then uses this criterion of *determinate force* to argue that a particular case of non-sentential utterance is not a "linguistic assertion, and indeed is not a genuine linguistic speech act" (Stanley, 2000, 407). In the case considered by Stanley, a thirsty man staggers up to a street vendor and utters, 'water'. Stanley argues that in this case it is indeterminate whether or not the thirsty man's utterance has the force of a request, or a command: "It would be equally consistent with the thirsty man's intentions to suppose that the utterance was a request, or a command" (Stanley, 2000, 407). And since the thirsty man lacks intentions that would determine a force appropriate to the act kind *assertion*, the utterance does not count as an assertion, and thus does not count as a "genuine linguistic speech act."

Unfortunately, Stanley's discussion of the thirsty man's utterance of 'water' takes the debate rather far astray. First, even if one grants Stanley's conclusion that the thirsty man's utterance does not count as a "genuine linguistic speech act," it is far from clear how this serves to rescue utterance compositionality. This principle is threatened because it predicts that non-sentential utterances do not express truth conditions, yet many such utterances seem to express truth conditions. Hence, what is relevant is whether or not the thirsty man's utterance expresses truth conditions — whether or not it counts as an *assertion*, or any other "genuine linguistic speech act" is beside the point.[11] Second, though I agree with Stanley that the thirsty man's utterance is not an assertion, and moreover does not express truth conditions, nothing relevant to the debate about non-sentential utterances follows from this.[12] Stanley is allegedly presenting a reason for supposing that "apparent non-sentential assertions" (Stanley, 2000, 407) do not really express truth conditions at all. The problem is that if an utterance lacked the force appropriate to assertion, then it simply would not be an "apparent non-sentential assertion" — it would not be a *prima facie* counterexample. Nobody claims that just any old utterance of a word or phrase constitutes a *prima facie* counterexample to utterance compositionality. Hence the example of the thirsty man *cannot* pose a problem for utterance compositionality; it does not even *seem* to express truth conditions. Only utterances that *seem* to express truth conditions can be *prima facie* counterexamples. In order to explain away such problematic utterances, Stanley must provide a reason for thinking that though such utterances *seem* to express truth conditions, they do not *really* express truth conditions. Stanley's first reason does not even attempt to do this.

Stanley's second reason for supposing that some apparent non-sentential assertions are not really genuine assertions is that linguistic speech acts "must express determinate contents" (407). Stanley then uses this criterion of *determinate content* to argue again that the thirsty man's utterance of 'water' to a street vendor is not a genuine linguistic speech act:

> ... in the case of the thirsty man's utterance ... there is no determinate content associated with the speech act. Suppose, for the sake of argument, that the speech act is an assertion. Then, the relevant sort of content is a proposition. But what proposition has thereby been expressed? The point is particularly acute if we assume that propositions are structured. Is the proposition thereby expressed the proposition that the thirsty man wants water? Is it the proposition that the vender should give the thirsty man water? The available facts simply do not determine a determinate propositional content for the alleged assertion. And when a communicative act lacks a determinate content, it is not a linguistic act. (408)

Stanley again mistakenly focuses on whether or not the thirsty man's utterance qualifies as an *assertion*, or any other sort of "linguistic act." Such issues of illocutionary force are, to repeat, beside the point — the relevant issue is whether or not the thirsty man's utterance really expresses truth conditions. But Stanley's second reason, unlike his first reason, can be interpreted so that it is relevant. That is, Stanley can be interpreted as endorsing a *criterion of determinate content*: An expression expresses truth conditions only if it has "determinate content."

*If* having "determinate content" is a necessary condition for an utterance's expressing truth conditions, then not only will the thirsty man's utterance not qualify as expressing truth conditions, but *all* non-sentential utterances that are not *obvious* cases of syntactic ellipsis will not qualify as expressing truth conditions. Consider again my seeming assertion of 'totally useless' in the policy meeting. Precisely which determinate proposition have I expressed? That the policy just proposed would be totally useless? That the policy they proposed is totally useless? That the policy being considered in this meeting would be totally useless, if we adopted it? Stanley's insight that speakers' intentions are not rich enough to determine how non-sentential assertions are to be *completed* yields the result that *no prima facie* counterexample involving a non-sentential utterance will qualify as expressing truth conditions. But the consequences of Stanley's insight extend even further: If having "determinate content" is a necessary condition for an utterance's expressing truth conditions, then no utterance requiring any sort of *completion or expansion* will qualify as expressing truth conditions.

Consider again a typical utterance requiring *expansion*:

(4) The bottle is empty.

Suppose this sentence is uttered by a desperate parent who is bottle-feeding a fussy child. And suppose that this utterance constitutes a *prima facie* counterexample — it is an apparently successful act of communication. To fix intuitions, suppose that as a consequence of uttering (4) the other parent says "OK," and is led to bring the speaker another baby-bottle, sufficiently full of baby formula. According to Stanley the utterance of the desperate parent expresses truth conditions only if it expresses "determinate content." But here again Stanley's insight clearly applies. Which, if any, of the following best expresses the "determinate content" of the speaker's assertion?

(4a) The bottle (in my hand) is empty.
(4b) The bottle (I have been using) is empty.
(4c) The bottle (I am looking at) is empty.
(4d) The bottle (in little Suzie's mouth) is empty.
(4e) The bottle (right here) is empty.
(4f) The bottle (I have been using just now to feed our child) is empty.

I have made the point elsewhere (Clapp, 2001), so I will not belabor it here, but clearly there is no more reason for thinking that, e.g., (4a) is the "determinate content" than there is for thinking that (4c) is the "determinate content." It is of course determinate *which bottle* the parent is *denoting* in uttering (4) — the utterance is successful. What is not determinate is how the "incomplete definite description" is made "complete," or more generally, how the quantifier is further restricted. Moreover, there is nothing extraordinary about the utterance of (4) we have been considering, and thus it is clear that this sort of indeterminacy is present in almost every utterance containing a quantifier term. And neither is this indeterminacy limited to utterances involving quantifiers.

Consider again a typical utterance requiring *completion*:

(1) John left.

Suppose we are at a painfully dull party, and somebody utters (1) in response to an inquiry as to the whereabouts of John. What is the "determinate content" of this utterance? Again, here are a number of plausible candidates:

(1a) John left (this dull party)
(1b) John left (the party)[13]
(1c) John left (this place)
(1d) John left (this apartment)
(1e) John left (the apartment we are now in)
(1f) John left (the party we are now at)

Again, in a typical utterance of (1) there is no more reason to suppose that, e.g., (1a) represents the "determinate content" or the utterance than there is to suppose that (1d) represents the "determinate content" of the utterance.

It would seem then that "indeterminacy of content" is, as Frege might have put it, a widespread deficiency of natural language. In particular, almost every *prima facie* counterexample to utterance compositionality will suffer from this deficiency; having "indeterminate content" is almost an essential feature of *prima facie* counterexamples.[14] The defender of utterance compositionality might suppose this to be a beneficial result; Stanley presented the criterion of *determinate content* as a means of explaining away only some *prima facie* counterexamples involving non-sentential utterances. But as it turns out the criterion can be used, indeed *must* be used, to explain away (almost) all *prima facie* counterexamples. Not surprisingly, the widespread applicability of the criterion of determinate content has a number of significant consequences for the defender of truth-conditional semantics.

One significant consequence is that the defender of truth-conditional semantics who follows Stanley in endorsing the "determinate content" criterion for expressing truth conditions has no need of the *syntactic strategy*. In other words, one consequence of Stanley's rejection of non-sentential utterances on the grounds that they do not have "determinate content" is that Stanley and Gendler Szabo's utilization of the syntactic strategy to account quantifier domain restriction is rendered otiose, as is Stanley's (2000) appeal to a process of *pragmatic ellipsis*.[15] If utterances of sentences containing quantifiers do not constitute genuine assertions because they lack "determinate content," then there is no need to posit sophisticated hidden syntactic structure to preserve utterance compositionality. It might be claimed, however, that this is good news for the defender of truth-conditional semantics. For such "hidden indexical" theories seem *ad hoc* and problematic for independent reasons.[16] If the *prima facie* counterexamples can be explained away without positing hidden syntactic elements and mysterious processes whereby "context provides" semantic values for these hidden elements, so much the better for truth-conditional semantics.

Another significant consequence of the widespread applicability of Stanley's criterion of "determinate content" is that it commits the defender of truth-conditional semantics to *semantic minimalism*: According to semantic minimalism, utterances that undergo a process of *completion* do not really express truth conditions at all, and utterances that undergo a process of *expansion* express only the minimal proposition that is semantically encoded in the utterance. Hence according to semantic minimalism the actual truth conditions of utterances are often, perhaps usually, quite different than what ordinary speakers take them to be. For instance, according to semantic minimalism, so long as there is more than one bottle in the universe, (4) cannot really be used to make an assertion, for its presupposition that there is only one bottle is always false.

A good example of semantic minimalism is provided by Salmon's (1986) and Soames' (1987) analysis of attitude ascriptions. Salmon and Soames maintain that, despite interpreters' recalcitrant judgments to the contrary, all utterances of attitude ascriptions report only the "determinate content" encoded in utterances, and consequently attitude ascriptions are *transparent.* Thus, despite speakers' firm judgments to the contrary, occurrences of 'John believes that Twain wrote' and 'John believes that Clemens wrote' express the very same truth conditions. Though, to my knowledge, neither Salmon nor Soames themselves motivates this Russellian analysis of attitude ascriptions by appeal to the criterion of determinate content, it is certainly open for them to do so. That is, against competing Fregean analyses — including "hidden-indexical" analyses — that posit reference to "modes of presentation" of some sort, they could follow Schiffer (1992) in rejecting such theories on the grounds that that they suffer from the "meaning intention problem" (Schiffer, 1992, 512). In brief, Schiffer's meaning intention problem is the fact that speakers do not have intentions that would determine which modes of presentation are referred to in an utterance of an attitude ascription. Therefore, since any content there might be involving modes of presentation is indeterminate, attitude ascriptions cannot involve reference to modes of presentation. The only determinate content expressed by an attitude ascription is the minimal Russellian proposition, and as a result attitude ascriptions must be *transparent.* In this way, following Schiffer's and Stanley's lead, Salmon and Soames could motivate their view that only the minimal, Russellian, propositions encoded in the (mostly) phonetically realized features of an attitude ascription are *really* expressed. As is always the case, any attempt at *expansion* results in a lack of determinate content thereby precluding the expression of truth conditions.

So, if the defender of utterance compositionality follows Stanley in endorsing the determinate content criterion for expressing truth conditions, then he is committed to semantic minimalism, and thus he must claim that fully competent speakers are often, perhaps even usually, incorrect in their judgements of the truth conditions of utterances. Is this consequence acceptable for the defender of truth-conditional semantics? It is not, for it is incompatible with the model of interpretation inherent in truth-conditional semantics. Or rather it is incompatible with that model of interpretation so long as that model is understood as an *empirical* theory attempting to explain how speakers actually interpret utterances, and is not, *a la* Frege, understood as a proposal for reconstructing and improving natural language semantics. Recall that the model of interpretation inherent in truth-conditional semantics proposes that the truth conditions actual interpreters judge actual utterances to have are derived through the following two-step process: In the first step the hearer uses her syntactic and phonological knowledge, together with whatever clues she can garner from the context of utterance, to determine the LF of the assertion. In the second step the hearer uses her knowledge of the LF of the utterance, together with her knowledge of the semantic theory for her language, and knowledge concerning the relevant context of utterance, to determine the proposition expressed, or equivalently the truth conditions of the utterance. In keeping with utterance compositionality, this two-step model of interpretation requires that the truth conditions interpreters assign to "typical assertions" must be "traced to logical form." We have now seen, however, that if semantic minimalism is true, then this model of interpretation does *not* correctly explain and/or predict speaker-hearers' judgements of truth conditions.

Stanley's utilization of the pragmatic strategy crucially depends upon his endorsement of the criterion of determinate content. This criterion leads to semantic minimalism, and the attendant result that interpreters are often, perhaps usually, incorrect in their judgments of truth conditions. But this result undermines the model of interpretation inherent in truth-conditional semantics, at least in-so-far-as that model is understood as an empirical theory of semantic performance attempting to explain how speakers actually interpret utterances. Like the fabled Viet Nam commander, Stanley has destroyed the village of truth-conditional semantics in attempting to save it.

One might agree that Stanley's way of utilizing the pragmatic strategy to explain away *prima facie* counterexamples involving non-sentential utterances fails, but only because he endorses the criterion of determinate content. Perhaps the problem is with this particular criterion for expressing truth conditions, and not so much with the pragmatic strategy generally. If one could formulate a more discriminating criterion according to which *prima facie* counterexamples involving non-sentential utterances do *not* qualify as expressing truth conditions, but other sorts of *prima facie* counterexample *do* qualify as expressing truth conditions, then perhaps one could apply the pragmatic strategy to non-sentential utterances without having to apply it to all sorts of *prima facie* counterexample. In other words, perhaps a more discriminating criterion for expressing truth conditions would allow the defender of truth-conditional semantics to save the village of truth-conditional semantics without destroying it. As I will now argue, however, the prospects for formulating such a discriminating criterion are bleak.

To argue that problematic non-sentential utterances do not really express truth conditions, one must formulate some sort of *general* criterion for expressing truth conditions that is incompatible with the judgments of actual speaker-hearers. The effect of this criterion will be that all utterances bearing some property, or set of properties, will be deemed to not express truth conditions, even through fully competent speaker-hearers interpret them as expressing truth conditions. But it is difficult to see how the property or set of properties described in the proposed criterion could serve to rule out *only* problematic non-sentential assertions and not other sorts of *prima facie* counterexamples. It would be question begging for the sententialist to maintain that only utterances that constitute complete sentences (at LF) qualify as really expressing truth conditions. The proposed criterion would have to be something along the lines of Stanley's proposed criterion, which does not depend upon the mere fact that the problematic non-sentential utterances are at least apparently non-sentential. But it is difficult to see how any such non-question-begging criterion would not apply to many, perhaps all, sorts of *prima facie* counterexamples. Moreover, once the door is open to this sort of *error theory*, it is difficult to see how it would not trump all utilizations of the syntactic strategy for explaining away *prima facie* counterexamples. Once it is allowed that competent speaker-hearers can be egregiously mistaken concerning the truth conditions of utterances, then, given any *prima facie* counterexample, the pragmatic strategy would be preferable to the syntactic strategy. Given the options of either (i) claiming that a *prima facie* counterexample is just *another* case where interpreters are wrong, or (ii) positing hidden syntactic machinery to account for the truth of interpreters' judgements concerning the truth conditions of the utterance — where it is wholly mysterious as to how the semantic values for the hidden machinery are "provided by context" — it would seem that (i) would always be preferable.[17]

Consequently it seems that any remotely plausible, non-question-begging, criterion would be applicable to many sorts of *prima facie* counterexample. But, to the extent that the criterion can be used to explain away *prima facie* counterexamples, the two-step model of interpretation inherent in truth-conditional semantics is undermined. If speaker-hearers regularly interpret utterances as having truth conditions that cannot be determined via the two-step model, then obviously speakers regularly do not utilize the two-step model to interpret utterances. So to the extent that the defender of truth-conditional semantics claims that competent speakers make incorrect judgments concerning the truth conditions of utterances, he raises counterexamples to truth-conditional semantics.

## 5. SEMANTICS AND PRAGMATICS, AND COMPETENCE AND PERFORMANCE

In light of the preceding, it is not obvious that it is even open to a theorist who is attempting to explain how interpreters actually determine the truth conditions of utterances to maintain that often interpreters make mistakes and interpret utterances as expressing truth conditions that they "really" do not express. If one of the tasks of truth-conditional semantics is to explain how interpreters actually do determine the truth conditions of utterances, then it is not clear that it even makes sense to claim that interpreters often *incorrectly* assign truth conditions to utterances. Stanley is aware of this tension in his view, and he attempts to resolve it by invoking a semantic *competence/performance* distinction. After noting that his utilization of the pragmatic strategy is incompatible with how speakers actually do interpret some non-sentential utterances, Stanley writes,

> But this is to be expected. Ordinary discourse often involves the use of complex expressions which would be counted as ungrammatical even by the utterer's own lights. For example, some people regularly start a new sentence halfway through an utterance of another sentence. Such discourse involves few sentences that the utterers themselves would classify as grammatical. It is absurd to suppose that we should count such discourse as grammatical, and thereby modify syntactic theory to account for it, and this despite its (statistically speaking) relative normalcy. It is just as absurd to suppose that our conception of semantics should be modified to account for every communicative action which involves the use of language. (Stanley, 2000, 408).

Stanley is here presenting an argument based upon an analogy between contemporary syntactic theory and truth-conditional semantics. He correctly points out that what speakers often, perhaps usually, utter is according to contemporary syntactic theory ungrammatical. And he correctly maintains that it does not follow from this that contemporary syntactic theory should be rejected. To make such an inference would be to confuse *competence* and *performance.* But, Stanley claims, the case of truth-conditional semantics is analogous. And thus Stanley maintains that although the way speakers often *interpret* utterances is incompatible with the predictions of truth-conditional semantics, it does not follow from this that traditional truth-conditional semantics should be rejected. To make such an inference, Stanley suggests, would be again to confuse *competence* and *performance.*

The analogy, however, does not hold. For, as was explained in section II, the defender of truth-conditional semantics defends a *performance* theory. Consider Chomsky's classic and influential description of the competence/performance distinction and its relevance to linguistics:

> Linguistic theory is concerned primarily with an ideal speaker-listener, in a completely homogeneous speech-community, who knows its language perfectly and is unaffected by such grammatically irrelevant conditions as memory limitations, distractions, shifts of attention and interest, and errors (random or characteristic) in applying his knowledge of the language in actual performance.... To study actual linguistic performance, we must consider the interaction of a variety of factors, of which the underlying competence of the speaker-hearer is only one.... We thus make a fundamental distinction between *competence* (the speaker-hearer's knowledge of his language) and *performance* (the actual use of language in concrete situations). Only under the idealization set forth in the preceding paragraph is performance a direct reflection of competence. A record of natural speech will show numerous false starts, deviations from rules, changes of plan in mid-course, and so on. (Chomsky, 1965, 3–4.)

And several pages later Chomsky further elaborates on the competence/performance distinction:

> To avoid what has been a continuing misunderstanding, it is perhaps worthwhile to reiterate that a generative grammar is not a model for a speaker or a hearer. It attempts to characterize in the most neutral possible terms the knowledge of the language that provides the basis for actual use of language by a speaker-hearer. When we speak of a grammar as generating a sentence with a certain structural description, we mean simply that the grammar assigns this structural description to the sentence. When we say that a sentence has a certain derivation with respect to a particular generative grammar, we say nothing about how the speaker or hearer might proceed, in some practical or efficient way, to construct such a derivation. These questions belong to the theory of language use — the theory of performance. No doubt, a reasonable model of language use will incorporate, as a basic component, the generative grammar that expresses the speaker-hearer's knowledge of the language; but this generative grammar does not, in itself, prescribe the character or functioning of a perceptual model or a model of speech production. (Chomsky, 1965, 9)

The reason that, as Stanley correctly notes, theories of generative syntax are to some extent insulated from the stops, starts, and muddles of actual speech is that syntactic theory is not a theory of the processes and procedures whereby actual speaker-hearers produce or interpret actual speech in actual situations. Syntax, as a part of generative grammar, is a theory of *competence*, not a theory of *performance.* That is to say the goal of contemporary syntactic theory is to provide an account of the syntactic rules and principles that constitute a speaker-hearer's implicit *grammatical knowledge.* In actual speech this grammatical knowledge interacts "with a variety of factors" to yield actual speech. From the perspective of generative grammar these other factors — which include other knowledge, processes and systems — are "noise" to be factored out. Thus a speaker's muddled actual speech is a result of this complex interaction, only one factor of which is grammatical competence. Thus it is not necessarily a problem for contemporary syntactic theory that it predict that much of what speakers actually say is ungrammatical. Nor, conversely, is it necessarily a problem for contemporary syntactic theory that some utterances speaker-hearers judge to be ungrammatical are predicted to be grammatical.

Truth-conditional semantics, however, is not in this way insulated from what speaker-hearers actually do. This is because the two-step model of interpretation inherent in truth-conditional semantics is a theory of *performance*; it is a theory about the processes and procedures speaker-hearers actually utilize in interpreting utterances.[18] Consequently, if the truth conditions speaker-hearers actually interpret utterances as having are incompatible with the predictions of the model, then this counts as evidence against the model.[19]

Stanley, on behalf of truth-conditional semantics, might claim that the two-step model of interpretation is not intended to yield predictions about how speakers *actually* interpret utterances; that is, he might claim that the two-step model is a theory of competence, not performance. But this would be simply to abandon *traditional truth-conditional semantics* in favor of *truth-conditional pragmatics* — the conception of semantics proffered by Bach, Sperber and Wilson, Carston, Stainton, Recanati, myself, and others. According to truth-conditional pragmatics, the truth conditions speaker-hearers actually judge utterances to have are *not* determined by LFs and the semantic values of relevant features thereof, and thus truth-conditional pragmatics rejects the principle of utterance compositionality. Rather, according to truth-conditional pragmatics the LF of an utterance and the semantic values of its semantically relevant features are only some of the factors contributing to the interpretation of the utterance. In addition, what have been thought to be mere *pragmatic* processes must also be invoked to yield truth conditions.

## 6. CONCLUSION: ARE THERE NON-SENTENTIAL ASSERTIONS?

The *pragmatic strategy* is not a live option for the sententialist. The problem, in brief, is that any reason the sententialist might provide in support of the claim that *prima facie* counterexamples involving non-sentential utterances do not express truth conditions will also apply to the many other sorts of *prima facie* counterexample. This widespread applicability has two significant consequences: First, it renders all utilizations of the syntactic strategy otiose. If speaker-hearers habitually treat utterances that do not really express truth conditions as if they did express truth conditions and thus are habitually grossly mistaken concerning the truth conditions of utterances, then there is no need to posit hidden syntactic structure to account for their interpretative judgements. If speaker-hearers are habitually *mistaken* about truth conditions, there is no need to posit hidden syntactic material to render them *correct.* Second, and more importantly, the result that speaker-hearers are habitually grossly mistaken concerning the truth conditions of utterances is incompatible with the two-step model of interpretation inherent in truth-conditional semantics. This model is a theory of *performance*; it alleges to describe, albeit in very general terms, the process whereby speaker-hearers actually determine the truth conditions of utterances. If this model predicts that speaker-hearers are often, perhaps usually, mistaken in their interpretations, then the model, and truth-conditional semantics generally, must be rejected.

It does not follow from the failure of the *pragmatic strategy* that sententialism is false, for perhaps the *syntactic strategy*, in various forms, can be utilized to explain away apparent non-sentential assertions and all the other sorts of *prima facie* counterexamples to utterance compositionality. But I am skeptical. Suppose, as is called for by the syntactic strategy, that the LFs somehow instantiated in the brains of *speakers* are much richer than what is phonologically represented in, or even suggested by, their actual speech. How is this additional phonetically unrealized material discerned by *hearers*? I believe that the problem posed by this simple question is in many cases insurmountable, and consequently that many non-sentential utterances constitute genuine counterexamples to utterance compositionality. If this is right, then truth-conditional semantics should be rejected in favor of truth-conditional pragmatics. To endorse truth-conditional pragmatics, however, is to take only a small step toward explaining how speaker-hearers actually manage to interpret one another's utterances.

## NOTES

* This paper benefited from helpful comments and criticisms from Robert Stainton, Jason Stanley, Andrew Botterell, and Robyn Carston.

1 Theorists have posited a number of different processes of ellipsis. The standard sort of syntactic ellipsis (e.g., Morgan, 1973) involves a process of "deletion" that results in structure that is not phonetically realized. Another proposal (Williams, 1977) involves a process of "copying" structure already present in the discourse of the elliptical utterance. Both sorts of process require identical syntactic structures to be already present in the discourse environment because only structure that is already phonetically realized in a discourse is allowed to be "copied to," or "deleted from," a subsequent utterance. This condition of identity precludes the standard processes from applying in cases where an apparent non-sentential assertion appears in discourse initial position. To account for these more problematic sorts of cases theorists proposed *pragmatic ellipsis*. (See Sag and Hankamer 1977, and Stanley, 2000). Pragmatic ellipsis does not require a *phonetically realized* linguistic antecedent — rather the material to be "copied" or "deleted" is provided by other features of the discourse context. The problem with *pragmatic ellipsis* is that it violates the condition of recoverability: other features of context often drastically underdetermine what the ellided information might be. (See Barton 1990 and Clapp 2001 for criticisms of *pragmatic ellipsis.*)

2 Though Stanley is correct that it is open to the sententialist to utilize both strategies, considerations of parsimony suggest that a unified account of all instances of non-sentential utterances is, *ceteris paribus*, to be preferred. That is, a fully adequate unified account is to be preferred over a fully adequate disjoint account.

3 In a previous paper (Clapp, 2001) I argued against the syntactic strategy, or more precisely against pragmatic ellipses. In this paper criticizing the other general strategy of response available to the sententialist, hence this paper complements the earlier paper.

4 I borrow the phrases 'truth-conditional semantics' and 'truth-conditional pragmatics' from Stanley (2000). The phrases are defined in section II.

5 Another strategy of response would be to maintain that at least one of the lexical items involved in my utterances is, despite appearances, context-sensitive, and thus is assigned different semantic values in different contexts. To my knowledge, no defender of truth-conditional compositionality has utilized this 'indexical strategy" in response to the *prima facie* counterexamples involving non-sentential utterances. The indexical strategy has, however, been used in various forms as a response to the *prima facie* counterexamples involving propositional attitude ascriptions (Richard, 1990) and quantifier domain restriction (Szabo and Stanley, 2000).

6 As Davidson (1968) notes, Frege (1893) himself violated this constraint in order to account for attitude ascriptions. A very similar violation of semantic innocence is proposed in Higginbotham (1991). It is controversial as to whether or not the violations of semantic innocence proposed by Frege and Higginbotham undermine the explanatory power of a truth-conditional semantic theory. But even if these violations are allowed it is, I believe, agreed among truth-conditional semanticists that, e.g., an adjectival phrase such as 'totally useless' cannot in some syntactic environments express truth conditions, and yet in other syntactic environments merely serve to contribute toward the truth conditions of complete sentences in which it appears.

7 I appropriate this usage of 'semantics' from Stanley (2000), though I think that much of what Stanley would classify as *semantic* would usually be classified as *pragmatic*. For example, the question of how indexical expressions are interpreted as having different semantic values in different contexts would typically be classified as a question for *pragmatics*. But on the usage I have appropriated from Stanley, this is, at least in part, a question for *semantics*. I think nothing important depends upon such terminological issues.

8 If the defender of truth-conditional compositionality attempts to explain away a *prima facie* counterexample by positing additional, phonologically unrealized, *non context-sensitive* material in the LF of the

expression, where the identity of this material varies across contexts, then he is claiming that the expression does not actually possess property (c). And if he attempts to explain away a *prima facie* counterexample by positing additional, phonologically unrealized, *context sensitive* material in the LF of the expression, where the identity of this material does not vary across contexts, then he is claiming that the expression does not actually possess property (d). It would also of course be possible to utilize a mixed strategy according to which both (c) and (d) are not possessed by a *prima facie* counterexample.

[9] Bach thus maintains that occurrences of sentences such as (2) express both a minimal and an expanded proposition, though the expanded proposition is the one the speaker intends to communicate. Bach's views thus differ from Recanati (1984), who denies that a minimal proposition is expressed. This issue is beside the point of my paper. All that matters for my purposes is that because occurrences of (2) can express the expanded proposition, expressions such as (2) constitute *prima facie* counterexamples to utterance compositionality.

[10] There are some difficult issues concerning presupposition that I am glossing over. An utterance of a sentence containing a definite description whose presupposition is not satisfied is neither true, nor false. (Or so I shall assume.) But does such an utterance nonetheless express truth conditions? I here assume that it does not, though I am not confident of this. Thankfully, the issue is not directly relevant to my concerns.

[11] As Stainton reminded me, many speech acts that seem not to be *assertions* nonetheless express truth conditions. For example, in finishing a joke one might utter, 'Pigs do fly!' Such an utterance expresses truth conditions — the utterance is clearly false — but the speaker is telling a joke and is not making an *assertion.* Hence, issues concerning the *illocutionary force* of non-sentential utterances are for the most part irrelevant to utterance compositionality, and thus also irrelevant to Stanley's thesis that "all truth-conditional effects of extra-linguistic context can be traced to logical form" (2000, 391).

[12] Stanley is correct that the thirsty man is neither asserting, nor requesting, nor commanding, but I think the man is performing a genuine sort of speech act with an appropriate sort of force. The thirsty man is *ordering*, where ordering is a sort of speech act that, in appropriate conditions, customers make to various sorts of employees in the service industry.

[13] Note that this could not be a complete specification of the "determinate content," as it contains an "incomplete" definite description itself in need of further restriction.

[14] I think it is conceivable that there be an apparent assertion in need of either *completion* or *expansion* that nonetheless has "determinate content," but I cannot provide an example of such an utterance. One reason for this is that it is not at all clear to me what it would be for an utterance to have "determinate content."

[15] Stanley (2000) presents purely *syntactic* arguments to support utilization of the syntactic strategy for *prima facie* counterexamples involving quantifiers and relational expressions. Stanley argues that certain phenomena involving binding relations require the sort of "hidden indexicals" posited by the syntactic strategy. Consequently, if Stanley's syntactic analyses are correct, there are *syntactic* reasons to utilize the syntactic strategy, despite the widespread applicability of the pragmatic strategy. So, if Stanley's syntactic arguments are sound, then some *prima facie* counterexamples can be explained away by *both* the syntactic strategy and the pragmatic strategy. But this presents the defender of truth conditional semantics with a dilemma, for the pragmatic strategy and the syntactic strategy "pull in different directions" — the former is an "error theory" that rejects the judgments of ordinary speaker-hearers, while the latter renders these judgments compatible with utterance compositionality. Hence something must give; one cannot allow both strategies to apply to a particular *prima facie* counterexample.

[16] The most significant problem is of course that there is nothing in most contexts of utterance that might fix the semantic values of the alleged hidden indexicals. In terms of Stanley and Gendler Szabo's hidden indexical account of quantified sentences, there is no mechanism that might fix the semantic value of the posited function indexicals ***f()***, and ***i***.

[17] Unless of course there is independent, perhaps syntactic, evidence for the existence of the posited hidden machinery, in which case the defender of truth conditional semantics would be faced with the dilemma described in note 15.

[18] This is not of course to say that the two-step model is offered by Stanley and Gendler-Szabo as a *complete* performance theory. They are quite clear that they are offering only a sketch of such a theory, but it is nonetheless a sketch of a *performance* theory, intended to describe the processes speakers actually utilize in interpreting actual utterances. In Stanley and Gendler Szabo (2000), they introduce the two-step model of interpretation with the following, "In order to interpret typical assertions of others, we normally need to know what sentence they used. . . . " (228). And in Stanley (2000) he writes, while describing the model, "It is often assumed that the objects of semantic interpretation, that is, syntactic logical forms, are free of lexical and structural ambiguity. However, sometimes the sounds we hear suffer from such ambiguity. One role context plays is in helping us to decide which logical form is the one that has been uttered" (399).

[19] Of course, even a theory of linguistic performance must allow for wholly non-linguistic factors — perceived fire alarms, bricks to the head, etc. — to affect actual speech production and interpretation. Even a *performance* theory is a theory in the special sciences, and thus is rife with *ceteris paribus* clauses.

## REFERENCES


Bach, K., "Conversational Impliciture." *Mind and Language* 9 (1994): 124–62.

Bach, K., "Do Belief Reports Report Beliefs?" *Pacific Philosophical Quarterly* 78 (1997): 215–41.

Barton, E., *Nonsentential Constituents: A Theory of Grammatical Structure and Pragmatic Interpretation.* Amsterdam: John Benjamins. 1990.

Carston, R., "Implicature, Explicature, and Truth-Theoretic Semantics." In S. David (ed.), *Pragmatics*. Oxford: Oxford University Press. 1991: 33–51.

Chomsky, N. *Aspects of the Theory of Syntax.* Cambridge: MIT Press. 1965.

Clapp, L., "What Unarticulated Constituents Could Not Be." In J. Campbell, M. O'Rourke and D. Shier (eds.) *Meaning and Truth*. New York: Seven Bridges Press. 2002: 231–256.

Davidson, D., "On Saying That." *Synthese* 19 (1968): 158–74.

Frege, G., "Uber Sinn und Bedeutung." *Zeitshrift fur Philosophie und Philosophische Kritik* 100 (1893): 5–50.

Frege, G., "Der Gedanke", 1918. Translated as "Thoughts" in Geach, 1977.

Geach, P. (ed.), *Logical Investigations.* tr. P. Geach and R. Stoothoff. New Haven, Conn.: Yale University Press. 1977.

Higginbotham, J., "Belief and Logical Form." *Mind and Language* 4 (1991): 344–69.

Larson, R. and Segal, G., *Knowledge of Meaning*. Cambridge: MIT Press. 1995.

Morgan, J., "Sentence Fragments and the Notion of 'Sentence'." In *Issues in Linguistics*, B. Kachru et al. (eds.) Urbana: University of Illinois Press. 1973: 719–751.

Recanati, F., "Domains of Discourse." *Linguistics and Philosophy* 19 (1996): 445–75.

Richard, M., *Propositional Attitudes: An Essay on Thoughts and How We Ascribe Them.* Cambridge: Cambridge University Press. 1990.

Sag, I., and Hankamer, J., "Syntactically vs. Pragmatically Controlled Anaphora." In *Studies in Language Variation*, R. Gasold and R. Shuy (eds.) Washington D.C.: Georgetown University Press. 1977.

Schiffer, S., "Belief Ascription." *The Journal of Philosophy* 89 (1992): 499–521.

Sperber, D., and Wilson, D., *Relevance.* Cambridge: Harvard University Press. 1986.

Stainton, R., "Using Non-Sentences: An Application of Relevance Theory." *Pragmatics and Cognition* 2 (1994): 269–84.

Stainton, R., "Non-Sentential Assertions and Semantic Ellipsis." *Linguistics and Philosophy* 18 (1995): 281–96.

Stanley, J., "Context and Logical Form." *Linguistics and Philosophy* 23(4) (2000): 391–434.

Stanley, J., and Z. Szabo, "Quantifier Domain Restriction." *Mind and Language* 15(2&3) (2000): 219–261.

Travis, C., "On What is Strictly Speaking True." *Canadian Journal of Philosophy* 15(2) (1985): 187–229.

Williams, E., "Discourse and Logical Form." *Linguistic Inquiry* 8 (1977): 101–139.

TIM KENYON

# NON-SENTENCES, IMPLICATURE, AND SUCCESS IN COMMUNICATION

> In the case of strong communication, the communicator can have fairly precise expectations about some of the thoughts that the audience will actually entertain. With weaker forms of communication, the communicator can merely expect to steer the thoughts of the audience in a certain direction (Sperber and Wilson, *Relevance*, 60).

> The aim of communication in general . . . is to increase the mutuality of cognitive environments and thereby the similarity of thoughts, rather than to guarantee a (generally unreachable) strict duplication of thoughts (Sperber and Wilson, "*Préçis*", 476).

## 1. INTRODUCTION

Linguistic communication, and verbal communication in particular, is miraculous. A speaker has some precise, highly structured thought, embedded as the object of a communicative intention that itself may comprise many embedding and embedded knowledge ascriptions to speaker and hearer both. On the basis of a mere utterance, a hearer somehow comes to hold precisely that same thought. Ironically, the communicative acts that are sometimes viewed as most basic or simple — "Slab!" — are potentially the *most* miraculous, since the minimality of the utterance itself forces speaker and hearer to use masses of background, implicit, and contextual knowledge in order to get the single, unique "thing-meant" from the speaker's mind into the hearer's mind — all of this usually happening in an instant, while the hearer is performing a variety of other cognitive and physical activities.

On the other hand, the process is a lot less miraculous, and much more explicable, if this is not how it happens. This would not be how it happens if, for instance, there is no such thing as thinking a precise, determinate thought. An antirealist about intentional content would certainly reject the idea that communication involves a univocal thing-meant and thing-grasped that starts as a thought in the speaker's mind and ends up as a thought in the hearer's mind, because, for an intentional antirealist, neither that starting point nor that end-point makes any sense. But suppose that we are intentional realists. On our view, the speaker starts with a determinate thought; the hearer winds up with a determinate thought. Still, we would find grounds to reject the description of the communicative process as miraculous, if we thought the success conditions on communication did not require that these be the *same* thought. There would be no single thing-meant, in at least some cases, not because there was no meaning, but because there is no type-identity condition on the thoughts of speaker and hearer in successful communication.



*R. Elugardo and R. J. Stainton (eds.), Ellipsis and Nonsentential Speech*, 131–147.

In the quote with which I opened this paper, Dan Sperber and Deirdre Wilson suggest this quite clearly.[1] In at least some cases, those they term "weak communication", a speaker can reasonably expect only to bring her audience around to some line of thought, loosely construed. Any more demanding characterization would be too strong a requirement for successful communication in such cases. And since *weak* and *strong* are here used to designate relative judgements about a communicative act's being a matter of "explicit content" or "implicit import", this is tantamount to the view that the success conditions on linguistic communication vary with the explicitness of an utterance. As intuitive as this thesis may seem (especially from within a relevance-theoretic perspective) it has non-trivial consequences in the philosophy of language and the metaphysics of meaning. For the variation in question is easily neglected when we attempt to characterize successful communication in the case of indirect, implicit, fragmentary, or otherwise heavily context-dependent utterances. Using explicit sentential communication as the model for what defines success, we are liable wrongly to assimilate it to success in the less explicit cases. This very mistake is committed, I argue, by Reinaldo Elugardo and Robert Stainton (2001). I consider the main argument of their paper in some detail, using it as a foil for the development of remarks on the relationship between success and explicitness in linguistic communication.

Elugardo and Stainton argue from an example of successful communication that employs a non-sentential utterance. This utterance, they claim, must have communicated a premise in an argument, and therefore must have communicated something with a logical form — viz., a proposition. The hearer is said not to have recovered a sentence in understanding the utterance; hence what the hearer recovers must be a proposition understood, and bearing its logical form, independent of any natural language sentence. And this establishes that there are propositions having their logical forms independent of any natural language sentence — potentially, a rather weighty conclusion.

The core of my reply is this: Elugardo and Stainton assume that success in their particular example requires a strict duplication of thoughts in speaker and hearer. In the most explicit sentential cases of communication this assumption may be reasonable, but for non-sentential or implicative communication it need not hold. Yet only on the basis of this assumption could one expect to work backwards from the success of a communicative exchange to the existence of a single "thing-meant", to use their term, realized in both speaker and hearer. The assumption can fail in at least two related ways: through the general indeterminacy of implicature; and through the ambiguity between successfully understanding the immediate *content* of an utterance, and successfully understanding its *point*. The latter observation in particular implicates communication as a dynamical process, the significance of which I also explore. In light of these reflections, non-sentential speech does not provide grounds for introducing propositions of the kind invoked by Elugardo and Stainton. I can also see some reasons *not* to introduce them, and will discuss these briefly as well.

## 2. VERNACULARISM AND CONTENT-REALISM

Elugardo and Stainton are concerned to argue against a thesis they call *Vernacularism*.

> *Vernacularism*: The view that logical forms are fundamentally assigned to expressions of natural language, and are only derivatively assigned to anything else: e.g., propositions, mental states, etc (Elugardo and Stainton, 394).

What does this view amount to? Even in light of Elugardo and Stainton's subsequent elaboration, it is not entirely clear. They focus exclusively on *sentences*, using a merely lexical utterance as their counterexample to Vernacularism. But the definition above is framed simply in terms of natural language, and the utterance of a mere word or phrase is no less linguistic, for all that. Taken at face value, Vernacularism extends to mere words and phrases, and so to reject it is to court the rejection of any constitutive connection between linguistic entities and acts, on one hand, and the existence and communication of propositions on the other. Probably Elugardo and Stainton do mean to say this, on the grounds that *only* sentences, among natural language expressions, could have complete logical forms.

But even interpreting Vernacularism as concerned with sentences, the relation between logical forms and sentences must be allowed to be loose or indirect, if the definition is to capture a genuine, if implicitly held, philosophical doctrine. Otherwise, for instance, Vernacularism would be difficult to reconcile with the apparent failure of many sentences to wear their logical forms on their faces. (The most familiar cases are identified by Russell's theory of descriptions.) Even for sentential cases there are philosophical grounds for sometimes taking the logical form of the uttered item to be canonically expressed by a *different* sentence. And Elugardo and Stainton certainly do not intend Vernacularism to rule out the Theory of Descriptions (though they believe the doctrine restricts one's options for dealing with ToD).

Vernacularism is claimed to have a mainly implicit effect, tacitly bolstering certain varieties of eliminativism towards propositions, among other philosophical views (398–400). Nevertheless, several prominent philosophers are mentioned as holding explicit doctrines that approximate Vernacularism, including Peter Geach, Wilfred Sellars, Donald Davidson, Peter Carruthers, and Jerrold Katz. An especially close fit is Katz's *Principle of Effability*, according to which every proposition "is expressible by some sentence of every natural language" (Katz, 226). Still, this principle does not in itself claim the *dependence* of propositions on sentences, which Elugardo and Stainton take to define Vernacularism. Katz moreover seems to base the principle upon a doctrine of what Quine called "eternal sentences".[2]

I take it, however, that this is not a necessary feature of Vernacularism. One can recognize the contextual co-determination of the semantics of many actual uttered sentences, while rejecting the doctrine of eternal sentences, and yet hold that every proposition is *canonically* expressed via the utterance of an associated sentence; that the communicability of a proposition non-sententially is derivative on its sentential communicability; and that the fundamental analysis, hence attribution, of logical form is conducted at the level of sentences. Taking this view of Vernacularism, it is reasonable to think that a counterexample would be a communicable proposition that *could not* be communicated sententially, except as a matter of implicature. Such a counterexample is just what Elugardo and Stainton propose to give. Now, since neither the content nor the consequences of Vernacularism is entirely clear to me, I have little to say directly in its defense. (I wonder, in particular, whether it is supposed to be a shorthand allusion to the Fregean "linguistic turn" in philosophy, or to Michael Dummett's (1994) related view that the fundamental analysis of the structure of thought proceeds through the analysis of language.) What I am concerned to do is reject the picture of communication, non-sentential and implicative communication in particular, that informs the argument *against* Vernacularism.

Having claimed a link between Vernacularism and eliminativism towards intentional content, Elugardo and Stainton proceed to further implicate the issue in their own argument. They see their opposition to Vernacularism as embodying a resistance to intentional irrealism, and introduce their paper with this caveat:

> [M]uch of what follows is plausible only given the assumption of content-realism. Some will take this as an argument, from the best explanation, for content-realism ... Others will complain that a central question has been begged (400).

I will not, however, press this complaint. Indeed, it is part of my thesis that content-realism is strictly orthogonal to the issues that matter for Elugardo and Stainton's argument. This is not to say that, for instance, issues of indeterminacy in interpretation are irrelevant. But the relevant sort of indeterminacy is one, not of content *tout court*, but of *implicature*. Consider something like a Fodorian Language of Thought view, clearly a strong variety of content-realism; on this view, to have a thought is to token a propositional content neurologically. Realism about the intentional does not get much more robust than this. While my observations in the following remarks often dwell upon the indeterminacy, ambiguity and ephemerality of what happens in communication, each such observation is entirely consistent with the neurological realization of intentional content. A content-realist can simply find Elugardo and Stainton's conclusions unacceptable on communication-theoretic grounds.[3]

## 3. THE NON-SENTENTIAL POINT

The case against Vernacularism hinges upon an imagined exchange between two people, Alice and Bruce. Bruce has recently expressed a philosophical scepticism about colour; objects are not actually coloured, he claims. When they meet on the following day Alice, in a Moorean mood, holds up a red pen and says, "Red. Right?"

> Bruce, guileless fellow that he is, happily agrees. Alice continues, "Red things are colored things. Right?" Bruce nods. At which point, Alice springs her trap: "So Bruce, there is at least one colored thing. This thing" (402–403).

Since Elugardo and Stainton are so clear about what they intend this example to show, it is worth quoting them at length:

> First, Alice is making an argument: She communicates propositions, which are premises in the argument; and these premises do indeed have implications with respect to the existence of colored things. And, of course, Bruce recognizes those implications. But premises that fit together into an argument, and are understood to do so, cannot help but have logical forms. So, what Alice communicated at each step had a logical form ... Second, given the lapse of time, it will not be clear to Bruce or to Alice what words were employed during their first exchange, although they both recall the general topic of discussion ... In which case, Bruce will not, during the second meeting, employ those specific expressions in interpreting what Alice meant. Notice, also, that all the evidence that Bruce actually uses is what we described. He does not need to ask Alice any questions, access further evidence that would be available to a third-party, etc. Nor does he need to wait until her argument is done to know what she has communicated with 'Red'. Finally, let us add that Bruce cannot say "which natural language sentence he used" to understand Alice. Plausibly, then, Bruce understands her just on the basis of her utterance of the word 'red' and the fact that she held up a red pen.
>
> Our contention is that, in this imagined case, Bruce did not recover any sentence in understanding Alice. What he did, instead, was to understand the predicate 'red', and apply its meaning to the salient object, the pen in Alice's hand. Doing this, he came to grasp a proposition. And that proposition had a logical form. If this description of what

> Bruce *did* is plausible, then it's also plausible that a real agent *can* in fact recover something that isn't a natural language expression, yet which has a logical form non-derivatively. Precisely because, in the described possible situation, this is just what Bruce does (403).

The crucial and most basic datum is that this communicative event was a success. Bruce *understands* Alice, recognizing the implications of her short speech. The interpretation given the datum by Elugardo and Stainton is this: what Alice intends above all to communicate is an argument. Her first utterance seems to communicate a *premise*, so what Bruce recovers from it has a logical form, and hence is a proposition. But Bruce does not recover what Alice intends to communicate by recovering a sentence — the only category of natural language expression to which complete logical forms are plausibly ascribed. So Bruce must be recovering something else: a propositional something-else, not associated, in the event, with any sentence.

To be sure, the argument's conclusion — that Bruce grasps what Alice's utterance communicates (the thing-meant) without recovering any particular sentence — is characterizable *via* a few distinct interpretations, including, at least, the following.

(C1) Bruce understands the thing-meant without *activating* an understanding of any natural language sentence which, uttered in that context, expresses it.

(C2) Bruce understands the thing-meant without *possessing* an understanding of any natural language sentence which, uttered in that context, expresses it.

(C3) Bruce understands the thing-meant even though there *exists* no natural language sentence which, uttered in that context, expresses it.

Clearly (C2) implies (C1), and (C3) implies both of them. While the upshot of their argument as they first express it — "Bruce did not recover any sentence in understanding Alice" — is most closely allied with (C1), there is reason to think that Elugardo and Stainton intend this to be an *a fortiori* implication of (C3), the strongest of the three interpretations. For they elaborate on the Alice-Bruce case, and defend its conclusion, by claiming that "the proposition which Alice communicated is essentially *less precise* than any fully sentential paraphrase of it" (p. 405, italics in original). This strongly suggests that they believe (C3) to hold, and to explain the weaker (C1). (C3), coupled with Elugardo and Stainton's view that the thing-meant has a logical form and hence is a proposition, generates the conclusion that there are propositions not explicitly communicable by the use of any natural language sentence, and that Alice asserts one of these. This strikes me as a bad idea, for reasons I discuss below. More important, however, is that even were it a good idea, Elugardo and Stainton's is not a good argument for it.

A final note before turning to analysis: Elugardo and Stainton conscientiously examine seven possible responses to their argument, each in considerable detail. In describing their view of the Alice-Bruce case, I canvass some remarks made in these replies, so I do engage their replies to some extent. Nevertheless, showing that my responses differ from *each* reply would be a long and fussy project — too long and too fussy to be worth doing, given that my more general goal is to sketch some ideas about communication. So, I must simply assert that the objections I raise to Elugardo and Stainton are not anticipated in their paper. The force of those objections, I am afraid, must remain hostage to the truth of this assertion.

## 4. THE AWKWARDNESS OF SENTENTIALLY INEXPRESSIBLE PROPOSITIONS

There might be many unhappy consequences of taking cases like Alice's to involve essentially imprecise propositions: one thinks of identity conditions, metaphysical profligacy and so forth. But I will dwell only briefly on two concerns. The first arises from the reliable knowledge one normally has of one's own communicative intentions. We can, it seems, tell our interlocutors what we have just asserted. Or, when we cannot, it is because we are confused, or have misremembered, or because some similar cognitive shortcoming intrudes. Normally a non-sentential utterance like Alice's "Red" can be offered in argument and then, in the face of some misinterpretation or failure of uptake on the part of the hearer, be clarified by the speaker via a subsequent utterance. ("No, I didn't mean specifically fire-engine red just any reasonably uncontroversial shade of it.") We are told that Bruce cannot tell us which sentence he employed in understanding Alice, a point to which we will return. But what of Alice herself? What weight may we give a speaker's sentential clarification of her *own* non-sentential utterance (possibly even a gesture) offered in argument? She is doomed to give an over-precisification of her original meaning, it seems, not by some contingent failure of self-knowledge, but by the metaphysics of speaker's meaning.

This violates what is at least a powerful intuition. It is an awkward consequence for Elugardo and Stainton if the utterer of a non-sentence *qua* premise cannot subsequently explain the very thing she had earlier meant, since, I submit, we routinely take ourselves to do just that. And we do so via sentences when we wish to be particularly clear on what we had initially meant to say. Who would take Alice to be reasonably clarifying the very thing she had meant to say if, in the face of Bruce's puzzlement, she simply repeated "Red! Red! Red!"? But on Elugardo and Stainton's view, this is all Alice could do if she wished to communicate the very proposition first employed. Saying *that very thing* with a sentence would be metaphysically impossible. I cannot prove that this is inconceivable, that it cannot possibly be correct, but it strikes me as grounds to avoid Elugardo and Stainton's conclusion if reasonably possible.

A second problem is contingent upon showing that non-sentences are an inessential complication in Elugardo and Stainton's argument. As I will argue, the soundness of the actual argument would surely transfer *mutatis mutandis* to cases of implicature involving full sentences. And if the point does transfer, then the problem just canvassed will surface again, this time as a problem for the cancellation of implicature. For Grice, it is a hallmark of conversational implicature that it can be cancelled by an explicit disavowal of the putative hidden meaning. Whether this is a *necessary* condition on implicature is an interesting question. That it is at least *possible* does not seem open to serious doubt. And yet, in what could such a disavowal consist, if delivered sententially, when the putative implicature is essentially less precise than any sentence? It looks like one cannot actually *say*, explicitly, sententially, what one did not intend to say. Hence one cannot cancel it.

Now, this looks like strong medicine. Why — one ought to reply on Elugardo and Stainton's behalf — would anyone think that the cancellation of an implicature requires that sort of precision? Surely close enough is close enough, in such cases! To which I reply: Yes, indeed. That is one point I hope to drive home in the remainder of this paper; close enough *is* close enough, and not just for the cancellation of implicatures. The point applies just as nicely to their communication, and itself undermines the argument based on Alice and Bruce's conversation. Before explaining how, though, I will explore the issue of the *generality* of the argument based on Alice and Bruce. There is reason to regard Alice's use of a non-sentential utterance as inessential to the case Elugardo and Stainton advance.

## 5. THE NON-SENTENTIAL POINT EXTENDS TO SENTENTIAL IMPLICATURE

The two points upon which the Alice and Bruce example hinges are that Bruce understands Alice's "Red" *immediately*, that he understands her as giving a premise, and that he cannot subsequently say what sentence he recovers in so doing. To these stipulations is added a methodological scruple: since Bruce cannot say which sentence he recovered, there is no principled way of selecting any one of the many sentences that intuitively approximate what Alice meant, as being *the* sentence recovered (404, 409). Elugardo and Stainton infer that Bruce's understanding of Alice's "Red" is not mediated by his understanding of any sentence, notwithstanding that he is said to grasp a proposition.

That Alice utters a non-sentence therefore seems quite important to the argument; along with Bruce's inability to specify a sentence-recovered, it appears to motivate that there is no *principled* means of selecting any one sentence as expressing the proposition-meant. And Elugardo and Stainton do suggest that it is non-sentential communication itself that creates the problem for Vernacularism, as if the example of Alice and Bruce simply draws out something implicit in the very phenomenon: "[W]e argue that Vernacularism is not as plausible as it first appears because of non-sentential speech" (393). However, the mere admission of non-sentential *assertions* to the ontology of pragmatics, as proposed by Stainton, does not provide grounds to reject Vernacularism (Stainton, "Using Non-Sentences"). A brief digression into Stainton's earlier work on non-sentential assertions makes this quite clear.

Stainton frames his account of non-sentential assertions in terms of relevance theory, following Dan Sperber and Deirdre Wilson, but with one important modification. Considering what separates mere communication from assertion, Sperber and Wilson appeal to the relation between the semantic and logical properties of some linguistic item, considered as a type, and the proposition communicated on some occasion of its use. They conclude: "An utterance . . . which communicates its propositional form, we will call an ordinary assertion" (Sperber and Wilson, *Relevance*, 181). That is, the linguistic item uttered (when enriched and disambiguated), taken as a type, has a propositional form. Assertion consists in the deliberate communication of that proposition by the utterance of that linguistic item. Assertion thus has a crucial element of explicitness to it, a view that forces a substantive distinction between assertion and implication. For it is very far from trivial whether the proposition made most contextually relevant by an utterance is one the form of which is expressed by the linguistic item uttered. Mere implicatures are not asserted propositions; for Sperber and Wilson, assertion is a matter of what they call *explicature*.

Stainton proposes a modification of this view, to allow for the assertoric use of linguistic items the logical form of which is not complete — i.e., not fully propositional. Among the things that can be "mutually manifest", or cognitively salient, in a context are various other incomplete logical forms, some of which will form propositions when conjoined with the incomplete logical form of the uttered non-sentence. The formal modification to Sperber and Wilson is this:

> Definition of Assertion (Revised): An utterance U is an assertion that P if and only if:
>
> (a) Either P is the propositional form of U (i.e., P results merely by completing the Logical Form of U — i.e., by disambiguating it, enriching it and assigning it reference) or P could result merely be completing the Logical Form of U and conjoining it with another manifest Logical Form of the appropriate semantic type; and
>
> (b) P is consistent with the presumption of optimal relevance (i.e., U actually communicates P) (Stainton, "Using Non-Sentences" 280).

In other words: when a non-sentential utterance communicates a proposition, and the context of discourse makes some incomplete logical form cognitively obvious to a hearer, and the incomplete logical form of the utterance can be conjoined with the cognitively obvious logical form to produce the very propositional form actually communicated by the utterance, then the non-sentential utterance counts as an assertion.

The revised criterion admitting non-sentential assertions into relevance theory (the second disjunct of condition (a) in Stainton's revised definition of assertion) alludes to the conjunction of the logical form of the uttered non-sentence "with another manifest Logical Form of the appropriate semantic type". But none of the listed assumptions required to make sense of the possibility that Alice's contribution is genuinely assertoric — none of Stainton's modifications to relevance theory — suggests that in the example at hand Alice's utterance communicates a proposition less precise than that explicitly expressed by any sentence-token. Quite the opposite: the revised criterion alludes specifically to the use of incomplete logical forms as a matter of conjunction with other logical forms cognitively manifest to a hearer, the result of which is, in Stainton's own exposition, sententially expressible ("Using Non-Sentences", 271). In short: accepting non-sentential assertions is not tantamount to rejecting Vernacularism.

A second main ingredient in the argument is Bruce's inability to *say* that he recovered this or that sentence. What follows from this, however, is also unclear. *Process Cartesianism* is the term sometimes applied to the historical thesis that agents have privileged access not only to the contents of their minds, but also to the mechanisms underlying cognition; probably no pre-theoretic intuition has been more decisively overturned by experimental psychology. Obviously it is *possible* that "Bruce may be perfectly unable to pick out 'the' sentence he recovered". He may also be unable to describe what he had for breakfast. Bruce's inability to say that he activated an understanding of such-and-such a sentence in grasping Alice's utterance has none of the important philosophical implications that Elugardo and Stainton extract from it, though, unless the modal strength of 'inability' is meant to be somehow absolute. If Bruce is to be understood as unable *in principle* to say what sentence he recovered, and not just as a matter of some contingent reporting difficulty, then of course his inability to report would be weighty here. But the idea that Bruce *could not* have sententially recovered the proposition Alice communicated is supposed to be the conclusion of the argument. It can hardly serve as an assumption. Nor can I see any argument for it, except to move from Bruce's not *knowing* what sentence he tokened to there *being* no sentence he tokened. How this squares with "staunch content-realism", when it looks like a typical epistemic argument for content-indeterminacy, is an interesting question.

Nevertheless, I am more interested in the importance of non-sentences to the anti-Vernacularism argument. We have seen that the mere non-sentential status of Alice's

"Red" does not carry the day against Vernacularism; it just sets up the further premise about the arbitrariness of selecting a particular sentential interpretation of what gets communicated. The idea is that any proposed sentential expression of what Alice communicates by her "Red" will arbitrarily rule out a variety of other equally good candidate sentences. For, given the choice between describing Alice as communicating "This thing is red", and describing her as communicating "This is red", Elugardo and Stainton conclude that picking the bare demonstrative over the complex demonstrative would be unprincipled. They add, "... why must the verb be 'be'? Why not 'instantiates' or 'exemplifies' or 'embodies'?" (404). Again, with no principled way of selecting one sentence as the correct expression of what Alice communicates, Elugardo and Stainton are driven to conclude that what Alice communicates is not sententially expressible.

> It seems to us, as it would likely seem to anyone who wasn't antecedently assuming something like Vernacularism, that the proposition which Alice communicated is essentially *less precise* than any fully sentential paraphrase of it. Just as none of 'vermilion', 'crimson', 'maroon' or 'scarlet' precisely captures the meaning of 'red', so no available sentence precisely and uniquely expresses what Alice meant (404–405, italics in original).

With this line of argument in mind, then, think of Grice's classic example of the faint-praise letter of recommendation.

> A is writing a testimonial about a pupil who is a candidate for a philosophy job, and his letter reads as follows: "Dear Sir, Mr. X's command of English is excellent, and his attendance at tutorials has been regular. Yours, etc." (Gloss: A cannot be opting out, since if he wished to be uncooperative, why write at all? He cannot be unable, through ignorance, to say more, since the man is his pupil; moreover, he knows that more information than this is wanted. He must, therefore, be wishing to impart information that he is reluctant to write down. This supposition is tenable only on the assumption that he thinks Mr. X is no good at philosophy. This, then, is what he is implicating) ("Logic and Conversation", 33).

We can safely suppose that the reader of this letter understands the conclusion to be drawn from it — *that the job should not go to Mr. X.* It follows that the faint-praise comment communicates a logical form-bearing entity, a proposition, that serves as a premise in the reader's reasoning. It also seems perfectly possible that the reader cannot subsequently say which of potentially many good candidates was *the* sentence recovered in understanding the comment and deriving the conclusion. In the Alice-Bruce case, Elugardo and Stainton claim that "nothing adequately justifies" settling on 'This is red' over 'This thing is red', as sentential paraphrases of the "thing-meant" (404). By parity of reasoning, any roughly equivalent statement of the *point* of the irrelevant praise will do as a gloss, but will be arbitrary relative to the other rough equivalents. So choosing one of these as the thing-meant would be unprincipled, which means that *the* proposition communicated must really be distinct from that expressed by any one such statement. We would over-precisify no matter which sentential gloss we were to choose. Add in the appropriate stipulations about what the writer and reader can and cannot say, to make the case parallel to that of Alice and Bruce, and the argument ought to run identically.

The problem is, Grice has already obligingly told us what proposition is communicated by implicature: that "Mr. X is no good at philosophy". Grice chooses this gloss over, for example, that Mr. X is not good enough to have a job in philosophy, but surely not on any principled grounds that Elugardo and Stainton can accept. So the argument seems to generalize. Non-sentential speech is an inessential complication, if the argument is a good one in the first place. This seems to raise the stakes, since all implicature is now apt to be characterized as communicating the sort of essentially imprecise propositions introduced by Elugardo and Stainton. It also illuminates one means of failure, for the approach of working backwards from communicative success to a definite thing-meant.

## 6. DETERMINACY AND IMPLICATURE

Having seen that Elugardo and Stainton's argument generalizes to sentential cases of implicature, we can see their non-sentential example as an instance of a broader over-simplifying assumption. In particular, it assumes or requires the determinacy of implicature; Bruce's understanding Alice's "Red", immediately *or* subsequently, is taken to establish outright that Bruce grasps a specific thing-meant by Alice, when it is far from obvious that the communication of implicature imposes any such requirement. Sperber and Wilson, for example, argue compellingly that the assumption of determinate implicatures has "obscured an important difference between explicit content and implicit import" in the pragmatics literature (Sperber and Wilson, *Relevance*, 196ff). They preface their argument with some useful observations.

> The proposal to ignore indeterminacy might be seen as a legitimate idealisation, a simplifying assumption of the kind which would pass unquestioned in other domains of scientific inquiry . . . However, not every idealisation is legitimate. An idealisation is not legitimate if, in simplifying the data, it introduces some significant distortion which puts theoretical work on the wrong track (196).

Arguing from the success of a communicative exchange to there being a determinate but essentially imprecise thing-meant in the exchange is, I suggest, a large step down a wrong track, one required neither by the success conditions on communication, nor by a commitment to content-realism. Let the intentional content of Alice's and Bruce's thoughts be carved in stone. That every conversational move they make must *communicate* a similarly determinate propositional content is a straightforward non-sequitur.

Grice's handling of the faint-praise letter makes this very clear; nothing in his suggested gloss even hints that the contents of the *thoughts* of writer or reader are somehow indeterminate. But his approach to the content of the communicative act itself is thoroughly pragmatic and goal-oriented. There is no hand-wringing over what "the thing-meant" must really have been, since, evidently, there is no sense that the definite article is appropriately used here. That Mr. X is not good enough to have a job in philosophy would do just as well as a gloss, because it too bears out the conclusion that the job should not go to Mr. X. Either interpretation would work equally well, for Grice, because there *is* no unique thing-meant. He makes this clear in the closing remarks of "Logic and Conversation", cited by Sperber and Wilson as evidence of Grice's indeterministic view of implicature:

> Since, to calculate a conversational implicature is to calculate what has to be supposed in order to preserve the supposition that the Cooperative Principle is being observed, and since there may be various possible specific explanations, a list of which may be open, the conversational implicatum in such cases will be a disjunction of such specific explanations; and if the list of these is open, the implicatum will have just the kind of indeterminacy that many actual implicata do in fact seem to possess (39–40).

Many distinct interpretations might bear out the manifest *point* of the faint-praise comment, and if nothing selects one of these as the clearest interpretation overall, then strictly understanding the implicature requires only settling on some one or other of the best-supported interpretations. Implicatures will very often count as "weakly" communicated, to return to Sperber and Wilson's distinction.

Contrast this with the line of thought sketched by Elugardo and Stainton, when considering the objection that in fact "several sentences taken collectively determine the logical form of the thing-meant" (409). Their reply to this proposal is that it reverses the proper order of explanation. Now, as in the faint-praise letter, there is a collection of roughly equally good sentential interpretations of Alice's "Red". Elugardo and Stainton argue that without a *prior* conception of the thing-meant, however, there is no making sense of such approximations as being better or worse interpretations, which some of them plainly are.

> To give an analogy, there are two ways of understanding the location of the bull's eye vis a vis an arrow. One might say, "The bull's eye is located just here because this arrow came very close, that arrow missed by a few inches, and that arrow was nowhere near". One might also say: "This arrow came very close because the bull's eye is just here, and the arrow struck just there". In the case of the bull's eye, it's clear that the former gets the order of explanation wrong: the bull's eye does not come to have its location because such-and-such an arrow missed. Now consider: in virtue of what is 'This thing is red' a quite good paraphrase of what Alice meant, whereas 'This doohickey exhibits red' isn't very good, and 'My plane is late' is nowhere near? Is "the target" determined by which things come close and which are far away? Or is the closeness of the paraphrase determined by where the target is? We take the latter line (409).

Certainly the idea that several sentences determine the logical form of some single thing-meant and thing-grasped is not a good one. It gets the order of explanation backwards. It is, rather, the fact that each plausible interpretation has the logical form it does that makes it plausible. Because, having the logical form it does, each such interpretation is apt to make the *manifestly intended* reasoning go through. Alice has a *point*, and it is this point that serves as the "bull's eye".

While Elugardo and Stainton also consider the objection that there is no single logical form-bearing thing-meant, they do so only by considering whether *the* thing-meant might have no logical form (410 *ff*) — an objection that predictably falls flat. But again, that there *is* exactly one thing-meant, that the success of the communicative exchange entails this, is assumed throughout their argument. Neither Grice nor Sperber and Wilson nor I share this assumption. Why not? In short, because we all seem to think that the interpretation of non-explicit speech proceeds via assumptions about the wider point of the utterance. And getting *this* right sets up the "bull's eye" that logically precedes the determination of candidate interpretations as better and worse. Elugardo and Stainton correctly point out the importance of this priority, but fail to consider that something really does play such a regulative (though not determinative) role in the context. When one works from a conjecture about what an implicative utterance is supposed to *do*, one acquires just such a bull's eye, in relation to which various interpretations are nearer to or further from the mark, depending on whether they would *do that*. There are constraints operating on the process of settling on a specific interpretation, chosen from within the class of functionally or logically equivalent interpretations, but these do not guarantee uniqueness. Relevance-theoretic considerations about processing effort can rule out especially long, baroque, or highly redundant interpretations, even when their logical form would sustain the desired reasoning, but may not decide between a range of surviving candidates.

Does this settle the issue of what Bruce *recovers* from Alice's "Red"? This is a bad question. "Recovery", while Elugardo and Stainton's preferred term, is not an innocent expression in this context, since it implies verisimilitude with some original proposition that served as the (partial) object of Alice's communicative intention. In no common context of use have you recovered something if what you got back is different from what you lost; the description of Bruce's understanding in terms of recovery thus assumes, or at least heavily favours, the assumption of a type-identical thing-meant. It eases the way for acceptance of the view that, if successful, the entire communicative process from Alice's intention to Bruce's ultimate reflections revolves around a single proposition. Once one sees grounds for rejecting this as criterial for successful communication, the assimilation of the content of Alice's intention to the content of Bruce's interpretation emerges as unmotivated.

None of which is to say that the success conditions on communication *never* include the determinacy — or better, a great clarity — of interpretation. They may well do, for example, in cases of explicit communication. Before discussing this, however, I turn to the question of how precisely the hearer's state of mind must track the content of a speaker's communicative intention *in real time*, in order for understanding, strictly speaking, to have occurred. As with the preceding observations, this is not a proposal to the effect that the content of a speaker's communicative intention is indeterminate, still less that intentional content in general is indeterminate. Grant the determinacy of both; Elugardo and Stainton's argument still does not go through without assumptions about when, in a conversational exchange, the question of what is communicated can be answered.

## 7. DYNAMICS: IMMEDIATE VERSUS RECONSTRUCTIVE INTERPRETATION

Taking seriously the details of cases like Alice and Bruce's requires recognizing the dynamical nature of communication and the cognitive processes that subsume it. In particular, the relevant phenomena are temporally "messy".

People take turns, in conversational exchanges, but not, usually, in a manner similar to turn-taking as it occurs in games. A chess game or a computer game may be halted or saved at an arbitrary point between moves, and then taken up at any later time; all that needs to be remembered is whose turn was next, in order for the game to be entirely preserved. In conversation, however, all sorts of moves are made that have "expiry dates". Conditional premises are granted, licenses to develop a point are tacitly or explicitly issued, and temporal aspects of context are invoked in utterances. None of these moves remains in force longer than the rather ephemeral cognitive processes that ground it. And these are grounds to be cautious about any very robust content attribution to a fleeting linguistic act, especially, as in this case, one based upon *post hoc* analysis.

Elugardo and Stainton have, I believe, a very sensible respect for this concern, and attempt to minimize it by having Bruce "happily agree" with Alice's "Red. Right?" (402). The idea is to have this a *settled* matter, before having Alice move on with her argument. This, however, does not assuage my worry, for what is at issue is precisely the wisdom of our reading a specific settled interpretation into Bruce's indication of agreement, on the basis of our knowing what Bruce, in the immediate event, does not: namely, the point Alice is in the process of developing. I am, in short, questioning the assimilation of an immediate understanding of an utterance like Alice's "Red" to an immediate grasp of some logical form-bearing entity. The former Elugardo and Stainton are free to stipulate; and must, in one sense, be correct. Alice says "Red", Bruce understands English; how could he not understand? Simply to run this together with the latter idea, however, is illicitly to stipulate a conclusion into what can only be a description of the data. Suppose for now that Bruce's happy agreement consists in his nodding his head, or just replying, "Right". Does he thereby indicate his grasp of a *propositional* content? Nothing compels us to think so.

That Alice gives an argument, in a perfectly legitimate sense of the phrase; that she intends Bruce to see her as giving an argument; that she intends Bruce to be able to describe the reasoning comprising that argument, in a manner acceptable to her; and that Bruce eventually can do this — these are all compatible with describing the immediate effect of Alice's "Red" *merely* as modifying Bruce's cognitive environment. She increases the relevance of the pen's being red, and Bruce, through whatever manifestation of "agreement", issues a license for Alice to make good on this increased relevance in some way. Taken from the perspective of Bruce's state of information in the moment of Alice's utterance, it is perfectly reasonable to understand his nod as saying, in effect, "Right — you've said 'Red', you're showing me this red pen — now, show me why this matters. I'm listening." In particular, this is consistent with the stipulation that Bruce understands Alice *immediately*. He immediately understands her to have said "Red", he knows what the word means, and he has picked up on Alice's cues that she is, loosely speaking, *up to something*. He is engaged in a cooperative project with Alice, trying out contexts of interpretation, processing information about Alice's gaze and facial expressions; he is awaiting and expecting elucidation.

It may seem a cheat to say that this satisfies Elugardo and Stainton's stipulated condition, that Bruce does not "need to wait until her argument is done to know what she has communicated with 'Red'". No doubt it does not comport well with their intention. But it is unclear how much stronger a reading of the stipulation itself can be granted. Patently it cannot be *stipulated* that Bruce immediately understands Alice's "Red" to communicate a logical form-bearing entity (never mind an essentially non-sentential one), since this is to be the conclusion of the argument. One can play by the rules of the thought-experiment, and accept the description of Bruce as somehow indicating *some* sort of agreement after Alice says "Red". But simply to have that datum is to leave it open what Bruce *does* with his indication of agreement, whatever it is. The datum itself in no way forces one to interpret it as an indication of Bruce's willingness to avow some particular truth he takes Alice to have expressed. Again, taking the details seriously leaves it open that Bruce is simply engaged in encouraging feedback, agreeing to follow whatever line of thought Alice is part-way through laying out.

Understanding speech, I submit, has a distinction analogous to that between contexts of discovery and contexts of justification in science; we account for everything in the case of Alice and Bruce if we suppose Bruce to *discover* Alice's point as she speaks, and to have access to a range of psychologically plausible and logically sufficient interpretations that will justify that point to some significant degree. Or, to borrow a metaphor from Michael Dummett (1993), very often in implicit speech we are in the position of not knowing an utterance's tactical role until we have seen its strategic intent. In this case, Bruce's appreciation of the tactical role of Alice's first word is likely to take shape very rapidly as she continues speaking, and will be quite firm when he sees her strategic intent by the end of their brief exchange. During which time the sort of interior monologue that Grice portrays in the case of sentential implicature becomes cognitively (if not phenomenologically) plausible: She must be bringing up that colour scepticism again; she was dead set against it last time; she's saying that *this pen is red*... Or whichever form of thought he happens to settle on.

Indeed, even sentential cases can be canvassed for evidence that the success conditions on communication are sometimes not defined *locally*, so to speak, but may be precise only with respect to the wider goal of an intended inference. Daniel Dennett gives a useful example.

> One of the most quotable lines Abraham Lincoln ever came up with is: 'You can fool all the people some of the time, and some of the people all the time, but you can not fool all the people all of the time'.
>
> What did Lincoln mean? Logic teachers are fond of pointing out that there is a "scope ambiguity" in the sentence... What are the odds that Lincoln never noticed the scope ambiguity and never actually got around to having one communicative intention rather than "the other"? Perhaps it just sounded so good to him when he first formulated it that he never picked up the ambiguity, *and never had any prior communicative intention* — except the intention to say something pithy and well cadenced on the general topic of fooling people (*Consciousness Explained*, 244, italics in original).

Dennett takes the content-indeterminacy route here, or at least the intention-indeterminacy route, which I have eschewed in the interest of playing by Elugardo and Stainton's rules. But a content-realist can extract substantially the same point from the example via the notion of communicative success conditions. We can sharpen the example by imagining Lincoln's epigram used in a situation with a single intended interlocutor and a more definite goal. Suppose an old veteran con artist is advising a young and brash con artist against being too relentless in committing fraud. "Kid," the veteran says, "you can fool all the people some of the time, and some of the people all the time, but you can't fool all the people all the time. Grifting someone who's not about to be fooled can get you put in jail. So pick and choose your opportunities."

This is clearly an argument. Its first premise is communicated by the utterance of Lincoln's epigram. But consider: the scope ambiguity in the epigram leaves it an open question as to which of two possible propositional forms is involved. And The Kid follows the argument effortlessly without being able, let us say, to report with any confidence which reading of the first premise he settled on at the time. Again, parity of reasoning with Elugardo and Stainton drives us to conclude that, since choosing either of the two possible propositional forms as the "right" one would arbitrarily exclude the other, the utterance must have communicated a third proposition instead, one essentially less precise than the two sentential disambiguations.

Surely not. The case is entirely clarified by the observation that there is, cognitively manifest to The Kid, a sententially expressible interpretation of Lincoln's epigram that bears out The Veteran's conclusion.[4] Even if The Veteran's intentions are precise with respect to this ambiguity, giving the existential quantifier wide scope, even if The Kid actually follows the intended inference by way of physically tokening the propositional content that gives the universal quantifier wide scope, *this was a communicative success*. By the standards appropriate to the occasion, defined by the speaker-intended and hearer-recognized validity of the argument, it went off without a hitch.

## 8. CONCLUDING THOUGHTS ON SUCCESS

I am suggesting that what counts as communicative success varies according to at least two factors: the explicitness of the utterance, and the clarity or obviousness of the broader goal(s) of the utterance. When someone utters a complete sentence, in a straightforward context, with the intention of communicating the proposition expressed by that sentence, then indeed "the communicator can have fairly precise expectations about some of the thoughts that the audience will actually entertain". But this is hardly an *a priori* condition on communicative success in general. It is an artifact of the typically overwhelming contextual relevance of one such specific proposition: the one expressed by the uttered sentence-type. In the case of implicature, and in the non-sentential case, however, the speaker's communicative intention is not displayed as the propositional content of uttered item. And in these cases, there is no clear reason to continue thinking of their success conditions as implicating a single shared proposition, or logical form; still less for concluding that this proposition must be essentially inexpressible by any sentence.

Had Alice said, "This thing is red", and had Bruce reported his interpretation of her utterance as "This here particular doohickey is, no doubt among other things, a property-instance of redness", we would have a precise criterion — the proposition expressed by the sentence-type she tokens — by which to judge him as having partly missed her meaning via over-specifying (even though his take on her utterance at least has the virtue of making her argument go through). But her utterance merely of "Red" affords us no such precise criterion. Now our judgement, and her expectation, of the success of this exchange must be evaluated relative to the broader or more general point of the utterance. Again, the "bull's eye" that conditions Alice's intention is some ultimate outcome she wishes to effect, and not some precise premise that Bruce must immediately *recover* from her utterance of "Red". I submit that a range of more or less relevant propositional forms, each, for all we know, associated with some sentence or other, is cognitively available to Bruce in the context described, and even were Alice specifically to have one of them in mind when she says "Red", there would be no reason to deny that genuine communicative success results when Bruce settles on *any* one or other of those propositional forms apt to *make the argument work*.

As we saw earlier, the issue here is not whether every proposition is expressed by some sentence-type. Nor is it even whether every thought is communicable by a sentence. Referring to a paper by Sperber and Wilson (1998), in which they argue that not all thoughts are sententially communicable, Elugardo and Stainton claim that this thesis "dovetails with ours in certain respects" (393). But without considering which respects might be the intended ones, I simply point out that Sperber and Wilson's reasoning is based on the notion that some concepts "may be too idiosyncratic to be even loosely communicated" ("Mapping Between the Mental and Public Lexicon", 200). Their incommunicability via the literal utterance of a sentence follows simply from their incommunicability *tout court*. This crucial implication, at least, crashingly fails to dovetail with the picture of communication presented in the case of Alice and Bruce, where what is incommunicable via the literal utterance of a sentence is supposed to be *obviously* communicated, nevertheless. I do not endorse Sperber and Wilson's view of mental idiolects; but it is useful for showing the independence of the relevant theses. While they argue that the "mental lexicon" is much larger than the public lexicon provided by natural languages — there being "many more concepts in our minds than words in our language" — this is turned into a critique, and not a defense, of the view advocated by Elugardo and Stainton. ("Mapping Between the Mental and Public Lexicon", 197). As Sperber and Wilson say of their own example of implicature:

> When Mary says that she is tired, her utterance gets its explicit meaning through adjustment to a set of weak implicatures: that is, implicatures whose exact content is not wholly determined by the utterance. The *ad hoc* concept of tiredness that Peter constructs . . . is unlikely to be exactly the same as the one Mary had in mind . . . This is not a failure of communication. It is an illusion of the code theory that communication aims at duplication of meanings (199).

Taking stock: While the indeterminacy of intentional content would guarantee that the object of communication is not to effect a sameness of thought, this conclusion is also perfectly compatible with intentional realism. Occurent thoughts, including those underlying communicative acts, may have propositional contents that are realized neurologically, without determining an implicature for those acts; there might well be no fact of the matter about what is implicated, even though the content of each participant's thought is robustly factual. Moreover, when implicature *does* appear determinate, the determining factors may obtain only in a context much wider than the immediate context of utterance. Indeed, such a wider context can be chosen as an interpretive tool precisely because it affords this determination. When the determinacy or clarity of an implicature emerges in non-explicit communication, it often obtains first at the level of the *point* of the utterance; the success is often primarily strategic and only secondarily tactical.

Not really knowing what it is, I have not defended Vernacularism. The more specific issue here has been the determination of what Alice communicates. Communication being a co-operative endeavour, its success no doubt consists in *something* being shared between speaker and hearer. The naïve way of capturing this idea is to depict communication as entirely a matter of encoding and decoding a proposition that travels as the kernel of meaning within a message, but this picture, the pure "code conception" of language, has long been recognized as unhelpful. Indeed, it is least plausible in precisely the non-sentential and alinguistic cases of communication that offer too little explicit syntax and semantics for the communication to be mediated by encoding and decoding, as opposed to the broader notion of inference-in-context that characterizes relevance theory.

I take the intuition to be a sound one, that the strict duplication of thoughts is rarely an immediate communicative aim. The success conditions on communication will, at some broad level of description, involve the speaker's and hearer's thoughts (dispositionally, at least) being describable by some single proposition — like, *The colour scepticism Bruce professed yesterday is in some tension with our ordinary way of describing things*. But this is very different from supposing that communication requires the duplication of thoughts, or thought processes, since this level of description may be quite far removed from whatever is determinate in the speaker's and hearer's immediate thoughts as the exchange unfolds. Alice and Bruce succeed, in that Bruce's eventual thought is describable in a manner that Alice will recognize as satisfying her communicative intention. But they succeed by standards quite different from those at work in literal sentential cases of communication.

## 9. NOTES

[1] Although the following remarks adopt and extend some of Sperber and Wilson's claims, I am not attributing to them the specific view I press in the following remarks. They may well not concur with the use to which I put their arguments.

[2] The idea is that any sentence $S_i$ containing indexical or otherwise context-sensitive elements could be reformulated, so that each proposition expressed by an explicit utterance of $S_i$ would be expressed by some context-insensitive sentence-*type* $S_e$, which would not have actually to be *tokened* in order to be entirely semantically evaluable.

[3] A comment is in order regarding the standard for what would count as a refutation of Elugardo and Stainton's case, since their central theses and arguments are presented quite cautiously. Consider the stated main goal of their paper, "to urge that [Vernacularism] is not obviously true, and to explain why that is important" (1). Vernacularism, regardless of whether anyone is explicitly committed to it, is a philosophical view about the dependence relations of logical form between various concrete and abstract levels of psycho-linguistic analysis. How could it be *obviously* true? Of course Stainton and Elugardo do not mean to suggest that any satisfactory defense of Vernacularism must involve a proof that it is utterly obvious; rather, they intend to shift the burden of proof, to establish that the congeniality of Vernacularism to naturalism, deflationism or plain parsimony is not sufficient to establish the doctrine. If their argument can be shown to be seriously flawed, therefore, we ought not regard Vernacularism as any the worse for still not being obviously true — an unfeasible standard for any thesis within a rarified domain of inquiry. Similarly, the argument by example that forms the heart of Stainton and Elugardo's case is introduced with the admission that it is "not, admittedly, an airtight demonstration" (9). In itself this is surely permissible, since few finitely expressible arguments aspire to airtight status. But it is not uncharitable to ask how *close* to airtight the argument is intended to appear — how far from airtight, in other words, it would have to be in order for it not to have performed as advertised. Here I have no useful conjecture to offer, and can only state that I intend to give detailed reasons for agreeing with Stainton and Elugardo on this point, that their main argument is not airtight.

[4] Indeed, in this case *either* interpretation would suffice, which is probably important. Not only must one available interpretation carry the reasoning through, but no interpretation that *fails* to support the reasoning should be more cognitively manifest, nor even equally so.

## 10. REFERENCES


Dummett, M., *Origins of Analytical Philosophy*. Cambridge, Mass.: Harvard University Press. 1994.

Dummett, M., "Mood, Force and Convention." *The Seas of Language*. Oxford: Oxford University Press. 1993: 202–223.

Elugardo, R. and Stainton, R., "Logical Form and the Vernacular." *Mind and Language* 16.4 (2001): 393–424.

Grice, H.P., "Logic and Conversation." *Studies in the Way of Words*. Cambridge, Mass.: Harvard University Press. 1989: 22–40.

Katz, J., *Language and Other Abstract Objects*. Oxford: Blackwell. 1981.

Sperber, D., and Wilson, D., "The Mapping Between the Mental and the Public Lexicon." In P. Carruthers and J. Boucher (eds.) *Language and Thought*. Cambridge: Cambridge University Press. 1998: 184–200.

Sperber, D., and Wilson, D., *Relevance: Communication and Cognition*. 2nd ed. Cambridge, Mass.: Blackwell. 1995.

Sperber, D., and Wilson, D., "*Préçis* of *Relevance: Communication and Cognition*." *Behavioral and Brain Sciences* 10 (1987): 697–711. Reprinted in H. Geirson, and M. Losonsky (eds.). *Readings in Language and Mind*. Cambridge, Mass.: Blackwell. 1996: 460–486.

Stainton, R.J., "Using Non-Sentences: An Application of Relevance Theory." *Pragmatics and Cognition* 2.2 (1994): 269–284.

ANDREW CARSTAIRS-McCARTHY

# THE LINK BETWEEN SENTENCES AND 'ASSERTION': AN EVOLUTIONARY ACCIDENT?

## 1. INTRODUCTION[1]

Stainton and others have argued that it is not necessary to use a sentence in order to assert. However, among philosophers of language it still seems uncontroversial that assertion is protoypically achieved through sentences rather than non-sentences. The very fact that this book has no companion volume dealing with assertion by means of sentences is evidence of that. Logicians and philosophers of language leave it to linguists to describe the syntax of natural languages. Nevertheless, logicians and philosophers of language do make assumptions about natural language syntax, in that, when discussing notions such as 'proposition', 'thought' and 'truth', they take it for granted that the syntactic unit most intimately associated with their subject-matter is the sentence. This axiom of the primacy of the sentence (as one might call it) is firmly stated by Dummett (1981:xxxi): 'the understanding of the fundamental structure of language and therefore of thought... depend[s] upon possessing, in a correct form, that explanation of the construction of and interrelationship between *sentences* which it is the business of logic to give [emphasis added]'. Logic is thus concerned primarily with the interrelationship between 'All men are mortal' and 'Socrates is a man', but not with the interrelationship between 'human mortality' and 'Socrates's humanity', Dummett seems to say.

In this chapter I will argue that the primacy of the sentence is illusory, in that assertoric force can just as well be achieved in the framework of a hypothetical natural language whose syntax contains nothing corresponding to the 'sentences' of English and other human languages. The position I adopt is therefore more radical than that of most contributors to this volume. An adequate defence of my position requires a book (Carstairs-McCarthy 1999) rather than an article. Here I will concentrate on a point not covered in the book, namely that two logical or epistemological distinctions that may seem to provide cognitive or semantic motivation for the distinction between sentences and noun phrases (NPs) fail to do so. These are the distinction between 'knowledge by description' and 'knowledge by acquaintance' (section 3) and the distinction between 'facts' and 'events' (section 4). First, however, I will set the stage by summarizing how an imaginable alternative to natural-language syntax may lack any analog of the distinction between sentences and noun phrases, and consequently any obvious analog of the distinction between 'being true' (or 'being false') and 'referring' (or 'failing to refer') (section 2).



*R. Elugardo and R. J. Stainton (eds.), Ellipsis and Nonsentential Speech*, 149–162.

A question remains. If the link between sentences and assertion is as tenuous as I claim, why is it so widely taken for granted? This, however, is not a philosophical question so much as a historical one, about why humans have acquired the kind of language capacity that they have. As such, it is a question for the biological anthropologist and the linguist, not the philosopher (section 5).

## 2. LANGUAGES WITHOUT THE DISTINCTION BETWEEN TRUTH AND REFERENCE

Language, like all human capacities, is a product of evolution. Why, then, has it evolved so as to incorporate a distinction between sentences and NPs?[2] One possible answer is that the distinction is inevitable, given that language is used for identifying things (objects, events, states of affairs) in the world, and making statements about the things identified. This outcome is as inevitable (one might argue) as the fact that, once humans developed the ability to count, their system of arithmetic should incorporate a distinction between odd and even numbers. But I will argue that such an analogy is false. If the distinction between identifying things and making statements about them had an inevitable counterpart in syntax, then a language whose syntax does not encode this distinction would be impossible. But that is not so, as I will show directly, first by reference to an imaginary language that is rather like English, and then by reference to one that differs radically from English and all other natural languages, yet would be perfectly serviceable as an instrument for communication and for the representation of experience.

Consider a language that I will call 'Nominalized English', which is just like English except that it contains no verbs, and consequently no verb-headed units such as clauses and sentences. At (1) is a short dialogue in English, and at (2) is a rendering into Nominalized English:

| | | |
|---|---|---|
| (1) | Bill | Hi! Where are you off to? |
| | Julia | Just the supermarket. We've run out of bread. |
| | Bill | Oh, while you're there, could you get some curry powder too? I've been meaning to get some for days. |
| | Julia | OK. Are you sure there's nothing else we're short of? |
| | Bill | I don't think so. I'll be taking the car there tomorrow anyway. |
| (2) | Bill | Greetings! My ignorance of your destination. |
| | Julia | Just the supermarket. Our total lack of bread. |
| | Bill | Oh, a suggested opportunity for a purchase of curry powder too on your part. My recent procrastination in respect of such a purchase. |
| | Julia | OK. A request for clarification of your awareness of other shortages. |
| | Bill | A fairly definite negative belief on my part. My fortuitous visit there by car tomorrow. |

Nominalized English is certainly quaint, and in its lack of a syntactic distinction between sentences and NPs it does not resemble in structure any language known to me. The issue, however, is not its quaintness but whether, if some language like it existed, it would really be unserviceable for communication because of failure to achieve 'assertoric force'. Would Bill and Julia in (2) inevitably be doing no more than listing a succession of states of affairs without any commitment to their actuality or any interest in their possibility? The answer is surely no. In English, as Ryle (1960) says, uttering the string of words 'Brutus, assassination, Caesar' does not amount to asserting that Brutus assassinated Caesar. Uttering in English the NP 'Brutus's assassination of Caesar' does not normally amount to making that assertion either. But we cannot say the same of Nominalized English, whose grammar is in a vital respect radically different from that of English.

I have presented Nominalized English as an imaginary language, unlike English in structure. However, there are situations where, by convention, something like Nominalized English is used even by English speakers. When announcing guests at a formal reception, a footman does not say 'Lord and Lady Blenkinsop have arrived!' or 'Here are Lord and Lady Blenkinsop!', but rather 'Lord and Lady Blenkinsop!' Likewise, pictures generally have nominal titles rather than sentential ones ('The Arrival of the Queen of Sheba', not 'The Queen of Sheba Arrives'), and some but not all newspapers permit nonsentential headlines, such as 'VICTORY FOR DEWEY' (Dewey being the Republican candidate in the 1948 American presidential election, who lost but was wrongly assigned the victory by at least one over-hasty newspaper).

A question now arises about how to describe inaccuracies in the use of these nonsentential expressions. If a flustered footman roars 'Lord and Lady Blenkinsop!' when the new arrivals are in fact the Duke and Duchess of Omnium, has he made a false statement, or has he merely misidentified two people? Similarly, is it appropriate to describe 'VICTORY FOR DEWEY' as untrue, or rather as an instance where identification of an existing object or state of affairs in the world has not been achieved, just like the much-discussed phrase 'the present King of France'? One may be inclined to say that 'untrue' (or 'false') is clearly an appropriate epithet in both instances, because the way in which they fail to correspond to reality is so similar to that of sentences such as 'Here are Lord and Lady Blenkinsop!' or 'DEWEY WINS'. However, the example of Nominalized English should give us pause, because it is a language in which sentences, as syntactic entities distinct from NPs, do not exist.

Consider Julia's use of the expression 'Our total lack of bread' in (2), on the assumption that the breadbin is indeed empty. Is she saying something true, or is she merely identifying an existent state of affairs? In order to answer that question, we would need to know how to distinguish in Nominalized English (as opposed to actual English) between telling the truth and achieving identifying reference. Yet it is hard to see on what basis this distinction could be made. Being true and successfully referring are both ways in which expressions, usually sentential and nominal respectively, can be applicable to the world as it is. Conversely, being false and failing to refer are ways in which expressions can be inapplicable. Now, the emptiness of the breadbin renders 'Our total lack of bread' in (2) applicable to the world. But I can see no basis, in terms of Nominalized English semantics, to distinguish two kinds of applicability. On the contrary, in a parallel world (the Nominalized world) where all actual languages are replaced by nominalized counterparts (Nominalized Chinese, Nominalized Swahili and so on), not even the most ingenious philosopher of language is likely to perceive any motivation to subdivide applicability into truth and reference. In that world, there will be scope for debate about the nature of the relationship between an applicable expression and the state of affairs that renders it applicable, corresponding to the philosophical debate in our own world about theories of truth; but that debate is independent of the truth/reference distinction that concerns us here.

Now imagine a language (let us call it 'Monocategoric') that can conveniently be described in terms of a categorial grammar with only one basic category.[3] Most categorial grammars that have been developed distinguish two basic categories, such as 's' and 'n' (Ajdukiewicz 1935) or 't' and 'e' (Montague 1973). These labels recall respectively the distinction between sentences and nouns and that between truth-values and entities, thus implicitly taking for granted either the syntax of actual languages or else the semantic distinction between truth and reference that is here at issue. In Monocategoric, by contrast, there is a distinction only between a basic category 'expression', which we can label 'x'[4], and derived categories 'x/x, x/xx, x/xxx . . . ', which act like operators (one-place, two-place, three-place, . . . ) that form complex expressions when combined with the appropriate number of expressions as arguments. Let us assume also that the semantic roles of these arguments (e.g. Theme, Agent, Goal) are encoded by linear order. Here is a tiny fragment of a vocabulary, at (3), and a syntax, at (4), for Monocategoric:

| | | | |
|---|---|---|---|
| (3) | Category | x | girl, dog, bone, boy, rat |
| | | x/x | hungry (Theme) |
| | | x/xx | eat (Agent, Theme) |
| | | x/xxx | give (Agent, Goal, Theme) |

(4) Members of derived categories, when preceded by the appropriate number of expressions (simple or complex), yield syntactically well-formed complex expressions.

Now here is a set of complex expressions in Monocategoric, and a selection of possible renderings in English:

(5) girl dog hungry bone give
- (a) 'The girl gave the hungry dog a bone'[5]
- (b) 'the girl who gave the hungry dog a bone'
- (c) 'the hungry dog that the girl gave a bone to'
- (d) 'the bone that the girl gave to the hungry dog'
- (e) 'the girl's gift of a bone to the hungry dog'

(6) (girl dog bone give) rat eat[6]
- (a) 'The dog that the girl gave a bone to ate a rat'
- (b) 'the rat eaten by the dog that the girl gave a bone to'

I expect readers to be puzzled by the variety of glosses for (5) and (6). This variety is intended to make the point that, because Monocategoric has no syntactic distinction between sentential and nominal expressions, there is no reason to privilege either a sentential or a nominal rendering for any of its expressions in English. What Monocategoric syntax does is encode a semantic representation of a state of affairs, while leaving it open whether any special informational salience attaches to one of the participants (for example, the girl in (5b), the dog in (5c) or the bone in (5d)) or to the activity (the gift in (5e)).

A skeptic may be tempted to deny that (5) and (6) really encode a semantic representation of a state of affairs, on the ground that (5) and (6) are more akin to singular terms than to sentences, and the role of singular terms is to pick out objects rather than describe state of affairs. But this objection will be futile unless it can be shown that a clearcut distinction between objects and states of affairs can be drawn independently of the linguistic expressions (noun phrase and sentence respectively) that, in natural languages, are typically associated with them. An inert, rigid phenomenon such as a pebble or a billiard ball may seem clearly classifiable as an object; but what about a field, a waterfall, a tree in a gale, a butterfly emerging from its chrysalis, or a battle? It is not clear that we are dealing here with a one-dimensional continuum, with 'object' and 'state of affairs' at its extremities; it is even less clear where on such a continuum the dividing-line between objects and states of affairs should be placed. In discussing alternatives to language-as-it-is, we must guard against relying too heavily on ontological classifications that may turn out to be mere ghosts of familiar linguistic ones.

A speaker of many actual human languages, such as English, may still have qualms about the apparent versatility of Monocategoric expressions, as illustrated by their multiple glosses. These qualms, however, reflect the unfamiliarity of Monocategoric rather than any shortcomings in their capacity to convey information. Three considerations will demonstrate this.

Firstly, the apparent versatility of (5) is no greater than the versatility of (7) in English, in a context where 'she' refers to an individual identified as (let's say) President Clinton's mother:

(7) She's talking to that man over there with red hair.

(7) is versatile inasmuch as it can serve as the answer to two questions that seek quite different information. It can serve to answer someone who wants to know what the President's mother looks like, and so asks (perhaps at a White House reception) 'Which woman is President Clinton's mother?' It can also serve to answer someone who is already acquainted with the President's mother but who wants to find out what she is up to at the moment, perhaps through asking 'Where's President Clinton's mother?' These two questions seek different information. One can therefore imagine how a speaker of a language unlike either English or Monocategoric might take it for granted that this difference should be reflected in a syntactic contrast between the replies to them. Yet the syntax of English allows this different information to be packaged identically, without arousing in us any qualms about its communicative adequacy.

One might argue that, in English, the context will nearly always make it clear which elements in any sentence are informationally salient. But precisely the same can be said of the Monocategoric expression at (5). In the context of a reply to the question 'Why did the barking stop?' (or its Monocategoric equivalent), the appropriate interpretation of (5) 'girl dog hungry bone give' will be (a) 'The girl gave the hungry dog a bone'; in reply to the question 'Who is that?' the appropriate interpretation will be (b) 'the girl who gave the hungry dog a bone'; and so on — but with the proviso that Monocategoric speakers are likely to be no more conscious of informational versatility in (5) than English speakers are conscious of it in (7). In describing English, we may indeed be inclined to ascribe to the sentence at (5a) a basic semantic value, independent of use or pragmatic context, that is different from the basic semantic value ascribed to the NP at (5b); but it would be rash to assume that this semantic difference is motivated independently of the English syntactic distinction that shadows it, and would consequently be pertinent to the semantics of Monocategoric.

The second consideration involves languages such as Diegueño and American Sign Language, which have 'head-internal' relative clauses (Liddell 1978). 'Head' here means the nominal element that the relative clause modifies; thus, in the English NP at (8), containing a relative clause in brackets, the head is 'bone':

(8) the bone [that the girl gave to the hungry dog]

In English, as (8) shows, relative-clauses are 'head-external'; that is, the head 'bone' lies outside the modifying clause, even though it is construed as the object of 'gave' in that clause. In languages with head-internal relative clauses, by contrast, these heads occupy the appropriate syntactic position within the relative clause itself, so that, in a hypothetical head-internal dialect of English, the counterpart of (8) would be (9):

(9) [the girl gave the bone to the hungry dog]

Correspondingly, the head-internal counterpart of the English sentence at (10) would be (11) (with relative clauses bracketed):

(10) The bone [that the girl gave to the hungry dog] is under the tree.
(11) [The girl gave the bone to the hungry dog] is under the tree.

However, (11) in this hypothetical head-internal English will correspond to two other actual English sentences also, namely (12) and (13):

(12) The girl [who gave the hungry dog a bone] is under the tree.
(13) The hungry dog [that the girl gave a bone to] is under the tree.

Does this mean that speakers of Diegueño, American Sign Langage and other head-internal languages have to put up with a relative clause construction that is intolerably ambiguous? No, for two reasons. Firstly, the ambiguity will very often be resolved by context. In (11) I deliberately chose a predicate, '. . . is under the tree', that is pragmatically about equally appropriate whether the subject is the girl, the dog or the bone; but other predicates such as '. . . is John's sister' or '. . . was rapidly gnawed to pieces' would effectively disambiguate the subject NP with its clause-internal head. Secondly, such languages may possess both syntactic and nonsyntactic means of effecting the disambiguation, while preserving the head-internal character of the relative clause. For example, in American Sign Language there are various optional devices to indicate explicitly the identity of the head (Liddell 1978:81–5).

This leads directly to the third consideration supporting the communicative adequacy of Monocategoric. Determining in (5) whether it is the girl, the dog, the bone or the whole state of affairs that is salient could well be achieved explicitly, for example by a one-place operator (a member of the category 'x/x') following the relevant expression. Let us call this operator 'focus'. By means of it, the sense of (5) glossed in English as (5a) would be rendered by (14); the sense glossed as (5b) would be rendered by (15); and so on:

(14) (girl (dog hungry) bone (give focus))
(15) ((girl focus) (dog hungry) bone give)

Importantly, this operator would not vitiate the status of 'x' as the single basic category of Monocategoric. In other words, it would not introduce a category distinction similar to that between 's' and 'n' in traditional categorial grammar, and would therefore do nothing to render Monocategoric syntax more akin to that of English. Example (15) is most naturally glossed in English as a noun phrase containing a relative clause ('who gave the hungry dog a bone') that modifies a head noun ('girl'). However, this does not mean that the Monocategoric expression 'girl' in (15) has somehow become a noun, any more than that the location of 'focus' in (14) somehow converts the expression 'give' there into a verb.

Monocategoric differs from actual English more radically than Nominalized English does. In Nominalized English it is only the verb/noun distinction that is effaced, whereas other major lexical categories (e.g. adjectives and prepositions) remain. In Monocategoric, by contrast, all these distinctions disappear, the traditional framework of lexical categories being replaced by a distinction between simple expressions and operators. Even so, I hope to have persuaded readers that the fact that Monocategoric uses only one basic syntactic category is not such a disadvantage as may at first sight appear — indeed, is no disadvantage at all.

It is important to appreciate that, even in a Monocategoric or Nominalized world, there can still be a distinction between expressions that are 'asserted', in some sense, and ones that are not, if 'asserted' is understood as 'meant to be taken seriously as a vehicle of information'. In a Monocategoric or Nominalized world there will be occasions when one uses linguistic expressions without intending them to be taken seriously: when thinking aloud, for instance. Just the same applies in the actual world: Sherlock Holmes may think aloud in Watson's hearing about the likely culprit in a murder case, but if it later turns out that Holmes was wrong, Watson does not accuse him of having made false assertions, or told lies, even if Holmes's audible thinking was carried out by means of sentences. What is different about the Nominalized and Monocategoric worlds, however, is that in them there is no syntactic unit prototypically associated with 'assertion'. There is therefore no temptation in that world to link such a unit with a certain kind of 'force', namely 'assertoric force', as its semantic or pragmatic counterpart, distinct from the semantic or pragmatic counterparts of other syntactic units. 'Assertoric force' thus emerges as a mere byproduct of syntax (specifically, of the primacy of the sentence), just as much as the truth/reference distinction does.

This radical claim would be undermined, however, if it could be shown that the sentence/NP distinction is genuinely based on some nonlinguistic distinction other than that between truth and reference. I explore two such possibilities in sections 3 and 4. In doing so, my role is rather unusual. I am not replying to arguments that have been publicly adduced, by philosophers or anyone else, in support of a nonlinguistic basis for the sentence/NP distinction. This is simply because the distinction has been so universally taken for granted by logicians and philosophers of language that its rationale seems almost never to have been seriously explored. Debate about this distinction has been so sparse that I myself, in questioning its basis, have had to undertake the task of hunting out anything, apart from grammar, that may motivate it.

## 3. EPISTEMOLOGY AND 'ASSERTORIC FORCE'

Many philosophers have distinguished two kinds of objects of knowledge: one kind to which our access is direct, perhaps infallible, and another kind to which our access is indirect, involving association of or deduction from objects of knowledge of the first kind, and subject to error. ('Subject to error' is a loose expression here, because what has been shown to be wrong can strictly never have been an object of knowledge, only of mistaken belief.) Sometimes this is associated with lexical distinctions such as that between *connaître* and *savoir* in French, or between *kennen* and *wissen* in German. For Russell (1912:69–70), the *connaître/savoir* distinction is associated with 'knowledge of things' versus 'knowledge of truths'. Our concern here is not with this distinction for its own sake, much less with comparing Russell's version of it to those of other philosophers, but rather with whether it may help to motivate a special 'assertoric' role for sentences.

Such motivation might work as follows. How syntax is organized can be expected to reflect in some degree the structure of our knowledge of the world. Therefore, it is reasonable to expect that there should be a syntactic unit typically associated with knowledge of things, and another typically associated with knowledge of truths; and perhaps noun phrases and sentences respectively are those syntactic units. Consequently (one might argue), since it is only knowledge of truths that is susceptible of error (speaking loosely), it is natural that only sentences should be fundamentally associated with a distinction between assertion and denial (denial being the ascription of error). So, even if sentences are not the only syntactic vehicles for assertion, they are still the prototypical vehicles for it.

This motivation will be undermined, however, if 'things' turn out to be as subject to error as 'truths' are, or nearly so. I will argue that Russell's distinction is flawed in just such a fashion. When he is being most careful epistemologically, Russell makes a distinction between what he calls 'knowledge by acquaintance' and 'knowledge by description'. So, for 'things' and 'truths' to have a firm epistemological basis, untainted by grammar, it is desirable that they should correspond exactly to these two kinds of knowledge. That is, both 'knowledge of things' and 'knowledge by acquaintance' should share the property of being immune from error. Sometimes Russell speaks as if this is indeed so (1912:172):

> [K]nowledge of truths raises a . . . problem, which does not arise in regard to knowledge of things, namely the problem of *error*. . . . This problem does not arise with regard to knowledge by acquaintance, for, whatever may be the object of acquaintance, . . . there is no error involved so long as we do not go beyond the immediate object . . . [Russell's emphasis]

The kinds of 'thing' which can be known in this error-free fashion include facts, or states of affairs, such as sunsets (1912:210–11):

> Our theory of truth . . . supplies the possibility of distinguishing certain truths as *self-evident* in a sense which ensures infallibility. . . . [Y]ou can, if the weather is fine, look to the west and actually see the setting sun: you then know [that the sun is setting] by way of knowledge of *things* [Russell's emphasis].

And, if not only routine objects such as tables and chairs but also events such as sunsets can be accessed by way of 'acquaintance', it looks as if potential objects of acquaintance may be neatly coextensive with the kinds of semantic content that NPs are typically used to express.

However, Russell also talks in ways that imply a much narrower view of what one can be 'acquainted' with. The particular objects of which one may have knowledge by acquaintance include not tables and chairs but merely the sense-data from which one can infer the presence of tables, chairs and suchlike (1912:170). Thus, not only 'truths' but also many 'things' turn out to be knowable not directly, 'by acquaintance', but only derivatively, 'by description'. Let us compare the implications of this doctrine for sunsets and for tables respectively. In respect of sunsets, this doctrine is immediately attractive; after all, to witness a sunset is to know that the sun is setting; yet the fact that the sun is setting is something about which one could conceivably be in error, if (for example) one wakes up in confusion and sees the sun low on the horizon without knowing whether one is facing west or east. But Russell goes further than this: even a physical object such as a table cannot be known directly, because to interpret a particular collection of sense-data as a table involves cognitive ingredients beyond the sense-data themselves (1912:170). Even a supposedly self-evident fact, such as that the sun is shining, does not suffice to guarantee the truth of the judgment 'The sun is shining', because '[i]n passing from the perception to the judgment... it is possible to commit an error' (1912:214).

Could it be, even so, that 'knowledge by acquaintance' motivates the sentence/NP distinction, inasmuch as it motivates the existence of NPs that are directly referential, containing no taint of description: indexicals ('me', 'you'), demonstratives ('this', 'that') and names of directly perceived sense-data? The answer is no. Russell's strict epistemological distinction between description and acquaintance lumps almost everything that we talk about (pebbles and billiard balls as well as trees, waterfalls and battles) into the known-by-description category. Consequently, if this distinction were to be the basis for syntactic categorization in natural language, we would expect to find one syntactic category for indexicals and demonstratives and another for all the territory actually covered by the category 'sentence' together with nearly all the territory covered by 'NP'. This would be closer to the syntax of Monocategoric than to that of English and other actual languages. So no basis for the sentence/NP distinction as it exists in natural languages can be derived from Russell's epistemology.

As I have said, the merits of Russell's account as a theory of knowledge are not at issue here. What matters is whether his distinctions between acquaintance and description and between things and truths yield a plausible motivation for a syntactic distinction which he did not discuss but to which they might conceivably be relevant: the distinction between a unit with prototypical assertoric force (the sentence) and a unit without (the NP). The conclusion has to be no. Russell's distinctions supply no reason to ascribe assertoric force to 'The sun is setting' but none to 'a sunset', when either is used in an appropriate context. If anything, the boot is on the other foot. One is tempted to think that that the distinction between things and truths, because it matches the distinction between acquaintance and description so imperfectly, reflects the infection of Russell's epistemology by a tacit preconception that, if some syntactic distinction (such as between sentences and NPs) is pervasive in natural languages, some important cognitive distinction must underlie it. Other theorists of knowledge may or may not have avoided such infection. For present purposes, what matters is that Russell's theory of knowledge in *The Problems of Philosophy* provides no basis for a link between sentencehood and assertion.

## 4. THE FACT/EVENT DISTINCTION AND 'ASSERTORIC FORCE'

There is a well-established distinction in semantics between facts and events (Peterson 1997). Events are concrete in that they may have a specific duration, may take place slowly or quickly, and so on. By contrast, facts are abstract; they may be expected or unexpected, exciting or sad, and they may be described accurately or inaccurately, but they cannot be fast or slow, and they have no location in space and time. Thus, in (16) 'the sinking of the Titanic' represents a fact, while in (17) it represents an event:

(16) The sinking of the Titanic was a terrible tragedy.
(17) The sinking of the Titanic took two hours.

These examples show that the linguistic expressions that represent events and those that represent facts can overlap, and indeed they do so to a considerable extent, but not entirely (Peterson 1997):

(18) That the Titanic sank was a terrible tragedy.
(19) *That the Titanic sank took two hours.

The potential relevance of this to the 'assertoric' role of sentences is as follows. Examples (18) and (19) show that, in some contexts, an embedded sentence ('that the Titanic sank') may have a 'fact' reading but no 'event' reading, while (16) and (17) show that a NP closely related to this sentence, in the sense of having an identical semantic predicate-argument structure, may have either a 'fact' reading or an 'event' reading. Now, to be a fact is to be something that can be truthfully asserted; therefore, to the extent that being a fact is associated with being expressed by means of either a sentence or a NP closely related to a sentence, the existence of facts motivates the existence of sentences as prototypical vehicles for expressing facts, that is, as prototypical vehicles for truthful assertion. By contrast, non-facts, or, to be more exact, kinds of content in respect of which the question whether it constitutes a fact or an event does not arise, will prototypically be expressed by some other syntactic unit, such as a NP (more specifically, a NP not closely related to a sentence in the way that 'the sinking of the Titanic' is).

This argument depends crucially on showing that the fact/event distinction really is limited to complex pieces of semantic content of the kind that can be expressed only by means of a sentence, or by means of a complex NP such as 'the sinking of the Titanic'. If it can be shown that the fact/event question (or something very like it) can also arise in respect of a simple NP containing no adjuncts or modifiers, such as 'the table' or 'those pebbles', then the fact/event distinction cannot motivate a kind of 'assertoric force' preferentially linked to sentences.

Let us consider the following sentence:

(20) Those pebbles undermined Professor Smith's theory about the history of this coastline.

Is there any fact/event indeterminacy in the interpretation of 'those pebbles' here, comparable with the indeterminacy of 'the sinking of the Titanic'? At first sight, it is hard to see how there could be, if only because a collection of pebbles can hardly be described as an event, in anything like the ordinary sense of that term. However, consider now the following two amplifications of (20):

(21) Those pebbles undermined Professor Smith's theory about the history of this coastline. They are not smooth enough to have undergone wave action for as long as he claimed.

(22) Those pebbles undermined Professor Smith's theory about the history of this coastline. If he were right, the beach would be composed entirely of sand.

In (21), the crucial aspect of the pebbles for Professor Smith's theory is a physical characteristic: their smoothness (or roughness). In (22), however, the crucial aspect is something more abstract: the pebbles' very existence. In (21), therefore, the pebbles function as a (quasi-)event, with spatiotemporally locatable properties; in (22) they function as a (quasi-)fact, in that what matters is solely the fact that they exist, not their size, smoothness, or any other characteristic.

Once one has got the feel for the distinction, in respect of physical objects, between quasi-events and quasi-facts, it is easy to find further examples of it. In what follows, the subject NP in the (a) examples is a quasi-event, whereas in the (b) examples it is a quasi-fact:

(23) a. The desk in the bedroom was a surprise. It had unusual corkscrew legs.
b. The desk in the bedroom was a surprise. People don't usually do office work in the same room that they sleep in.

(24) a. Those glasses make Roger seem older than he is. He chooses such heavy oldfashioned frames.
b. Those glasses make Roger seem older than he is. Few boys as young as he is have to wear spectacles.

(25) a. Princes William and Harry are both expert skiers.
b. Princes William and Harry make it unlikely that Prince Andrew will ever succeed to the throne.

In (23a) and (24a), 'the desk in the bedroom' and 'those glasses' stand for quasi-events, because the focus is on physical characteristics of them (the shape of the legs, the heaviness of the frames). In (23b) and (24b), however, they stand for quasi-facts, because what matters about them is their mere existence. Similarly, in (25b) it is the mere existence of Princes William and Harry, as sons of Prince Charles, that places Prince Andrew fourth in line for the British throne rather than second, as he would be if Prince Charles were childless. On the other hand, in (25a) the princes count as quasi-events, because something more than their mere existence is at issue.

The terms 'quasi-fact' and 'quasi-event' that I have used so far may suggest that I think there is a real nonlinguistic distinction, relevant to 'assertoric force', between quasi-facts and facts, and between quasi-events and events. However, I can see no basis for any such distinction. With quasi-facts and facts alike, what matters is the mere existence of an object or state of affairs, whether simple ('those glasses') or complex enough to be analysed into a predicate and one or more arguments ('the sinking of the Titanic'). With quasi-events and events alike, what matters is some characteristic of that object or state of affairs, going beyond its mere existence (for example, the design of the glasses, or the speed of the sinking). There is thus no special connection between (quasi-)facts and sentences of a kind that might furnish sentences with a special fact-linked 'assertoric' role. One might argue, perhaps, that, if what matters about an object-or-state-of-affairs is its mere existence, then that object-or-state-of-affairs is likely to be semantically complex (to have a predicate-argument structure, for example) rather than semantically simple; therefore, given the tendency for minimal non-elliptical free-standing utterances to be both syntactically sentential and semantically complex, (quasi-)factual content is likely to be more frequent among sentences than among NPs. But, if so, this difference is a mere byproduct of the sentence/NP distinction, and cannot count as an explanation for it. More specifically, this difference is a mere byproduct of the tendency for minimal non-elliptical free-standing utterances to be sentences — a fact that still cries out to be explained.

## 5. THE PREHISTORIC ORIGINS OF THE SENTENCE/NP DISTINCTION

I have suggested that the distinction between sentences and NPs is not motivated by any prototypical 'assertion' role for sentences, because no relevant difference between what sentences do and what NPs do can be identified that is independent of the sentence/NP distinction itself. Neither the distinction between knowledge by description and knowledge by acquaintance (as described by Russell) nor the distinction between facts and events turns out to differentiate sentences and NPs in a relevant fashion. Why, then, does the sentence/NP distinction exist?

As I said in the first section, this is an empirical question to which the philosopher of language has less to contribute than the prehistorian of language. The prehistory of language (or language evolution) is a notoriously obscure topic, which was banned from discussion by the Linguistic Society of Paris in 1866 as being intractable, and which most linguists ignore even today. However, anthropologists, psychologists, primatologists and even philosophers (e.g. Bennett 1976:202–10; Quine 1997) have not been so shy, and since about 1990 there has been a revival of linguistic interest in it too, as well as increasing interdisciplinary cooperation (Hurford, Studdert-Kennedy and Knight 1998; Knight, Studdert-Kennedy and Hurford 2000). Squarely on the research agenda, and much debated, is the question whether syntax is an adaptation or an exaptation (that is, a byproduct of an adaptation), its origin in either case being a biological phenomenon, or whether it is an outcome of physical and chemical processes rather than biological ones (rather as the hexagonal shape of honeycomb cells is due to physics rather than to any biological characteristic of bees).

There is no generally agreed answer to this question, nor even a view that is sufficiently widespread to be called orthodox. However, one answer that has been proposed (Carstairs-McCarthy 1999; 2000) takes seriously the idea that syntax could have been radically different from how it is. According to this proposal, basic syntactic structure, including the sentence/NP distinction, is a byproduct of neural mechanisms associated not with cognitive functions but with changes in the vocal tract resulting from bipedalism. Briefly, these changes in the vocal tract facilitated a new kind of vocalization divisible into syllables, and, when the neural mechanism for controlling vocalization acquired a syntactic role too, the internal structure of the syllable was pressed into service to supply a blueprint for syntax (I have suggested).

This is not the place to rehearse arguments for and against this hypothesis, which is novel and controversial. For present purposes, what matters is that it shows that an answer is possible, in principle, to a doubt that may assail some readers. If the sentence/NP distinction is really as unmotivated logically and epistemologically as I have claimed, why is it so universal in languages generally and so readily taken for granted by even the most searching philosophical critics of natural language? The answer may be that its universality is a matter of neurophysiology rather than logic, and that its unquestioned status reflects no more than the fact that all logicians and philosophers of language so far, like all linguists, have been native speakers of some natural human language. In consequence, understandably but regrettably, most of them have not recognized the need to overcome, by an effort of the imagination, their natural tendency to assume that, in fundamental respects, syntax-as-it-is is the only way syntax could have been.

## NOTES

[1] I am grateful to Jack Copeland, Martin Davies, Ray Elugardo, Kate Kearns and Rob Stainton for comments on an earlier draft. They are not to be assumed to agree with what I say, however, and are not responsible for faults that remain. This work is a development of a project on language evolution that was supported by a grant from the Marsden Fund of New Zealand.

[2] That this distinction is found in all known languages is sufficiently well established so that denials of it, as by Gil (1994) in respect of the Riau Indonesian, are few and controversial.

[3] I am grateful to Jay Garfield for pointing out to me that (as is obvious, on reflection) the kind of language that I had already christened Monocategoric (Carstairs-McCarthy 1999) can be described in terms of a categorial grammar with only one category. He is not responsible for the use that I make of Monocategoric, however.

[4] It will do no harm if 'x' here recalls to some readers Jackendoff's (1977) use of 'X' as a label for an arbitrary lexical category or word class (noun, verb, adjective or preposition).

[5] I assume that in Monocategoric, as in Chinese, there is no obligatory overt expression of tense. In the sentential glosses at (5a) and elsewhere, where English grammar forces a choice of tense, the past is chosen. But nothing hangs on this.

[6] The parentheses here are meant to facilitate parsing, but are strictly superfluous, just like parentheses in the Polish logical notation.

## REFERENCES

Ajdukiewicz, K., "Die syntaktische Konnexität." *Studia Philosophica* 1 (1935): 1–27. (English translation 'Syntactic connexion' in *Polish Logic*, ed. by Storrs McCall. Oxford: Oxford University Press. 1967: 207–31.)

Bennett, J., *Linguistic Behaviour*. Cambridge: Cambridge University Press. 1976.

Carstairs-McCarthy, A., *The Origins of Complex Language: An Inquiry Into the Evolutionary Beginnings of Sentences, Syllables and Truth*. Oxford: Oxford University Press. 1999.

Carstairs-McCarthy, A., "The distinction between sentences and noun phrases: an impediment to language evolution?" In Knight et al. (eds.), 2000: 248–63.

Dummett, M., *Frege: Philosophy of Language* (2nd edn.) Cambridge, MA: Harvard University Press. 1981.

Gil, D., "The structure of Riau Indonesian." *Nordic Journal of Linguistics* 17 (1994): 179–200.

Hurford, J.R., Studdert-Kennedy, M. and Knight, C. (eds.). *Approaches to the Evolution of Language: Social and Cognitive Bases*. Cambridge: Cambridge University Press. 1988.

Jackendoff, R., *X-syntax: a study of phrase structure*. Cambridge, MA: MIT Press. 1977.

Knight, C., Studdert-Kennedy, M., and Hurford, J.R. (eds.). *The Evolutionary Emergence of Language: Social Function and the Origins of Linguistic Form*. Cambridge: Cambridge University Press. 2000.

Liddell, S., "Nonmanual signs and relative clauses in American Sign Language." In *Understanding Language through Sign Language Research*, P. Siple (ed.). New York: Academic Press. 1978: 59–90.
Montague, R., "The proper treatment of quantification in ordinary English." In *Approaches to natual language*. Proceedings of the 1970 Stanford Workshop on Grammar and Semantics, ed. by Jaakko Hintikka, Judith Moravcsik and Patrick Suppes. Dordrecht: Reidel. 1973: 221–42. (Reprinted in: *Formal philosophy: selected papers of Richard Montague*, ed. by Richmond H. Thomason. New Haven: Yale University Press. 1974: 247–70.)
Peterson, P.L., *Fact Proposition Event*. Dordrecht: Kluwer. 1997.
Quine, W. van O., "The flowering of thought in language." In *Thought and Language*, J. Preston (ed.), 171–6. (Royal Institute of Philosophy Supplement 42.) Cambridge: Cambridge University Press. 1997.
Russell, B., *The Problems of Philosophy*. London: Thornton Butterworth. 1912.
Ryle, G., "Letters and syllables in Plato." *Philosophical Review* 69 (1960): 431–51. (Reprinted in: *Collected papers, i: Critical essays*. London: Hutchinson. 1971: 54–71.)

# PART II

# IMPLICATIONS

ANDREW BOTTERELL

# KNOWLEDGE BY ACQUAINTANCE AND MEANING IN ISOLATION*

## 1.

Bertrand Russell is justly famous for the following thesis, which I will call, for obvious reasons, the *Meaning in Isolation Thesis*:

> Meaning in Isolation Thesis: phrases of the form 'the so-and-so' lack 'meaning in isolation.'

The Meaning in Isolation Thesis features prominently in Russell's writings on definite descriptions.[1] In those writings Russell sets out to defend the view that definite descriptions "never have any meaning in themselves." (Russell, 1905, pg. 42) He proceeds to say that a definite description "is essentially part of a sentence, and does not, like most single words, have any significance on its own account." (Russell, 1905, pg. 51)

The Meaning in Isolation Thesis is an attractive thesis about the nature and role of definite descriptions in natural language, and Russell provides a number of arguments in support of it. Despite its attractiveness, however, the thesis appears to lead to problems when it is conjoined with another plausible thesis, which I will call, for equally obvious reasons, the *Non-Sentential Assertion Thesis*:

> Non-Sentential Assertion Thesis: speakers can assert propositions using non-sentences.

To see why these two theses appear to lead to problems, suppose that Smith, having been the victim of a robbery, is called down to the police station to look at a line-up. Confronted with five men, Smith utters the following phrase:

(1) The second man from the right.

It is plausible to suppose that in uttering (1) Smith has asserted that there exists a unique second man from the right and that that man is the man who robbed him. But Smith did this by uttering an isolated definite description, that is, by uttering a definite description that is not itself a sentence and does not appear to be part of any larger sentence. So according to the Meaning in Isolation Thesis, Smith uttered something that has no meaning.[2] But if what he uttered has no meaning then how could Smith have asserted that the second man from the right is the man who robbed him? This is the puzzle with which I will be concerned in the present paper.

To help focus discussion, I will concentrate on a certain conditional linking the Non-Sentential Assertion Thesis with the Meaning in Isolation Thesis. This conditional claims that if the Non-Sentential Assertion Thesis is true, then Russell was mistaken



*R. Elugardo and R. J. Stainton (eds.), Ellipsis and Nonsentential Speech*, 165–184.

in thinking that phrases of the form 'the so-and-so' lack 'meaning in isolation'. Call this conditional *(C)*:

(C) If the Non-Sentential Assertion Thesis is true, then the Meaning in Isolation Thesis is false.

This conditional seems to me to be of interest for several reasons. First, because there are very good reasons for thinking that the conditional is true. Second, because — as I shall argue — the antecedent of the conditional is also very likely true. Third, because the truth of the conditional threatens some central aspects of Russell's views on semantics and epistemology. And fourth, because the truth of the conditional raises some interesting methodological issues concerning the relation between empirical facts about language use and general philosophical theses about knowledge and understanding.

The paper proceeds as follows. In section 2 I discuss the conditional (C) in more detail. In sections 3 and 4 I turn to the phenomenon of non-sentential assertion, and indicate why I think we ought to accept the Non-Sentential Assertion Thesis.[3] In sections 5 and 6 I turn to the Meaning in Isolation thesis. I consider a popular view of the meaning of definite descriptions — the so-called *Generalized Quantifier view* — and ask why Russell didn't avail himself of something like the Generalized Quantifier view, given that he had the resources to formulate something very close to it. I argue that the answer to this question turns on issues having to do with Russell's epistemological views and, in particular, with his Principle of Acquaintance. Finally, in section 7 I make some speculative remarks about how the phenomenon of non-sentential assertion bears on questions of philosophical methodology.

## 2.

Let me begin with the conditional (C):

(C) If the Non-Sentential Assertion Thesis is true, then the Meaning in Isolation Thesis is false.

Part of my aim in this paper is to argue that this conditional is true. In order to assess the truth of this conditional, however, some preliminary remarks are in order.

As I noted earlier, Russell's aim in "On Denoting" is to argue quite generally "that denoting phrases never have any meaning in themselves, but that every proposition in whose verbal expression they occur has a meaning." (Russell, 1905, pg. 43) What exactly does Russell mean by a 'denoting phrase'? By a denoting phrase Russell has in mind "a phrase such as any one of the following: a man, some man, any man, every man, all men, the present King of England, the present King of France, the center of mass of the solar system at the first instant of the twentieth century, the revolution of the earth round the sun, the revolution of the sun round the earth." (Russell, 1905, pg. 41) In Russell's view, to say that an expression has meaning in isolation is to say that there is some *meaning-relatum* that is paired with the expression in question. According to Russell meaning-relata are of two sorts. Names have particulars as meaning-relata; other linguistic items, with one class of notable exceptions, have concepts as meaning-relata. So in particular, adjectives have properties as meaning-relata, and verbs have relations as meaning-relata.

The class of notable exceptions are, unsurprisingly, so-called denoting phrases. At the time of *The Principles of Mathematics* Russell thought that the meaning-relatum of a denoting phrase is "a definite something... which must, in a sense, be an object, but is characterized as a set of terms combined in a certain way, which something is denoted by all men, every man, any man, a man or some man; and it is with this very paradoxical object that propositions are concerned in which the corresponding concept is used as denoting." (Russell, 1903, pg. 62) As is well known, however, Russell came to have doubts about this account of the meaning of denoting phrases, and the 'paradoxical objects' that Russell mentions in connection with such expressions were eventually rejected in favor of an alternative account of the meaning of denoting phrases.

It should be clear, then, that when Russell claims that denoting phrases never have meaning in themselves, he does not mean that when considered by themselves they are meaningless. For denoting phrases are obviously meaningful in a way in which the expression 'mimsy', say, is not. That is, they are not gibberish. Does it therefore follow that such phrases must have some meaning, that there must be some meaning-relatum with which they are paired? It does not. For example, 'and Mary met on' is a string which has a *semantic impact* on the meaning of 'Jane and Mary met on Friday'. But we cannot say what thing this string stands for. So it is arguable that an expression could fail to be gibberish and yet also fail to have meaning. Again, what Russell was denying when he denied that denoting phrases have meaning in isolation was that denoting phrases have meaning-relata. That is, Russell's claim was that unlike a proper name such as 'Smith' that refers to, or picks out, an individual, or a predicate such as 'is red' that refers to, or picks out, a property, descriptions do not refer to or pick out anything.[4] In his terminology, they *denote*, but do not refer.

In support of this position, Russell offers the following argument. Consider the proposition 'Smith is tall'. Russell takes this proposition to be composed of the meaning of 'Smith' and the meaning of 'is tall'. That is, the proper name 'Smith' contributes its meaning, namely the individual Smith, to the proposition; and the predicate 'is tall' contributes its meaning, namely the property of being tall, to that same proposition. But what about the proposition 'The second man from the right is tall'? What are the meaning constituents of this proposition? It seems likely that one of the meaning constituents of this proposition is going to be the meaning of 'is tall'. But what entity might be contributed by the expression 'the second man from the right'? Perhaps the meaning of 'the second man from the right' is whoever *is* the second man from the right. Thus, suppose that Smith is the second man from the right; then it might be thought that the meaning of 'the second man from the right' is Smith.

But Russell thinks that this will not do. He reasons as follows: suppose that Smith is the meaning of 'the second man from the right'. Then 'the second man from the right' and 'Smith' would have the same meaning. However, suppose that I am out for a walk and I happen to meet Smith. Then while it might be false to say 'I met the second man from the right, but I did not meet Smith' it is not contradictory, which it surely would be if 'the second man from the right' meant the same as 'Smith'. So the 'second man from the right' cannot mean the same as 'Smith'. And since 'Smith' means Smith, it follows that 'the second man from the right' cannot mean Smith. But, furthermore, there is no reason to suppose that any other man could be the meaning of 'the second man from the right'. Thus, we are forced to conclude that 'the second man from the right' does not mean or refer to any particular individual. Russell was thus led to conclude that descriptions did not stand for entities, and hence, that descriptions lacked meaning-relata.

So much for Russell's reasons for thinking that denoting phrases lack meaning-relata, and hence, are not meaningful in isolation. How does the truth of the Non-Sentential Assertion Thesis bear on this thesis of Russell's? As follows. If, as I will argue, speakers can indeed assert propositions using unembedded definite descriptions, this can only be because such expressions are meaningful by themselves, i.e., because such expressions are meaningful in isolation. I take the truth of this claim to be an instance of a more general claim linking language use with meaning. For I take it that if anyone can *grasp* and *deploy* a thing, then that thing must exist. But if a speaker can assert a proposition using a non-sentential expression $E$, then in doing so that speaker must be capable of grasping and deploying the meaning of $E$, from which it follows that there is something that *is* the meaning of $E$. In Russell's terminology, this can only be because $E$ has a meaning-relatum. This suggests very strongly that the conditional (C) is true: if speakers are capable of asserting propositions using isolated definite descriptions, then descriptions have meaning in isolation, contrary to what Russell supposes. With this is mind, let me turn to consideration of the antecedent of (C), the Non-Sentential Assertion Thesis.[5]

## 3.

It can hardly be denied that people sometimes appear to utter non-sentences.[6] Take (1) again:

(1) The second man from the right.

I take it that there are strong *prima facie* reasons for thinking that (1) really is a non-sentence. For one thing, (1) doesn't look like a sentence; rather, it looks like a definite description. I also take it that there are strong *prima facie* reasons for thinking that a speaker can use (1) to assert a proposition. For example, it seems to me that Smith is able to use (1) in the situation described to get his audience to understand that the second man from the right is the man who robbed him. And this, I think, counts as a genuine case of assertion. Granted, these reasons are only *prima facie*, and as such are surely defeasible. Still, in the absence of some compelling reason for thinking otherwise, it seems to me that the conclusion that ought to be drawn from these observations is that (1) is a non-sentence, and that Smith has succeeded in asserting some proposition in uttering (1).

It might be thought that we have here a straightforward case of non-sentential assertion and hence, that the Non-Sentential Assertion Thesis is true. But in fact the existence of utterances like (1) is not sufficient to establish the truth of the Non-Sentential Assertion Thesis. I say this for two reasons. First, because (1) may not *be* a non-sentence. Rather, (1) may be merely an *elliptical* sentence. And second, because even if (1) *is* a non-sentence it may nonetheless be false that Smith is able to use (1) to assert a proposition. For example, perhaps in uttering (1) Smith has merely succeeded in *communicating* or *implicating* some proposition, but has failed to *assert* that proposition. With this in mind, let me briefly discuss some reasons for thinking, first, that (1) really is a non-sentence; and second, that it is possible for speakers to assert propositions by uttering non-sentences like (1).

When confronted with the apparent fact that speakers use non-sentences like (1) to assert propositions, many are inclined to respond as follows: look, if Smith really does succeed in making an assertion by uttering (1) then, since only sentences can be used to make assertions, it must be the case that (1) really is a sentence. By way of illustration, consider Michael Dummett's remark that "[t]he primary case is . . . the utterances of *sentences*; the utterance of a singular term in response to a question can be considered an abbreviated form of utterance of a sentence[.]" (Dummett, 1981, pg. 298) Setting to one side Dummett's remark about questions the view suggested by this passage is that if Smith utters 'The second man from the right', what Smith has done is utter something that is an abbreviated form of, or is elliptical for, a sentence like 'The second man from the right is the man who robbed me'. On this view, in other words, all apparent cases of non-sentential assertion are merely apparent: whenever we come across a putative case of non-sentential assertion, what we have really come across is a case of an elliptical sentential assertion.

If this view can be made to work, then we will have a reason for rejecting the claim that (1) is a non-sentence. In order to adequately assess this view, however, we first need to ask: What is a sentence? Although this question appears to be straightforward, it is not.[7] This is because there are a number of different things that could be meant by 'sentence'. Perhaps the most natural view is that a sentence is something that has a certain sort of form.[8] This might be called the *syntactic* sense of 'sentence'. For example, according to recent linguistic orthodoxy a sentence is an inflectional phrase that is derived from the so-called *X-bar schema*. The details don't matter much for present purposes, but the basic idea is simple enough. According to X-bar theory, phrases are hierarchically structured projections of their heads. Simplifying somewhat, the general form of a phrase is:

$$\begin{aligned}&XP \rightarrow Spec;\ X'\\&X' \rightarrow X;\ YP\end{aligned}$$

By substituting in appropriate category variables for the categories in the X-bar schema particular expression types are obtained. So, for example, the X-bar schema for an inflectional phrase (IP), i.e., a sentence, is as follows:

$$\begin{aligned}&IP \rightarrow NP;\ I'\\&I' \rightarrow I;\ CP/VP\end{aligned}$$

By then filling in appropriate formatives under the category variables, we obtain a particular sentence.[9]

I earlier suggested that (1) is not a sentence. We are now in a position to see why I said this. If (1) were a sentence in the syntactic sense, then it would have to fit into the X-bar schema for an IP. How might (1) be made to fit in the X-bar schema for an IP? We would replace each of NP, I, and CP/VP with various different lexical items to yield an inflectional phrase. But notice: since (1) lacks an inflectional element, and since it lacks a verb, it cannot receive either an I or a CP/VP completion. Thus, since (1) cannot be made to fit in the general form of a sentence it is not a sentence in the syntactic sense.

Despite its intuitive appeal, however, this argument is merely an opening for discussion; it does not end it. This is because a proponent of the ellipsis hypothesis has a response available to her. For she can argue that at some appropriate level of syntactic analysis the relevant syntactic material *is* present and hence, that at some appropriate level of syntactic analysis (1) really does have the form of a sentence. Call this the *syntactic ellipsis hypothesis*. I won't go into the reasons in detail, but let me briefly consider the syntactic ellipsis hypothesis and suggest some reasons for thinking that we would do well to reject it.

How might a proponent of the syntactic ellipsis hypothesis show that (1) is syntactically a sentence? By arguing that there is some syntactic material that, although phonetically unrealized, is nonetheless present at some suitable syntactic level. But what syntactic material? Here are some possibilities: (i) [pres/sing] be the one who robbed me: (ii) [past/sing] rob me: (iii) [pres/sing] be the robber: (iv) [pres/sing] be the man I believe to be the robber. But which one of (i)–(iv) is the *unique* syntactic material that is phonetically unrealized? It is impossible to say. Thus, in the absence of some reason for thinking that (ii), say, as opposed to (i) or (iii) is the phonetically unrealized syntactic completion for (1), it seems that we must conclude that *none* of (i)–(iv) is the syntactic completion for (1), and hence, that the syntactic ellipsis hypothesis is false.[10]

Although this discussion has been extremely brief, it seems to me that there are good reasons for rejecting the idea that whenever a speaker utters an isolated definite description like (1), what she has done is utter something that is elliptical for some other sentence. At any rate, I'll assume that this is the case for the remainder of the paper.

## 4.

In the previous section I argued that (1) is not a sentence. I now want to argue that speakers can assert propositions by uttering expressions like (1). This will suffice to establish the Non-Sentential Assertion Thesis.[11]

In the normal case, it seems clear that if a speaker *S* were to utter (2):

(2) The apple is red.

with appropriate force and in appropriate circumstances, *S* would have asserted that there exists a unique apple and that that apple has the property of being red. The present suggestion is thus that if a speaker *S* were to utter (1):

(1) The second man from the right.

with appropriate force and in appropriate circumstances, *S* would have asserted that there exists a unique second man from the right and that that man is the man who robbed him.[12] It seems to me that this claim is both true and defensible. However, it is also controversial, and its truth is clearly going to depend on how assertion works. This is by no means a settled issue. For example, one account of assertion maintains that assertion is a matter of convention. Very roughly, this view holds that a speaker *S* asserts the proposition that *P* iff *S* utters a sentence s that is recognized as being used according to some convention to mean that *P*. However, since (1) is not a sentence, (1) clearly cannot be used to make an assertion. Michael Dummett is perhaps the most influential proponent of this sort of view. Says Dummett,

> the fact that a sentence expresses an act of assertion is as much a matter of linguistic convention as is its having the sense it has (in Frege's use of 'sense'). This is not to deny that there are sentences which can be used to perform any one of a number of linguistic acts: I may say, 'You will learn a sonnet', as a prediction, as an expression of my intention,

> or as a command. What constitutes my *meaning* the sentence in any one of these ways is my intention to be understood as performing that one of these linguistic acts. What makes it possible for me to have such an intention is the existence of general convention endowing the utterance of certain sentences — and this one in particular — with a certain significance. (Dummett, 1981, pg. 300)

Nonetheless, despite what Dummett says there seem to me to be decisive reasons for rejecting this view about assertion, reasons which I won't go into in detail here.[13] For the purposes of this discussion, therefore, I will adopt an alternative picture of how assertion works. In order to adequately explain how I mean to understand the notion of assertion, I will first appeal to the notion of communicating a proposition. Having explained that notion, I will then cash out the notion of assertion in terms of the notion of communication. What will emerge is an account of assertion that owes much to the relevance theory of Sperber and Wilson (1986).

Following Stalnaker (1978) I will take it as given, first, that asserting is something that people do; second, that assertions take place within a context; and third, that what context an assertion takes place within can affect the content of the assertion. I will also assume that the notion of a context can be made sense of in terms of propositions.[14] Thus, let us define a conversational context $C$ as the set of propositions that individuals in the context assume or presuppose to be true for the purposes of that conversation.

What does it mean for a proposition to be *communicated* by an utterance? Following Sperber and Wilson (1986) let us say that a speaker $S$ communicates a proposition $P$ by uttering $U$ in a context $C$ — or more simply, that an utterance $U$ communicates a proposition $P$ — if:

(a) $P$ is relevant enough to make it worth the addressee's while to process the utterance $U$; and
(b) $U$ is among the most relevant utterances the speaker could have used to communicate $P$.

Propositions are relevant relative to contexts. So to say that a proposition $P$ is relevant to a context $C$ is to say that $P$ makes a difference to $C$. The greater the difference made by $P$ to $C$, the more relevant $P$ is to $C$. Recall that I am assuming that a conversational context is the set of propositions presupposed to be true by the participants in the conversation. A proposition is then said to be relevant to that context if it changes the context in some way, either by reducing the number of propositions assumed to be true in the context, or by augmenting that number. Thus, consider again our speaker Smith who utters (1) in a context where all parties to the conversation know that Smith was recently robbed, know what a line-up is, and know that Smith is trying to pick an individual out of a line up. Is it reasonable to assume that in such a context both (a) and (b) are satisfied by Smith's utterance of (1)? It seems to me that it is. For what does an utterance of (1) do in such a context? It indicates to the participants in the conversation that Smith believes that the second man from the right is the man who robbed him, and so changes the context. For it eliminates some possibilities that were previously left open, for example, that Smith believes that the third man from the right is the man who robbed him, that Smith believes that the butler was the man who robbed him, and so on. Thus, in such a context the proposition that the second man from the right is the man who robbed Smith is relevant enough to the context to make it worth the addressee's while to attend to and process the utterance of 'The second man from the right'; and second, because there is no utterance more relevant than (1) that could have been used to communicate that proposition, it follows (1) is among the most relevant utterances Smith could have used to communicate that proposition.[15] Thus, Smith succeeded in *communicating* the proposition that the second man from the right was the man who robbed him.

So far, so good. But how do we go from a claim that many would accept, namely that in uttering (1) Smith *communicates* the proposition that the second man from the right is the man who robbed him, to a claim that many would deny, namely that by uttering (1) Smith also *asserts* the proposition that the second man from the right is the man who robbed him? There is clearly a gap between these two claims. Thankfully, however, it is not an insurmountable one. According to Sperber and Wilson (1986), and simplifying somewhat, assertion works as follows:

*Assertion* An utterance $U$ is an assertion that $P$ iff
(a) $U$ communicates the proposition that $P$; and
(b) $P$ is the propositional form of the utterance $U$.[16]

I have already explained what (a) amounts to, and I attempted to establish that (1) does in fact communicate the proposition that the second man from the right is the man who robbed Smith. But what about (b)? What is the propositional form of an utterance $U$? According to Stainton "[a]n utterance $U$ has a propositional form [$PF$] just in case [$PF$] is a completion of $U$'s Logical Form $L$ — i.e., [$PF$] results from assigning reference to all indexicals in $L$, disambiguating $L$ and enriching $L$." (Stainton, 1994, pg. 279) By way of illustration, consider the following sentence:

(3) He is the man who robbed the bank.

The propositional form [Jones is the man who robbed the financial institution] is a possible propositional form for (3), because it could result from assigning Jones to be the reference of the pronoun 'he' and disambiguating the word 'bank' to mean financial institution rather than river bank. But of course, other propositional forms are also possible. For example, Bloggs could have been assigned to be the reference of the pronoun 'he' and the word 'bank' could have been disambiguated to mean river bank, in which case we would have ended up with the propositional form [Bloggs robbed the river bank].[17]

How does this account of assertion support the claim that speakers can assert propositions using *non*-sentences? Take (1) again. What propositional form might be assigned to (1)? Here there is trouble. For since (1) is not a sentence it cannot be assigned a propositional form as its logical form. Does this mean that no proposition can be asserted by an utterance of (1)? It does not. What it does suggest, however, is that we need to look more closely at Sperber and Wilson's definition of assertion. The problem with the current account of assertion is that it does not make room for utterances like (1). But this is easily remedied if we replace (b) in our definition of assertion with (b*):

(b*) $P$ is the propositional form of $U$; *or* $P$ could result by completing the logical form of $U$ and merely conjoining it with another salient logical form of the appropriate semantic type.

This yields the following account of assertion.

*Assertion-Revised* An utterance *U* is an assertion that *P* iff
(a) *U* communicates the proposition that *P*; and
(b*) *P* is the propositional form of *U*; or *P* could result by completing the logical form of *U* and merely conjoining it with another salient logical form of the appropriate semantic type.

Let us apply this revised definition of assertion to (1). We have a conversational context in which all parties to the conversation presuppose that Smith was robbed, that he is looking at a line-up, that he is trying to identify the man who robbed him, and so on. Smith utters (1), and a logical form is assigned to it by participants in the conversation, viz., the logical form [The second man from the right]. Other logical forms are also salient, however. In particular, given the context there is another logical form that is salient to the participants in the conversation, namely the logical form [*x* is the man who robbed Smith]. When this logical form is conjoined with the logical form assigned to (1), what results is the following *propositional* form:

(4) [The second man from the right is the man who robbed Smith]

But as we have already established, this is the proposition *communicated* by (1). So we have met both conditions on our revised definition of assertion. For since in uttering (1) Smith communicates the proposition that the second man from the right is the man who robbed Smith, and since that proposition could result by completing the logical form of (1) and merely conjoining it with another logical form of some appropriate semantic type, it follows that in uttering (1) Smith asserts the proposition that the second man from the right is the man who robbed him. But since (1) is a non-sentence it therefore follows that speakers can use non-sentences to assert propositions, and hence, that the Non-Sentential Assertion Thesis is true.

## 5.

Where are we? I have been arguing that we ought to accept the conditional (C). I have also been arguing that the antecedent of (C) — the Non-Sentential Assertion Thesis — is true. It therefore follows that the consequent of (C) is also true. But the consequent of (C) just is the claim that the Meaning in Isolation Thesis is false. So we have here an argument for rejecting Russell's claim that definite descriptions — phrases of the form 'the so-and-so' — lack meaning in isolation.

It might be thought that this ends the discussion: Russell was simply mistaken in thinking that definite descriptions lack meaning in isolation. To be sure, I do think that this is the conclusion we ought to draw. But I also think that this conclusion, and the argument employed to reach it, raises a number of interesting and important issues. One issue is the following. A popular view that assigns meanings to definite descriptions is the so-called *Generalized Quantifier view* (hereafter the *GQ view*). Interestingly, however, given Russell's notion of a propositional function, it turns out that Russell had the logical and semantic resources to formulate something very close to the generalized quantifier view. This naturally leads to the following question: why *didn't* Russell assign meanings to phrases of the form 'the so-and-so', even when they occur in isolation, given that he had the resources to do so? The answer to this question turns, I think, on issues having to do with Russell's views on epistemology, and in particular, on his Principle of Acquaintance. Consequently, what I would like to do in the next sections is describe the GQ view in a bit more detail, and compare it to Russell's view in "On Denoting". Using Stephen Neale as a representative example, I will argue that the relation between the GQ view and Russell's theory of descriptions is more subtle and more complex than it might initially appear.

In tracing the development of Russell's views on the meaning of definite descriptions and other denoting phrases, the impression that one gets is that Russell abandoned the view he espoused in *The Principles of Mathematics* not because he had any strong objections to the idea that denoting phrases could have meaning-relata, but rather because he couldn't figure out what such meaning-relata could be.[18] The idea that there could be an indefinite man, say, that was the meaning-relatum of the denoting phrase 'a man' struck him, as it must surely strike us, as being implausible. However, one can't help but feel that, had Russell been shown a way to assign meanings to denoting phrases, he would quite happily have done so. And it seems to me that this is something that, first, can be done; and second, that Russell *himself* could have done.

Let us therefore suppose that the Meaning in Isolation Thesis is false, and that definite descriptions do have meaning in isolation. This raises an obvious question, namely: what might the meaning of a definite description be? One proposal is that the meaning of a definite description 'the $F$' is whatever object happens to be the unique $F$. Thus, if Jones is the unique second man from the right, then on this view Jones is the meaning of 'the second man from the right.' Like Russell, however, this position does not seem to me to be an attractive one, and I will set it aside.

Another, more plausible, suggestion is that the meaning of a definite description is not an individual, but is rather a function of some kind. The GQ view is a particular instance of this more general idea.[19] According to the GQ view, the meaning of a definite description is a generalized quantifier. What are generalized quantifiers? It is easiest to think of generalized quantifiers as properties of sets, or more simply, as functions from sets to propositions.[20] Thus, the generalized quantifier corresponding to 'some $F$s' is that function $f$ from sets $\Sigma$ to propositions such that the proposition $f(\Sigma)$ is true iff the intersection of the set of things that are $F$ with $\Sigma$ is non-empty.[21] Similarly, the generalized quantifier corresponding to 'all $F$s' is that function $f$ from sets $\Sigma$ to propositions such that the proposition $f(\Sigma)$ is true iff the set of things that are $F$ is contained within $\Sigma$. Finally, and most importantly for our purposes, the generalized quantifier corresponding to 'the $F$' is that function $f$ from sets $\Sigma$ to propositions such that the proposition $f(\Sigma)$ is true iff there exists a unique thing that is $F$ and everything that is $F$ is contained within $\Sigma$.

The GQ view is quite attractive. For one thing, it gives us a uniform way of assigning meanings to definite descriptions and other so-called denoting phrases. On this view a definite description is treated like any other quantificational phrase, and receives the same sort of meaning. Thus, we can treat the definite article 'the' as being semantically similar to more obvious quantifiers like 'all' and 'some', and we can treat descriptions of the form 'the $F$' as being semantically similar to quantificational phrases of the form 'some $F$s' and 'all $F$s'. For another thing, this view allows us to assign meanings to descriptions that occur in isolation.[22] And finally, this view comports nicely with the account of assertion described above.

It is important to realize, however, that the adoption of the GQ view is by no means an innocent addendum to Russell's theory of descriptions. To the contrary, it raises a number of important questions. Perhaps the most salient question for our purposes is the following: What is the relation between the GQ view and Russell's own theory of descriptions? One position — which I will call the *equivalence thesis* — maintains that the two views are in fact identical. For example, Stephen Neale suggests that there is a deep affinity between his *Restricted Quantifier* (RQ) interpretation of Russell's theory of descriptions and the theory of descriptions proposed by Russell in "On Denoting".[23] In his book *Descriptions* and in his article "Grammatical Form, Logical Form, and Incomplete Symbols" Neale argues that his RQ interpretation of the theory of descriptions isn't even in competition with Russell's own formulation. Says Neale,

> it seems to me that the RQ account of descriptions is just Russell's theory stated in a way that allows us to see the relationship between surface syntax and logical form more clearly. By virtue of being Russellians about descriptions, we are not committed to the view that the only way to represent the logical form of a sentence *S* containing a description is to translate *S* into a formula of the language of *Principia Mathematica* (or a similar language). As far as explicating the logical structure of sentences containing descriptions, treating them as restricted quantifiers results not in a falling out with Russell but in an explanation of where the Theory of Descriptions fits into a more general theory of natural language quantification, a theory in which determiners like 'every', 'some', 'all', 'most', 'a', 'the', and so on, are treated as members of a unified syntactical and semantical category. (Neale, 1993, pg. 91)

According to Neale, "[t]he purpose of the theory [of descriptions] is to make available a class of propositions to serve as the meanings of (utterances of) sentences of the form 'the *F* is *G*', whether or not anything answers to 'the *F*'." (Neale, 1990, pg. 20) However, while this certainly captures part of the content of the theory of descriptions, it by no means exhausts it. For if Russell had merely wanted to make available a class of propositions to serve as the meanings of sentences of the form 'the *F* is *G*' whether or not such a thing as the *F* exists, then his proposal in *The Principles of Mathematics* would have been sufficient. There Russell remarked that "words all have meaning, in the simple sense that they are symbols which stand for things other than themselves." (Russell, 1903, pg. 47) So in particular, according to Russell "such proper names as are derived from concepts by means of [the word] *the* can be said to have meaning[.]" (Russell, 1903, pg. 502) Thus, on this view the (so-called) proper name 'The King of France' has meaning, in the sense that it is a symbol that stands for something other than itself. While it is exceedingly difficult to determine what exactly Russell meant by 'meaning', he apparently thought that the meanings of descriptions were similar to Fregean senses. As he says, Frege's "distinction between meaning (Sinn) and indication (Bedeutung) is roughly, though not exactly, equivalent to my distinction between a concept as such and what the concept denotes." (Russell, 1903, pg. 502) At the time of *The Principles of Mathematics*, then, Russell seemed to think that descriptions had meaning in the technical sense explained above — they stood for things other than themselves — that they contributed their meaning to propositions in whose verbal expression they occurred, and that this was the case whether or not any particular thing satisfied, or fell under, the relevant concept as such. Evidently, this proposal differs from Russell's mature theory of descriptions.

Neale seems to think that because his theory and Russell's mature theory make the same truth conditional predictions for sentences containing definite descriptions, the two theories are equivalent. However, given that Russell *rejected* the proposal of *The Principles of Mathematics*, a proposal that made the same truth conditional predictions about sentences containing descriptions as his mature theory of descriptions, but which assigned meaning-relata to descriptions, it's hard to see how Neale's proposal can be viewed as a mere notational variant of Russell's.

A second position — which I will call the *compatibility thesis* — maintains that, while not equivalent, the GQ view and Russell's view are nonetheless compatible. According to the compatibility thesis, in other words, we can graft the generalized quantifier view onto Russell's mature theory of descriptions without altering the overall shape of Russell's semantic theory. Indeed, it may be that this is what Neale has in mind when he says that the RQ view just is Russell's view 'stated in a way that allows us to see the relationship between surface syntax and logical form more clearly.' The main problem with this proposal is a simple one: according to the GQ view definite descriptions have meaning in isolation. But it is central to Russell's mature theory of descriptions that definite descriptions *lack* meaning in isolation. Consequently, it might be hard to see how it could turn out that the GQ view is compatible with Russell's views on descriptions. For although Russell was interested in the truth-conditions of sentences, Russell was also interested in the meanings of individual words and phrases. The fact that two semantic theories make the same truth-conditional predictions about a given class of sentences does not mean that the two theories are equivalent. For there might be other respects in which they differ.

On the other hand, having considered Russell's views on definite descriptions, and the differences between the theory of *The Principles of Mathematics* and that of "On Denoting", somebody might be tempted to reason as follows: while it's true that Russell abandoned the theory of descriptions in *The Principles of Mathematics*, Russell's formulation of the theory of descriptions in "On Denoting" is not based on any principled objection to the assignment of meanings to descriptions. Rather, Russell's reasons for rejecting the treatment of descriptions proposed in *The Principles of Mathematics* are traceable to the fact that he was unable to see what the meanings of descriptions could be. Had he been presented with a reasonable proposal about the meanings of descriptions, he would not have needed to formulate his theory of descriptions in the manner in which he did formulate it. But, so the present thought goes, such a proposal was available to Russell given that he already had a theory of propositional functions. According to this line of reasoning, in other words, not only is it the case that Russell *should* have taken generalized quantifiers to correspond to descriptions, it is also the case that he *could* have done so.

Let me elaborate. Central to Russell's theory of quantification is the notion of a propositional function. A propositional function is a function from entities to propositions. According to Russell, if we replace the expression 'John' in the phrase 'John is bald' with a variable ranging over individuals, and then apply a circumflex accent to the variable, what results is a phrase that denotes a propositional function. Call such a phrase a *function abstract*.[24] According to Russell the function abstract '$\hat{x}$ is bald' denotes a function that takes an individual as argument and yields the proposition with respect to that individual that that individual is bald.[25] If functions are properties, then function abstracts will denote properties. So far, so good.

Suppose, however, that we allow second-order quantification. Then there seems to be no reason why 'John is bald' could not yield another propositional function. For suppose we replace the expression 'bald' in 'John is bald' by a variable ranging over properties and apply a circumflex accent to that variable. Then the function abstract 'John is $\hat{F}$' will denote a function that takes a property $F$ as argument and yields the proposition whose first constituent is John and whose second constituent is the property $F$.[26] Again, on the assumption that functions are properties, the function abstract 'John is $\hat{F}$' will denote a property. In this case the property denoted will be a property of properties. But this is precisely what the generalized quantifier proposal amounts to. For according to the generalized quantifier proposal, a generalized quantifier just is a property of properties, or a property of sets.

## 6.

Somewhat surprisingly, then, it turns out that there is a sense in which Russell's theory of descriptions *is* compatible with the GQ view. This is because Russell had at his disposal the resources to define a class of entities to serve as the meaning-relata of definite descriptions. So why, given that Russell had the resources for formulating a version of the GQ view, didn't he do so? One possibility is that Russell's view that descriptions disappear on analysis led him to believe that a description cannot contribute anything to propositions in which it occurs. But this seems open to dispute. For example, while it may be true that the sugar I put in my cake disappears upon further mixing, it would be a mistake to say that the sugar contributes nothing to the cake.

It might be objected that this analogy is strained, which, no doubt, it is. Another more plausible possibility is that Russell's principle of acquaintance prevented him from formulating a version of the GQ view.[27] The principle of acquaintance, Russell's "fundamental epistemological principle in the analysis of propositions containing descriptions" is this: "*Every proposition which we can understand must be composed wholly of constituents with which we are acquainted.*" (Russell, 1911, pg. 23, emphasis in original) He further remarks that "a constituent with which we are not acquainted is unintelligible to us." (Russell, 1911, pg. 31) Thus, according to the principle of acquaintance, if an entity is a constituent of a proposition then it must be the kind of thing with which we can be acquainted.[28]

According to Russell, "we have *acquaintance* with anything of which we are directly aware, without the intermediary of any process of inference or any knowledge of truths." (Russell, 1912, pg. 46) Russell had fairly definite ideas about the sorts of things with which we are acquainted. The most fundamental sorts of objects with which we are acquainted are what Russell called *sense-data*. Russell does not provide an explicit definition of 'sense-data', but he does provide examples of them, saying that "[w]hen I see a colour or hear a noise, I have direct acquaintance with the colour or the noise." (Russell, 1911, pg. 17) The color and the noise are thus sense-data, objects that are given to us in perception. In addition to direct awareness of objects, Russell also allows that we can be acquainted with objects via memory and introspection, and he also allows — somewhat tentatively — that we can be acquainted with ourselves.[29]

Now, according to the GQ view propositions of the form 'the $F$ is $G$' contain as constituents a generalized quantifier corresponding to 'the $F$' and a property denoted by 'is $G$'. Let us assume that we can understand such propositions. Then according to Russell we must be capable of being acquainted with their constituents. But among the constituents of such propositions are generalized quantifiers. So the question to be asked is: can we be acquainted with generalized quantifiers? On the face of it, yes. For Russell grants that we can have awareness of, and so be acquainted with, universals as well as particulars. For example, Russell says that "[n]ot only are we aware of particular yellows, but if we have seen a sufficient number of yellows and have sufficient intelligence, we are aware of the universal yellow." (Russell, 1919, pg. 18) Since properties are universals — if we are realists about properties — and since generalized quantifiers are properties, albeit of a highly complex sort, there would appear to be no reason why we couldn't be acquainted with generalized quantifiers and hence, no reason why they couldn't be constituents of propositions. Indeed, it appears that Russell explicitly allowed this latter possibility in some cases, since he held that the proposition that everything is a man is equivalent to the proposition that the propositional function denoted by '$\hat{x}$ is a man' is always true. And the latter proposition clearly contains the propositional function '$\hat{x}$ is a man'. So Russell's acknowledgement that propositional functions could be constituents of propositions lends some support to the view that the GQ view is compatible with Russell's views on definite descriptions.

On the other hand, the principle of acquaintance would seem to count against this view. For when Russell talks about awareness of universals he suggests that we become aware of universals only after having been acquainted with particular instances of them. But then it becomes mysterious how we could be acquainted with a generalized quantifier: for what could count as being acquainted with a particular instance of a generalized quantifier? Perhaps it could be said that we are acquainted with particular instances of generalized quantifiers by being acquainted with particular utterances of definite descriptions and other denoting or quantificational expressions. But again, it is hard to know what it would mean to be acquainted with a generalized quantifier. Moreover, the sorts of things with which we can be acquainted are, for Russell, epistemological primitives. For example, we can be acquainted with redness because such an item can be a foundational piece of knowledge. But can it seriously be suggested that the generalized quantifier corresponding to 'all cyclists' is a foundational item of knowledge? That it is indubitable and certain in the way in which 'red here now' is indubitable and certain? It seems to me that it cannot.

Another reason to be skeptical about the idea that we can be acquainted with generalized quantifiers is that it is arguable that somebody cannot understand a generalized quantifier without having some knowledge of truths. For example, consider again the generalized quantifier corresponding to 'all cyclists'. In order for somebody to understand this function it would be necessary for that person to know that the generalized quantifier corresponding to 'all cyclists' is that function $f$ from sets $\Sigma$ to propositions such that the proposition $f(\Sigma)$ is *true* iff the set of cyclists is contained within $\Sigma$. That is, in order to understand the generalized quantifier corresponding to 'all cyclists' it is necessary to know how it combines with sets or with properties to yield truths. But if we cannot have direct awareness of generalized quantifiers without having knowledge of truths, then on Russell's view we cannot be acquainted with generalized quantifiers. To this extent generalized quantifiers seem to be different from other properties. For it seems that I can have direct awareness of redness without knowing any truths whereas this does not seem to be the case with generalized quantifiers.[30]

A third possibility for why Russell did not formulate a version of the GQ view — and one which is related to the Principle of Acquaintance — has to do with Russell's distinction between *complete* and *incomplete* symbols. On Russell's view descriptions are incomplete symbols, symbols that 'disappear on analysis'. Interestingly, however, what makes an expression a complete or an incomplete symbol is not a matter of the expression's form, but is instead a matter of the expression's semantic characteristics. Thus, what Russell means by the claim that definite descriptions are incomplete symbols is that they do not stand for objects and do not contribute objects to propositions in whose verbal expression they occur. Notice that on this view even proper names count as incomplete symbols for Russell, since according to him proper names do not contribute objects to propositions in whose verbal expression they occur.

Why is this important? Because according to the GQ view, descriptions *do* contribute objects to propositions in whose verbal expression they occur, although the objects contributed are properties — in particular, generalized quantifiers — rather than individuals. It is clear, however, that Russell's distinction between complete and incomplete symbols is intimately related to his principle of acquaintance. For if an expression is complete only if it contributes an object to propositions in whose verbal expression it occurs, and if objects contributed to propositions must be objects with which we can be immediately acquainted, then an expression is complete only if it contributes an object with which we can be immediately acquainted to propositions in whose verbal expression it occurs. Thus, another reason why Russell might not have formulated something like the GQ view is that it entails that definite descriptions are complete symbols.

I admit, however, that the issue is a complicated one. I have been arguing that the GQ view carries with it a commitment to the idea that definite descriptions have meaning-relata, and contribute those meaning-relata to propositions in whose verbal expression they occur. This amounts to the claim that descriptions ought to be viewed as complete, rather than incomplete, symbols. But this is open to dispute. For instance, Neale (1993) argues to the contrary that the GQ view does *not* entail that descriptions stand for objects or have meaning-relata, and so does not entail that descriptions are complete symbols. Says Neale, "for Russell a *complete* symbol stands for some entity and contributes that entity to the propositions expressed by utterances of sentences containing that symbol." (Neale, 1993, pg. 91) But Neale goes on to say that in an expression of the form '[the$_1$ king $x_1$]$_1$($x_1$ likes Russell)' "the quantifier '[the$_1$ king $x_1$]$_1$' that binds the variable is an incomplete symbol. It doesn't even purport to stand for an object... There is no sense, then, in which the RQ account of descriptions conflicts with Russell's conception of descriptions as incomplete symbols." (Neale, 1993, pg. 92)

Whether Neale is right to say that there is no conflict between the RQ account — or the GQ view; I am not here distinguishing between the two — and Russell's theory of descriptions is going to depend, among other things, on what is meant by 'entity', 'object', 'stands for', and 'contribute'. It is tempting to say that an expression is a complete symbol if it is a referring expression, incomplete if not. But this cannot be right. For Russell allows that predicates are complete symbols even though they do not contribute individuals to propositions in whose verbal expression they occur. Consequently, the fact that an expression is not a referring expression is no bar to that expression's being a complete symbol. Neale slides from talk of expressions contributing *entities* to propositions in whose verbal expression they occur to talk of expressions contributing *objects* to propositions in whose verbal expression they occur. It is true that on the GQ view descriptions do not contribute objects, i.e., individuals, to propositions; but they *do* contribute entities to propositions in the form of generalized quantifiers. It therefore seems to me that, *pace* Neale, there is a sense in which the GQ account *does* conflict with Russell's conception of descriptions as incomplete symbols. At any rate, the fact that there is room for disagreement on this issue again indicates that the adoption of the GQ view is not a problem of terminology alone.[31]

7.

To recapitulate, I have been speculating about the relation between the GQ view of the meaning of definite descriptions, Russell's theory of descriptions, and Russell's Principle of Acquaintance. I have been arguing that there are good reasons to think that definite descriptions stand for generalized quantifiers. I have also been arguing that adopting this position results in a view which, although not incompatible with the semantic and logical resources available to Russell, violates certain of his epistemological principles. The upshot of this discussion is that adoption of the GQ view threatens Russell's theory of descriptions. This is because on the GQ view descriptions are complete symbols that stand for entities other than themselves, and contribute those entities to propositions in whose verbal expression they occur.

Let me conclude with some very brief, and very speculative, methodological remarks. To this point I have been concerned with a fairly narrow question: given that Russell had the resources to formulate something like the generalized quantifier view, why didn't he do so? My diagnosis was that Russell's foundationalist epistemology, and in particular, his Principle of Acquaintance, barred him from taking seriously the idea that definite descriptions might have generalized quantifiers — or entities similar to generalized quantifiers — as meaning-relata. But this narrow question leads naturally to a much broader question, namely: Is it plausible to suppose that results about everyday speech and language processing could end up threatening Russell's foundationalist epistemology?

Russell's views on linguistic understanding are intimately linked to his views on epistemology. On Russell's view, as we have seen, if an expression has meaning — in the technical sense of having a meaning-relatum — then that meaning must have certain epistemological characteristics. In brief, it must be something with which we are capable of being acquainted. As we have also seen, this places severe constraints on the sorts of meanings that expressions can have. But suppose that the arguments of the present paper are correct: that speakers can use unembedded definite descriptions to assert propositions; that this requires that definite descriptions have meaning-relata; and that the natural candidates for such meaning-relata are generalized quantifiers. Then it does appear that Russell is faced with a difficult choice: either reject the Principle of Acquaintance; or retain the Principle of Acquaintance and endorse the idea that we can be acquainted with generalized quantifiers and other complex linguistic meanings.

Now, it might be thought that abandoning the Principle of Acquaintance and the foundationalist epistemology that supports it might not be such a bad thing for Russell given the problems that infect sense-data theories quite generally. But what is surprising is that an argument against foundationalism in epistemology might come from reflections on what speakers do with words. After all, one would have thought that if foundationalism is mistaken it would be shown to be mistaken for other reasons.

Could Russell retain the Principle of Acquaintance by making appropriate adjustments elsewhere in his theory? He could. But that would require accepting the idea that we can be acquainted with generalized quantifiers. And as we have seen, this is not an altogether plausible idea. For one thing, generalized quantifiers do not seem to have the right epistemological characteristics to be the sort of things with which we can be acquainted: they are not indubitable in the required sense, nor can we be directly aware of them. For another thing, it appears that to understand a generalized quantifier we require knowledge of truths, which again suggests that we cannot be acquainted with them. What is clear is that if Russell were to allow that we can be acquainted with generalized quantifiers and other complex meanings the overall shape of his epistemology would be greatly altered.

That reflections on what speakers do with words might lead us to reconsider foundational issues in epistemology might seem initially implausible, but on reflection it should come as no surprise. Recent developments in Chomskyan linguistics have forced philosophers to rethink what it means for something to be an item of knowledge, or what it means for an item of knowledge to be innate, or what it means for attributions of linguistic knowledge to be correct. If linguistic understanding is but one of the many ways in which we find out about the world, it should not surprise us to learn that reflections on how language is used threaten to spill over into other areas of philosophical inquiry, including epistemology as it has been traditionally conceived.

## 8.

To conclude. My primary aim in this paper has been to argue that the conditional (C) is true. My reasons for focusing on this conditional were threefold. First, because there are good reasons for accepting the antecedent of (C), and hence, good reasons for accepting its consequent. Second, because the truth of (C) has consequences for Russell's theory of descriptions. And third, because the truth of (C) indicates that the relation between empirical facts about how language is used and philosophical theses concerning language and epistemology are more intimate than they might otherwise appear to be. Along the way I argued that there are good reasons for thinking that the meaning of a definite description is a generalized quantifier. I also argued that the adoption of what I called the GQ view about the meaning of definite descriptions is not obviously compatible with Russell's theory of descriptions and should not be viewed as a mere notational variant of Russell's theory. Investigation of Russell's theory of descriptions continues to be fruitful in part because it is one of those genial areas of philosophical inquiry where issues having to do with semantics, syntax, epistemology, and natural language processing collide, with interesting and sometimes surprising results.

## NOTES

* I am indebted to Alex Barber, Richard Cartwright, Lisa Sereno, and, especially, Robert Stainton for extremely helpful comments on previous versions of this paper. I would also like to thank Ray Elugardo and Robert Stainton (again) for their support and patience while the final version of this paper was being prepared.

1 It should be emphasized that Russell does not restrict himself in his writings to consideration of definite descriptions alone. Rather, Russell is concerned with so-called 'denoting phrases' in general. For simplicity, however, I will confine myself to discussion of definite descriptions. I believe that the conclusions I draw about definite descriptions can be extended to other so-called denoting phrases.

[2] I realize that this claim is controversial and requires further spelling out. I will return to discussion of it below.

[3] Readers who are already convinced that the conditional (C) is plausible and that the Non-Sentential Assertion Thesis is true should feel free to skip these first sections.

[4] Of course, Russell did not think that proper names in natural language refer to individuals. Rather, Russell would view a proper name like 'Smith' as being short for a definite description of the form 'the $x$ such that $\phi x$', where $\phi$ stands for some set of properties had by Smith. However, it will simplify matters somewhat if we assume here and throughout that proper names in natural language *do* refer to individuals. I will return to this issue below in connection with Russell's Principle of Acquaintance.

[5] Just so there is no confusion: what's important here isn't so much that speakers are capable of *asserting* propositions using non-sentences, but rather that in so doing they are *grasping* and *deploying* the meanings of non-sentences. Thus, the reason that the ability of speakers to assert propositions using non-sentences is of interest is that it is a particular instance of a more general claim linking meaning and understanding. So if the particular claim can be established — if, that is, the Non-Sentential Assertion Thesis can be established — then we will have succeeded in establishing the more general claim that speakers can grasp and deploy the meanings of non-sentences and hence, that such expressions *have* meaning in isolation.

[6] What follows is by no means original. The arguments I give below borrow heavily from Barton (1991), Stainton (1994, 1995, 1998), and Yanofsky (1978).

[7] For a nice discussion of the complexities that accompany this question, see Stainton (2000).

[8] For the purposes of this discussion, I will restrict myself to discussion of this interpretation.

[9] For a more thorough overview of X-bar theory, see Haegeman (1994).

[10] For a more thorough discussion of this style of objection, see Clapp (2001).

[11] What follows owes much to Stainton (1994) and Sperber and Wilson (1986). It should be emphasized, moreover, that the claim that speakers are capable of asserting propositions using non-sentences is a controversial one, and is not universally accepted. For arguments against the sort of view presented here, see Stanley (2000).

[12] There is nothing special about (1). If the Non-Sentential Assertion Thesis is true many other non-sentences can be used to make assertions.

[13] For arguments to this effect, see Stainton (1997).

[14] This assumption is controversial. For defense of this idea see Stalnaker (1978, 1998).

[15] For it is surely true that an utterance of the sentence 'The second man from the right is the man who robbed me' is no more relevant than an utterance of (1). Indeed, it might even be thought to be *less* relevant than an utterance of (1) since it repeats information that is already present in the context.

[16] The '?' indicates that this account of assertion is subject to revision.

[17] Although there are many possible propositional forms that sentence (3) could have, it is important to note that there are also many propositional forms that (3) could *not* have. For example, [Bloggs is the man who robbed the 4th of July parade] is not a possible propositional form for (3) because there is no way that 'bank' could be disambiguated to mean 'the 4th of July parade'. So we know that in assigning propositional forms to sentences, not anything goes.

[18] For a fascinating discussion of the origin and development of Russell's theory of descriptions, see Cartwright (1987).

[19] See Barwise and Cooper (1981) for a more thorough discussion of the nature of generalized quantifiers and their relationship to natural language expressions. Stainton (1998) contains more detailed arguments in favor of the GQ view.

[20] Why functions from sets to *propositions* rather than functions from sets to *truth values*? Because treating generalized quantifiers in this way leaves open the possibility that the generalized quantifier corresponding to 'some unicorns' is distinct from the generalized quantifier corresponding to 'all round squares.' If generalized quantifiers were merely functions from sets to truth values, then these two generalized quantifiers would be semantically equivalent.

[21] Note that it is the entire quantificational phrase 'some $F$s' that is assigned a generalized quantifier as meaning, not the determiner 'some'.

[22] Why prefer a view that assigns to a definite description of the form 'the $F$' a generalized quantifier to a view that gives the meaning of *sentences* in which definite descriptions occur according to a recursive rule, a view, that is, according to which, although 'the $F$' is not assigned a meaning, all sentences of the form 'the $F$ is $G$' are assigned the value true iff there exists a unique $F$ and that $F$ is $G$? The reason should be familiar by now: since it is plausible to suppose that definite descriptions do have meaning in isolation — since they can be used by speakers to assert propositions — *some* meaning must be assigned to them when they occur unembedded.

[23] So far as I can tell, Neale's RQ account and the GQ view are notational variants of each other, or at least can be treated as such for our purposes. By a restricted quantifier, Neale has in mind an expression of the form $[Qx\colon Fx]$, where the domain of the quantifier $Q$ is restricted to the class of things that are $F$. On this view, 'the' can be viewed as a device that operates on two predicates, $F$ and $G$, to yield an expression of the form $[\text{the } x\colon Fx](Gx)$ which is true just in case the unique thing which is $F$ is also $G$, in much the same way that 'most' can be viewed as a device that operates on two predicates, $F$ and $G$, to yield an expression of the form $[\text{most } x\colon Fx](Gx)$ which is true just in case there are more $F$ things which are $G$ than there are $F$ things which are not $G$. If we make the assumption that restricted quantifiers express properties, then Neale's RQ account would appear to be equivalent to the GQ view.

My primary worry with this interpretation of Neale's RQ account is that Neale always provides truth conditions for complete sentences containing definite descriptions, and never explicitly says what the meaning of a restricted quantifier is. Moreover, in arguing (in Neale (1993)) that restricted quantifiers are *incomplete symbols* — in Russell's sense of the term — Neale seems to commit himself to the view that restricted quantifiers do not stand for any object, and do not contribute any object to propositions in whose verbal expression they occur. I will return to discussion of the distinction between complete and incomplete symbols below. For the time being, it suffices to note that if Neale's RQ account is equivalent to the GQ view, then what goes for the one goes for the other. And if Neale's RQ account differs from the GQ view, then my remarks below concerning its relation to Russell's proposal in *The Principles of Mathematics* would still seem to apply.

[24] This terminology is due to Mark Sainsbury. See (Sainsbury, 1979, pg. 280).

[25] Russell is not entirely consistent on this issue. Sometimes Russell talks as if propositional functions are extra- or non-linguistic entities; at other times he talks as if propositional functions are linguistic entities. Hence it is not clear whether Russell thinks that the function abstract '$\hat{x}$ is bald' is a propositional function, or whether he thinks that what the function abstract '$\hat{x}$ is bald' denotes is a propositional function. Despite this inconsistency, I will adopt the latter interpretation in what follows. For an interesting discussion of this issue, see (Sainsbury, 1979, pg. 278).

[26] It is worth noting that this proposal corresponds almost exactly to Richard Montague's proposal for the semantics of proper names in a natural language like English. According to Montague (1974), the English expression 'John' translates to the expression $\lambda P[P\{\mathbf{j}\}]$ (where $P$ is a variable ranging over properties). This expression denotes the set of properties of John, i.e., a function from properties to truth values (or propositions). Hence, according to Montague 'John is bald' is true just in case the property of being bald is a member of the set of properties of — i.e., possessed by — John. For a more detailed exposition, see Dowty et al. (1981).

[27] For similar speculations, see Sainsbury (1979).

[28] Although the principle of acquaintance receives its most extended treatment in Russell (1911, 1912, 1919), it surfaces in Russell (1905) as well. Thus in "On Denoting" Russell says that "in every proposition that we can apprehend (i.e. not only in those whose truth or falsehood we can judge of, but in all that we can think about), all the constituents are really entities with which we have immediate acquaintance." (Russell, 1905, pg. 56)

[29] Cautions Russell: "although acquaintance with ourselves seems *probably* to occur, it is not wise to assert that it undoubtedly occurs." (Russell, 1912, pg. 51)

[30] Of course, somebody might object that in order to understand the property corresponding to the predicate 'is red' one must know that redness is that function $f$ from individuals $e$ to propositions such that the proposition $f(e)$ is true iff $e$ is red. But this seems rather dubious as an account of what is required to understand the property of being red.

[31] For a more thorough discussion of this issue, see Linsky (1992) and Neale (1993).

## REFERENCES

Barton, E., "Nonsentential Constituents and Theories of Phrase Structure." In K. Leffel and D. Bouchard (eds.) *Views on Phrase Structure*. Dordrecht: Kluwer Academic Publishers. 1991.

Barwise, J., and Cooper, R., "Generalized Quantifiers and Natural Language". *Linguistics and Philosophy* 4 (1981): 159–219.

Cartwright, R., "On the Origin of Russell's Theory of Descriptions." In *Philosophical Essays*. Cambridge, MA: MIT Press. 1987.

Clapp, L., "What Unarticulated Constituents Could Not Be." In J. Campbell, M. O'Rourke, and D. Shier (eds.) *Meaning and Truth: Essays in Philosophical Semantics*. New York: Seven Bridges Press. 2001.
Dowty, D., Wall, R., and Peters, S., *Introduction to Montague Semantics*. Dordrecht: Kluwer Academic Publishers. 1981.
Dummett, M., *Frege: Philosophy of Language*. Cambridge, MA: Harvard University Press. 1981.
Haegeman, L., *Introduction to Government and Binding Theory*. Oxford: Blackwell. 1994.
Linsky, B., "The Logical Form of Descriptions." *Dialogue* 31 (1992): 677–83.
Marsh, R., (ed.), *Logic and Knowledge*. London: George Allen and Unwin, Ltd. 1956.
Montague, R., "The Proper Treatment of Quantification in English." In R. Thomason (ed.), *Formal Philosophy: Selected papers of Richard Montague*. New Haven, CT: Yale University Press. 1974.
Neale, S., *Descriptions*. Cambridge, MA: MIT Press. 1990.
Neale, S., "Grammatical Form, Logical Form, and Incomplete Symbols." In A. Irvine, and G. Wedeking (eds.), *Russell and Analytical Philosophy*. Toronto: University of Toronto Press. 1993. Reprinted in Ostertag (1998). [Page references are to the Ostertag reprint.]
Ostertag, G., *Definite Descriptions: A Reader*. Cambridge, MA: MIT Press. 1998.
Russell, B., *The Principles of Mathematics*. New York: W.W. Norton & Co. Ltd. 1903.
Russell, B., "On Denoting." *Mind* 14 (1905): 479–493. Reprinted in Marsh (1956).
Russell, B., "Knowledge By Acquaintance and Description." *Proceedings of the Aristotelian Society*, 11 (1911). Reprinted in Salmon and Soames (1988). [Page references are to the Salmon and Soames reprint.]
Russell, B., *The Problems of Philosophy*. Indianapolis, IN: Hackett Publishing Company. 1912.
Russell, B., "Descriptions." In *Introduction to Mathematical Philosophy*. London: George Allen and Unwin, Ltd. 1919.
Sainsbury, M., *Russell*. Routledge, London. 1979.
Salmon, N., and Soames, S. (eds.), *Propositions and Attitudes*. Oxford: Oxford University Press. 1988.
Sperber, D., and Wilson, R., *Relevance: Communication and Cognition*. Cambridge, MA: Harvard University Press. 1986.
Stainton, R., "Using non-sentences: An application of Relevance Theory." *Pragmatics & Cognition* 2(2) (1994): 269–284.
Stainton, R., "Non-sentential Assertions and Semantic Ellipsis." *Linguistics and Philosophy* 18(3) (1995): 281–296.
Stainton, R., "What Assertion is Not." *Philosophical Studies* 85(1) (1997): 57–73.
Stainton, R., "Quantifier Phrases, Meaningfulness in Isolation, and Ellipsis." *Linguistics and Philosophy* 21(3) (1998): 311–340.
Stainton, R., "The Meaning of 'Sentences'." *Noûs* 34(3) (2000): 441–454.
Stalnaker, R., "Assertion." In P. Cole (ed.), *Syntax and Semantics*, volume 9. New York: Academic Press. 1978. Reprinted in Stalnaker (1999).
Stalnaker, R., "On the Representation of Context." *The Journal of Logic, Language, and Information* 7, 1998. Reprinted in Stalnaker (1999).
Stalnaker, R., *Context and Content*. Oxford: Oxford University Press. 1999.
Stanley, J., "Context and Logical Form." *Linguistics and Philosophy* 23(4) (2000): 391–434.
Yanofsky, N., "NP Utterances." *Chicago Linguistics Society: Papers from the Regional Meeting*, 14 (1978): 491–502.

ALEX BARBER

# CO-EXTENSIVE THEORIES AND UNEMBEDDED DEFINITE DESCRIPTIONS

Non-sentential assertion is a potentially rich source of evidence in both syntax and semantics. Suppose we have two theories that are indistinguishable in the predictions they make about the grammaticality of a given range of sentences (relative to an interpretation of each) yet make incompatible claims about the internal structure of those sentences. It may be possible to discriminate in favour of one of the pair by virtue of a difference in the predictions each makes for sub-sentential acceptability judgements. In this paper I consider the extent to which this potential is realised for a case that has received some attention in this regard: definite descriptions.

In §1 I look at syntax, and the lessons that may be drawn from the use of definite descriptions such as (1) that, though not embedded in any sentence, can be used to communicate (and perhaps to assert) a proposition — in this case, that the best candidate was the person who has just left the room:

(1) The best candidate [uttered after the final interviewee has just left the room].

I ask whether such uses speak in favour of treating the determiner *the* as part of a restricted quantifier, rather than as a binary operator as claimed by Gareth Evans (1977, 1982). The results here are inconclusive.

In §2 I turn to semantics. Once again two theories are available that resemble one another in respect of what truth conditions they assign to all sentences yet where we might hope to be able to discriminate between the theories by considering the meaningful use of subsentential expressions. Andrew Botterell (this volume) and Robert J. Stainton (1998) have urged us to see the phenomenon of unembedded definite descriptions as calling for treatment using generalized quantifier theory rather than a more authentically Russellian syncategorematic theory. By drawing parallels between their argument and Donnellan's 1966 criticisms of Russell 1905 (as criticised by Kripke 1977), I aim to show that their case against syncategoremicity is unpersuasive and that both semantic theories are compatible with the phenomenon in (1).

In §3 I show how this negative result in §2 undermines Botterell's claim that Russell's principle of acquaintance is refuted by the phenomenon of unembedded (yet meaningful) definite descriptions.



*R. Elugardo and R. J. Stainton (eds.), Ellipsis and Nonsentential Speech*, 185–201.

## 1. UNEMBEDDED DEFINITE DESCRIPTIONS AND SYNTAX

Early in his 1990 book *Descriptions*, a sustained defence of Russell's 1905 theory of descriptions, Stephen Neale considers how best to think of the syntax of determiners, and in particular of *the*: as an element in a unary restricted quantifier, or as a binary quantifer. The difference doesn't seem to matter at the sentence level, either to truth conditions or to syntax.

If we take the restricted-quantifier option, Russell's theory would be expressed thus:

> $\ulcorner$[the $x$: $Fx$] ($Gx$)$\urcorner$ is true iff there is exactly one F and all Fs are G[1]

where the structural description offered here is a simplification of the representation at LF. Following the binary-quantifier option, by contrast, it would be expressed thus:

> $\ulcorner$[the $x$] (F$x$ ; G$x$)$\urcorner$ is true iff there is exactly one F and all Fs are G

That is, the assignments of truth conditions to sentences containing definite descriptions are indistinguishable. Both are what we can call *weakly Russellian*: they assign truth conditions even when nothing is denoted (*pace* Strawson 1950; strong Russellianism will be defined in §2).

The rules of syntactic composition are different, being (after Neale, 1990, p. 59 n. 54):

> (1) If $\phi$ is a well-formed formula that contains at least one occurrence of $b$, and if $D$ is one of 'the', 'some', 'no', etc., then $\ulcorner[Dx\text{: }\phi(\text{b}/x)]\urcorner$ is a well-formed quantifer phrase, where $\ulcorner\psi(\text{b}/x)\urcorner$ is the result of replacing at least one occurrence of $b$ in $\psi$ by $x$; (2) If $\psi$ is a well-formed formula that contains at least one occurrence of $b$, and if $\ulcorner[Dx\text{: }\phi]\urcorner$ is a well-formed quantifier phrase, then $\ulcorner[Dx\text{: }\phi](\psi(\text{b}/x))\urcorner$ is a well-formed formula.

and:

> (1) 'the', 'some', 'no', etc., are all determiners; (2) If $\phi$ and $\psi$ are well-formed formulas each containing at least one occurrence of $b$, and if $D$ is a determiner, then $\ulcorner[Dx](\phi(\text{b/x});\psi(\text{b}/x))\urcorner$ (where $\ulcorner\psi(\text{b}/x)\urcorner$ is the result of replacing at least one occurrence of $b$ in $\psi$ by $x$) is a well-formed formula.

respectively; but these rules are co-extensive in respect of which strings they classify as sentential. In view of this semantic and syntactic co-extensionality (at the sentence level), what *should* guide us in our choice of LF representation? And in particular, ought the existence of non-sentential utterances to make a difference?

It is of course artificial to pretend that ignoring evidence from non-sentential utterances would put us in the position of Buridan's ass, faced with the paralysing task of choosing between two syntactically and semantically co-extensive theories of equal standing. Evidence from syntax is likely to speak in favour of restricted quantifiers, for at least two reasons. First, within the context of the same sentence:

The F is G
The F is G

the single underlined string manifests far greater stability as a constituent than does the double underlined string. Second, the two syntactic composition rules are merely Neale's adaptations of the formation rules for $\forall$ and $\exists$ in first-order logic, not for natural language. Once one introduces real-world contingencies and complexities such as quantifier raising and the desirability of an X-bar format, the clause for the binary operator looks to be a less promising starting point.[2]

But there are arguments in favour of the opposite perspective. In particular, Gareth Evans claims that certain phenomena of anaphoric dependence and scope are incompatible with a restricted quantifier treatment.[3] Rather than go into the details of this I will simply assume that it would be useful to have evidence from some independent source, and in particular that it is worth examining utterances of unembedded definite descriptions to see if we can discriminate between the two theories.

Perhaps the observation that it is impossible to utter (2) in isolation (save in ellipsis) speaks in favour of a restricted quantifier treatment. For this contrasts with (3), which could be used in a fishmonger's shop to communicate the proposition that the utterer wishes to purchase the halibut next to the mackerel.

(2) *The
(3) The halibut next to the mackerel

It is true that (2) could be used in ellipsis, as in (4):

(4) A to C: *A bed in your room is made up for you.*
(5) B to C: *The* [meaning that there is no other bed]

By calling (4) elliptical I have in mind that some fragment of discourse salient in the environment is borrowed to complete the phrase. (I say more about ellipsis in §2.) A rare and so perhaps discountable exception to this claim about *the* might be (6), where there is no ellipsis in this sense:

(6) The! [on the unveiling of a magnificent new bed, which the utterer has been anticipating all week]

Is it reasonable to infer from the contrast between (2) and (3) that definite descriptions have a restricted quantifier syntax and not a binary quantifier syntax?

Any intuitive confidence we feel in this inference seems to rest on a flawed maxim, namely, that *one should identify as constituents those phrases that can be used meaningfully in isolation*. But this maxim is highly questionable, and it has no obvious acceptable surrogate.

One complication has to do with the fact that sentences have more than one level of representation. What is a constituent at one level of representation may turn out not to be so at some other. In the case at hand, it would be open to Evans to insist that although *The F* is a constituent under a binary quantifier treatment at PF, it is not so at LF.

Moreover, the general principle that would render the maxim a reasonable one is false. Consider the assignment of structure to (7) (with an intended interpretation that has the table rather than the keys being qualified as inside the front door) in (8). It is no objection to this assignment that one could, in a suitable context, express the same proposition using (9), which is not a constituent of the longer sentence. The assignment in (10) conforms with the maxim and the acceptability of (9) but gets the (intended) interpretation wrong.

(7) The keys are on the table inside the front door
(8) The keys are [on [the table inside the front door]]
(9) On the table
(10) The keys are [on the table][inside the front door]

We can conclude from these examples that there is no simple generic link between constituency and potential for unembedded use.

Still, there may be specific reasons for preferring restricted quantifiers to binary quantifiers, reasons that turn on semantic considerations. In the next section I consider whether the meaningful use of unembedded definite descriptions is more readily accommodated by generalized quantifier theory than by a syncategorematic competitor, as Stainton and Botterell have claimed. Restricted quantifier syntax combines more readily with generalized quantifier theory than does binary quantifier syntax,[4] so if they are right, a preference for restricted quantifiers would follow as a corollary. (Notwithstanding the inconclusive outcome of the present section, I will assume throughout §2 that sentences containing definite descriptions have quantified noun phrases as constituents at LF and focus on the task of providing a suitable semantic clause. I indicate why this is an innocent assumption in the conclusion.)

## 2. UNEMBEDDED DEFINITE DESCRIPTIONS: SEMANTICS

Stainton and Botterell argue from the fact that we often use isolated quantified noun phrases, including definite descriptions, to perform meaningful utterances to conclusions about the semantic rules that underpin our competence in this domain. Stainton 1998 argues that generalized quantifier theory is more comfortable with the existence of unembedded quantified noun phrases than any theory that interprets quantifiers syncategorematically. His argument is reiterated and endorsed by Botterell (this volume) for the specific case of definite descriptions.

Botterell, moreover, uses this conclusion to reinterpret and reassess Russell's 1905 treatment of denoting phrases (i.e. quantified noun phrases, including definite descriptions). He suggests that Russell's principle of acquaintance was a likely source of Russell's failure or refusal to regard generalized quantifiers as the meaning of definite descriptions, and for his opting instead for the theory that definite descriptions do not have any meaning save in an attenuated sense. Botterell then turns the tables on Russell, arguing that the principle of acquaintance is undermined by the phenomenon of unembedded descriptions.

In this section I present then reject the argument for generalized quantifier theory, suggesting that it is lacking in the same way that Donnellan's 1966 criticism of Russell 1905 was lacking. I turn to the principle of acquaintance only in the next and final section.

What is at stake in the debate over whether definite description phrases have 'meaning in isolation' is helpfully boiled down by Stainton (1998, section 1) to a question concerning what semantic clause we should adopt for these constructions. To claim that they do not have meaning in isolation is to claim that they should be understood syncategorematically (i.e. in accordance with Neale's first suggestion in the previous section):

$\ulcorner$[the $x$: $Fx$] ($Gx$)$\urcorner$ is true iff there is exactly one F and all Fs are G

Call a semantic theory with this as its key clause a syncategorematic theory. To claim that definite descriptions *do* have meaning in isolation is to claim that they have a semantic value assigned to them independently of their appearance in a sentence schema. A semantic theory is *strongly Russellian* if, like the syncategorematic theory, it denies this.[5]

One way of assigning a semantic value to definite descriptions is to use generalized quantifier theory. On this theory, quantifier phrases in general, and so definite descriptions in particular, refer to generalized quantifiers. (A terminological clarification: generalized quantifiers are not phrases; rather, they are what quantifier phrases refer to.)

Generalized quantifiers are functions, mapping sets to propositions.[6] For example in the case of *every cat*, and *some cat*, the semantic value will be the functions $f_{\forall cat}$ and $f_{\exists cat}$ respectively, defined as follows for arbitrary set G as argument:

$$\begin{aligned} f_{\forall cat}(\mathrm{G}) &= \text{a true proposition if } \{x\text{: } x \text{ is a cat}\} \subseteq \mathrm{G}; \\ &\quad\ \text{a false proposition otherwise} \\ f_{\exists cat}(\mathrm{G}) &= \text{a true proposition if } \mathrm{G} \cap \{x\text{: } x \text{ is a cat}\} \neq \varnothing; \\ &\quad\ \text{a false proposition otherwise} \end{aligned}$$

In the case of a definite description phrase, *the cat*, the relevant clause is:

$$\begin{aligned} f_{\mathrm{THE}cat}(\mathrm{G}) &= \text{a true proposition if } |\{x\text{: } x \text{ is a cat}\}| = 1 \text{ and } \{x\text{: } x \text{ is a cat}\} \subseteq \mathrm{G}; \\ &\quad\ \text{a false proposition otherwise} \end{aligned}$$

Both the generalized quantifier theory and the syncategorematic theory explain how the presence of an embedded definite description phrase in a sentence feeds into the determination of the truth condition of that sentence. And they both predict the same assignment of truth conditions. The difference is that under the syncategorematic theory the determination will be in one step, whereas under the generalized quantifier theory determination is in two steps. The first of these two steps is the assignment of a semantic value — a function — to the quantified noun phrase as above; the second is the determination of a truth condition using a phrasal clause along the lines of:[7]

$$\mathrm{val}([Qx\text{: } Fx]\ (Gx)) = \mathrm{val}([Qx\text{: } Fx])(\mathrm{val}(Gx))$$

The argument against the syncategorematic theory, and so against the strong Russellian claim that definite descriptions do not have meaning in isolation, is easy to state. The syncategorematic theory's schematic clause gives no clue as to what the meaning of definite descriptions would be if they were not embedded within a sentence; hence it gives no clue as to how they could be used meaningfully when not so embedded. But they can be used meaningfully in this way. So the syncategorematic theory is at best incomplete, and to the extent that it implicitly asserts its own completeness, it is false (Stainton 1998, p. 316).

The generalized quantifier theory faces no such difficulties. It tells us that definite descriptions, like other quantifier phrases, refer to generalized quantifiers. Specifically they refer to the generalized quantifier defined above in the case of *the cat*, and more generally the function defined by the relevant instance of:

> val⌜[*the* $x$: $Fx$]⌝ $= f(\mathrm{G})$: a true proposition if $|\{x\text{: Fx}\}| = 1$ and $\{x : \mathrm{F}x\} \subseteq \mathrm{G}$; a false proposition otherwise

An account is still needed of how the identity of the proposition expressed by utterances of isolated definite descriptions comes to be interpreted correctly. But such accounts are available.[8]

My task in the remainder of this section is to find fault with this inference from the phenomenon of isolated but meaningful uses of definite descriptions to the claim that definite descriptions have meaning in isolation (in the sense that they cannot have a solely syncategorematic semantics). I begin by drawing a moral from an earlier debate.

Keith Donnellan (1966) objected to Russell's 1905 analysis of the semantics of definite descriptions by claiming that it was incompatible with the existence of the phenomenon he describes as a referential versus attributive ambiguity in definite descriptions.[9] (Weak) Russellianism may be right for the attributive sense of definite descriptions, but it is wrong for the referential sense. Saul Kripke (1977) replies on Russell's behalf by asking us to imagine a community whose language, call it Russellese, is stipulated to be Russellian in its treatment of definite descriptions but otherwise like English.[10] That is, in Russellese, sentences involving definite descriptions are semantically unambiguous. Would the phenomenon Donnellan describes nevertheless manifest itself among this community? It is very plausible to suppose that it would, since a pragmatic mechanism for the recognition of the speaker's intention in so-called 'referential uses' is readily available.[11] This shows how Russellian logical form is compatible with the phenomenon. So the presence of the phenomenon among speakers of English does not show that a (weakly) Russellian semantics is false of English.

The beginning stages of the same dialectic are implicit when we look at unembedded definite descriptions being used meaningfully, and the use of this phenomenon to object to (strong) Russellian semantics. The moral to carry over from Kripke 1977 is given by the schema:

> *Kripke's methodological principle*
> An objection to semantic theory $\theta$ for typical idiolects of English, to the effect that it is incompatible with the phenomenon $\phi$ found among typical speakers of English, is refuted if $\phi$ would be manifest among a community of speakers of $L_\theta$, stipulated as having a semantics in accord with $\theta$.

'$\theta$' this time is strong rather than weak Russellianism: a syncategorematic semantics for definite descriptions. (As I have indicated parenthetically, Donnellan was objecting even to weak Russellianism, and in this regard the generalized quantifier theory and the syncategorematic theory are on all fours; both would equally have been a target.) The substituens for '$\phi$' in Kripke's deployment was the so-called referential use of definite descriptions; in the present context, it is the phenomenon of communicating a proposition using an unembedded definite description.

Following Kripke's methodological recipe, then, consider a community of speakers of what I will call $L_{SYN}$, the language that is just like English save in having a syncategorematic semantics for definite descriptions (if indeed this is a difference). Would the practice arise in such a community of using unembedded definite descriptions to communicate entire propositions? Implicit in Stainton's and Botterell's discussions is a negative reply to this. And they do, in effect, consider and reject some of the ways in which the phenomenon might arise among speakers of $L_{SYN}$. However, they do not consider all the ways.

One *flawed* reason for supposing that the phenomenon actually prevalent among typical speakers of English would arise among speakers of $L_{SYN}$ is to hold that they would speak elliptically, with the definite description alone represented at PF and a hidden sentence having a syncategorematic semantics. (Strictly, the phenomenon described so far as the use of *unembedded* definite descriptions would then need to be recharacterised long-windedly as the use of PF-unembedded but LF-embedded definite descriptions.)

Stainton shows (1995, 1997a, 1997b, and 2000), convincingly, that this recharacterisation cannot be allowed to go through. Depending on what is meant by 'ellipsis', the thesis that ellipsis is at work when we perform sub-sentential utterances is either false or unhelpful. For it to work in the present context, the only thesis that will do is that there is a level of representation that is still plausibly called syntactic, but which is the result of filling in appropriate formatives in the following:

$$IP \longrightarrow NP;\ I'$$
$$I' \longrightarrow I;\ CP/VP$$

to yield an inflectional phrase, i.e. a sentence.[12] But the formatives, syntactic material to serve as the fillers for 'I' and 'CP/VP' (with 'NP' being the definite description itself), are simply not available for this to happen. The difficulty comes along with the massive overabundance of candidates for being the filler. Suppose a potential witness utters 'The tall one' at an identity parade. A proposition is expressed, but candidates for being the filler include: [past/sing] *rob me*; [pres/sing] *be the one who robbed me*; [pres/sing] *be the robber*; and [pres/sing] *be the man I believe to be the robber*. The problem is not that we cannot tell which of these is the right filler. All that is required for the syncategorematic theory is that one of them *be* the right filler, not that we *know* which one is. The problem, rather, is that there does not seem to be any fact in virtue of which it is one rather than the other.

One tempting thought is that there is something that determines one from among the surfeit of candidates to be successful, and it is a matter of what goes on in the speaker's brain as they perform the utterance. A model for this would be, for example, the manner in which the filler in bona fide syntactic ellipsis is determinate. In the exchange in (11), B's utterance is elliptical of (12) because a determinate I', as spelled out here, is represented in the speaker's mind through its salience *as syntactic material* in the context of discourse (as a constituent of the sentence uttered by A, underlined).

(11) A: *Who <u>is at the door?</u>*
B: *The pizza delivery boy*

(12) $[_{IP}[_{NP}$*The pizza delivery boy*$][_{I'}[_{I}$pres/sing$][_{VP}$*be at the door*$]]]$

But not all uses of unembedded definite descriptions are such that the syntactic material is available to be borrowed in this way. And there is evidence that when this crutch is missing, nothing determinate comes in its stead. B's utterance in III in (13) is such a case, in which an unembedded definite description occurs discourse initially.

(13) I B: *That's the beer shop*
C: *And its manager is your biological father*
II A: *What's that?*
B: *The beer shop*
C: *And its manager is your biological father*
III B: *The beer shop* [uttered to identify the premises]
C: ??*And its manager is your biological father*

Although B's utterance communicates the same proposition in all three scenarios, C's attempts at ellipsis differ in their success in a way that is dependent on what happens antecedently. When B's utterance is of a sentence, whether overt (I) or bona fide elliptical (II), syntactic material can be borrowed. The contrasting inadequacy of C's utterance in III suggests that, when an unembedded definite description is discourse initial, no complementary syntactical material is available, even in ellipsis, for C to borrow.

I will take this to show that in at least some meaningful uses of unembedded definite descriptions there is no elliptical sentence present. But a caveat to this concession is needed. On the syncategorematic theory, definite descriptions are what might be termed *incomplete sentences*. An incomplete expression of type $X$ is an expression that receives a determinate semantic interpretation only when complemented by some other expression to form a larger phrase of type $X$. If incomplete sentences are classified as a species of elliptical sentence, then my concession is only that no elliptical completed sentences are present in meaningful uses of unembedded definite descriptions. What I want to show is that a definite description, thought of as an incomplete sentence, could be used to communicate a proposition. But this is not because a complete sentence, with suitable instantiations of the required formatives hung onto an I' within an IP, is hidden at LF. Instead the proposition would be communicated in a thoroughly pragmatic fashion.

Before turning to this pragmatic account, I should note that Stainton and Botterell both anticipate appeals to pragmatics designed to undermine their inference from the unembedded-use phenomenon to the failure of the syncategorematic theory. Stainton anticipates the thought that the proposition is non-linguistically communicated, and presents an independent worry. Botterell anticipates the thought that the utterance is not an assertion of the proposition communicated. I consider their three concerns in turn, before turning to my pragmatic proposal.

Stainton wonders whether a use of, say, *The pizza delivery boy*, to communicate that a contextually unique pizza delivery boy is at the door, could be like the brandishing of an umbrella, used to communicate the fact that it is raining outside. Acts of the latter type have non-natural content (in Grice's 1957 sense) but they lack a semantic content. In other words, the use of unembedded definite descriptions would be non-linguistic, albeit meaningful and communicative, acts. So perhaps meaningful uses of unembedded definite descriptions would arise among speakers of $L_{SYN}$ as a pragmatic but non-linguistic phenomenon.

Stainton points out that this thought is not promising. After all, meaningful but unembedded definite descriptions can be a complex as you like, iterated, and susceptible to systematic transformation as in (14) and (15):

(14) The pizza delivery boy who would have won a Fulbright last year but for the judging panel's lack of imagination

(15) The pizza delivery boy who would have been winner of a Fulbright last year but for the judging panel's lack of imagination

To the extent that compositionality and systematicity of this kind are typical marks of the linguistic, the use of unembedded definite descriptions seems to be linguistic.

Stainton considers and then, again rightly, rejects a second way in which competent interpreters of $L_{SYN}$ could be held to get by without assigning a semantic value to unembedded definite descriptions: their 'mak[ing] use of the context' to 'come up with some predicate' and 'combine this predicate with the heard quantifier phrase to form sentence' (1998: 320), and then using their syncategorematic semantics to interpret accordingly, and correctly if they managed to come up with the *right* predicate. But that is just the problem, says Stainton: there is no account of how the right predicate could come to be selected:

> Pretty clearly, the quantifier phrase [i.e. the definite description] must play a central part in the search for the "right predicate". . . . [But] the hearer, in his search for the right predicate, cannot rely on the *meaning* of the unembedded quantifier phrase since, by hypothesis, [this meaning] doesn't come into play until *after* the missing predicate has been found. But, if the quantifier phrase offers *no semantic clue* about where in the context to search, there are going to be far too many "salient predicates" to choose from. Arriving at an interpretation of the speaker would end up being a fabulous stroke of luck.

The problem is that the hearer is supposedly in the position of hearing an expression that is meaningless to them until they combine it with a predicate. Given the plethora of candidates, the number that would need to be tried out would be vast.

One could attempt to ride out this concern of Stainton's by insisting that a suitable predicate is *not* that difficult to isolate. In the case of a sudden and loud knock on the door, this is not so difficult to imagine: 'is at the door' will be one of the first one tries out. But even if such cases were the norm, there are others where this is not so. Suppose the utterance were of (16):

(16) The man who you think looks like the local newsreader for BBC South-West

where a suitable predicate would need to be expressive of the attribute of being an apt dinner party guest for next week, and where a search for someone possessing this attribute had been occupying the conversants the night before. If the utterance had been of the name 'Roberto Simonetti', the search for the predicate would have been far more straightforward, and the audience would not have had to try, only to reject, all predicates expressive of the attributes of being, respectively, likely to commit suicide, in need of being fetched from the kitchen, a film on at the local cinema, *etc*. Only attributes of Roberto Simonetti, the individual, would be assessed for salience, hugely narrowing down the processing task. But because the syncategorematic clause fails to associate any individual with the definite description, this narrowing down is not possible. And without any such narrowing down, the search is simply too vast.

In a short while I hope to show that speakers of $L_{SYN}$ would be able to narrow down the search in the same way that they could if a straightforward name were used in place of a definite description. I agree with Stainton that they could not do this by sticking to the letter of the semantics. But there is no reason to suppose they stick to the letter of the semantics. Before showing why not I will consider two final objections-in-principle to pragmatic solutions.

Botterell (this volume, section 4) claims that the phenomenon under discussion consists of using unembedded definite descriptions to *assert* the communicated proposition, and not in merely implicating or conveying it. His claim matters to me since, at least in normal uses of the term 'assertion', the resources to which one may appeal in associating a proposition with the utterance are semantic.

Botterell notes that unembedded definite descriptions fail to assert a proposition in the following sense of 'assert':

An utterance *U* is an assertion that *P* iff:
(a) *U* communicates the proposition that *P*; and
(b) *P* is the propositional form of the utterance *U*.

Unembedded definite descriptions do not have a propositional form (i.e. an interpreted logical form that is propositional — apt for truth valuation — in character). He therefore adds a clause to (b) to give (b*):

An utterance *U* is an assertion that *P* iff:
(a) *U* communicates the proposition that *P*; and
(b*) *P* is the propositional form of the utterance *U*; or *P* could result by completing the logical form of *U* and merely conjoining it with another salient logical form of the appropriate semantic type.

With this addition to what is meant by 'assertion', it is more conceivable that unembedded definite descriptions could be used to make assertions. But how does this definition of 'assertion' sit with my desire to show the syncategorematic semantic theory to be compatible with the phenemonon at issue?

There is some residual unclarity concerning whether, were the syncategorematic theory true, definite descriptions should or should not be said to have a completed (i.e. interpreted) logical form. Fortunately this is an unclarity that we need not resolve. If they do, then there is nothing here that stands in the way of offering a pragmatic account of how this completed logical form gets conjoined with another salient logical form of the appropriate semantic type, to deliver the communicated proposition. If this pragmatic account could eventually be provided, there would be no incompatibility between the syncategorematic clause and the phenomenon of non-sentential assertion, thus described. On the other hand, if definite descriptions treated syncategorematically could not be said to have a completed logical form in isolation, then all that needs to happen is that the phenomenon we are interested in accommodating no longer be unquestioningly described as non-sentential assertion. 'The use of unembedded definite descriptions to communicate a proposition' would be less contentious. (In his contribution, Botterell does not explain why we have to accept his description of the phenomenon as one of assertion; at most he indicates a use of 'assertion' in which the phenomenon *could* turn out to be assertion, not that it *must* so turn out.)

There is one final concern about the possibility of a pragmatic account: implicature tends to manifest cancellability. Consider the example of the philosophy-job applicant for whom I am writing a reference letter, communicating that she is a poor philosopher by remarking on her excellent handwriting and punctuality. This implicature can be cancelled without self-contradiction by my asserting, immediately after, that she is a very gifted philosopher. By contrast, if I utter (3):

(3) The halibut closest to the mackerel

I do appear to contradict myself if I later assert that I wanted the halibut farthest from the mackerel.

In fact, the proposition communicated *is* cancellable. As the fishmonger hands me the halibut that was closest to the mackerel and asks for payment, I could without contradiction claim that I didn't want to *buy* the thing, I just wanted to know a little more about it, to smell it for freshness, or even to know if it was male or female. (I couldn't do this if my utterance was preceded by a question, 'Which fish would you like to buy?'; but in that case my utterance would be elliptical in the narrower of the two senses of p. 192, and so easily accommodated.)

Cancellability, I claim, is a feature that frequently accompanies pragmatically communicated propositions, but is not an essential feature of them as such (unless trivially stipulated to be so). Cancellability seems always to attach to that which is not explicit to the utterance. I can cancel the suggestion that I *want to buy* the denoted object; I cannot cancel the suggestion that it is *the denoted object* that I want to buy. That is to be expected since the attribute of the denoted object — being wanted for purchase — was left covert, implicit to the context, whereas what object is being denoted is explicit in the utterance. In standard examples of implicature, it is not explicit in the utterance what the pragmatically communicated proposition is. It is for this reason, and not for the reason that it is pragmatically communicated, that a pragmatically communicated proposition will typically be cancellable.

## THE PRAGMATIC ACCOUNT

I need to show how competent speakers of $L_{SYN}$ would be able to interpret utterances of unembedded definite descriptions successfully, i.e. in accordance with the utterer's intention and expectation that they interpret them this way. My claim is that they could do so pragmatically, using the semantic information available to them in the syncategorematic clause as a springboard.

We cannot help ourselves to the more familiar pragmatic paradigms. These tend to take the semantic input from which the pragmatic account takes off to be truth conditional or propositional. That is, they assume that what is uttered is a *whole sentence*. This is presupposed throughout much of Grice's 1975 account, for example. For him, the trigger for a search for an implicated proposition is almost always a failure of the semantically expressed proposition to satisfy the maxims of quality, quantity, manner, etc.[13] When the uttered expression is subsentential one could try to fall back on failures of semantic actions of some kind other than that of stating — such as referring — to be (say) relevant in the context. But when the semantic theory is the syncategorematic theory, no semantic significance *at all* seems to attach to the utterance of an unembedded definite description.

In the account I propose, the $L_{SYN}$ audience use the information they have by virtue of knowing the semantic clause for definite descriptions to isolate the objected *denoted* by the uttered definite description, assuming there is one, and then figure out what salient property is being attributed to this entity.[14] This gets the order of isolation — object, and only then the salient property — correct relative to Stainton's concern that there would otherwise be too many salient properties to choose from.[15]

The $L_{SYN}$ audience could be expected to figure out what property is being attributed to the denoted object in three steps. First, they realise that they need to figure out what object the utterer has in mind from the uttered definite description. Second, once this need has been recognised they come to fix on the object denoted by the definite description. Third, they identify the salient attribute of this object.

The first of these steps may seem too obvious to bother stating, but remember: on the syncategorematic theory, definite descriptions are not assigned any determinate semantic significance by the relevant clause save when conjoined to some or other predicate. Hearing an unembedded definite description should seem like hearing half a word, which is to say, not like witnessing any kind of semantic event at all. Actually, it is worse than hearing half a word. In the latter case one can look around for ways to finish the word to deliver one that is meaningful in the context. But trying to 'finish the word' in the unembedded-definite-description case would lead to our undertaking the foolhardy quest Stainton rightly warns against: trying to complete the sentence by finding the salient predicate *before isolating the denotation*.

The seeds of an answer to the question of why the $L_{SYN}$ audience would seek an object can, after all, be found in Grice 1975. The first debt to Grice comes in the form of an appeal to his co-operative principle, which commands us to 'make your conversational contribution such as is required, at the stage at which it occurs, by the accepted purpose or direction of the talk exchange in which you are engaged'. Clearly, to utter a meaningless fragment or half-word is not as such to live up to this demand. But if the audience member nevertheless *assumes* the utterer to be operating under the principle, she will begin to look beyond anything the semantics of the fragment alone can provide. We can also assume she is in a position to notice that the fragment is of a kind that must be conjoined with a predicate before it becomes semantically interpretable. After all, this is written into her semantic clause for definite descriptions.

Let us assume temporarily that this is the first time she has heard a definite description in isolation. She might wonder what the predicate is, and begin to look for the most contextually salient attributes in order to then try out predicates expressive of them. But at that point she will run up against the fact that this is a foolhardy quest: there are so many salient predicates (being likely to commit suicide, in need of being fetched from the kitchen, a film on at the local cinema, etc.) that it is unlikely she will hit on the right one. Rather than persevere, she is likely to look for assisting evidence, with confidence that it is there since she is taking the utterer to be operating under the co-operative principle, and to be abiding in particular by the *maxim of manner*, according to which one ought to seek to be 'perspicuous ... [and] avoid ambiguity and obscurity' (our second debt to Grice 1975). One thought likely to strike her as of overriding significance is that, since it is an attribute that is being sought (because it a predicate that would complete the utterance, 'finish the word', and predicates express attributes), and since attributes are attributes *of* things, she should first isolate some thing or things. Optimistically, she turns to the definite description itself in the hope that it is meant to provide insight into the object or objects to which some salient property is being attributed.

That completes the first step, the second being to understand how she could discriminate the *denoted* object or objects as the one(s) for which she must seek out a relevant attribute in step three. Her reasoning so far has been laborious, and described in a way that is at odds with the undeniable speed and unreflective character of our normal processing of unembedded definite descriptions. But this is because I am operating under the artificial assumption that she is coming across these constructions for the first time. If implicature can operate in these artificial circumstances, the cognitive routines that allow us to operate within a pervasive practice would account for speed and unreflectivity. And as Stainton himself points out, the practice is pervasive: 'quantifier phrases are very frequently used and understood in isolation... [T]ake a cursory glance at a speech corpus' (1998: 314, n. 2).

Suppose we are in a community in which utterances consisting of *The cat* conjoined grammatically with *is G* are known to be true just in case there is exactly one thing that is a cat, and that thing has the property expressed by *G*. Faced with the task left from the first step, of associating some object with *The cat*, it beggars belief to suppose that members of this community would not look around for a salient cat. In fact they would be so likely to shape their search in this way that even if Russell were to explain to them that it cannot be the *semantic* function of definite descriptions to pick out and refer to an object, up to half of their philosophers of language and semanticists would remain unpersuaded a whole century later. Of course, it would not suit my purposes to maintain that referring to a contextually unique cat is the semantic function of *The cat*. If that were the case, the syncategorematic theory would be wrong (as would the generalized quantifier theory). All I want to claim is that, faced with an interpretative need to associate some object or objects with *The F*, her familiarity with the truth conditions of entire sentences involving phrases of this kind would likely lead her to settle on some thing that uniquely satisfies *F* — to settle on the thing denoted by the definite description, in other words.

I have described a two step process whereby members of an $L_{SYN}$ speaking community could come to associate an object with a definite description uttered in isolation. Once they have done this they could set about taking the third step, of finding an attribute that is salient with respect to this object. How they do this is something everyone has to worry about. But at least they would, I am claiming, have avoided the problem of having to select the attribute with no helping hand in the form of an appreciation of what object is being denoted. (END OF PRAGMATIC ACCOUNT)

I have been arguing that, because the phenomenon of meaningful but unembedded definite descriptions would occur among the $L_{SYN}$ community, the actual existence of the phenomenon among English speakers does not lower the prior probability of the syncategorematic theory. I want to close by offering some very tentative reasons to think that the phenomenon of unembedded definite descriptions may actually tip the balance *away* from the generalized quantifier account and towards the syncategorematic one.

Use of unembedded definite descriptions is not always for the purpose of expressing a proposition. In the right context, an isolated use of the expression in (17):

(17) The beer shop

can be used in context to express or convey the proposition that some salient consumer outlet is the place to purchase a cigarette lighter. This is the kind of use we have been looking at so far. But it could also be used as the name of the establishment, displayed on the shop front. Call this the *labelling usage* of unembedded definite descriptions, to contrast with the *propositional usage*.

There is a plausible principle about labelling that is in tension with the generalized quantifier theory:

> *The labelling principle*
> When expressions are used as labels, what they label is the same entity as their normal semantic value in propositional usage.

Cases where this is clearly true are the labels we call proper names. Nelson Mandela goes under the label 'Nelson Mandela' (among others). And when this same expression is used propositionally, the contribution it makes, as a default, is given by:

val(*Nelson Mandela*) $= x$ iff $x =$ Nelson Mandela

If the labelling principle and the generalized quantifier theory are both true, and definite descriptions can and do function as labels, then the expression *The beer shop* would be a suitable label, not for a shop but for a function from sets to propositions.

The syncategorematic theory is not much better off. Syncategorematic clauses for definite descriptions do not deliver labelled objects as semantic values, either, for the simple reason that they do not assign anything as semantic values. Assigning no semantic value and assigning the wrong one are equally unacceptable, and taken together this shows that the labelling principle cannot be right for definite descriptions. But definite descriptions do nevertheless seem well designed to serve as labels, and how they manage to do so is something that may tell in favour of one over another of our competing semantics.[16]

The explanation of how a practice could grow up of using definite descriptions, with a syncategorematic semantics, to label an individual object, would both piggy-back on and reinforce the explanation of how the practice could grow among speakers of $L_{SYN}$ of conveying whole propositions using unembedded definite descriptions. With the latter practice in place, hearing a definite description in isolation would automatically trigger a search for an object denoted. In such an environment, use of definite descriptions to label objects they denote would become commonplace. In fact it would become such a stable phenomenon that definite descriptions could be used to label entities they do not strictly denote:

(18) Le grain de sel

is the name of a restaurant, not of a grain of salt. By giving it this label, the proprietor was presumably intending us to think of her or his premises as being the unique bearer of certain metaphorically-expressed qualities.

When we turn to the generalized quantifier theory, things are not so straightforward. Stainton's account of how unembedded definite descriptions come to express propositions does not similarly lend itself to conversion into an explanation of how definite descriptions could acquire the labelling function. It runs roughly as follows. Like any phrase whose interpreted logical form is non-propositional, quantifier phrases when uttered in isolation are combined with logical forms that are contextually salient so as to generate a propositional form, the propositional form that expresses what is asserted by the utterance. At no point is it the case that the interpreter is called on to isolate the denoted object in order to come to know the truth condition of the utterance, or the proposition it expresses. What they isolate, rather, is a propositional function.

Of course, it may be possible that a practice would emerge, among speakers of $L_{GQ\Theta}$ (like English but stipulated to have a generalized quantifier theoretic semantics for definite descriptions), of using definite descriptions as labels. But showing this will have to involve isolating pragmatic factors that would lead to an association between a definite description and some object that it actually or putatively denotes. These pragmatic factors are likely to stem from recognition that the conditions for truth of sentences involving definite descriptions are met only when there is some object denoted. But in just this way a practice of using unembedded but syncategorematic definite descriptions to convey propositions could arise. So accounting for the labelling usage of definite descriptions will force the generalized quantifier theorist into the awkward position of defending the supposition that the phenomenon of conveying propositions using unembedded definite descriptions would manifest itself among speakers of $L_{SYN}$.

## 3. CONCLUSION

In §1 I suggested that unembedded definite descriptions fail to speak in favour of either restricted quantifier syntax or binary quantifier syntax. I ended that section by raising the possibility of a reversal of this negative result through vindication of generalized quantifier theory and so, indirectly, restricted quantifier syntax. But against this hope I argued in §2 that unembedded definite descriptions fail to speak strongly in favour of either generalized quantifier semantics or a syncategorematic semantics. (The discussion in §2 operated for simplicity using restricted quantifier syntax, but the assumption was an innocent one: the pragmatic account would seem to be available no matter what the syntax.)

I will conclude with yet another negative claim: that the argument in §2 undermines Botterell's argument (this volume) against Russell's *principle of acquaintance*:

> Every proposition which we can understand must be composed wholly of constituents with which we are acquainted (Russell, 1911: 23)

Botterell argues that the phenomenon of unembedded definite descriptions being used to communicate propositions shows Russell's principle to be mistaken. For independent reasons I think the principle of acquaintance is flawed. But if I am right in what I have said so far, the reasons Botterell offers are not sufficient to undermine the principle.

Botterell's argument can be summarised as follows:

P1 Unembedded definite descriptions can be used to communicate propositions;
P2 Only by treating generalized quantifiers as the semantic values of definite descriptions is it possible to account for this;
P3 We are not acquainted with generalized quantifiers;
C The principle of acquaintance is mistaken.

Botterell advances this as a case of a linguistic phenomenon being used to argue for a philosophical claim — a thin silver lining for Russell, who was keen on such reasoning.

My objection to the argument is not that it uses linguistic premises to argue for epistemological and metaphysical conclusions. Rather, it is that the second premise is false. It is possible to treat definite descriptions syncategorematically, and yet still be able to explain their use for the communication of propositions when not embedded.[17]

## NOTES

[1] 'At least one F' if 'F' is plural. See Neale 1990, pp. 41–2, 46. See also his 1993.

[2] Neale goes some way towards offering a realistic syntax for restricted quantifiers (1990, section 5.6; 1993, section 5); for more see Larson and Segal 1995, Ch. 9.

[3] The problem concerns anaphors that on a restricted quantificational syntax are not c-commanded by the quantifier on which they are referentially dependent. They are like '$\forall x(\exists y Fxy \,\&\, Gy)$', which is a non-sentence. A binary-quantificational syntax avoids the problem. See Evans 1977, pp. 136–9; 1982, p. 59. Neale attempts to undermine Evans' reasoning (1990, p. 42 and section 6.3; 1993, section 7) by introducing a special kind of 'D-type' pronoun that needn't be c-commanded by its antecedent.

[4] Indeed it suits Botterell's purposes to treat Neale's restricted quantifier view and the generalized quantifier view as notational variants. For my purposes it is important that I keep them distinct. It is possible to give a syncategorematic reading of restricted quantifiers.

[5] A further claim of Russell's, that proper names are disguised definite descriptions, is neutral with regard to the distinction between weak and strong Russellianism in the sense defined. This claim about proper names is the target in Kripke 1972 but does not figure in the present discussion.

[6] Or to truth values in versions of the theory dropped by Stainton (1998, p. 316) and Botterell (this volume) in favour of that in the main text. Since it does not bear on the present discussion I will follow them.

[7] Abstracting as before from the real-to-life complexities set out in more detail in e.g. Larson and Segal 1995, chs. 6–8 (though they present a truth-values version — see previous note).

[8] See Stainton 1998, sections 7 and 9 for quantifier phrases; and in greater depth and generality, Elugardo and Stainton 2003. The main components of the account are implicit in Botterell's outline (this volume) of how unembedded definite descriptions could be used to assert a proposition.

[9] Donnellan illustrates the difference in intended senses (as he might put it, though as Kripke 1977 notes, only some of the time is Donnellan clearly committed to the distinction being a semantic rather than pragmatic one) with the following kind of contrast: *Attributive:* "Smith's murderer is deranged" (uttered at the scene of the crime, beside the mutilated corpse of Smith); *Referential*: "Smith's murderer is deranged" (said of a man who is frothing at the mouth in the dock, on trial for Smith's murder, when he is in fact innocent).

[10] Kripke is better known as a critic of Russell, particularly in 1972. But there he is criticising Russell's claim that proper names are disguised definite descriptions. He does not contest Russell's analysis of overt definite descriptions, save to the extent of expressing concern over the familiar problem of definite descriptions that fail to achieve uniqueness.

[11] Neale (1990), Ch. 3, esp. 3.5, offers an attractive exposition along Gricean lines.

[12] See Botterell, this volume. I also lean heavily on his witness example in my reconstruction and elaboration of the objection to the ellipsis thesis, below.

[13] Neale's Gricean derivation of the phenomenon of so-called referential uses of definite descriptions, for example, begins: '(a) *S* has expressed the proposition that [*the x: Fx*](*Gx*); (b) There is no reason to suppose that *S* is not observing the CP and maxims; (c) . . . '. See 1990, p. 89.

[14] *Terminological note:* An object is *denoted* by a definite description of the form ⌜*the F*⌝, iff it is F and nothing else is. If strong Russellianism is correct then an object denoted by a definite description is not *referred to* by it since definite descriptions do not refer, ever. They never refer because the logical form we must assign to definite descriptions on account of their occasionally lacking denotation means that we cannot treat them as referring — having semantic value — even when they have denotation.

[15] Curiously, and for solely explicatory purposes, Stainton exploits the niche in logical space for just such a theory in the course of laying out his own account of how quantifier phrases, understood in accordance with generalized quantifier theory, could come be interpreted as expressive of a full proposition (1998: 331–2). It may be that he fails to distinguish it from the infinite-quest account discussed above.

[16] Other exceptions to the labelling principle exist. A band in the 1980s was called *Frankie Goes To Hollywood* after a newspaper headline. The point about definite descriptions is that they seem so naturally suited to a labelling function. Over 90% of pubs in my local yellow pages have names beginning with a definite article. Just one is named after a sentence (*The Geese Flew Over the Water*, the first line of an Irish song).

[17] My thanks for helpful comments on earlier drafts to Jenny Saul, Rob Stainton, and an audience at Cardiff University.

## REFERENCES

Botterell, A., "Knowledge by acquaintance and meaning in isolation," this volume.

Donnellan, K., "Reference and Definite Descriptions." *Philosophical Review* 77 (1966): 281–304.

Elugardo, R., and Stainton, R.J., "Grasping Objects and Contents." In A. Barber (ed.), *Epistemology of Language*. Oxford: Oxford University Press. 2003: 257–302.
Evans, G., "Pronouns, Quantifiers and Relative Clauses (I)." *Canadian Journal of Philosophy* 7 (1977): 467–536. Reprinted in his *The Collected Papers*, Oxford: Oxford University Press. 1985: 76–152.
Evans, G., *The Varieties of Reference*. Oxford: Oxford University Press. 1982.
Grice, H.P., "Meaning." *Philosophical Review* 66 (1957): 377–388.
Grice, H.P., "Logic and Conversation." In P. Cole, and J. Morgan, (eds.) *Syntax and Semantics, Volume 3: Speech Acts*. New York: Academic Press. 1975: 41–58. Reprinted as Ch. 2 of his *Studies in the Ways of Words*. Cambridge, Mass.: Harvard University Press. 1989.
Kripke, S.A., "Semantic Reference and Speaker Reference." In P.A. French, T.E. Uehling, Jr., and H.K. Wettstein (eds.) *Contemporary Perspective in the Philosophy of Language*. Minneapolis: University of Minnesota Press. 1977: 6–27.
Kripke, S.A., *Naming and Necessity*. In D. Davidson and G. Harman (eds.) *Semantics of Natural Language*. Dordrecht: Reidel. 1972: 253–355 and 763–769.
Larson, R., and Segal, G., *Knowledge of Meaning*. Cambridge, Mass.: MIT Press. 1995.
Neale, S., *Descriptions*. Cambridge, Mass.: MIT Press. 1990.
Neale, S., "Grammatical Form, Logical Form, and Incomplete Symbols." In A.D Irvine and G.A. Wedeking (eds.) *Russell and Analytic Philosophy*. Toronto: University of Toronto Press. 1993: 97–139. Page references are to the reprint in G. Ostertag, *Definite Descriptions: A Reader*. Cambridge, Mass.: MIT Press. 1998: 79–122.
Russell, B., "On Denoting." *Mind* 14 (1905): 479–493.
Russell, B., "Knowledge by Acquaintance and Description." *Proceedings of the Aristotelian Society*, 11 (1911). Reprinted in N. Salmon and S. Soames (eds.), *Propositions and Attitudes*, Oxford: Oxford University Press.
Stainton, R.J., "Non-Sentential Assertions and Semantic Ellipsis." *Linguistics and Philosophy* 18 (1995): 281–296.
Stainton, R.J., "What Assertion Is Not." *Philosophical Studies* 85 (1997a): 57–73.
Stainton, R.J., "Utterance Meaning and Syntactic Ellipsis." *Pragmatics and Cognition* 5 (1997b): 49–76.
Stainton, R.J., "Quantifier Phrases, Meaningfulness 'in Isolation', and Ellipsis." *Linguistics and Philosophy* 21 (1998): 311–340.
Stainton, R.J., "The Meaning of 'Sentences'." *Noûs* 34 (2000): 441–454.
Strawson, P.F., "On Referring." *Mind* 59 (1950): 320–344.

MARGA REIMER

# THE ELLIPSIS ACCOUNT OF FICTION-TALK

## 1. INTRODUCTION

Suppose that, in the appropriate sort of conversational setting, I were to assertively utter the following sentence:

(1) Saul Kripke used to teach at Princeton.

I would surely have said something *true*. How is this fact to be explained? Well, there's this guy, Saul Kripke, and he used to teach at Princeton — which is what I just said! But then what about an assertive utterance of a sentence like the following:

(2) Sherlock Holmes lives at 221B Baker Street.

Suppose that I were to assertively utter this sentence in a setting where the topic of conversation was the famous Conan Doyle character. Here too, I would seem to have said something *true*. But how can that be? Can we simply say: There's this guy, Sherlock Holmes, and he lives at 221B Baker Street? — and because that's what I've just said, I've said something true? No; of course not. The problem is that there is no such guy — Sherlock Holmes does not exist, not really; he is a purely fictional character after all. Or, perhaps there *is* a Sherlock Holmes — perhaps he is a Meinongian entity — an entity that can be referred to, despite its lack of existence. At least then there might be some hope of accounting for the apparent fact that we can say something true by assertively uttering a sentence like (2). But there are well-known difficulties with Meinongianism,[1] a doctrine which should thus be avoided if possible. The advocate of the ellipsis account of fiction-talk thinks that such avoidance *is* possible. We need only regard sentences like (2) as *elliptical for* sentences like (3):

(3) According to the Conan Doyle stories, Sherlock Holmes lives at 221B Baker Street.

For the truth of a sentence like (3) does not require that the name 'Sherlock Holmes' refer to *anything* — existent or not; it requires only that the stories contain the ellipsed sentence or sentences that (together perhaps with certain background assumptions) imply it.[2] The result is an ontologically cautious account of fiction-talk — but is it a *plausible* one?

My intention in what follows is two-fold. First, I would like to take a close, critical look at ellipsis accounts of fiction-talk. Second, I would like to propose, motivate, and



*R. Elugardo and R. J. Stainton (eds.), Ellipsis and Nonsentential Speech*, 203–215.

develop an alternative account of fiction-talk — one that preserves the virtues of ellipsis accounts, while avoiding their drawbacks.

The format of this paper is as follows. I begin by setting out the data to be explained, data which concern the apparent fact sentences like (2) can be used to make true assertions. I then present the ellipsis account of the data. I go on to discuss an apparent difficulty with the account, after which I discuss some alternatives that have been proposed in its place. I object to these alternatives on the grounds that they fail to preserve the intuition that fiction sentences can in fact be *true*, after which I go on to suggest yet another account of fiction-talk — one according to which fiction sentences of the sort in question can be true, *when interpreted relative to the appropriate context*. Yet the proposed account is committed neither to Meinongianism nor to the view that the sentences in question are anything other than what they appear to be — simple (unellipsed) subject/predicate sentences. After arguing on behalf of this alternative view, I anticipate and respond to some likely objections, and then conclude with a few brief remarks concerning the advantages and disadvantages of the ellipsis account of fiction-talk.

## 2. THE DATA

The data in question concern the fact that we appear to be able to make true statements/assertions[3] via assertive utterances of sentences purportedly about fictional entities. Consider, for instance, the following three sentences:

(4) Sherlock Holmes is a brilliant detective.
(5) Pegasus has wings.
(6) Santa Claus lives at the North Pole.

When these sentences are assertively uttered in the appropriate sorts of conversational settings, they appear to express *truths*; indeed, when uttered in such settings, they appear to *be* true.[4] The question is: What is the best explanation of this apparent fact? More particularly, is an explanation available that avoids the postulation of Meinongian entities?

## 3. THE ELLIPSIS ACCOUNT

### *3.1. General*

The central claim of the ellipsis account of fiction-talk is that sentences like (4) through (6) are elliptical for sentences that are explicitly about the relevant fiction(s). In this way, we are able to explain the fact that such sentences can be used to make true claims without having to endorse Meinongianism. For so long as the fiction contains or (somehow) implies the sentences in question, those sentences count as true, *according to that fiction*. Thus, pre-fixed sentences like (3) emerge as true, as do the elliptical sentences that "abbreviate" them — sentences like (2).

At least two versions of the ellipsis account have been proposed in the literature. Let us turn to these now.

### *3.2. Variations*

According to David Lewis (1978), instead of taking fiction sentences at "face value," we should

> regard them as abbreviations for longer sentences beginning with an operator, "In such-and-such fiction . . . " Such a phrase is an intensional operator that may be pre-fixed to a sentence $\phi$ to form a new sentence. But then the prefixed operator may be dropped by way of abbreviation, leaving us with what sounds like the original sentence $\phi$ but differs from it in sense. (Lewis, 37–38)

Lewis then goes on to devote the remainder of his paper to devising an intuitively satisfactory truth conditional analysis of fiction sentences like (4) through (6). He proposes that such sentences be analyzed as counterfactuals. As he puts it, "what is true in the Sherlock Holmes stories is what *would be true* if those stories were told as known fact rather than fiction." (emphasis added) We are thus able to explain the fact that an assertive utterance of a sentence like (2) might be true.[5] After all, were the Conan Doyle stories told as known fact rather than fiction, it *would be true* that Sherlock Holmes lives at 221B Baker Street.

As Lewis acknowledges, the ellipsis account is unable to explain the (apparent) fact that sentences such as the following can be used to make true assertions/statements:

(7) Sherlock Holmes is a fictional character.
(8) Pegasus is a mythical horse.
(9) Santa Claus is an imaginary figure.

(We will return to these problematic cases later.)

Michael Devitt's (1981) account of fiction-talk is similar in spirit to Lewis's.[6] Devitt suggests that two distinct sentential operators are required, one (S) for story-telling and another (F) for statements made about fiction. The former is to be read as 'it is pretended that', the latter as 'in fiction'. He then claims that when one asserts 'Tom Jones is illegitimate' the sentence token is paraphrasable by 'F (Tom Jones is illegitimate)'. This token is true, provided that 'Tom Jones is illegitimate' appears in Fielding's novel. He further suggests that the speaker's communicative intentions determine whether or not a particular sentence token is to be construed as pre-fixed by a fictional (or story-telling) operator.[7]

## 4. A PROBLEM/SOME PROPOSED ALTERNATIVES

Rod Bertolet (1984a) and Kent Bach (1987) have both claimed that the ellipsis account of fiction-talk conflates *sentences* with the *statements* they are used to make. Bertolet claims that while a sentence such as (2) might be used to state the truth that, in the Conan Doyle stories, Holmes lives at 221B Baker Street, *the sentence itself* is not true (or false). Of sentences like (4) through (6), he writes:

> . . . these sentences *are not themselves true*, any more than a sentence such as 'I don't like him' is *itself* true. These sentences are neither true nor elliptical nor covert for the various and sundry things which might be said by uttering them. We might say that the speaker spoke elliptically, in that he uttered a sentence which does not itself represent what he was saying, but that is another matter. (Bertolet, 191)

Bach makes the same basic point when he claims that,

> ... there is really no need to suppose that the *sentence* 'Polonius was an old buffoon' should be read as 'In *Hamlet* Polonius was an old buffoon.' Rather the sentence is being used non-literally. The sentence is being used to state that in *Hamlet* Polonius was an old buffoon, but no special operator needs to be assigned to the sentence being used non-literally to make that statement. Of course a speaker could always make fully explicit what he means by including 'In *Hamlet*' in his utterance. (Bach, 216)

Despite the obvious similarities between the accounts of Bertolet and Bach, there are important differences. For Bach, sentences like (4) through (6) are *false*. On his view, all proper names, including those of fictional entities, are to be analyzed as meta-linguistic descriptions of the form *the individual named 'N'*, descriptions which are then subjected Russell's (1905) Theory of Descriptions. Sentences of the sort in question invariably come out false on account of a failed existence condition. For Bertolet, fiction sentences have *no truth value* — as is the case with non-eternal sentences generally.[8]

I agree with Bertolet and Bach that fiction sentences are not elliptical for sentences of the form *In such-and-such fiction, ...* Sentences (2) and (3) are not synonymous — not even when the former is uttered with the intention of saying something about the character in the Conan Doyle stories.[9] To suppose otherwise seems unintuitive, and there are no compelling reasons to suppose that intuitions here are misleading.[10] For as we will see, the data in question are easily explained *without* having to claim that the sentences in question are elliptical for sentences explicitly about the relevant fiction. However, I believe that fiction sentences can themselves be *true*, when relativized to the appropriate context; they are not invariably false or invariably without truth value. In this respect, I am in agreement with the advocate of the ellipsis account; I too would like to preserve (rather than explain away) the intuition that fiction sentences are capable of being true (or false).

## 5. AN ALTERNATIVE ACCOUNT OF FICTION TALK

Ideally, an account of fiction sentences like (4) through (6) would have the following three features. *First*, it would preserve (rather than explain away) the intuition that such sentences can indeed be true, when uttered in the appropriate sorts of conversational settings. Suppose a colleague writing on fiction sentences asks me whether Santa Claus lives at the North Pole or the South Pole. When I respond by assertively uttering (6), that *sentence* is true, given the conversational setting in which it was uttered.[11] I do not have to preface or suffix the sentence with the proviso, "according to the myth," in order for that sentence to emerge as true. *Second*, the account would preserve the intuition that such sentences are *not* elliptical for sentences explicitly about the relevant fiction. Although what I *mean* by an utterance of (2) might be made more explicit by an utterance of (3), the former is not elliptical for the latter: the sentences are not synonymous. And *third*, the account would avoid Meinongianism; it would avoid the postulation of entities that don't exist.

The following is such an account. Simple subject-predicate sentences, whether fictional or not, are interpreted and truth-evaluated *relative to a context* — which may be actual or counterfactual, real or imagined.[12] The context of interpretation[13] and evaluation is determined by the communicative intentions of the speaker, intentions which are, in "normal" cases, discernible to the hearer. (Some exceptions will be discussed below.) Sentence (1) is evaluated as true — when the context of interpretation is the actual/real world. Sentence (2) is evaluated as true — when the context of interpretation is a counterfactual/imagined one in which the Conan Doyle stories are told as known fact rather than fiction. But this does not entail that (2) *means* (3) — anymore than it entails that (1) means (10):

(10) *In the actual world*, Saul Kripke used to teach at Princeton.

Nor does the proposed view entail that the various objects and individuals imagined to exist (in a counterfactual context), have "being" of *any* sort. And why should it? One might suppose that to say (for instance) that sentence (2) is true relative to imagined context *c just is* to say that it expresses a *true singular proposition* relative to *c*: one to the effect that *a* lives at 221B Baker Street, where *a* is the non-existent (perhaps Meinongian) referent of "Sherlock Holmes." But as I will argue below, this is simply not the case. Not only does the contextually relativized sentence not express a true *singular* proposition, it does not express a *true* proposition. Indeed, it does not (so I shall argue) express any *proposition* at all — not if "propositions" are construed as abstract, structured, truth-conditional entities containing such things as objects and concepts, properties and relations. How, then, is the truth of (2) to be explained? Simply by appeal to the fact that *its truth conditions are satisfied*: were the Conan Doyle stories told as known fact rather than fiction, a true singular proposition *would have been* expressed.

## 6. EXTENDING THE ACCOUNT

One of the virtues of the proposed account is that it can easily be extended to handle a variety of different sorts of cases. In particular, it can be extended to handle the problematic fiction sentences mentioned by Lewis, certain cases of number-talk, and cases involving speakers mistaken about the ontological status of what they purport to be talking about.[14] Let's consider these in turn.

### *6.1. Problematic Cases of Fiction-Talk*

Consider again sentences (7) through (9).

(7) Sherlock Holmes is a fictional character.
(8) Pegasus is a mythical horse.
(9) Santa Claus is an imaginary figure.

Intuitively, to assertively utter any one of these sentences in the appropriate sort of context would be to say something true. But assertive utterances of their unellipsed counter-parts would not be true. For it is surely not true that, *according to the Conan Doyle stories*, Sherlock Holmes is a *fictional* character! How, then, are these sentences to be accommodated?

The proposed account would have no trouble handling these sentences. They are evaluated as true simply because they are interpreted relative to a context in which the names 'Sherlock Holmes', 'Pegasus', and 'Santa Claus' denote *fictional/mythical/imaginary* characters. Such sentences are *not* interpreted relative to the counterfactual contexts with respect to which sentences (4) through (6) are interpreted — contexts in which these "characters" are imagined to be *not fictional but real*. If they were interpreted relative to *those* contexts, they would of course be evaluated as false rather than as true.

Because the "ordinary man" tends to think that there are fictional and mythical characters,[15] he will insist that sentences like (7) through (9) express truths, even if the philosopher claims to have ontologically-motivated doubts. But even if the philosopher's doubts are well-founded, that does not mean that the sentences are other than true — *unless sentences can be true only when interpreted relative to the real world*. But I see no reason to suppose that this is so. A proof of the non-existence of abstract objects might convince someone that there are (in actuality) no abstract objects without *thereby* convincing him that contextually relativized sentences like (7) though (9) are anything other than true. How can this be? Perhaps the answer is simple: The context against which such sentences are interpreted, and according to which they are deemed true (or false), needn't be the actual world. In particular, the context in question will contain fictional and mythical characters, *even if the actual world does not*. If we adopt this sort of approach, we can still insist that sentences like (7) through (9) are true — even if we grant that the proof against abstract objects is a sound one.

*6.2. Number-Talk*

Consider the following three sentences:

(11) $2 + 3 = 5$
(12) There are many numbers.
(13) There is one even prime number.

Intuitively, assertive utterances of these sentences would express truths. But how can that be if, as the nominalist claims, numbers don't really exist? Well, perhaps the nominalist is wrong and numbers do exist, but even assuming they don't, we can explain the intuitions in question. Assertive utterances of number sentences are interpreted and truth-evaluated relative to a context in which numerals are assumed to refer. But does that explain the fact that the sentences are true? Yes — provided (as just suggested) that the operative notion of truth is one that allows relativization to counterfactual contexts. And surely it must be. After all, most — if not all — sentences that appear to be true are thought to be true — only given certain assumptions, assumptions that *could* (for all we know) be false. Does the fact that the world might not be as we take it to be pose any threat to the claim that the sentence 'Snow is white' is true? It does not appear to. Does the fact that our talk about mental states might be deeply confused have any tendency to make us question the truth of the sentence: 'OJ killed his wife out of jealously'? Surely not; the arguments of the eliminative materialist may well lend credence to his favored doctrine, but they do absolutely nothing to support O.J.'s claims of innocence. For to interpret those claims against a context *not* containing jealousy and other emotions (as ordinarily conceived) is to *misinterpret* those claims.

*6.3. Confusions Concerning Ontological Status*

Consider an assertive utterance of the following sentence:

(1) Saul Kripke used to teach at Princeton.

Suppose that the speaker thinks that Kripke is a *fictional* philosopher — the character in a particular work of fiction. In that case, his utterance should be interpreted and evaluated relative to an imagined context — one according to which the Kripke stories record known fact rather than fiction. But there are no Kripke stories of the relevant sort, and so the context to which the speaker is tacitly appealing does not exist. The utterance thus has no truth value. Intuitions to the effect that it expresses a truth are the result of supposing the intended context to be the real world — but by hypothesis this is not the intended context, even if the hearer might suppose it to be. The analogy would be to assertive utterances of sentences like (4) through (6), where the speaker is under the misimpression that the proper name is one of a real, rather than fictional, character. In that case, nothing is expressed by the sentence. For although the context to which the speaker is tacitly referring does exist in this case, it does not contain any individuals whose names occur in works of (pure) fiction.[16] This accounts for the intuition that there would be something odd about such utterances — that they do not express truths, at least not straightforward truths.[17]

## 7. OBJECTIONS AND REPLIES

### *7.1. No Truth Without Reference*

You say that sentences like (4) through (6) can be true when interpreted relative to the appropriate sort of context. But how can this be if the subject terms fail to refer? For if the subject terms fail to refer, it simply makes no sense to assume that, in assertively uttering such a sentence, a property is predicated of some object. In that case, how can *anything* be asserted — let alone something true?

The mistake here is to suppose that if such sentences are true, that can only be because *they express true propositions*. What *is* arguably true is that such sentences *would* express true (and presumably singular) propositions *were* the imagined context a real one. But this is precisely what makes the fiction sentence true, relative to the imagined context — that it *would* express a true (singular) proposition, *were* the imagined context a real one.[18] To respond that there is a true proposition that is *actually expressed* — one to the effect that, were the counterfactual context actual, a true singular proposition to such-and-such an effect would be expressed, is to confuse the truth conditions of a sentence with what the sentence expresses.[19] The sentence expresses no such proposition, though its assertive utterance no doubt conveys (pragmatically) that its truth conditions are satisfied.

What, then, are we to make of the intuition that, in cases of sentences like (2) and (4) through (6), a true singular proposition *is* expressed and (typically) grasped? In such cases, the intuition that such a proposition is expressed might be explained as the result of misconstruing what *would be* expressed under such-and-such conditions with what is *actually* expressed. We feel as though, in grasping what the speaker says, we are grasping the singular proposition that *would* be expressed under such-and-such conditions. But of course, we are grasping no such thing — for there is, by hypothesis, no entity to fill the subject position of the singular proposition allegedly expressed. In our less reflective moments, we might well overlook this fact — after all, genuine singular propositions — like the one expressed by (1) — have the same "phenomenological feel" as do "virtual" singular propositions of the sort seemingly expressed by sentences like (4) through (6).

*7.2. Wayward Intuitions*

It seems *obvious* that sentence (1) is true; it seems somewhat less obvious that sentence (2) is true. After all, although Kripke *really did* teach at Princeton, Holmes doesn't *really* live anywhere on Baker Street. How is this to be explained if sentence (2) is no less true than sentence (1)?

(1) Saul Kripke used to teach at Princeton.
(2) Sherlock Holmes lives at 221B Baker Street.

My response is two-fold. First, if sentence (2) does not seem obviously true, perhaps that's because it's not obvious to the hearer that the context of interpretation is an imagined one. Once this is made clear, as when the speaker says (something like) "I'm talking about the world of the Conan Doyle stories" — the truth of (2) becomes obvious. To attempt to challenge this by claiming that Holmes doesn't *really* live at 221B Baker Street, is simply to shift the context of interpretation from the counterfactual one where the stories are told as known fact, to the actual one, where they are told as fiction. The shift is effected by means of the intensifying expression "really" — an expression that implies that the real world is the world being talked about. Second, while (1) expresses a true singular proposition, (2) — though true — does not express *any* proposition, let alone a true one. This difference in expressed content no doubt contributes to the intuition that an assertive utterance of (1) is somehow "more true" than an assertive utterance of (2). (I elaborate on this point immediately below.)

*7.3. Is Counterfactual Truth Really Truth?*

In response to the proposed view, Kent Bach has asked (in personal correspondence):

> Why is truth with respect to a fictional circumstance truth? Why is counterfactual truth truth?

In response to the proposed view according to which counterfactual truth is to be understood as truth with respect to a context of interpretation, Bach remarks:

> Philosophers speak of truth with respect to a world or, following Kaplan, a circumstance of evaluation (this in the model of model theory, i.e., truth relative to a model). But when *people* say that something is true, they mean true, period. They don't mean true with respect to a world, not even the actual world.

My response to Bach is two-fold. *First*, I have no difficulty with the view that truth with respect to a fictional/counterfactual context of interpretation is — in a sense — not *genuine* truth. Indeed, it would seem that I am *committed to* something like a distinction between counterfactual and genuine truth, as I claim that sentences that are true (only) with respect to a counterfactual context of interpretation do not express truths — they do not express true propositions (or *any* propositions for that matter).[20] In this respect, such sentences contrast with sentences evaluated with respect to ordinary (factual) contexts — sentences which *do* arguably express propositions. In those cases, where the expressed proposition is true, the sentence that expresses it is nevertheless true only *relative to* a context of interpretation. However, because the context of interpretation is the real world, such sentences are (in a strong sense) *genuinely* true: they *represent the facts*, one might say.[21]

*Second*, I agree with Bach that when non-philosophers say that something is true, they mean true *period*. However, this does not mean that these speakers do not interpret and truth-evaluate sentences with respect to contexts of interpretation. In this particular respect, the case of counterfactual truth is not different from the case of truth involving sentences containing so-called "incomplete" quantifiers. When I say to my students "There's no chalk," and they interpret what I say as true, they do so only because they interpret the sentence uttered relative to a context not extending beyond the room in which I am lecturing. Nevertheless, in interpreting the sentence uttered as true, they think of it as being true, *period* — not as true *relative to* any context. These considerations suggest that ordinary speakers think in terms of sentence tokens, rather than sentence types. They accordingly construe true sentences as true *simpliciter*, rather than as true relative to a certain circumstance, world, or context. In contrast, the philosopher of language, in an attempt to get clear on just how our truth-evaluations are arrived at, draws a distinction between the sentence (type) uttered and the context of interpretation. He thus speaks of sentences being true *relative to* such-and-such a circumstance, world, or context.

### *7.4. Easy Truth*

Suppose we grant that sentences can be true when the context with respect to which they are interpreted is a counterfactual one. In that case, all sorts of obviously false sentences might emerge as true. Consider, for instance, a scenario where both the speaker and hearer are under the misimpression that the earth is flat. In that case, the sentence:

(14) The earth is flat.

would be true as uttered by the speaker. After all, it would surely express a truth were the imagined context a real one — were the world a place where the earth was flat.

The response here is simple. The sentence in question would not emerge as true because the context against which it is to be interpreted is the real world — a world *mistakenly believed* by the speaker and hearer to contain a flat earth. The real world is, after all, the intended context of interpretation. But suppose that speaker and hearer were aware of the facts, but were imagining that the facts were other than they are. In that case, the sentence 'The earth is flat' could indeed emerge as true.

But we are faced with a difficulty if we attempt to extend this line of reasoning. Suppose that there are no numbers, that there are no abstract objects — those who think otherwise are simply mistaken. This would appear to suggest that sentences like (11) through (13) are not necessarily true. In particular, it would seem to suggest that while such sentences would be true in the mouth of the *nominalist*, they would be false or untrue in the mouth of the *realist*. For the nominalist believes that there are no numbers, while the realist believes that there are. Thus, when the realist utters sentences (11) through (13) he says something false or untrue — *assuming the intended context of interpretation is the actual world*. (Since the realist thinks there really are numbers it is plausible to construe the intended context in this way.) The nominalist, in contrast, says something true when he utters those same sentences — *assuming the intended context is a counterfactual one in which numerals refer*. (Since the nominalist thinks there are no numbers, it is plausible to construe the intended context in this way.) But surely this is an undesirable consequence: the sentences should come out true in the mouths of *anyone* who assertively utters them.[22]

Although admittedly surprising, I don't believe this consequence to be an undesirable one. The ordinary speaker would presumably claim that the sentences in question were true *regardless of who utters them*, but the ordinary speaker has formed no opinion on whether or not there "really are" numbers. He is an "ordinary" speaker after all, not a metaphysician. So, how do we explain the ordinary speaker's truth-evaluation of (11) through (13) in view of this fact? By supposing that he regards the context of interpretation as one in which numerals are assumed to refer — *without a considered view as to whether this context is the actual world*. So, the ordinary speaker would claim that the sentences are true — whoever utters them. But if the realist philosopher takes himself to be making claims *about the actual world* when he asserts the sentences in question, then I think we must claim that what he says is *not* true, *assuming there are no numbers* — even though the ordinary speaker is bound to interpret him as saying something true.[23] For again, the ordinary speaker will simply assume that the context of interpretation and evaluation is one in which numerals refer, while remaining neutral on the issue of whether the context is the actual world. (To remain neutral on this issue is simply to remain neutral with respect to the nominalism/realism debate about numbers.) This may sound counter-intuitive, but on reflection it makes a lot of sense. After all, how is it different from claiming that an assertive utterance of (2) is untrue if the speaker purports to be talking about the real world?

### *7.5. The Indeterminacy of Imagined Contexts*

You talk of "imagined contexts" which are how things would be were the relevant fiction told as fact rather than fiction. But such contexts are obviously going to be indeterminate — and thus make for the possibility of indeterminate truth conditions. What, for instance, are we to make of an assertive utterance of a sentence like:

(15) Santa Claus has no siblings.

The context of interpretation is one in which the Santa Claus story records known fact rather than fiction. But in that context *does* Santa Claus have siblings? The stories don't say, so we cannot say whether (15) is true or false.

My response here is to concede the point, while denying that it is in any way problematic. Intuitively, (15) is not clearly true or false — precisely because the Santa Claus stories don't state or imply whether or not Santa Claus has siblings. I thus agree with Bertolet (1984b) when he writes:

> ... it will sometimes be difficult to determine whether what someone says by uttering a sentence 'about a fictional character' is true. But this *is* sometimes quite hard, and it is not obviously a defect in a view that it preserves this difficulty. Indeed, I should rather take it to be a defect in a view that it gave clear and unhedged answers to these questions when we are unclear and anxious to hide in the hedges. (Bertolet, p. 212)

## 8. CONCLUDING REMARKS

Ellipsis accounts of fiction-talk have their virtues. In particular, they preserve the intuition that fiction sentences are capable of being true *when uttered in the appropriate sorts of conversational settings.* Moreover, they preserve this intuition while avoiding Meinongianism.

The problem with such accounts is a simple one — there is no evidence for the view that sentences of the sort in question *are* elliptical for sentences explicitly about the relevant fiction. But the solution is not (*pace* Bertolet and Bach) to deny that the fiction *sentence* is true; that it's only the *statement* made that's true. Rather, it is to claim that the sentence can indeed be true provided it is interpreted relative to a counterfactual context in which the relevant fiction is told as fact rather than fiction. If the sentence would express a true (singular) proposition were the counterfactual context actual, then the sentence is true (relative to that context). But one can endorse these truth conditions without having to claim that fiction sentences are *elliptical for* sentences explicitly about the relevant work of fiction. Instead of positing hidden linguistic meaning, as does the ellipsis theorist, one need only relativize the sentence to the appropriate sort of context — a (counterfactual) context in which the relevant fiction is told as known fact.[24]

## NOTES

1 Some of the more obvious of these are pointed out by Lewis (1978).

2 Lewis's (1978) version of the ellipsis account is more subtle than this rather rough characterization of the account might suggest. See below for details.

3 I use these notions interchangeably, and distinguish statements/assertions from the sentences used to produce them.

4 This is just an *intuition* — which I take to be a pre-theoretical one. As is well known, some philosophers have argued that propositions/assertions/statements are the primary or sole bearers of truth. My point here is simply that, intuitively, *the sentences*, when uttered in the appropriate sorts of conversational settings, appear to be true. Rod Bertolet has pointed out to me (in personal correspondence) that the intuition that such sentences are true is not as strong as the intuition that the assertions/statements made are true. I agree with Bertolet here and think that the comparative weakness of our (pre-theoretical) intuitions concerning the truth-evaluability of sentences is due simply to the fact that the pre-theoretical notion of an assertion/statement is more familiar to us than is the pre-theoretical notion of a sentence. Unless we are philosophers of language (or grammarians), we talk and think far more frequently of assertions and statements than of sentences.

5 Or, as Lewis would put it, we are able to explain the fact that the *sentence* itself might be true.

6 However, there may also be important differences between the accounts of Lewis and Devitt. See note 9.

7 Lewis (1978, 38) claims that "content, context, and common sense" will generally suffice to make the intended interpretation clear.

8 Bertolet (1984a) considers and rejects the idea that fiction sentences can be true (or false) if *relativized to a context.*

9 It is important to bear in mind that when I speak of "sentence meaning," I am construing such meanings as *conventional*. To see this, suppose we were to adopt a notion of sentence meaning according to which sentence *tokens* are the primary bearers of semantic properties, and according to which the meaning of such sentences is determined at least partly by what the *speaker* means by the uttered token. This is the sort of view endorsed by Michael Devitt (1996). Given such a view, one might claim that while sentences like (2) and (3) are not synonymous if such meanings are thought of as *conventional*, they might well be synonymous if such meanings are thought of as contingent upon what the *speaker* means in uttering those sentences. The question to be answered (though not in this paper, alas) is: Which conception of sentence meaning is preferable? I assume throughout this paper a conventionally-based account of

sentence meaning. I would like to thank Michael Devitt for drawing my attention to this point (in personal correspondence).

[10] For more on this issue, see Bertolet (1984a).

[11] Of course, this would not preclude the possibility that the utterance, assertion/statement made, and proposition expressed are also true. The point is simply that, intuitively, *the sentence itself* — given the conversational setting in which it is uttered — is true.

[12] Predelli (1997) proposes a similar account, but there are significant differences in terms of scope, motivation, and content between the proposed account and Predelli's. In terms of scope, Predelli's account concerns names of *real* individuals, as those names occur in descriptions of counterfactual contexts. The proposed account, in contrast, concerns such names *as well as* names of purely fictional characters like Santa Claus, Sherlock Holmes, and Pegasus. For differences regarding motivation and content, see notes 14 and 20.

[13] The locution "context of interpretation" is borrowed from Predelli (1997) and, following Predelli, it is intended to contrast with the (Kaplanian) context of utterance. Although the two contexts coincide in ordinary cases, they diverge in cases of fiction-talk.

[14] Predelli (1997) motivates his account of fiction-talk (involving names of real individuals) by arguing that we need to distinguish between the context of interpretation and the context of utterance in order to explain and preserve our intuitions concerning certain cases involving indexical expressions. Thus, consider for instance, the following sentence, as it appears in a history text:

> It is May 1949. Germany outflanks the Maginot line. Now, nothing stands between Hitler's troops and Paris.

(The example is from Predelli.) In order to preserve our intuition that what the passage says is (or might be) true, the context *of interpretation* must be May of 1949.

[15] He can even give examples of some such creatures — Sherlock Holmes, Pegasus, Santa Claus. However, to say that the ordinary man believes that there are such things, is not necessarily to say that he believes that they *exist*. For the ordinary man has no trouble with the notion of there being things that don't exist. (See Reimer 2001a and 2001b) for details.

[16] Of course, the actual world will no doubt contain individuals with *homonymic* names.

[17] This suggests that Dummett (1983) is right when he complains that Evans (1982) fails to realize that reference to *x* is not possible unless the speaker *intends to refer* to *x*.

[18] And were the context in question the speaker's *intended* context of interpretation/evaluation.

[19] Strawson (1950) makes a similar point against Russell (1905). He claims that while Russell is correct to think that an assertion of 'The king of France is bald' is true just in case there is exactly one king of France and he is bald, he is wrong to think that the proposition expressed by the sentence is that there is exactly one king of France and he is bald.

[20] Predelli's account, in contrast to the proposed account, carries no such commitment.

[21] Thus, on the proposed view, sentence (3) — in contrast to sentence (2) — is genuinely true.

(2) Sherlock Holmes lives at 221B Baker Street.
(3) According to the Conan Doyle stories, Sherlock Holmes lives at 221B Baker Street.

Lewis's view entails that, uttered in the relevant sort of conversational setting, (2) is no less genuinely true than (3), as it is *synonymous with* that sentence. My intuitions, which I take to be widely shared, are that (3) is true in a way in which (2) is not. Such intuitions thus favor the proposed view over Lewis's.

[22] See Yablo (2000) for a similar point.

[23] It might be possible for a realist to drop his metaphysical convictions in non-philosophical talk, and say something true. For a similar point, see Yablo (2000).

[24] I would like to thank Kent Bach, Rod Bertolet, Michael Devitt, and Stefano Predelli for helpful comments concerning the topic of this paper.

## REFERENCES

Bach, K., *Thought and Reference*. Oxford: Clarendon Press. 1987.
Bertolet, R., "On A Fictional Ellipsis." *Erkenntnis* 21 (1984a): 189–194.
Bertolet, R., "Inferences, Names, and Fictions." *Synthese* 58 (1984b): 203–218.
Devitt, M., *Designation*. Cambridge, MA: MIT Press. 1981.
Devitt, M., *Coming to Our Senses*. Cambridge: Cambridge University Press. 1996.

Dummett, M., "Existence." In *Humans, Meanings, and Existences*, D. P. Chattopadhyaya (ed.) Delhi: Jadavpur Studies in Philosophy. 1983.
Evans, G., *Varieties of Reference*. Oxford: Oxford University Press. 1982.
Lewis, D., "Truth in Fiction." *American Philosophical Quarterly* 15(1) (1978): 37–46.
Predelli, S., "Talk about Fiction." *Erkenntnis* 46 (1997): 69–77.
Reimer, M., "A 'Meinongian' Solution to a Millian Problem." *American Philosophical Quarterly* 38 (2001): pp. 233–248.
Reimer, M., "The Problem of Empty Names." *Australasian Journal of Philosophy* 79 (2001): 491–506.
Russell, B., "On Denoting." *Mind* 14 (1905): 479–493.
Strawson, P.F., "On Referring." *Mind* 59 (1950): 320–344.
Yablo, S., "Go Figure: A Path Through Fictionalism." unpublished typescript, 2000.

STEVEN DAVIS

# QUINEAN INTERPRETATION AND ANTI-VERNACULARISM

It is common in ordinary conversation for participants to use non-sentences to communicate what they mean. Consider the following conversation:

1. Alice: Rain, again.
2. Sam: No picnic today.

One view about 2 is that it is really a sentence with missing parts and what Sam means can be captured by 3. What Sam means and Alice understands, then, is the proposition expressed by the full sentence

3. There'll be no picnic today.

On this view, to get at the proposition expressed and understood, Alice and Sam pass through the sentence, 3. So, we can say that it is 3 that wears the trousers; the proposition that Sam expresses in 2 is derivative. It depends on the proposition that 3 expresses. Not only is the proposition expressed in 2 derivative of 3, but so too is the proposition's logical form. The logical form of the proposition expressed in uttering 2 is just the logical form of 3. We can generalize this point and say that the logical form of all non-linguistic entities, propositions, mental states, etc. is derivative of the sentences that express them. An underlying assumption of this view is that only complete sentences express what speakers mean, even when they utter non-sentential phrases.

Another view, found in a recent paper of Ray Elugardo and Robert Stainton (henceforth, E & S), is that 3 is not available to Alice and thus, her grasping of the proposition expressed does not pass through 3. Moreover, the logical form of the proposition that Alice grasps in understanding what Sam means in uttering 2 does not depend on her recognizing the logical form of 3. It is has its logical form non-derivatively. To make this position plausible, E & S present an argument against the view in the previous paragraph that they call 'vernacularism' that they claim shows it to be false (E & S, 393).[1] I shall show that their argument does not establish their conclusion, but this leaves open which of the two hypotheses is correct.[2] Before turning to this argument and my criticism of it, I shall lay out E & S's considerable groundwork that leads up to their argument. As I shall show, it is not problem free. Let us begin with what E & S take vernacularism to be.[3]

> Logical forms are fundamentally assigned to expressions of natural language, and are only derivatively assigned to anything else: e.g., propositions, mental states, etc. (E & S, 394).



*R. Elugardo and R. J. Stainton (eds.), Ellipsis and Nonsentential Speech*, 217–235.

So vernacularism has it that propositions, **P**, and expressions, **E**, have logical forms and that the former has its logical forms derivatively from the latter.[4] I take the thesis to be that for every **P** there is an **E** of a natural language that is appropriately associated with **P**, perhaps by being expressed by **E**, such that **P**'s logical form is **E**'s logical form. As it stands, vernacularism is ostensibly a thesis about the relationship between sentences and propositions. What is key to understanding vernacularism is 'logical form' and 'derivatively.' Once we have before us E & S's gloss on these key notions, it will become evident that for E & S vernacularism is a psychological thesis about understanding that can be viewed as an epistemological hypothesis about how hearers come to know what has been said.

My first goal is to try to get a clear picture of what E & S take vernacularism to be. My strategy in this regard is to consider the key notions above and E & S's understanding of them. Once we are clear about their account of these notions, they shall be incorporated into vernacularism. My second goal is to lay out E & S's argument against vernacularism and their construal of it. When we have these before us, we shall have a further understanding of what E & S take to vernacularism to be. My third goal is to present criticisms of E & S's argument against vernacularism. Finally, I shall close with some remarks about what is at stake in the dispute between vernacularism and E & S's view. To anticipate my conclusion, I show, I believe, that E & S's arguments do not establish that vernacularism is false, but I remain open as to its truth or falsity.

There are three questions that arise with E & S's account of vernacularism above.

4. What is it for something to have a logical form?
5. What is the logical form that it has?
6. What is it to have a logical form derivatively?

Let us begin with E & S's answer to 4.

$\alpha$ has a logical form if and only if

7. $\alpha$ is capable of being true or false
8. $\alpha$ stands in structural entailment relations in virtue of its structure; and
9. An agent, [**S**], recognize[s] $\alpha$'s structural entailment relations in virtue of "the item's logico-structure" (E & S, 394).

It seems that in 8, 'structure' and in 9, 'logico-structure' just are $\alpha$'s logical form. So, 8 and 9 should read

10. $\alpha$ stands in structural entailment relations in virtue of its logical form.
11. **S** recognizes $\alpha$'s structural entailment relations in virtue of $\alpha$'s logical form.

This in turn gives us a partial answer to 5. For E & S, the logical form of $\alpha$ just is the structural properties of $\alpha$ by virtue of which it has its entailment relations and by virtue of which **S** recognizes these. Thus, something without such structure cannot have entailment relations.[5]

Let us consider 11, one of the conditions that E & S give for something's having a logical form and thus, part of their answer to 4. In 11, how is 'recognize' to be understood? E & S make the standard distinction between competence and performance and cash out recognition as a capacity, a competence, to assign entailment relations to sentences abstracting away from limitations of memory, time, etc. (E & S, 395). The parallel here, one would suppose, is with the competence-performance distinction applied to syntax in which speakers are taken to have tacit knowledge of their language's grammar that enables them to assign syntactic properties to the sentences of their language and to judge whether any given sentence is grammatical. A tacit grammar is not the capacity to assign syntactic structure to a sentence or to determine its grammaticality, for that would be a capacity to perform some mental act. Rather, a speaker's internalized tacit grammar contains the necessary information (tacit knowledge) for assigning a syntactic structure to a sentence and for determining whether the sentence is grammatical.

I do not think that the competence-performance distinction borrowed from Chomskyian linguistic meta-theory slides neatly over to entailment relations. For most sentences, whether a sentence is grammatical is determined by speakers' intuitions. There is no truth to the matter independently of these intuitions.[6] The same does not hold for entailment relations. What entailment relations a sentence has does not depend on speaker's intuitions, but on the sentence's logical features and the logical theory that is applied to it to give an interpretation of these features. Beginning students in logic are notorious for making simple logical errors, for example, affirming the consequent. And the work of Kahneman and Twersky show that subjects, even logically sophisticated subjects, systematically make logical mistakes in reasoning. The point is that intuitions of subjects about entailment relations do not exhaust the facts about these relations; there is a fact of the matter independent of these intuitions. Given this, a theory of the entailment relations of sentences cannot be constructed simply on the basis of intuitions.

As E & S recognize, their view can dispense with vexed question about the competence-performance distinction applying to entailment relations (E & S, 395, n. 6). They drop talk of the competence-performance distinction and replace it with a necessary condition for an expression's having a logical form. More precisely, they hold that

12. If $\alpha$ has a logical form, then if **S** recognizes $\alpha$'s entailment relations, then he does so (in part) by virtue of $\alpha$'s logical form.

A moment's reflection shows that 12 is false. Suppose that **S**, a non-speaker of English, is given a list of English sentences, including $\alpha$, paired with the sentences' entailment relations. Since **S** is not an English speaker, he does not understand the sentences. Let us suppose that he is able to recognize the sentences by their shape. Now, suppose further that **S** is given $\alpha$ and a list of sentences that includes $\alpha$'s entailment relations. **S** is asked to identify which sentences on the list are $\alpha$'s entailment relations, something that he is able to do, since he remembers the list's pairings. **S** has not matched $\alpha$ with its entailments by virtue of its logical form, since not understanding $\alpha$, he has no knowledge of its logical form. I believe that 12 can be repaired to avoid this counterexample without doing violence to E & S's intent.

13. If $\alpha$ has a logical form, then if S understands $\alpha$ and recognizes thereby $\alpha$'s entailment relations, then he recognizes them to be so (in part) by virtue of $\alpha$'s logical form.[7]

Let us turn to question 5. What do E & S take logical forms to be? They claim that

14. The logical form of $\alpha$ is that in virtue of which agents recognize $\alpha$'s structural entailment relations (E & S, 394).

14 too must be changed to accommodate the counterexample that I offered above against 12. As it stands, 14 would allow the shape of a sentence to be its logical form. Let me propose the following as a replacement for 14.

15. The logical form of $\alpha$ is that in virtue of which agents who understand $\alpha$ recognize thereby $\alpha$'s structural entailment relations (E & S, 395).

There are two questions that arise here:

16. What is to be included in the set of structural entailment relations?
17. What is that in virtue of which agents who understand $\alpha$ recognize thereby $\alpha$'s structural relations?

The structural entailment relations of something include what E & S call its *structural semantic and logical entailments* (E & S, 396). There are two sorts of entailment relations that E & S claim are excluded. First, they do not include an item's *meaning based entailments*, the entailment relationship, for example, between 18 and 19.

18. Sam knows that Quebec is a province.
19. Sam believes that Quebec is a province.

The relationship between 18 and 19 supposedly holds between the meaning of 'knows that' and 'believes that' that is not captured by what E & S regard the logical form of 18 to be. Second, E & S's notion of logical form does not account for the fact that all sentences that can be true or false entail every necessary truth (E & S, 395, n. 5). Third, it does not account for the necessity of sentences like,

20. Water is $H_2O$.

E & S claim that if 20 is necessary, it is so by virtue of "its semantic content, semantic meaning, or modal facts" (Ibid.). What is important, according to E & S, is that it is an "expression's structural properties" by virtue of which it has the logical form that it does. There is nothing in 20's structure that marks it as being necessary.

If I have understood E & S correctly, their claim is that expressions have their structural entailment relations by virtue of their structural properties and their structural properties are their syntactic constituent form. This does not mean that a syntactic constituent is the same as an element in logical form. But I think that it does mean the following: if an expression, $\alpha$, has an element, $\varphi$, in its logical form that plays a role in entailment relations, then there is a constituent structure of $\alpha$ that corresponds to $\varphi$. Given this, I am not sure I understand exactly what is being included or excluded in an expression's logical form. Consider the following pairs where the second represents the standard logical form of the first.[8]

21. Unicorns don't exist
22. $\sim (\exists x)(UX)$
23. All men are boring.
24. $(x)(Mx \supset Bx)$

The existential quantifier is a constituent of the logical form that 22 represents, but not of 21 and the material conditional is a constituent of the logical form represented by 24, but not of 23. In partial reply to this point, E & S claim that "EXISTENCE may be a higher order structural property of both [21 and 22]."[9] On E & S's view of structural property, this makes 'EXISTENCE' a syntactic constituent of 21. However, if 'constituent structure' is to make any sense, it must be related to syntactic theory. Let us assume that this can be made out for 21. Since there is no constituent structure in the surface form of 21 that corresponds to 'EXISTENCE,' 'EXISTENCE,' if it is a constituent of 21, must occur at some other level of syntactic structure than what is available in the surface structure of 21. That E & S accept such 'hidden' constituents will become important when we turn to their main argument. Even if we grant this, I think that E & S have a harder case to make with respect to 23. In no syntactic theory of which I am aware is there any constituent structure in 23 that corresponds to the material conditional; it might be argued that "All.... are....," does the trick, but "All.... are.... " is not a syntactic constituent of 23. This does not show that E & S are incorrect in their views about constituent structure and logical form, but a much longer story must be given than the one E & S have presented to make out the relationship.

Let us turn to questions 5 and its clarification in 17. The discussion so far does not tell us what logical forms are. E & S wish to remain silent on this question, since they claim that it is not important for their purposes to adjudicate among the different views on offer. For all E & S care, logical forms could fall into a range of ontological categories. E & S maintain that what is important for their central argument is to determine "when it's correct to say that a thing *has* a logical form." (E & S, 394, n. 2) As we have seen, something has a logical form if it has structural entailment relations by virtue of having constituent structure and it is by virtue of recognizing this constituent structure that an agent recognizes the items structural entailment relations.

This now brings us to the next question, question 6, what is it for something to have its logical form derivatively? As we shall see, it is E & S's answer to this question that turns vernacularism into a psychological thesis. Recognition plays a role in E & S's account of what it is for something to have its logical form derivatively.

> If, in order to recognize the entailment relations of $\alpha$ an agent must find some other item $\beta$ that has logical form, then $\alpha$ does not have its logical form fundamentally. Rather, $\alpha$ has its logical form derivatively from $\beta$. In contrast, if a hearer can recognize the entailment relations of $\alpha$ without finding any other logical form-bearing item $\beta$, $\alpha$ has its logical form non-derivatively (E & S, 398).[10]

This is not meant as an analysis of the pair 'derivative/fundamental,' but is supposed to serve as a psychological test for "$\alpha$ gets its logical form from $\beta$" (E & S, 397 and 398, n. 8). I am not sure that I understand this. If something has a logical form, I would suppose that it has that logical form essentially. For E & S, a thing's logical form is a function of its constituent structure. Imagine that a sentence, $\alpha$, has constituent structure $\Phi$, and thus, logical form $\Psi$. Could a sentence be $\alpha$ and not have logical form

$\Psi$? If the sentence did not have $\Psi$ as its logical form, then it must have a different constituent structure. But if it did not have $\Phi$ as its constituent structure it could not be $\alpha$, since sentences have their constituent structures essentially. The same argument can be used for anything that has logical form and thus, on E & S's view has constituent structure, to show that it has its logical form essentially. If this is the case, nothing that has a logical form can 'get' its logical form from anything else. Although things that have logical form do not get them from anything else, it might well be the case that agents only recognize the logical form of one class of entities by recognizing the logical form of another class of entities. This, I believe, is how E & S's derivative/fundamental distinction should be understood. It is a distinction that applies to how agents recognize the logical forms of entities and thereby distinguish among entities that have logical forms.

Let us reconsider E & S's description of vernacularism.

> Logical forms are fundamentally assigned to expressions of natural language, and are only derivatively assigned to anything else: e.g., propositions, mental states, etc. (E & S, 394).

Before incorporating the distinction between derivative/fundamental into this account, one matter must be cleared up. Talk of 'assigning logical forms' seems to me to be confused. According to E & S, sentences and propositions have their logical form by virtue of their constituent structures. But constituent structures are not assigned to sentences or propositions (who or what would do the assigning), since as I have noted, they have their constituent structures essentially. I think that a better way to put E & S's point is to talk about sentences and propositions having logical forms. Another reason for making this emendation is that it connects up with E & S's discussion of what it is for an entity to have a logical form.

The derivative/fundamental distinction plays a key role in E & S's vernacularism. In light of their account of the distinction, we can restate vernacularism. Vernacularism presupposes that a range of entities have logical forms, including natural language expressions, propositions and mental states, but it differentiates between entities that have logical form by the way that agents recognize their logical forms. Agents recognize the logical forms of natural language expressions that have logical forms without recognizing the logical forms of any other entities, while they recognize the logical forms of other entities, propositions etc., by recognizing the logical form of some other class of entities.[11] Seen in this light, E & S's vernacularism is a psychological thesis that distinguishes classes of entities by virtue of how agents recognize their logical forms. Moreover, it plays a role in the epistemology of understanding, since it is part of an account of how hearers understand what is said. Combining these point and my remarks about 'assigning logical forms,' we can recast vernacularism in the following way:

25. $\alpha$, an expresson of a natural language, is such that it has a logical form and if **S** recognizes its logical form, then he does not do so by first recognizing the logical form of any other ontological different kind of entity.[12]
26. $\beta$, a proposition, etc., is such that it has a logical form and if **S** recognizes its logical form, then he does so by first recognizing the logical form of some other ontological different kind of entity.

We can simplify 25 and 26 by supposing that **S** recognizes the logical form of the expression or proposition in question, that is, knows what it is. This gives us

27. $\alpha$, an expresson of a natural language, is such that it has a logical form and **S**, who recognizes its logical form, does not do so by first recognizing the logical form of any other ontological different kind of entity.
28. $\beta$, a proposition, etc., is such that it has a logical form and **S**, who recognizes its logical form, recognizes it by first recognizing the logical form of some other ontological different kind of entity.

27 and 28, respectively, are about expressions of natural language and propositions that have logical forms. As we have seen, the following is a necessary condition for something's having a logical form.

29. If $\alpha$ has a logical form, then if **S** understands $\alpha$ and recognizes thereby $\alpha$'s entailment relations, then he recognizes them (in part) by virtue of $\alpha$'s logical form.

In turn, the logical form of something is that by virtue of which an agent recognizes the thing's structural entailment relations.

30. The logical form of $\alpha$ is that in virtue of which **S** who understands $\alpha$ recognizes thereby $\alpha$'s structural entailment relations (E & S, 394) .

Putting these together we obtain,

31. If $\alpha$ has a logical form, then if **S** understands $\alpha$ and recognizes thereby $\alpha$'s entailment relations, then he recognizes them (in part) by virtue of that in virtue of which **S** who understand $\alpha$ recognizes thereby $\alpha$'s structural entailment relations.

According to E & S, agents recognize an entity's structural entailment relations by virtue of its syntactic constituent structure. This then gives us,

32. If $\alpha$ has a logical form, then if **S** understands $\alpha$ and recognizes thereby $\alpha$'s entailment relations, then he recognizes them (in part) by virtue of $\alpha$'s constituent structure.

Let us make the simplifying assumption with respect to 32 that we made with respect to 25 and 26 and suppose that there is some agent, **S**, who understands $\alpha$ and thereby recognizes its entailment relations. From this and 32, it follows that

33. If $\alpha$ has a logical form, then **S**, who understands $\alpha$ and recognizes thereby $\alpha$'s entailment relations, recognizes them (in part) by virtue of $\alpha$'s constituent structure.

Let us incorporate 33 into 27 and 28 to yield a revised version of vernacularism.

34. $\alpha$, an expresson of a natural language, is such that it has a logical form and **S**, who understands $\alpha$ and recognizes its logical form by virtue of it constituent structure, does not recognize its logical form by first recognizing the logical form of any other ontological different kind of entity.

35. β, a proposition, etc., is such that it has a logical form and **S**, who understands β and recognizes its logical form, recognizes it by first recognizing the logical form of some other ontological different kind of entity by virtue of its consituent structure.

According to E & S, vernacularism[13] plays a role in certain views about conversation. There are two sorts of cases that I shall consider.[14] Suppose a speaker, **S**, utters **E**, which has **P** as its semantic value, and in doing so means that **P**.[15] A hearer, **H**, understands what **S** means in uttering **E**, if he understands that **S** means that **P**. How does **H** do this? By assigning **E** its semantic value, **P**, **H** is able to infer that in uttering **E S** meant that **P**. For **H** to understand **P**, he must understand its logical form. In this case, the logical form of **P** is the logical form of **E**. Thus, the logical form of **P** is not fundamental, since **S** comes to recognize the logical form of **P** by recognizing the logical form of **E**.

There are cases involving ellipsis in which the semantic value of **E** does not yield what **S** meant. Suppose that **S** utters the following two sentences, meaning by the first, **Q** and by the second, **R**.

36. John weighs more than Bill.
37. John plays the piano and so too does Bill.

Since 36 and 37 are cases of ellipsis, we can say that **S** implicitly meant respectively that

38. John weighs more than Bill weighs. **[Q]**[16]
39. John plays the piano and Bill plays the piano. **[R]**

To understand that in uttering 36, **S** meant that **Q** and in uttering 37, **S** meant that **R**, **H**, then, supplements the sentences uttered yielding 38 and 39. Next, he assigns a semantic interpretation to 38 and 39 resulting in each case in a hypothesis about what **S** meant that is captured by 38 and 39. For **H** to understand what **S** meant in the two cases, he must recognize the logical forms of respectively, **Q** and **R**. He does this by recognizing the logical forms of 38 and 39. Since these sentences express **Q** and **R**, respectively, **S** recognizes the logical forms of the latter by first recognizing the logical forms of these sentences. Consequently, **Q** and **R** do not have their logical forms fundamentally. Supplementation is not the only method at **H**'s disposal that he can use to determine what **S** means. Imagine that **S** is at a party and that Al is putting forth some wild theory about the war in Kosovo. **S** picks up a banana that everyone can see and points to the banana and then to Al. In so doing, **S** means that Al is crazy. To arrive at the correct interpretation of what **S** meant in pointing to the banana and then to Al, **H** does not supplement **S's** action. Rather, he hypothesizes that what **S** meant implicitly is captured by the English sentence

40. Al is crazy.

**H**, then, assigns 40 a semantic value to arrive at a hypothesis about what **S** meant in pointing to the banana and then pointing to Al. The way in which logical form enters into this case is similar to the role it plays in the previous case.

To summarize, there are two sorts of cases in which vernacularism plays a role. The simple case is one in which **S** utters **E** meaning that **P** and the semantic value of **E** is **P**.

By understanding **E**, **H** forms the hypothesis that **S** means that **P**. The more complicated case is one in which **S** utters **E** and means that **P**, but the semantic value of **E** is not **P**. In this case, **H** finds an **E**′, the semantic value of which he takes **S** to have implicitly meant, assigns it a semantic value, thus, understanding **E**′ and thereby, recognizing its logical form. In doing so, he forms the hypothesis that **S** means that **P**. In both cases the assumption (vernacularism) is that for every **E**, that **S** utters in meaning that **P**, there is, available to **H**, an **E**′, which can be equal to **E**, the semantic value of which is **P** that **S** meant either explicitly or implicitly in uttering **E**. Moreover, **H** comes to recognize the logical form of **P** by virtue of recognizing the logical form of **E**′ and hence, **P** does not have its logical form fundamentally. This, of course, does not show that vernacularism is true; all that it shows is that there are some cases to which vernacularism appears to apply, cases in which hearers recognize the logical forms of propositions by first recognizing the logical forms of sentences. Thus, these propositions do not have their logical forms fundamentally. The question is whether vernacularism applies to all cases of a hearer's understanding a proposition.

What E & S wish to show is that 35 is false by showing that there are cases in which **H** understands what **S** means in uttering **E**, namely, **P**, and thus, comes to recognize the logical form of **P** without **H** first recognizing the logical form of any other entity. That is, E & S wish to show that there are cases of propositions that have their logical form fundamentally. As E & S put it, "[**H**] need not assign the logical form to [**P**] by recovering some item of language that encodes [**P**]. He can do so directly . . . ." (E & S, 402). Let us turn to E & S's main argument against vernacularism, an argument that I found very surprising. The reason for my surprise is that E & S's argument starts with what appears on the surface to be a Quinean premise and ends with a conclusion that affirms the existence of propositions! E & S claim to have shown that there are things other than natural language expressions that have their logical form fundamentally (E & S, 406). There are two parts to E & S's presentation of their argument: first, the argument and their gloss of it and second, their defense of their argument against various objections. Let us begin with E & S's argument and their interpretation of it. By looking at these closely, we shall see that it calls for a further revision of what E & S take vernacularism to be.

E & S imagine two characters, Alice and Bruce, who have had a discussion about whether there are coloured things and who resume their discussion several days later. They have forgotten the exact words they used in their previous discussion,[17] although they remember what is at issue between them, namely, whether there are colored objects.

| | | |
|---|---|---|
| 41. Alice (picking up a red pen): | (A) | Red. |
| | (B) | Right? |
| Bruce nods[18] | | |
| Alice: | (C) | Red things are colored things. |
| | (D) | Right? |
| Bruce nods | | |
| Alice: | (E) | So Bruce, there is at least one colored thing |
| | (F) | This thing. (E & S, 402–403) |

E & S claim that in (A)–(F), Alice is giving an argument in which (A) and (C) are premises and (E) and (F), the conclusions. As a consequence, (A) and (C), since they are steps in an argument, have logical forms. Moreover, E & S maintain that given

Bruce's replies, he understands Alice's argument and thereby, recognizes that (A) and (C) are premises in the argument and have logical forms.

How does Bruce understand what Alice meant and the argument that she presents in 41? E & S concentrate their attention on (A). they argue that

> Bruce did not recover any sentence in understanding Alice. What he did, instead, was to understand the predicate 'red', and apply its meaning to the salient object, the pen in Alice's hand. Doing this, he came to grasp a proposition. And that proposition has a logical form (E & S, 403).

If this is in fact what Bruce did, then Bruce understands what Alice meant in uttering 'red' and recognizes the logical form of the proposition that she meant without first recognizing the logical form of a sentence.[19] This, however, does not show that vernacularism in 35 is false, since 35 has it that for a proposition to have its logical form fundamentally an agent must not recognize its logical form by recognizing the logical form of any other entity. But Bruce does recognize the logical form of the proposition that Alice meant by understanding 'red.' It is by doing so that he understands the proposition that Alice meant and supposedly thereby recognizing the logical form of the proposition. Doesn't Bruce recognize the logical form of the proposition that Alice meant in uttering 'red' by first recognizing the logical form of 'red'? Isn't this sufficient to show that (A) is not a counterexample to 35? It isn't, since what Alice uttered is the word, 'red' and its logical form, if it has one, cannot be the logical form of the proposition that Alice meant in uttering 'red.' The reason is that the proposition that Alice meant has a truth-value and whatever 'red' expresses it is the wrong logical category to have a truth value and thus, cannot have the same logical form as the proposition that Alice meant (E & S, 408 and 411).

This calls for a reinterpretation of vernacularism, or at least that part of vernacularism, 35, against which E & S wish to argue. To show 35 to be false, then, we must find a case of a subject's coming to recognize the logical form of a proposition, **P**, without first, understanding another entity and thereby recognizing the logical form of this entity *that has the same logical form as **P***. It is not, moreover, just sameness of logical form that E & S seem to have in mind. E & S suggest that Bruce's route to understanding the proposition that Alice meant in uttering 'red' is not by "... recovering some item of language which encodes the proposition." (E & S, 402). This seems to suggest a stronger version of vernacularism that can be incorporated by modifying 35 in the following way:

42. $\beta$, a proposition, etc., is such that **S** understands $\beta$ by understanding a natural language sentence, $\alpha$, that expresses $\beta$, in part by recognizing the logical form of $\alpha$ by virtue of its constuent structure.

Let us reexamine E & S's argument against vernacularism and the background conditions that apply to it. According to E & S, Bruce understands

43. What proposition Alice expresses in uttering 'red' in 41(A). [Let us call this proposition **P**]
44. That **P** is a premise in an argument.
45. That **P** has implications for whether there are coloured things.
46. That **P** has a logical form.
47. What logical form that **P** has (E & S, 402–403).

There are several conditions that E & S place on how Bruce understands 'red.' E & S contend that

48. All the evidence that Bruce uses in understanding 43–47 is in 41 and in what he can remember of his previous conversaton with Alice.
49. Bruce does not have to wait until the end of Alice's argument to understand what Alice means in uttering 'red'.
50. There is no English language sentence that is available to Bruce that he used in understanding 43–47 (E & S, 403).

Clearly, if Bruce understands 43 and 47 and 50 is true, then vernacularism as in 42 is false. Let us grant E & S that Bruce understands 43 and 47.[20] It is 50 that has to be established. I shall examine the two arguments that E & S give for 50. I shall find them wanting. Then, I shall present a Quinean argument for the falsity of 50.

One argument for 50 is E & S's claim that

> If Bruce had recovered a sentence, it would be easy for *him* to say which sentence it was. And yet it surely cannot be denied that Bruce may be perfectly unable to pick "the" sentence he recovered (E & S, 14).[21]

I find this implausible. I would imagine that if Bruce were asked at any point in his conversation with Alice what she meant, say, when she utters 'red' in 41(A), he would be able to say what she meant. I would also think that the form of his report would be something like

51. Alice meant that **P**

where **P** is a sentence that would express what Bruce thought Alice meant. Why wouldn't this be the sentence that Bruce uses in understanding what Alice meant in uttering 'red' in 41(A)? In reply to this, E & S could say that the dialogue between Alice and Bruce is a thought experiment in which it can be imagined that Bruce cannot come up with a sentence that reports what Alice meant (E & S, 402). So, we appear to be trading intuitions.

Let us grant E & S their intuition. Why should it follow from this that he is not using a sentence in recovering what Alice meant? I believe that E & S have another principle with which they are operating, namely, that anything that Bruce uses in understanding Alice must not be something that is consciously available to him. The reason that E & S give for this assumption is that they take vernacularism to be committed to

> restrict[ing] the relevant mental states involved in communication to public language things, e.g., dispositions to utter, affirm, deny, etc., public language sentences. On [the vernacularist's] view, positing tacit mental states, which cannot be analyzed as public linguistic dispositions, is out of the question (E & S, 409, n. 18)

Let us call this the *availability principle*.[22] E & S claim that "some philosophers tacitly hold Vernacularism, which is enough to take it seriously even if no one ever explicitly endorsed it" (E & S, 398–399, n. 11). But on E & S's view of vernacularism, it would commit these philosophers to the availability principle. One of the philosophers that E & S cite as having a view close to vernacularism is J. J. Katz who certainly does not hold the availability principle. Leaving this aside, since vernacularism is not held by anyone explicitly, what it is is up for grabs. Consequently, E & S can set any conditions they wish for it, including the availability principle along as they are consistent. In their description of vernacularism, E & S, however, commit it to the utilization of tacit mental states in accounting for understanding. On their account of vernacularism, a subject understands a proposition by his understanding a sentence that expresses the proposition. In understanding the sentence, the subject makes use of the sentence's logical form that he recognizes by virtue of its constituent structure. But most speakers, I would suppose, have no conscious knowledge about the logical form or the constituent structure of the sentences that they understand. Logical forms and constituent structures are not readily available to speakers and they cannot be analyzed as dispositions of the sort to which E & S make reference in the availability principle.[23] What we can conclude is that either E & S give up the availability principle as a condition on vernacularism or they drop vernacularism's appeal to logical form and constituent structure in a subject's understanding a proposition. It is difficult to see how E & S could give up the second of these, since it is central to their view about how subjects understand sentences and propositions. But if the availability principle is given up, then E & S's argument against vernacularism that we are considering here is open to the criticism above.

E & S's second argument for 50 goes through 48. E & S contend that the evidence available to Bruce is not sufficient for him to pick out from 52, 53 or a range of other sentences, compatible with the evidence, which sentence is *the* sentence that captures what Alice meant in uttering 41(A).

52. This thing is red.
53. This is red.

E & S raise questions about what warrant Bruce has for including 'thing,' 'this,' and 'is.' Why include in a report of what Alice meant, ask E & S, 'thing' rather than 'object' or 'doohickey,' 'be' instead of 'instantiate' or 'exemplify' and 'this' rather than 'the pen in my hand' (E & S, 404–405)? E & S claim that there is no good reason for any of these choices. I think that there is, if we consider more closely the evidence that Bruce has at hand. Let us assume with E & S that in uttering 'red,' Alice has uttered a word. In understanding the word, Bruce has access to the dictionary entry of 'red.' Among the entries is $[_{\text{adj.}}\text{red (x)}]$; on this reading 'red' is a one place predicate. In addition, Bruce understands that by picking up the pen, Alice is demonstrating the pen. Further, Bruce knows that acts of demonstrating can be linguistically realized by English speakers in conjunction with a use of 'this' or 'that.' Since the item is in Alice's hand and thus proximate, Bruce can opt for 'this,' rather than 'that,' as a demonstrative that he can suppose that Alice could have used in the circumstance, accompanied by her demonstrating the pen. This hypothesis, then, leads him to select the adjective reading of 'red.' With this, he now has 'Red(that).' Moreover, Alice's demonstration is of something that presently is red. So, Bruce can conclude that what Alice wants to express is a thought that refers to the present. This is indicated sententially, given 'Red(that),' by present tense affixed to 'be,' yielding 53. Of course, Bruce could have arrived at a more complicated hypothesis on the basis of the evidence that he has available.[24] But there is no reason to suppose that his ability to understand is not constrained by a principle of simplicity.[25]

Let us for sake of argument suppose that there is some English sentence, **R**, that expresses the proposition, **P**, that Alice meant in uttering 'red' in 41(A) and that Bruce is capable of formulating **R** given his linguistic capacities. Now, E & S take it that Bruce has sufficient evidence to understand what Alice meant in uttering 'red,' namely **P**, but not sufficient evidence for him to recognize **R**. One would think that if the evidence that Bruce has is sufficient for him to recognize **P**, it is sufficient for him to recognize **R**, the sentence that by supposition expresses **P**.[26] If it is not, then a reason has to be given to show why it is not. There are a number of ways to defeat the criticism. One way would be to argue that there is a difference in the evidence that Bruce needs to determine **P** from the evidence that he needs to determine **R**. The evidence, one might claim, could be sufficient for Bruce uniquely to determine the former, but not uniquely to determine the latter. There might well be this sort of difference, but more has to be said than what E & S have presented to make out a difference. Another way to defeat my argument is to say that even though there is as much evidence for Bruce to determine **P** as **R**, it does not follow that Bruce uses **R** in his recognizing **P**. This, I believe, misses the point of my criticism. I am not trying to show that vernacularism is true, that Bruce uses an understanding of **R** in his understanding of **P**. What I am trying to show is that E & S's argument against vernacularism that turns on what evidence that Bruce has available is not conclusive. Thus we can conclude that if we grant E & S's assumption that given the evidence that Bruce has available he can determine **P**, then from the same evidence he can determine **R**. If this is not the case, then E & S owe us an explanation for why it is not the case.[27]

E & S's claim is that the evidence available to Bruce in the conversation does not enable him to choose from among a range of incompatible sentences which unique sentence among them expresses what Alice means in uttering 'red.'[28] What we have here is similar to Quine's indeterminacy of translation. Let us assume that Quine is correct in claiming that translation of terms is indeterminate and that in interpreting what someone says we are in the position of radical interpreters.[29] Let us apply this to the conversation in 41. Bruce is to be the linguist whose job it is to interpret Alice and Alice is his native informant. Let us assume that E & S are right about Bruce. He has no evidence for choosing among a range of equally good translations for 41(A) and for the other premises and conclusion of 41. What E & S rightly rule out is that this set of possible translations of 41(A) collectively determines the logical form of what Alice communicated in uttering 41(A) (E & S, 408–409). But what they have not ruled out is that from a set of equally good translation schema Bruce decides on a schema of radical translation and with it a translation and logical form for 41(A) that carries with it an assignment of a logical form for the rest of the sentences in 41.

Let us look more closely at the grounds that E & S give for ruling out the set of equally good translations of 41(A) as determining collectively the logical form for 41(A). E & S claim that the reason that there is a set of sentences that are equally good paraphrases of 41(A) is that each member of the set is close in meaning to the proposition that Alice expresses in uttering 41(A), a proposition that cannot be captured by any of the equally good sentential paraphrases of 41(A). But this, it seems to me, begs the question against the Quinean move here. Notice that if this were a legitimate move, then Quine's argument for indeterminacy of translation could be defeated by a similar strategy. All one would have to do is to say that 'Gavagai' expresses a proposition, but not one that can be captured by any sentence available to the linguist or native informant! Since I do not think that the indeterminacy of translation can be so easily defeated, I do not think that E & S's argument for there being propositions that have their logical form non-derivatively is successful.

E & S have a move against the criticism that I raised above. They could claim that their anti-vernacularism is not Quinean indeterminacy of translation. In their own defense, E & S could say that all that they are claiming is that in the context of the conversation in 41 there is no sentence that is available to Bruce that expresses what Alice means in uttering 41(A), a sentence that plays a psychological role in Bruce's interpreting what she meant. But this does not rule out the possibility that there is a sentence in some language or other that expresses exactly what Alice meant in uttering 41(A), but it is not a sentence to which Bruce has access. This sentence, then, would be an exact specification of what Alice meant in uttering 41(A).[30] Quine's thesis is more radical. Quine's claim is that there are equally good translation manuals, compatible with all possible evidence, for translating Alice's utterance of 41(A) and of the countless other expressions she has uttered, will utter and could utter. Hence, there is no possible evidence that could yield a choice of one translation that is *the* correct translation into a sentence of what Alice meant in uttering 41(A). E & S do not seem to rule out the possibility that there could be evidence that Bruce could bring to bear to determine exactly what Alice meant in uttering 41(A), only that this evidence is not available to Bruce in the circumstance in which he understands what Alice meant. So possible evidence can play no psychological role in Bruce's understanding of what Alice meant.

There is a similarity, however, between Quine's thesis of indeterminacy of translation and E & S's anti-vernacularism. I understand E & S's claim to be that in the context of the conversation, there is no evidence that is psychologically available to Bruce that would determine what Alice meant by her utterance of 41(A).[31] There is compatible, then, with the evidence *available* to Bruce, not all possible evidence, as Quine would have it, a set of translation manuals that yield incompatible translations of 41(A). In the context of his understanding Alice, there is no principled way for Bruce to choose among the translation manuals. Hence, what Alice meant in uttering 41(A) is indeterminate. What E & S's reply to my Quinean considerations does not rule out is that Bruce *operates* with one translation manual from among the set of psychological available translation manuals and uses this in interpreting what Alice means in uttering the expressions in 41. It would not have to be the case that the translation manual is consciously available to Bruce in his interpreting Alice's utterance of 'red' and her other utterances in 41, no more than it is the case that the syntax of Bruce's idiolect has to be consciously available to him in his use and understanding of the expressions in 41.[32] So it would not be the *set* of translation manuals that would assign a sentence to Alice's utterance of 41(A), yielding what Alice meant in uttering it, but one translation manual among the set, a translation manual that Bruce uses tacitly in interpreting what Alice meant. Hence, even if we accept E & S's claim that there is no evidence available to Bruce in the context of the conversation for uniquely determining a translation of Alice's utterance of 41(A), anti-vernacularism does not follow.

E & S have a Quinean rejoinder to my argument. We, as theoreticians, are in exactly the same position with respect to Bruce as he is with Alice. On the basis of the available evidence about Bruce's behavior, we can construct different theories about how he understands Alice, that is, different theories about what translation manual with which he is operating that are incompatible with one another, but that are compatible with the evidence that we have about Bruce's conversational behavior with Alice. Since for Quinean reasons, there is no fact of the matter about what Alice means; there is equally no fact of the matter about what translation manual with which Bruce is operating in understanding Alice. I think that this problem can be resolved. Let us allow Bruce to become the theoretician, or better yet let us become Bruce. We then have before us a range of translation manuals and we use one of them to go from Alice's utterance of 'red' to the sentence on that translation manual that we take to express what she means. No anti-vernacularism yet. But of course the one we have chosen to use in this instance is not the one which we need to use; we could have used any of the others. But for any one we choose, we end up with a sentence that we take to express what Alice means. Still, no anti-vernacularism. Let us go back to Bruce. We have no principled way to determine with which translation scheme he is operating. But for anyone we choose to attribute to him, we do not get anti-vernacularism. All the translation schemes with which he could be operating yield a sentence as the one he would take to express what Alice meant. Since none of the possible translation manuals that we could attribute to Bruce as the one with which he is operating in understanding Alice fails to yield a sentence as expressing what Alice means in uttering 'red,' we are still left without an argument for anti-vernacularism.

I want to take a step back from a consideration of E & S's arguments against vernacularism and consider what is at stake. As we have seen, for E & S vernacularism is a thesis about understanding. It claims that

54. If **H** understands what **S** means, namely, the proposition, **P**, in uttering the non-sentence, **r**, then he does so by first understanding some sentence, **R**, that in the context has **P** as its semantic value.[33]

E & S have what we might call a direct view about how hearers understand non-sentences.

55. If **H** understands what **S** means namely, the proposition, **P**, in uttering the non-sentence, **r**, then he does so directly and not by first understanding some sentence, **R**, that in the context has **P** as its semantic value.[34]

There is no reason why E & S's view must be restricted to hearers and cannot be applied to speakers as well. When Alice utters 'red,' she performs a speech act; she expresses the proposition, **P**, that she intends to communicate to Bruce. In extending E & S's view to Alice, we can suppose that in having the requisite intentions for performing the speech act and expressing the proposition, she need not use a sentence in formulating her speech act and communicative intentions. That is to say, no sentence of English need float through her head either consciously or unconsciously for her to perform the speech act. By extending E & S's view to speakers, it should no longer be construed to be limited to a thesis about understanding, but must also be seen as a hypothesis about speech acts and communication. Correspondingly, vernacularism need not be formulated as a thesis solely about hearers; it too can be extended to speakers and the acts they perform in uttering non-sentences. Thus, we have two opposing views about the use and the understanding of communicative linguistic acts.

Competence, we can say, is knowledge, either tacit or conscious, about a particular domain; performance is the use of this competence on a particular occasion.[35] A theory of competence of a domain is a specification of the knowledge with respect to the domain that is constitutive of that competence; a theory of performance is an account of how this knowledge is used on particular occasions. Chomsky introduced the distinction between competence and performance to draw attention to the distinction between a speaker's tacit knowledge of his language, his grammar, and his use of this knowledge on particular occasions. On this view of competence, a linguist's grammar is a theory of the syntactic, phonological and semantic knowledge that speakers of a particular language have about their language and a theory of performance is an account of how speakers use this knowledge in understanding and speaking their language.

Does the competence/performance distinction in Chomsky's sense play a role in the dispute between E & S and the vernacularist?[36] Let us return to E & S's thought experiment and the conversation between Bruce and Alice. E & S claim that when Alice utters 'red,' Bruce does not have available to him any sentence that expresses what Alice means, but despite this, he understands what she means. Vernacularism argues that Bruce does have available a sentence that plays a role in his understanding what Alice means. In both, it seems, then, that it is Bruce's performance that is in question, since the theories make different claims about how Bruce is able to understand what Alice means. Bruce's linguistic competence, as well, plays a role in his understanding Alice. The two theories differ, however, about how much a role and what role it plays in Bruce's understanding Alice.

According to vernacularism, Bruce understands **P**, the proposition that Alice expresses in uttering 'red,' by first finding a sentence, **R**, that has **P** as its semantic value. It is here that Bruce's linguistic competence comes into play. It is by virtue of his linguistic knowledge that Bruce is able to assign to **R** that part of its semantic value that is not a function of context. This can be generalized. Let us assume that speaker, **S**, and hearer, **H**, speak the same language, **L**. Let us suppose further that **S** uses an expression, **r**, of **L** and means that **P**. For **H** to understand what **S** means he must find a sentence, **R** of **L**, the semantic value (in context) of which is **P**. **R** must either be **r** or some other sentence that is related in a systematic way to **r**, to which **H** applies his linguistic knowledge contained in his grammar. If **H's** linguistic knowledge assigns to **R** a complete semantic value, then he is thereby successful in understanding what proposition **S** expresses. If only a partial value is determined, then this serves as input to the **H's** pragmatics the function of which is to assign **R** its semantic value and as a result, **H** understands **S**.

E & S's model of understanding also has a role for competence, but one that is much more limited. On this view, Bruce understands **P**, the proposition that Alice expresses in uttering 'red' by first assigning to 'red' its syntactic and semantic properties that are contained in the lexicon of Bruce's internalized grammar. This information, with other information that Bruce has from the context of his conversation with Alice, is the input to his pragmatics that provides Bruce with the proposition that Alice expresses. There is no step in the process of Bruce's understanding Alice in which an interpretation is given to a sentence that serves towards discovering the proposition that Alice means. E & S's model cannot be extended to all linguistic interventions, since it applies only to non-sentential speech acts and some speech acts are performed with complete sentences.

To sum up, one difference between vernacularism and E & S's model is the role that linguistic competence plays in understanding. In the former, in every case of a hearer's understanding what proposition a speaker expresses in uttering an expression the hearer finds a sentence to which he applies his linguistic competence that yields a partial or complete semantic value. In the latter, in cases in which a speaker utters an expression that is not a sentence or an elliptical sentence, the hearer understands what proposition that the speaker expresses by applying his linguistic competence to the expression yielding syntactic and semantic information about the expression. But no semantic value, either partial or complete is given to a sentence in the process of the hearer's understanding the speaker.

Our discussion of the role of speaker competence in the two views leads into another related difference between vernacularism and E & S's model. These are the roles that semantics and pragmatics play in understanding. Vernacularism would, I believe, take there to be a rather limited role for pragmatics; it is semantics that does the heavy lifting in understanding. As we have seen, on this view in every case of a hearer's understanding a speaker, the hearer's grammar yields at least a partial interpretation of a sentence the semantic value of which is the proposition that the speaker means. The role for the pragmatics is to fill in gaps in the interpretation, if there are any.[37] In contrast, on E & S's view, there are cases in conversation of non-sentential speech, quite frequent cases, where the main burden in understanding what the speaker means is born by the pragmatics. The only information that the hearer's grammar provides about the non-sentential expression that the speaker uses is limited information about the expression's semantic and syntactic properties. Along with other information, this is provided to the hearer's pragmatics that yields the proposition that the speaker expresses in the conversation.

Let me conclude by saying what I think that I have shown. I have considered E & S's argument against vernacularism and argued that it does not support E & S's claim that vernacularism is false. My counter arguments, however, are not meant to show that vernacularism is true. Nor do my arguments have any bearing on the truth of E & S's view. I believe that it is still an open question which of the two views is correct. I think that one thing that my counter arguments to E & S's arguments suggest is that there is some doubt about whether the method that E & S use in trying to establish the falsity of vernacularism, their thought experiment, is the right way to go about it. I believe that the best approach for E & S is to develop their own theory for understanding of non-sentential speech that does not appeal to sentences. When such a theory can be shown to explain what the vernacularist can't or when it is shown to be a simpler theory than the vernacularist's, we'll be able to make a clear choice between the two.

## NOTES

1 In the abstract of their paper E & S hold that their argument shows vernacularism to be false, but they also advance a weaker claim that what they intend to show is that vernacularism "... is not obviously true" (E & S, 401). This is puzzling since the argument that they present, if it were a good one, would show that vernacularism is false. Consequently, I shall regard the goal they have as trying to show that vernacularism is false.

2 Elugardo and Stainton's paper is divided into three sections. The first section, "Preliminaries," sets out what they take vernacularism to be, the second section, "Logical Form and Speaker's Meaning," lays out their argument against vernacularism and their defense of their argument against possible objections and the third and final section, "Vernacularism Assumed: Incompleteness and Russell's Theory of Descriptions," tries to show that vernacularism is important, since it is assumed by certain criticisms of Russell's theory of descriptions. In this paper, I shall only be concerned with the first two sections of Elugardo and Stainton's paper.

3 E & S claim that vernacularism is not a view that can be traced to a particular philosopher, but many express philosophical views that are in the neighborhood (E & S, 398–399, n. 11). I shall return to this.

4 E & S use 'logical form' in the philosophical semantic sense of logical form, not in the linguists sense where logical form is a level of syntactic representation that accounts for such properties as scope and anaphoric relations (E & S, 394, n. 3).

5 On E & S's view about propositions and mental representation, this does not exclude them from having entailment relations, since they too have constituent structure.

[6] There are, however, grammatical sentences like 'Oysters oysters oysters eat eat eat' that speakers of English would mark as ungrammatical. In such a case, it is the linguist's grammar of English that decides the issue. But the grammar itself has been constructed on the basis of clear cases in which linguistic facts about grammaticality are determined by speakers' intuitions. There is no gap between such linguistic facts and linguistic intuition. Such a gap makes no sense.

[7] This might seem to be a trivial emendation, but it will become important when I come to criticize E & S's main argument against vernacularism.

[8] E & S have helped me at this point with useful remarks on an earlier version of this paper.

[9] Private communication.

[10] There is a problem with E & S's account of the derivative/fundamental distinction. Take a proposition, $\alpha$, that has $\{\beta_1 \ldots\ldots \beta_n\}$ as its entailments. For someone to recognize $\alpha$'s entailment relations, he must recognize that $\alpha$ entails $\beta_i$ and hence, he must find some other item, $\beta_i$ that has logical form. It follows from this that no proposition can have its logical form fundamentally, a result, I am sure, E & S would find unacceptable.

[11] There is nothing in E & S's account of how agents recognize the logical forms of proposition, etc. that excludes linguistic expressions that do not have logical forms from this class.

[12] Expressions of natural language can be syntactically ambiguous and thereby, have more than one logical form. I shall disregard this complexity.

[13] It should be clear that the view presented here is a view that E & S attribute to the vernacularist, but it is not their own view.

[14] These do not exhaust all the cases of speaker meaning that are relevant here, but they are illustrative of the role that vernacularism can play in conversation.

[15] I make the simplifying assumption that **E** is unambiguous.

[16] In what follows, when I use '**Q**' or '**R**' I shall mean the propositions associated with the sentences, 38 and 39. When I use the numbers, 38 and 39, I shall be referring to the sentences, themselves.

[17] The way that E & S put it is: "It will not be clear to Alice or to Bruce what words were employed during their first exchange" (E & S, 403).

[18] This is not the way that E & S describe Bruce's response to Alice's opening remarks. They have it as, "Bruce... happily agrees." But this is an interpretation of what Bruce did, not a 'verbatim' description of his behaviour. It is important to keep these distinct, since what is at issue is how to interpret Alice and Bruce in 41.

[19] This presupposes that 'red' is not a sentence, a contentious issue in light of Quine's discussion of 'Gavagai.' E & S recognize the possibility that 'red' is a sentence and argue against so construing it. I shall return to this point.

[20] 47 is redundant, given 43, since on E & S's view, a necessary condition for understanding a proposition is understanding its logical form.

[21] Italics in original.

[22] It is not clear how this is to be understood. Does it exclude, for example, tacit grammars that include syntactic, semantic and phonological rules? It would seem so, since these cannot be analyzed as dispositions to 'utter, affirm, deny, etc. public language sentences.'

[23] See the discussion of the existential quantifier above.

[24] Bruce could have hypothesized that it is 'That + NP' where NP can be filled in by a range of noun phrases. This hypothesis is more complicated than the more simple hypothesis that it is 'that' that is needed. Simplicity should prevail here.

[25] The route from the evidence that is available to Bruce to his understanding Alice cannot be generalized to every situation in which a hearer understands a speaker who utters a non-sentential expression. Let us consider another example of a non-sentential expression (E & S, 404–405, n. 405). Suppose that Bruce is in a pub in England and sidles up to the bar and says to the publican, "A pint of bitters." Although the route from this expression to a sentence is not the same as the one that I proposed for Bruce in his conversation with Alice, a route there is nevertheless. The publican can suppose that someone that sidles up to a bar and says "A pint of bitters" is asking for a pint of bitters. A sincerity condition for such an act is that a speaker wants what he asks for. So the publican can conclude that in saying "A pint of bitters," Bruce wants a pint of bitters. In so thinking this, the publican can represent this as a sentence. Thus, we have our sentence which might well go through the publican's head. E & S could reply to this that the publican might well go directly to the indirect report of Bruce's desire without passing through a sentence. This won't do. What E & S must show is that there is no sentence available to the publican and clearly in this example this is not the case.

[26] I am not suggesting that if anyone has sufficient evidence for recognizing **P**, it follows that he has sufficient evidence for recognizing **R**. It wouldn't follow, for example, if Bruce were a monolingual

speaker of Spanish and Alice of English and Bruce has been told in Spanish what Alice meant in uttering 'red.' But given that Bruce and Alice speak the same language, it is plausible to suppose that if Bruce has evidence for recognizing **P**, then he has evidence for recognizing **R**, on the assumption that in the context, **R** expresses **P**.

[27] E & S's conclusion would follow if there is no sentence of English that exactly expresses **P**, but E & S give no argument for such a radical thesis.

[28] E & S conclude from this, however, that Bruce can determine precisely what Alice means, but without invoking a sentence in the process.

[29] It need not be assumed here that Alice's 'red' is a sentence, an assumption that would beg the question.

[30] E & S make precisely this suggestion (E & S, 412, n. 20).

[31] E & S explicitly exclude from the range of evidence psychological plausible extensions of the conversation, Bruce's asking her what she meant, for example (E & S, 403).

[32] See my remarks above about the availability principle.

[33] I leave out here the role that logical form and constituent structure play in E & S's theory of understanding.

[34] Background conditions must be provided for 55 of the sort that E & S have given for their Alice/Bruce example that make it plausible that **H** does not have available some sentence that he uses in understanding what **S** means. In addition, as in 54, I leave out here the role that logical form and constituent structure play in E & S's theory of understanding.

[35] This is not the only use of 'competence.' It can also be used about a subject's ability to do something.

[36] This is not the same performance/competence distinction to which E & S appeal; they apply the distinction to entailment relations.

[37] There is still a great deal of room for disagreement even within the vernacularist's picture about the role of semantics and the pragmatics. Some argue that the grammar provides the semantics with a partial interpreted semantic value with place holders, variables, for the gaps in the semantic value that are to filled in by the pragmatics using contextual information. Others claim that no such variables are provided, but that the pragmatics fills in missing components in the interpretation freely. See Bach, Carston, Recanati and Stanley for recent discussions of this dispute.

## REFERENCES


Bach, K., "Conversational Implicature." *Mind and Language* 9 (1994): 124–162.

Bach, K., "The Semantics-Pragmatics Distinction: What it is and Why It Matters." In Ken Turner (ed.) *The Semantics/Pragmatics Interface from Different Points of View* (CRiSPI 1). Oxford: Elvesier Science. 1999: 65–84.

Bach, K., "Quantification, Qualification and Context: A Reply to Stanley and Szabo." *Mind and Language* 15 (2000): 262–283.

Carston, R., "Implicature, Explicature and Truth Theoretic Semantics." In R. Kempson (ed.) *Mental Representation: The Interface between Language and Reality.* Cambridge: Cambridge University Press. 1988: 155–81.

Carston, R., "Enrichment and Loosening: Complementary Processes in Deriving the Proposition Expressed?" In Ken Turner (ed.) *Mental Representations: Interface from Different Points of View* (CRiSPI 1). Oxford: Elvesier Science. 1999: 85–125.

Elugardo, R., and Stainton, R.J., "Logical Form and the Vernacular." *Mind and Language* 16(4) (2001): 393–424.

Kahneman, D., Slovic, P., and Tversky, A., *Judgment under Uncertainty: Heuristics and Biases.* Cambridge: Cambridge University Press. 1982.

Quine, W.V.O., *Word and Object*. Cambridge, MA: M.I.T. Press. 1960.

Récanati, F., *Direct Reference: From Language to Thought.* London: Longman. 1993.

Récanati, F., "Unarticulated Constituents." *Linguistics and Philosophy* 25 (2002): 299–345.

Stanley, J., and Szabó, Z., "On quantifier domain restriction." *Mind and Language* 15(2&3) (2000): 219–262.

EMMA BORG

# SAYING WHAT YOU MEAN: UNARTICULATED CONSTITUENTS AND COMMUNICATION

In this paper I want to explore the arguments for so-called 'unarticulated constituents' (UCs). Unarticulated constituents are supposed to be propositional elements, not presented in the surface form of a sentence, nor explicitly represented at the level of its logical form, yet which must be interpreted in order to grasp the (proper) meaning of that sentence or expression. Thus, for example, we might think that a sentence like 'It is raining' must contain a UC picking out the place at which the speaker of the sentence asserts it to be raining. In §1 I will explore the nature of UCs a little further, and, in §2, suggest that we can recognise two different forms of argument for them in the literature. I will argue that ultimately neither is convincing, and they will be rejected in §3 and §4 respectively. The claim will be that, though the need for an appeal to such things as time and speaker are undoubtedly necessary in order to specify what a speaker said in a given context, advocates of the semantic relevance of UCs have failed to hold apart crucially different aspects of our understanding: first, the difference between knowledge of truth-conditions and the knowledge that truth-conditions are satisfied; second, the difference between knowledge of meaning and the understanding of communicative acts. Instead of ceding contextual information the kind of semantic role envisaged by advocates of UCs, we should, I will argue, see it as part of a theory of speech acts.[1]

I will suggest that what we need to recognise here is the proper division of cognitive labour, for once this division is in place we can recognise the role and function of the information attributed to UCs, and its crucial relevance to communication, without ceding it semantic value. Sketching a model of our cognitive architecture which can underpin this stance, and showing why it might be thought independently attractive, will be the task of §5. Clearly, then, although the main focus of this paper rests with UCs, there are some big issues hovering in the wings here, and perhaps before we turn our attention squarely on the main target it would be in order to say why I think discussion of UCs cannot be had in isolation from these bigger issues.

The reason, as I see it, is that arguments for UCs are part and parcel of a particular perspective on semantic theorising, one which is over-ambitious about the aims of a semantic theory. Consider the tasks we might expect an adequate semantic theory to fulfil: on the one hand, we might be concerned that such a theory explain quite 'low level' linguistic data, such as the meaning possessed by basic lexical items and how, given this base, our language displays properties like systematicity and productivity, which have been made so much of in recent linguistics and cognitive science. On the other hand, however, we might think that an adequate theory should do this and *more*,



*R. Elugardo and R. J. Stainton (eds.), Ellipsis and Nonsentential Speech*, 237–262.

say incorporating the knowledge required for our general communicative competence, or perhaps even underpinning our epistemic or metaphysical access to the world.[2] The information the theory need contain to achieve the first, limited function might, it seems, be given by a recursive, truth-conditional theory of the kind initiated by Davidson, where the input to the theory is given by structural descriptions of (for the most part) the surface level constituents of sentences;[3] but it is pretty clear even from the outset that such a theory will not take us very far in satisfying the latter kind of constraint. What then makes the existence of UCs seem so compelling to so many theorists, I will argue, is a certain conception of the role of a semantic theory: if we approach a semantic theory from an over-ambitious perspective, then, regardless of the force of any particular argument for UCs, their existence will come to seem inevitable. While, if we limit our ambitions, the semanticist can and should do without such additional, covert elements which receive no linguistic representation. It is for this reason, then, that once I have argued against the specific arguments for UCs (§§1–4), I will go on to say something briefly (§5) about the role and function proper to a semantic theory, arguing that such a theory should be of the limited form which makes the need for UCs otiose. However, let us begin on more solid terrain by examining the nature of UCs and the arguments on offer for their existence.

## (1) WHAT ARE UNARTICULATED CONSTITUENTS?

Determining the precise nature and role of UCs unfortunately proves a little harder than was suggested in the introduction. For although all theorists in this area seem happy to agree that a feature like the location where it is said to be raining in an utterance of 'It's raining' constitutes a paradigm case of a UC, the precise account which makes this the case can differ. In this section I want to outline two distinct notions of what might constitute an unarticulated constituent: the first stems from Bach, and the second from theorists such as Sperber and Wilson, and Recanati. Having distinguished these positions, we will then focus our attention on the second — for it is in this latter guise that UCs have recently come to prominence and it is under this guise that their existence proves problematic for standard truth-conditional approaches to meaning. In order to state these two approaches clearly, however, it will be useful initially to consider the way in which syntax and semantics in general relate.

At the start of his *Talk About Beliefs*, Crimmins sketches a principle of compositionality he calls 'full articulation'. This is easiest to state if propositions are viewed as structured entities (containing individuals and properties), then full articulation holds that each element of the proposition literally expressed by an indicative utterance of a sentence must itself be the content of some component expression of that sentence.[4] To put matters crudely, the idea is that the constituents of the proposition expressed by the sentence are *exhausted* by the contributions of the component expressions in that sentence and their mode of combination — we don't get anything 'for free' at the propositional level. Now, as Crimmins notes, for this constraint to play a role in practice we need to clarify what counts as a 'component expression'. One thought might be that component expressions are equivalent to vocalised (or orthographic) words, so that propositional constituents can be read (more or less) directly from surface form. However, there are cases which seem to show that this version of the articulation constraint is too strong. For consider cases such as 'syntactic ellipsis', where the proposition a sentence can be thought literally to express contains more constituents than can be traced to the surface form of the sentence itself (emerging instead from the linguistic context in which the sentence is to be found).[5] So, consider the following (where the material inside brackets is unpronounced):

(1) A: 'Has Bill gone?'
B: 'Yes, he has [$_{VP}$ gone]'
(2) A: 'Whose dog is that?'
B: 'It's Bill's [$_{NP}$ dog]'

In both of these cases, B's utterance appears to express a proposition containing a constituent not found at the vocalised, surface form level. However, because the additional material *is* present in the immediate linguistic environment of the utterance, and can be simply recovered from here, it is often assumed that the unvocalised material can be treated as a genuine constituent of the sentence B produces. The material is present at the syntactic level, it is suggested, but elided at the surface level. If this is possible then such cases do not contravene the principle of full articulation, though they do require it to operate at the level of syntactic, not surface, form.

A second respect in which syntactic component expressions may diverge from straightforward accounts of surface form has recently been explored by Taylor and Recanati.[6] For they suggest that a full description of the syntactic constituents of a sentence should include those elements represented at what we might call the 'sub-syntactic' level. So, for instance, say we have a transitive verb, the lexical entry for which tells us that it possesses 'slots' for two arguments. If only one argument place is filled in the surface form of a particular utterance of that expression, the presence of the other argument place is nevertheless guaranteed by the sub-syntactic form. For instance, take the lexical entry for a verb like 'kicks', treated as a transitive verb with one argument place for the agent and one for the object (so that the form of the relation is '*x* kicks *y*'). Then, if we get a surface level description of a sentence utilising this expression, but with only one argument place explicitly filled (e.g. 'John kicks'), the syntactic level description of that sentence will nevertheless supply the second argument place, with an existentially bound variable acting as a placeholder, yielding 'John kicks something' or '$(\exists x)$ John kicks $x$'.[7]

The principle of full articulation is obviously at its strongest if it holds between the surface form and the proposition expressed by the sentence; however, at this level, as we have seen, the constraint seems too strong. For we need to allow elements to appear at the level of proposition expressed which are not mirrored by component expressions at the level of surface form. Perhaps, then, the right place to state the articulation principle is not at the level of surface form; perhaps instead we should require each element in the proposition expressed by an indicative utterance of a sentence to be contributed by a component expression in that sentence's syntactic form. With this principle in mind, it now becomes easier to state our distinct definitions of unarticulated constituents, according to whether they reject or accept full articulation; so let's turn to this task now.[8]

The first take on UCs allows them to figure as elements of a thought entertained on hearing the utterance of a given sentence, but holds them to be quite extraneous to the proposition literally expressed by that sentence. Full articulation, mapping syntactic form to semantic form, is endorsed for the proposition literally expressed by the utterance of a given sentence, though it is explicitly recognised that the thought entertained on hearing such an utterance may have a content which diverges from the proposition expressed by that sentence.[9] Specifically, the thought entertained may contain constituents not found in the linguistic item under consideration. This is the position we find with respect to Gricean implicature and (more importantly from our respects) in Bach's notion of impliciture (to which we return in §4). It should be clear that this first definition of UCs does not threaten the principle of full articulation nor the project of standard truth-conditional approaches to semantics. It merely highlights the fact that literal, truth-conditional semantic analyses may not be the only kinds of analyses of meaning we are interested in in communicative exchanges. So, if UCs are thought to undermine the standard programme of formal semantics, they must be understood in some other way.

Our second definition of UCs, however, does directly threaten standard truth-conditional approaches to semantics. On this model (familiar from, for instance, Sperber and Wilson's 1986 Relevance Theory) the output of the formal (context-independent) portion of our semantic theory stands in need of several pragmatic refinements prior to arrival at the proposition a sentence-token expresses: for instance, as well as the processes of disambiguation and reference assignment, familiar from the standard truth-conditional picture, the output of the formal theory may also require the introduction of novel pragmatically triggered elements, through a process Sperber and Wilson have termed 'free enrichment'. These elements, these 'unarticulated constituents', are not mirrored by elements in the surface form or the logical form of the sentence under consideration, they simply figure in the proposition expressed, which may be analysed truth-conditionally, to give the 'explicature' (Sperber and Wilson's term) of the sentence uttered — the semantic analysis of what the sentence, as produced in that context, means. This approach denies the principle of full articulation, whether it runs off the surface form *or* the syntactic form of a sentence: *not all* propositional elements are contributed by component expressions at the syntactic or surface level. For Sperber and Wilson, amongst others, pragmatic mechanisms come to figure, not just 'post-semantically' (as in Gricean implicature), but as an inherent part of the truth-conditional analysis; we must engage in pragmatic reasoning *prior to* arriving at something which is truth-evaluable.[10] It is for this reason that Recanati has labelled such positions 'truth-conditional pragmatics' and it should be clear that such approaches are *incompatible* with the standard truth-conditional approach to semantics.

It seems, then, that we have two quite different definitions of 'unarticulated constituents' to hand:

i. a UC is an element which figures in the thought entertained on presentation or production of a sentence, but which is not relevant to the semantic analysis of that sentence (i.e. it does not figure in the proposition expressed by that sentence token).
ii. a UC is an element required for grasping the proposition literally expressed by an indicative utterance of a sentence, S (i.e. S's explicature), yet an element which receives no linguistic (i.e. syntactic) representation.[11]

I want now to set aside the former definition and concentrate instead on (ii). For on this analysis the contextual information captured by UCs comes to figure in the proposition expressed by a sentence. If this is correct, then the standard, formal approach to semantics, which sees the specification of truth-conditional content as a process which is context-independent, must be rejected.[12] In what follows I want to suggest that, contrary to the arguments of Recanati, Sperber and Wilson, Carston, et al, there is no role in a semantic theory for these additional, pragmatically introduced elements; rather we should see them as part of a broader theory of thought, independent of language. So let us turn now to the argument for the existence of UCs, understood along the lines of (ii) above.

## (2) THE ARGUMENTS FOR UNARTICULATED CONSTITUENTS

Since unarticulated constituents (UCs) are, *ex hypothesi* (and on any definition) not 'visible to the naked eye', as it were, arguments for their existence must be of an indirect form: they will be vindicated as theoretical postulates necessary to explain and underpin the recognised behaviour of the sentence. Prima facie, arguments for their existence then fall into two distinct camps:

(1) For at least some sentences, given just the syntactic constituents of the sentence, no truth-evaluable proposition can be recovered (without UCs the sentence simply lacks truth-conditions).

(2) For at least some sentences, given just the syntactic constituents of the sentence, the wrong truth-conditions will be recovered (truth-conditions based solely on verbalised constituents do not fit our intuitions about the circumstances in which the sentence will be true or false).[13]

A clear advocate of the first form of argument for UCs is Carston 1988, who argues that, for a range of cases, we simply lack anything truth-evaluable if we restrict elements of the 'explicature' (the literal content of what is said) to what we find on the surface of the sentence or at the level of logical form.

For instance, considering an utterance of 'She didn't get enough credits and can't continue', in a context where the most plausible interpretation of the utterance is: 'Jane didn't pass enough university course units to qualify for admission to second year study and, as a result, she can't continue with university study. Jane is not feeling at all happy about this', Carston writes that:

> The question then is which aspects of this interpretation are explicitly expressed (that is, part of the explicature) and which are implicit (implicated)? The disambiguation of 'get' and 'units' and the referent assignment of 'she' are surely part of the explicit content, while the assumption that Jane isn't feeling happy is surely implicit. But what about 'to qualify for admission to second year study' and 'with university study', which enrich and complete the two clauses of the conjunction, and the 'as a result' linking the two conjuncts. Are these part of what is explicated or what is implicated? Since they are not given linguistically, one might think they must be implicated, but then what is the explicature of the utterance? It must be 'Jane didn't pass enough university course units and Jane cannot continue (something??)'. It's not clear that this constitutes a propositional form, that is, it isn't possible to specify what conditions in the world must obtain for it to be true.[14]

It seems clear that Carston here envisages an argument along the lines of (1): without the addition of relevant contextual information, despite the fact that it does not figure in the syntactic form, the sentence is not truth-evaluable, we cannot specify the conditions under which it would be true. Furthermore, even some theorists who would disagree with Carston about the existence of truth-conditionally relevant UCs, agree with the claim under consideration here, viz. that at least some indicative sentences are semantically underdeterminate. For instance Bach writes:

> An (indicative) sentence is semantically underdeterminate if it fails to express a complete proposition — determine a definite truth-condition — even after ambiguity and vagueness are resolved and indexical references (including the time of the utterance) are fixed. . . .In these cases what the conventional meaning of the sentence determines is only a fragment of a proposition or what I call a *proposition radical*; a complete proposition would be expressed only if the sentence were elaborated somehow, so as to produce a *completion* of the proposition.[15]

Again, then, the thought seems to be that, unless we are willing to take the sentence as possessing more content than it superficially appears to have, we will simply be unable to assign a truth-value. The sentence as it stands is simply not truth-evaluable.

However, as noted above, this is not the only kind of argument possible for UCs, for it may be that, concentrating just on the explicitly represented elements of the sentence, we get something which *is* truth-evaluable, but that what we get is, in some sense, the *wrong* truth-conditions for what is said.[16] Arguments of the form of (2) are most evident in the discussions surrounding quantifier restriction. So, for instance, consider the following exchanges:

(3) A: How was the party?
B: Everyone was sick.[17]
(4) A: I've invited my boss for dinner.
B: But there is nothing to eat!
(5) A: Can I let Fido in from the garden?
B: Yes, the door is closed.

In (3) it seems B's utterance is true just in case everyone at the party was sick (as opposed to, say, everyone in the world); in (4) B clearly doesn't mean an unrestricted claim concerning the lack of food, but something like 'there is nothing to eat in the house' or 'there is nothing appropriate and available to eat'. While in (5), the special case of quantifier restriction that arises with respect to definite descriptions treated as quantified phrases, it seems B's utterance may be true in a situation where the door to the street is closed, even if one or more internal doors are open. If we take our T-sentences to be given simply by the overt elements of the sentence, we must treat (B) in each case as saying something (trivially) false, whereas our intuition in each case is that they have spoken truly.

Another set of cases which seem to lend support to the second argument for UCs can be found in examples like that made famous by Partee:

(6) A: I turned off the oven.

Here, unless there is some implicit reference to a time (and on the assumption that the speaker has turned off the oven more than once in the past) the speaker seems to be saying something trivially true; but this seems wrong. Certainly, the natural way to interpret (6) is along the lines of:

(7) I turned the oven off then.

The problem in (3–6) is not, then, that the sentences uttered entirely lack truth-conditions, but rather that they lack *suitable* truth-conditions. This disparity between our intuitive judgements of what is said (i.e. the conditions under which what is said will be true) and the paucity of the verbalised content of the sentence is again thought to provide evidence for the existence of unrepresented but semantically relevant constituents.[18]

In what follows I want to reject both these forms of argument for the existence of syntactically unrepresented but semantically relevant UCs.[19] Contrary to the first argument given above, I will argue (in §3) that even sentences like 'She can't continue' are truth-evaluable, though we need to hold apart the truth-conditions a sentence possesses and the actual situation which serves to make it true on any given occasion (which in turn may link to judgements of what is pragmatically communicated in that situation). While contrary to the second argument above, I will suggest that we have good reason to take the notion of *appropriateness* as a non-semantic one — one which goes hand in hand with determining what a speaker can or could convey in a given context, but not what a sentence literally means. Although I do not want to query our intuitions about what is said by the speaker in these cases, I will argue that judgements about what is said are of little help in determining what the sentence literally expresses. (Thus I will be *rejecting* the assumption, common from Grice on, that there is some privileged notion of 'what is said' which is informative as to the precise semantic content of the original sentence; seeing why this is so will be one of the tasks of §5.) So, let us turn now to the first argument for UCs.

## (3) (SOME) SENTENCES ARE NOT TRUTH-EVALUABLE WITHOUT UCs

The initial argument, endorsed in Carston 1988, claims that some sentences are not truth-evaluable without appeal to UCs. Prima facie, however, it seems that the opponent of UCs — e.g. someone who advocates a disquotational T-theory running (more or less) simply off the surface constituents of sentences — might wonder what exactly the problem is supposed to be here. Why, she might wonder, can't we simply disquote the sentences in question to yield theorems of the form:[20]

a. 'It is raining' is true (in L) iff it is raining.
b. 'Jane can't continue' is true (in L) iff Jane can't continue.[21]

Now, what is clear with truth-conditions of this form is that they don't specify a unique set of conditions which must pertain in order for the sentence to be true; or, better, they allow a range of more specific conditions each of which would serve to make the sentence true.[22] For instance, in the case of (b), we might envisage a range of possible situations, each unilaterally an instance of Jane's failure to continue; e.g. a world where Jane can't continue sleeping, a world where she can't continue running, and a world where she can't continue university education, to name but three.

However, this permissiveness in the precise conditions which make the object language sentence true doesn't immediately seem either problematic or particularly unusual. Take the sentence 'Jane is happy', which, we might think, is a less likely candidate for containing UCs than either (a) or (b). Given a disquotational T-theory we arrive at something of the form:

c. 'Jane is happy' is true (in L) iff Jane is happy.

Yet (c), no less than (b), fails to uniquely constrain the range of possible situations in which the object language sentence will be true. A world in which Jane is happy because it is her birthday but not because her boyfriend has left her, or where she is happy now but not five minutes ago, or where she has never been unhappy, are all worlds which serve to make the object language sentence true. And verifying whether or not the sentence is in fact true will involve finding out if any one (or more) of these possible situations is actual; i.e. it will require determining the precise conditions which, in this instance, satisfy the truth-condition. Yet, I would suggest, this is *no* different to what happens in a case like (b): determining the truth or falsity of the object-language sentence (b) will require finding out which (if any) of a range of possible situations are actual. Finding out whether Jane is happy, then, involves undertaking exactly the same kind of investigation as finding out whether Jane can't continue, it is just that we might think (speaking somewhat crudely) that there is a 'broader' range of situations which would make it true that Jane can't continue than there are which satisfy 'Jane is happy'.

Yet we clearly need much further argument to show that this intuitive difference in range must result in a difference in meaning, i.e. that there is some recognisable degree of variation in the possible situations which serve to satisfy a truth-condition, below which no introduced unarticulated constituents are needed, but above which the semantic requirement for UCs comes into play. Who, we might wonder, is responsible for setting this line, what exactly are the parameters of difference which it is supposed to be measuring, and what do we do with borderline, disputed or vague cases? To the extent that this proposal can actually be (non-metaphorically) understood, it seems entirely arbitrary and artificial. Of course, one option here would be for the advocate of UCs to deny an initial assumption we made above, viz. that 'Jane is happy' is not a good candidate for containing UCs. Perhaps 'Jane is happy' is precisely on a par with 'It is raining' or 'Jane can't continue', requiring UCs to specify the location, duration and kind of happiness Jane is enjoying. However, any intuitive support for the imposition of UCs seems to dissolve when we turn to sentences like 'Jane is happy'; although a multitude of different situations (perhaps an infinite number) can satisfy the T-sentence:

'Jane is happy' is true iff Jane is happy

this does not, I suggest, in any way encourage us to enrich the semantic content of the sentence in order to narrow down this number of situations. Yet as for 'Jane is happy' so for 'Jane can't continue', *unless* the advocate of UCs can convince us that there is some principled distinction between the two.[23] So, it seems, either the advocate of UCs pursuing this first line of argument (given as (1) in §2) must be willing to draw a line at some point, below which UCs are not required (however, in this case they face serious questions concerning how to make this border appear non-arbitrary), or they find themselves on a slippery slope which can only end with the requirement that the literal meaning of every sentence be exactly as precise as the particular worldly conditions used to verify it on a given occasion of utterance. Yet neither of these positions seems appealing.

From the start, then, it seems to me that the burden of proof rests with the advocate of UCs to show us what is wrong with the kind of liberal truth-conditions a formal theory would supply, for though they don't tie the world down to a unique state of affairs nor, it seems on closer inspection, do many other sentences.[24] Yet there is no intuitive appeal to the idea that all these other sentences (like 'Jane is happy') are good candidates for UCs. In response to this kind of argument, however, I think the advocate of UCs can marshal further putative problems with the kind of truth-conditions currently under consideration, problems which may still show us that liberal truth-conditions are unacceptable. The three objections I envisage here are as follows: first, there seems to be a problem regarding the fact that the world may both satisfy and fail to satisfy a given truth-condition at the same point in time; second, we may worry about how assessments of truth and falsity actually get made for sentences; third, it may be objected that the contextual conditions in play simply demand semantic accommodation through the role they are playing. I want to explore each of these putative objections in turn, but the conclusion will be that none of them support the claim that at least some sentences are non-truth evaluable without UCs.

A first objection to liberal truth-conditions concerns the recognition, given voice to by Perry, that at any given time, bits of the world may satisfy a truth-condition like (1), while other bits don't. Of his son's utterance of 'It's raining', Perry writes: "What my son said was true, because it was raining in Palo Alto. There were all sorts of places where it wasn't raining".[25] Of course, it is unarguable that the fact that it is raining in Palo Alto serves to make Perry's son's statement true in this situation. However, the claim we might envisage being made here is that this fact requires semantic recognition because otherwise we will be faced with a liberal truth-condition which one area of the world satisfies while another does not. The question we face, then, if we adopt truth-conditions like (a) or (b) is: is a world where it is raining in Palo Alto but not in London a world where the sentence 'It is raining' (without UCs) is true or false?[26]

Recall, however, that the argument currently under consideration is whether or not the sentence is *truth-evaluable* without appeal to UCs (not yet whether the truth-conditions are appropriate), and nothing in the recognition that a part of the world may satisfy the condition in question, while another part of the world does not, serves to show that the sentence is not truth-evaluable: a world where it is raining *anywhere* is, I would suggest, a world where the sentence 'It is raining' is true. For the sentence 'It is raining' to be false, it has to be the case that there is no (current) instance of raining going on at all.[27] If the speaker wanted to assert something which further constrained the set of circumstances which would make her sentence true, then she could and should have done this; but knowing how communication proceeds, she did not feel it was necessary in this case. (I'll return to the question of how much interlocutors can assume in communication, without explicitly asserting, in §5.)

Furthermore, that the sentence 'It's raining' must at least sometimes be analysed along the lines of (a) is reinforced by consideration of cases like the following: say we are concerned to measure the level of rainfall worldwide, perhaps in the light of fears about global warming.[28] To do this we set up a machine which rings a bell whenever there is an instance of rain anywhere in the world. Hearing the bell, it seems I may utter 'It's raining', aiming to express just the proposition that it is raining in some, quite unspecified location. There is no precise location where I wish to assert the rain is falling, nor does the recognition that it is not raining in very many places seem to affect the truth of what I say. So, the recognition that different parts of the world may (concurrently) satisfy or fail to satisfy a given truth-condition is not as yet reason to reject liberal truth-conditions like (a) and (b). However, there is a related problem which begins to surface now, for if truth-conditions really do (for the most part) run off the explicit contents of our sentences then we will be left with a vast range of truth-conditions whose actual satisfaction we cannot verify. Is the sentence 'it's raining', as uttered by S at t, literally true or false, we might ask? Well, without a relativisation to a place, it can turn out to be extremely hard to tell.

Once again, however, it's not clear that the advocate of standard truth-conditional semantics should be unduly worried by this claim. For it seems that the claim made by this kind of approach to semantics is that grasp of meaning is grasp of truth-conditions, not knowledge of whether those truth-conditions are satisfied, nor possession of a method by which to discover if those truth-conditions are satisfied; to think otherwise is, I believe, to fall prey to a kind of creeping Verificationism. What we are allowing is that the competent interlocutor can grasp the truth-conditions of the sentence, she knows how the world would have to be for the sentence to be true. To think that, in addition to this, the agent must be in a position to ascertain whether or not that condition is satisfied in order to count as understanding the meaning of the sentence is to run together notions of meaning and verification which (the history of Verificationist approaches to meaning tells us) are best kept apart. What matters for understanding a sentence is that it have a truth-condition, i.e. that it be (in principle) truth-evaluable, and that the interlocutor grasp that truth-condition, and this is not at all the same thing as requiring that, at any given time, we must be in a position to actually determine the sentence's truth-value. (It should also be born in mind that any such failures to verify concern *only* the proposition literally expressed by a sentence. It is perfectly possible that speakers of these sentences will convey some more precise proposition through their utterance of the sentence in question, and that the truth-value of this pragmatically conveyed proposition will be easily verifiable by interlocutors; a point returned to in §4.)

We need to hold apart knowing the truth-conditions of a sentence (a semantic matter) and knowing whether or not those truth-conditions are satisfied on some particular occasion of utterance (a non-semantic matter). What is obviously the case, given our limited cognitive resources and the speed of communicative exchanges, is that we simply don't have the time or ability to check all possible situations satisfying the conditions on any given occasion; but we should also note that very often we don't have to. Take the sentence 'John went for a walk', which can be made true by a world in which he went for a quick walk by a lake half an hour ago, or by a world in which he went for a slow walk over a bridge two weeks ago (and countless many other worlds as well). To find out if this sentence is true, I will begin by investigating those circumstances which are most likely to have provided the evidence for my interlocutors production of the sentence. If I discover, amongst these relevant alternatives, a situation which makes the sentence true, then I can simply stop there; if my interlocutor is speaking truly, then I can usually expect to find a confirming situation fairly quickly, say discovering that John did indeed go for a quick walk by a lake a short time ago.[29] Clearly, then, attempts to *verify* whether or not a given truth-condition is satisfied may well be something of a limited or curtailed endeavour. Specifically, we may confine ourselves to what seem to be the *relevant* possibilities here. We may decide that, even though a world in which Jane can't continue sleeping is a world in which 'Jane can't continue' is true, it is not a very relevant circumstance for us to investigate. Rather, from the conversational exchange in which the sentence is embedded, it seems that we can figure out a much more relevant set of circumstances to devote our attention to; namely, whether or not Jane can continue university education. But, to repeat, unless we think that meaning is to be located in our methods of verification, there is simply no argument from the role of a particular place, speaker, type of footwear, etc, in our verification of a sentence's truth-value to the necessary inclusion of such elements in a specification of semantic content.

It seems, then, that the advocate of disquotational T-theories can maintain that disquotation (based solely on syntactic constituents) is adequate for generating semantic content, whilst admitting that the conditions interlocutors look to to verify whether a given truth-condition is satisfied or not are severely curtailed, i.e. that the kinds of features Carston et al want to add to the semantics actually figure outside the semantics in the realm of how agents go about verifying the truth or falsity of a given utterance. In this case, sentences like 'Jane can't continue' are perfectly truth-evaluable (all we need to do is to grasp the appropriate disquotational T-sentence), though verifying the truth-value of the sentence, i.e. determining if its truth-condition is satisfied, may well advert to the kind of contextual information appealed to by advocates of UCs. So, I want to suggest that simple, disquotational T-sentences, like (a) and (b), are perfectly acceptable: first, though they do not pin the world down to a unique state of affairs, we have no reason to expect or require them to do so. Secondly, though this entails that the propositions literally expressed by many sentence tokens will not be verifiable, this only constitutes a problem if we lose sight of the fact that knowledge of meaning is knowledge of truth-conditions, not possession of a method of verification for those truth-conditions.

Finally, however, this brings us to the third and last objection to permissive truth-conditions that I want to consider. For we may worry that, if it's really the case that judgements about the truth or falsity of 'It's raining' stand or fall with how the weather is *here*, or *at X*, as indicated above, then this should be a fact which is reflected in our semantics. Not because without appeal to a place the sentence is non-truth-evaluable, but because without such appeal the sentence is not *appropriately* truth-evaluable. Truth-conditions like (a) and (b), though not ill-formed, are not suitable; they fail to capture our intuitive judgements about when the sentence should be taken to be true or false. The real worry here, then, does not seem to be, as initially suggested, that we simply can't get anything remotely truth-evaluable without appeal to UCs, rather it is to suggest that we can't get anything approaching *appropriate* truth-conditions without appeal to UCs. The objection is that, without the proposed presence of UCs, the only kinds of truth-conditions we can deliver for sentences like 'Jane can't continue', 'It's raining', or 'There's nothing to eat', are ones which fail to capture our judgements about when sentences like these are true or false. This, of course, is the second argument given above for the existence of UCs, so let us turn to this alternative form of argument now.

## (4) UCs ARE NEEDED FOR APPROPRIATE TRUTH-CONDITIONS

It seems, then, that the first argument (that some sentences are literally not truth-evaluable) ultimately collapses into the second argument; viz. that truth-conditions based solely on the syntactic contents of (at least some) sentences are in some way inappropriate. What a speaker says when they utter the sentence 'Everyone was sick' is that every person *in some relevant group* was sick, and what the speaker who says 'It's raining' means is that it is raining *in some particular place*. To treat the sentences as possessing the more general truth-conditions delivered by their overt constituents is to fail to capture what the speaker means, and to make predictions about the circumstances in which the sentence will be true or false which do not fit with our intuitive view of the subject matter. For instance, it is to hold 'Everyone was sick' is false in a situation in which everyone at the party was sick, but where some irrelevant individual, whom no one was talking about or thinking about, was well. Or that 'It is raining' is true when it is bone dry for hundreds of miles around the interlocutors, but, unbeknownst to all participants in the conversation, it is raining in a small corner of Timbuktu. This result, the advocates of UCs object, is unacceptable.

Initially, then, the claim seems to be that someone who utters, say, 'It's raining', can or must be viewed as meaning that it is raining *in X*, etc. However, as we all know thanks to Grice, because a speaker means a proposition, p, by her utterance of a sentence, s, this does not necessarily mean that the sentence uttered should be treated as having the semantic value that p.[30] The speaker who says, ironically, 'It's a nice day' when it's raining, means *it's a nasty day*, but this isn't the literal meaning of the sentence uttered. While the speaker who says pointedly 'someone hasn't handed in their essay again' may mean, and may be taken to mean, that the recalcitrant Jones has failed to turn in work once again, but this isn't what she literally expresses. So, the advocate of a restricted (non-UC) view of semantics might wonder why the cases to hand are any different. Why should we think that, because it is often uncontentious to say that the speaker uttering 'It's raining' means that *it's raining here* (or wherever) that this more informative proposition must give the literal, semantic content of the sentence produced?

I think there are probably three factors at play in the advocate of UCs assumption that the richer proposition must give the literal meaning of the sentence. First, the kinds of cases which the advocates of UCs appeal to intuitively look pretty different to typical cases of Gricean speaker-meaning. In the latter, we have an intention on the part of the speaker to say something non-literal (they intend to be ironic, hyperbolic, metaphorical, etc), whereas in the kinds of 'underdetermined' utterances focused on for UCs any such non-literal intent is absent. Why, then, think speakers are knowingly uttering literal falsehoods or trivial truths on these occasions, even when they are in possession of a range of perfectly simple sentences which would convey the substantive thoughts they really wish to communicate (i.e. why don't they say 'It's raining here' as opposed to just 'It's raining')? This thought seems especially pressing since our intuitions in these cases tell us that the speakers are in fact doing fine — producing fitting utterances and (often) asserting truths. So, even if the Gricean distinction is right in certain cases, still, the advocates of UCs contend, there is no reason to think these cases are (and every reason to think they are not) instances of speaker-meaning rather than semantic-meaning.

This connects to a second reason to treat the richer propositions as giving the literal meaning (as opposed to being Gricean implicatures), for it often seems both natural and correct to report a speaker who produces a (putatively) underdeterminate utterance using a 'completed' content sentence. For instance, the speaker who says 'It's raining' will usually be reported as having said that *it's raining here* (or wherever). Finally, as we saw at the close of the last section, it seems that when we look at the conditions appealed to in order to make judgements of truth or falsity for sentences as uttered on a given occasion, they are the states of affairs picked out by the richer propositions involving time, place and speaker, etc. If I want to find out whether Perry's son's utterance of 'It's raining' was true or false I need to consider not how the weather is with me now but how the weather was with him then (even though finding out the latter state of affairs is a much harder task than the former). Yet if this is right, then it seems undeniable that the statement Perry's son made must have contained elements picking up on his particular context of utterance (or the intended context for his utterance), i.e. that the semantic content of the sentence uttered contained UCs.

Let's take these three points in order: first, the claim that these cases are radically different to paradigm Gricean examples of speaker-meaning. It's obvious that speakers producing such sentences lack the kind of explicit non-literal intentions Grice appealed to. Yet this is not necessarily to concede that the speakers in these cases are intending to be taken literally; that is to say, we shouldn't think of non-literality as necessarily exhausted by cases where the speaker is trying to be ironic, metaphorical, etc. For instance, as Bach has pointed out (in discussion of what he terms 'impliciture'):

> [T]here are many sentences which are almost always used non-literally as elliptical for other sentences. For example, "Ed doesn't look tired, he is tired" would likely be used with a suppressed "merely" before "look" to be inferred by the hearer, since the speaker would not be stating that Ed does not look tired but is tired anyway. Similarly, if I say "I drink only Scotch", I would not be stating that I drink nothing but Scotch but merely that the only liquor I drink is Scotch.... The phenomenon of elliptical speech is commonplace; indeed, it often seems stilted not to suppress words that can easily be inferred as expressing part of what one means, as opposed to what the uttered sentence means.[31]

The claim that, in utterances like 'It's raining', the speaker is not trying to be *explicitly* non-literal (in the sense of trying to be ironic, etc) only entails that the speaker is not being non-literal if this is the only kind of non-literality we allow. What Bach points out in the above quote (and elsewhere) is that this last claim is extremely tendentious: we seem to allow a wide range of cases of non-literality, stretching much wider than the mere intention to speak metaphorically or ironically, etc.[32] It seems instead that a speaker can be viewed as speaking non-literally just in case there is a divergence between the thought the speaker wants to express and the literal meaning of the sentence produced, and this kind of phenomenon happens frequently, especially when there are elements already in play in the context which it would be stilted to repeat in one's speech, even though they form a part of the content of the thought to be conveyed. So, is there any evidence that speakers in the kinds of cases under consideration here are being non-literal in this (broad) sense?

Clearly the answer to this question is 'yes', for there is evidence that interlocutors are willing to hold apart literal sentence-meaning and speaker-meaning even in these cases. For instance, in an utterance of "I will go to the store" it always seems open to the mischievous speaker, on being chided to actually go, to reply that she did not say *when* she would go and that she merely meant to express the proposition that at some time in the future she would be visiting the store. No doubt such a speaker contravenes all sorts of communicative or conversational constraints, but it doesn't seem that she explicitly *contradicts* herself (as must be the case if her original sentence literally meant that, for some specific value of $t$, she would go to the store at $t$).[33] Or again, take the cynical response to 'Everyone is coming to my party' of 'Oh really? Will the Queen be there?' — the respondent here may be charged with being pedantic and uncharitable, but surely not with failing to understand the literal meaning of the English sentence. The retreat to the general proposition acquired from the surface contents of the sentence may be pedantic, and a speaker who insists on such unhelpful interpretations will quickly prove an exasperating interlocutor, but the mere fact that we allow such retreats, without charging the speaker with inconsistency or failure to grasp the meaning of the sentence, seems to demonstrate that we have here precisely the kind of sensitivity to speaker-meaning versus sentence-meaning outlined by Grice. So, the first argument against treating the richer propositions as non-literal can, it seems, be deflated.

Moving to the second point, concerning indirect speech reports, it seems that the shared intuition — that, for instance, an utterance of 'It's raining' can often be reported using the richer content sentence 'A said that it's raining *at l'* — can be accommodated without embracing semantically relevant UCs. For it seems that this intuition may be best viewed as concerning not the literal meaning of linguistic expressions in natural language, but speaker's exploitation of these signs in successful communication, as highlighted in reported speech. That is to say, just because, in many contexts, it is entirely natural to report a speaker utilising a content sentence which is richer than the sentence originally uttered, this does not mean we need refine our semantic evaluation of the original sentence to incorporate every element present in an acceptable content sentence of an indirect speech report. For, in general, it seems quite clear that facts about reported speech cannot be used in any straightforward way to demarcate facts about semantic content.[34] The first thing to notice is that the move from proposition expressed to correct indirect speech reports is not one:one. A single utterance can always be adequately reported by a number of indirect speech acts. So, 'It's raining' as uttered by S, at time t and location l, may be reported in (at least) the following ways:

S said that it is raining.
S said that it is raining where she is.
S said that it is raining at l.
S said that it was raining at l on t.

Furthermore, given the right context of reporting, the utterance may support a range of more 'liberal' indirect speech reports, like:

S said that it was raining 50 miles south of the Grand Canyon.
S said that it was nice weather for ducks at t in l.
S said that the drought was over.

So, if we were to assume that facts about indirect speech limn facts about semantic content, we would have to allow that a single sentence possesses an indefinite number of distinct semantic contents, depending on the range of acceptable ways in which it may be reported.[35] Yet, with concerns surrounding the systematicity and creativity of natural language (and the constraints of language learning) in mind, this seems totally unacceptable. It simply seems wrong to think that part of the semantic content of 'It's raining' could include reference to droughts or ducks.

Of course, the natural move for the advocate of UCs here is to claim that it is not *every* indirect speech report which is informative as to semantic content, but only some subset of them (e.g. those which capture what the speaker 'really' said, in some sense).[36] However, as Cappelen and Lepore have stressed, once one starts reflecting on how permissive indirect speech reporting can be, the idea that it can tell us anything useful about semantic content becomes extremely doubtful. For instance, given the right context of utterance and report, the content sentences in indirect speech reports may swap co-referring or synonymous terms from the original sentence (e.g. exchanging 'John' for 'that boy'), and they may exchange referring terms for quantified noun phrases ('John' for 'the oldest boy in class').[37] We may also allow the omission of conjuncts or disjuncts ('p & q' reported by 'S said that p'), and the picking up of implicatures ('someone hasn't done the washing-up' reported by 'John complained that Jill hadn't washed up again', or Blair's claim that 'I will endeavour by the office of this government to bring once again within the direct control of the Nation those systems of public transportation that form the lifeline of so much of this country's wealth and well-being' reported as 'Blair said that he wants to renationalise the railways'). Yet given this degree of liberality, it seems very hard to see how the discrete subset of indirect speech acts which are intended to be genuinely informative as to semantic value are to be distinguished.[38] Rather, it seems, facts about reported speech *per se* entail very little about what meaning should be ascribed to the original sentence uttered. Thus, there is no direct move from the intuition that 'It is raining at l' may be a correct report of an utterance of 'It is raining' to the theoretical claim that the former gives the correct semantic analysis of the latter.

To recap: it seems that the first and second motivations for assigning UCs semantic relevance in order to arrive at appropriate truth-conditions can be dissipated. For, on the one hand, there is evidence that the cases in question do fit the speaker-meaning/sentence-meaning divide introduced by Grice (since we are willing to take the speaker's rejection of assigned, richer propositions — like *it is raining here* — and their retreat to the more general proposition yielded by syntactic constituents alone — e.g. *it is raining* — as non-contradictory and legitimate, though almost certainly conversationally improper and pedantic). While, on the other hand, it seems that the data here properly resides with facts about reported speech (viz. the unarguable fact that speakers can be correctly reported using content sentences which overtly appeal to such elements as speaker, location and time); but, as I have tried to show, for this undisputed fact to be relevant here, we need to assume an extremely close connection between how a speaker can be reported (i.e. what the speaker succeeded in communicating) and the literal meaning of the sentence uttered, a connection which in general does not seem to hold. Though how a speaker can be reported must be *in some sense* constrained by the sentence she produces, the assumption that we can extract facts about semantic meaning from facts about reported speech seems wrong. In §5 I will offer an explanation of why this is the case, sketching a view of the cognitive architecture of the agent which makes it clear why we cannot hope to begin with facts about speaker-meaning and hope to move from there to facts about sentence-meaning. However, the claim for now is simply that an advocate of the semantic relevance of UCs owes us much further argument from the claim that contextual information figures in indirect speech reports to the idea that such information figures semantically in the initial sentence produced.

However, the advocate of UCs is not to be silenced yet, for as noted at the start of this section, there is a third argument she may appeal to in rejecting the pragmatic explanation of these cases. For perhaps the motivation for ceding the richer propositions semantic relevance can be found in consideration of the conditions under which we seem willing to judge the sentences in question true or false. As noted above, it seems that the speaker saying 'It's raining', in a context where the relevant location is X, will be judged to have spoken truly *if it's raining at X* and falsely even if it's raining elsewhere (and not at X). While the speaker who says 'There is nothing to eat' may be judged to have spoken truly, despite the absence of global famine. So, how can we claim contextual information is irrelevant to sentence-meaning when the conditions under which utterances of these sentences are held true or false are just the kind of constrained conditions delivered by the incorporation of UCs? It is not only that the kind of information appealed to by UCs figures in correct indirect speech reports, but also that it figures in our assessments of the truth and falsity of the original utterance; what more evidence could we need, the advocate of UCs will object, to grant the information a semantic role?

I think there are two points to notice in respect of this argument: first, we need to bear in mind the distinction between knowledge of truth-conditions and the verification of those truth-conditions, and, secondly, we need to ask ourselves *which* proposition interlocutors will be most interested in verifying the truth of in any given context — will it be the literal, semantic content expressed, or will it be the proposition (or propositions) the speaker wants to (and succeeds in) communicating? On the first point: as we saw in the last section, we need to be very clear that the conditions interlocutors appeal to to verify a sentence are not necessarily identical to the truth-conditions of the sentence produced. I may verify the truth of 'John went for a walk' by finding out that he went for a slow walk over a bridge, or a fast walk beside a lake, but neither the speed of the walk nor the route taken (need) figure as part of the semantic content of the sentence. Similarly, I may verify an utterance of 'It's raining' by seeing that there is a downpour outside my window, or being told by a reliable source that there is a light drizzle in Palo Alto, but, I contend, this gives us no reason to think the weight of waterfall or the place where it is falling figures in the literal meaning of the sentence produced. To think otherwise would be to demand the literal meaning of the sentence produced be precisely as fine-grained as the particular condition used to verify it; but we have no reason to think every sentence we produce must specify a completely unique way the world must be in all its myriad detail. Furthermore, such a position would run roughshod over any principle of 'semantic innocence' we might have, by seeing the contents of sentences like 'John went for a walk' as containing concepts like bridges and lakes, strolls and wanderings.[39] Rather it seems that verifying the truth of a sentence is simply not the same thing as understanding the truth-conditions of that sentence, and it seems that the final argument for UCs is guilty of running together these two notions: maintaining that just because we appeal to a specific condition in determining the truth-value of the sentence, this condition must be part of the semantic content of the sentence produced.

Furthermore, even though I believe we should hold apart the notions of truth-conditions and the verification of truth-value, it still seems that the opponent of semantically relevant UCs can accommodate the crucial role contextual features play in understanding communicative acts. To see this, we need to be clear about the nature of the debate here, for matters are somewhat delicate. The issue here is not 'does contextual information have a role to play or not?' (a question to which all parties will answer in the affirmative), but 'does this information have a peculiarly semantic role to play?' (the issue is one of division of labour). The opponent of UCs can grant relevant contextual information a crucial role to play in understanding and verifying the truth of *what is said* (non-semantic) by the utterance of the sentence in the given context, even whilst denying it a semantic role in the literal meaning of the sentence produced. That is to say, they can explain why we may judge 'It's raining' as false when it is not raining *here*, though it is raining (at some irrelevant) *there*; or why we judge 'There is nothing to eat' true, even when there is a well-stocked food shop nearby, for in these cases we are judging not what is literally expressed but what is communicated. Contextual information is of crucial importance for understanding what speakers mean, but this is not to say that it must have an inherent role in the literal meaning of those sentences speakers use to communicate what they mean.[40] What advocates of semantically relevant though syntactically omitted elements should recognise, I think, is that there is a perfectly standard discrepancy between sentence-meaning and speaker-meaning, and that features vital for determining both the truth-conditions and the truth-value of the latter need not be in any way relevant for determining the former.

So I believe we should reject all three of the proposed reasons for treating the richer propositions resulting from the inclusion of contextual material as semantically relevant, treating them instead as quite standard cases of speaker meaning (as opposed to sentence meaning). Yet if this is right, then the second argument for UCs fails: *appropriate* truth-evaluation is a pragmatic matter, thus the fact that UCs are required for this goes no way towards establishing their semantic relevance. Combined with the failure of the first argument for UCs (namely, that some sentences are non-truth-evaluable without UCs, rejected in §3), it seems that we are left with no compelling argument for the existence of semantically relevant, though syntactically unmarked, constituents. Finally, however, this brings us back to the bigger issues touched on at the outset; for it seems to me that to reject the existence of such unarticulated constituents it is not enough simply to reject the specific arguments for them. For it seems that, in actual fact, for many theorists the real motivation for UCs comes from the embracing of a particular perspective on semantic theorising — a perspective which makes such elements almost inevitable. The suggestion we have to consider now is that, regardless of any specific argument for the existence of UCs, if we want a semantic theory which is in any way adequate, we will simply be forced to accept the existence of UCs; arguments about the semantic relevance of UCs are ineliminably connected to arguments about the role of a semantic theory itself.

The advocate of UCs apparently sees the semantic realm as primary — as responsible not only for our understanding of linguistic items, but also for our understanding of what speakers can use these items to say. The assumption seems to be that a semantic theory which is not sensitive to the range of thoughts conveyed in a communicative exchange must fail as a theory of meaning. Alternatively, opponents of UCs see the semantic theory as contributing just *one* element to the understanding of what was said by the speaker, with elements such as knowledge of the speaker, knowledge of the context, identification of the referent, etc, forming equally crucial, though non-semantic, elements. Thus so-called 'pragmatic' features (a label which, I think, really serves just as a 'catch-all' term for non-semantic knowledge) are different to, but absolutely no less vital than, semantic features. In the final section, then, I want to consider briefly wider questions concerning the semantic/non-semantic divide, examining how we might construe the boundary between language and thought, how it might be crossed, and in which direction. The argument will be that we have no reason to amalgamate all the information required to understand communicative acts as properly part of the semantic theory and that, with the more constrained view of semantics in place, the need for semantically relevant though syntactically unarticulated constituents drops away.

## (5) THE BOUNDARY BETWEEN LANGUAGE AND THOUGHT

The positive view I want to put forward is that understanding a language is just one, necessary but far from sufficient, step on the road to understanding linguistic communicative acts. Understanding a language is not, as Wittgenstein told us, understanding a way of life; rather it is understanding a constructed code, a system of representation with finite basic parts and recursive rules, which can be used by speakers to express (elements of) their thoughts. Of course, this claim as it stands is probably uncontroversial: all theorists, advocates of UCs, truth-conditional pragmatics and standard formal semantic theories alike, want to recognise the important role of postsemantic, pragmatic features in affecting speaker's meaning. However, where the view to be advocated diverges, I think, from the commonly accepted claim, is in the degree of responsibility attributed to, and the range of, non-semantic information. The thought is that semantic interpretation yields only an extremely minimal level of understanding and that what we need to do to build up to anything like an adequate understanding of a communicative act is to subject this semantic interpretation to a vast range of further information we possess concerning the world and one another.[41] We need, to put matters somewhat hyperbolically, to move from language to thought.

To make matters more concrete, let's borrow from the picture made familiar by theorists like Chomsky and Fodor. Within this framework, then, what I want to claim is that agents possess a language faculty containing discrete bodies of information, say, orthographics/phonetics, syntax, and semantics. The semantic information contained in the language faculty is, however, of a quite minimal kind, namely just what is required to explain the kind of low-level semantic facts given in the introduction (meanings of primitives, properties like productivity, etc). On its own, then, the language faculty is not equipped to explain fully our communicative competence. To know what someone has said (non-semantic) by an utterance of a given sentence, an interlocutor needs to begin with the calculation of the literal meaning of the sentence produced, but this information is then fed out of the language faculty and into what we might call an agent's 'generalised intelligence' (in current jargon, sometimes the 'central processing unit'). It is at this point that the specifically semantic information becomes subject to a vast range of other kinds of information possessed by the agent, including the output of the perceptual system, commonsense psychology, commonsense physics, etc. The point, which is often paid lip-service but not, I think, always fully appreciated, is that what matters in (even linguistic) communication is *just as much* what is not said as what is.[42] To arrive at an understanding of what is said a great deal of language-independent information must come together; though we *start* with an understanding of the meanings of words and their modes of combination, we proceed almost automatically to an assessment of what that literal meaning itself means in the current context and in the mouth of the current speaker. The literal meaning may be enriched, altered, rejected or refined in the light of an agent's non-semantic knowledge. It is for this reason that trying to recover the purely semantic contribution from an assessment of what is communicated is so difficult: we cannot start with the coalescence of all these different features and hope to drag out the semantic contribution from here, for it has been submerged within our general understanding. Though there is a function which takes us, in any particular case, from the sentence produced and the context in which it is uttered, given our background grasp of the world and one another, to the proposition communicated, we can do no more than offer a functional definition of this operation in terms of its input and output.[43]

To understand what is literally meant by 'It's raining' all we need to know is the meaning of the parts of the sentence (as indicated by the surface elements of the sentence) and their mode of combination, however to know what is communicated by an utterance of this sentence we need to know so much more. For a start, we need to understand some crucial facts about language-based communication, such as that when a speaker comes to conveying a particular idea in a given context she may choose to use words and phrases which do not entirely match her thought. This may be because the thought is (for her) inexpressible — she simply cannot find the right words for it; or it may be because she wishes to flout some conversational rule to a given end — perhaps she wishes to be ironic or metaphorical; or it may be because at least some of the information she wishes to convey is already in the public domain, as it were, so that she can use a short-hand linguistic version of what she means to communicate. It is this 'conversational short-hand' that I want to suggest is in play with the sort of contextual information appealed to by UCs.[44] In addition, given that her grasp of communicative practices tells the interlocutor that information from the wider context of utterance, or background information she possesses about objects or people, will be relevant for determining what thought the speaker means to convey, she needs to know *which* non-semantic features of the context and her background knowledge are relevant for determining what is said, i.e. that in an utterance of 'It's raining' it is more useful to determine which location the speaker has in mind than the kind of rainfall she believes to be occurring, though sometimes determining factors like the speaker's attitude to the rainfall may be equally important. Furthermore, we need to know non-semantic information about the concepts deployed in the literal meaning itself, such as that two drops of water probably don't constitute an instance of rain, or that if it is raining in an area of drought then the drought is over;[45] and we need to know non-semantic information about how agents usually act in response to rain, e.g. that if it is raining then any picnics will be cancelled, or that in the rain people tend to use umbrellas.

The point I want to stress is that the semantic contribution to judgements of what is said forms just one (crucial) part of a much bigger picture, and that without the bigger picture semantic meaning is an impoverished thing. To know a language, if one doesn't know about the world or one another, is not yet to know very much.[46] Thus to position contextual elements as necessary to understanding communicative acts, though not necessary to understanding semantic content, is not to undervalue these additional elements, rather it is just to recognise that they are playing a different (though equally important) role in coming to understand what a speaker means by her utterance of a given sentence. This difference in role may be obscured by the fact that it is both natural and immediate to move from understanding the sentence to understanding what the speaker of the sentence conveys in a given context, together with the fact that, once we have arrived at this latter meaning, it is extremely difficult to retrace our steps to discover the purely semantic contribution to the communicative act (as natural language speakers we are adept at crossing the boundary from language to thought and back again, but as theorists the interaction of different aspects of our knowledge remains a very poorly understood domain).

Yet this is not to say that the distinct contributions should not be held apart: we know the kind of information a semantic theory must contain, I suggest, because we know the kind of data a semantic theory has to explain, viz. the systematic nature of linguistic understanding and our ability to produce an indefinite range of sentences despite our limited cognitive resources. Furthermore, we have some idea of how this data might be explained, i.e. by positing a recursive, truth-conditional theory as responsible for semantic understanding. Thus it is from *this* perspective that we can isolate the semantic contribution of sentences to judgements of what is said (non-semantic); the mistake made by (some) advocates of UCs is to try to *begin* with judgements of what is said and abstract semantic contributions from there. At present, this latter task is simply beyond us: we cannot in any particular case work back from the result of processes utilising our 'generalised intelligence' to discover the specific contribution of the language faculty, because the kind and amount of other information which figures in a calculation of what is said is simply too vast and too complex.[47] To repeat: if we understand the task of a semantic theory (as I think we should) to be explaining features like the productivity and systematicity of natural language, and how an infant can come to acquire such a language, then there is no place for syntactically unrecognised but semantically relevant UCs. In general, the input to such a theory will be simply a structural description of the surface level features of the sentence. This leaves a great deal still to be said about how we understand the communicative acts in which linguistic items may play a part, for such an approach holds out no hope of a semantic theory coming to serve as a general account of communicative competence. That is to say, such an approach still leaves the door wide open for 'unarticulated constituents' understood in the first way given in §1 (stemming from Bach), for this is just to recognise that the thoughts properly engendered by an utterance of a sentence, S, may diverge from the semantic content of (i.e. proposition expressed by) S to a greater or lesser extent.

In conclusion, then, I have argued that we should reject both the specific arguments for, and the wider perspective which underpins, the move to embrace truth-conditionally relevant but syntactically unarticulated constituents. In the first place, we should reject the claim that (many) sentences are not truth-evaluable without the appeal to such constituents: for by holding apart specification of truth-conditions from verification of truth-value, we can see that this claim is unfounded (the argument of §3). Secondly, we should recognise that the richer propositions containing additional contextual information are well treated as forms of *impliciture*: first, since interlocutors do recognise a distinction between literal and speaker meaning, even in these cases, and, second, because facts about reported speech seem to tell only indirectly on facts about semantic content (the arguments of §4). Finally, I have suggested that we have no reason to lump together all the apparently disparate knowledge required for understanding a communicative act under the general heading of 'semantic'. Rather, we do far better to retain a more austere view of the task of a semantic theory, seeing it as required to explain some quite precise features of our linguistic understanding, but allowing that it contributes just one, necessary but far from sufficient, element to our understanding of communicative acts. Yet within this perspective on semantic theories there is simply no need for syntactically unarticulated but semantically relevant constituents. When I work out that by your utterance of 'It's raining' you mean to convey the thought that it is raining *here* what I learn is something about you, using information about you, our speech community and our current (conversational and other) context; what I learn is not something about the meaning of our language.[48]

## NOTES

1 This position is not novel — it is, for instance, advocated in Bach 1994a and by Cappelen and Lepore (manuscript). Furthermore the general strategy should be familiar to all from such arguments as Kripke's rejection of the semantic relevance of referential definite descriptions. However, I hope the precise arguments deployed against the 'semantic relevance' camp are new.

2 Theorists who endorse the epistemic role for a semantic theory include those who, following Russell, see fit to posit a special class of linguistic items which require 'acquaintance' (or a similar privileged epistemic relation) to understand. While those endorsing the metaphysical role of semantics include those who predict that we can read our ontology in some way from our language.

3 The interpolation 'for the most part' is needed to provide the degree of latitude required for cases like syntactic ellipsis, to be explored in §1.

4 Crimmins 1992, pp. 9–10.

5 See Elugardo and Stainton 2003 for a somewhat more extended discussion of ellipsis, especially with respect to non-sentential cases. For a challenge to the idea that there is syntactically real though unvoiced material even in cases like (1–2) see Dalrymple (this volume).

6 Taylor 2001; Recanati 2002.

7 If we allow that sub-syntactic features are relevant to semantic articulation then, as Recanati stresses, many of the cases standardly treated as instances of unarticulated constituents will not be genuinely unarticulated at all (articulated, as they are, sub-syntactically). I will return to this point in the next section.

8 It is worth noting in passing a third possible explanation for the kind of material typically accorded to UCs, which stems from Perry 1986 (where I believe the term 'unarticulated constituent' first appeared). Though Perry himself opts for something more akin to the second definition to be given below, he begins (1986, p. 147) with a discussion of information which figures, not as a propositional constituent, nor even as an element of the thought entertained by the agent, but instead as parameter against which the proposition a sentence expresses gets assessed for truth or falsity. It might be thought that a similar treatment, where contextual information is introduced by the character or lexical rule associated with a linguistic item (and is thus not directly incorporated into the truth-conditional content of the uttered sentence) could be available for all the kinds of information attributed to UCs. While I do not have the space to discuss this approach here, two points should be noted: first, such a move will result in a *vast* increase in the number and kind of contextual parameters supposedly introduced by lexical items, which may not be credible. Second, however, even if such a move could be made to work, it would not be in conflict with the standard conception of truth-conditional semantics, and thus does not form a genuine opponent in this respect.

9 Matters are delicate here, for it may be objected that, in general, it is wrong to think of sentence *types* as expressing propositions, rather we must speak of sentence types *relativised to a context* (to account for the resolution of indexicality). The question then is whether we can think of a context in this respect along broadly Kaplanian lines (i.e. as consisting of a set number of contextual parameters — e.g. speaker and time — which can be settled independently of investigation of richer notions like speaker intentions), or whether the notion of context we need is a far fuller one which itself introduces the kind of elements typically appealed to for UCs. As Rob Stainton has urged on me, this is a crucial issue here, but I hope it is clear that I construe 'standard truth-conditional semantics' as committed to something like the former picture; indeed, the arguments of this paper could be construed as aiming to show that the richer notion of context is not necessary for determining linguistic meaning.

10 Matters here are additionally complex given that Bach *agrees* that sometimes pragmatic reasoning must be entered into to arrive at something which is truth-evaluable, but *disagrees* with Sperber and Wilson et al about the status of this 'completed' proposition. For Sperber and Wilson it gives the literal explicature of the sentence produced, while for Bach it forms a non-literal, pragmatic supplement to the semantically relevant 'propositional radical' (I return to this point briefly in §2).

11 Recanati's, 2002, p. 316, chosen definition for these elements is slightly different again. He writes: "*In context*, it may be that the unarticulated constituent is 'required'; but then it is required *in virtue of features of the context*, not in virtue of linguistic properties of the expression-type. A constituent is mandatory in the relevant sense only if *in every context* such a constituent has to be provided (precisely because the need for completion is not a contextual matter, but a context-independent property of the expression-type). This, then, is the criterion we must use when testing for (genuine) unarticulatedness: Can we imagine a context in which the same words are used normally, and a truth-evaluable statement is made, yet no such constituent is provided? If we can imagine such a context, then the relevant constituent is indeed

unarticulated; if we cannot, it is articulated, at some level of linguistic analysis." Clearly, then, Recanati's class of UCs will be narrower than many other truth-conditional pragmatists, though he suggests it still includes elements such as the location of rain in 'It's raining'. This narrower definition of UCs impacts on the range of arguments available to Recanati. To anticipate §2: he will allow arguments of the second form for UCs (viz. that without them inappropriate truth-conditions are delivered), but not the first (viz. that without them sentences are non-truth-evaluable). However, since I aim to reject *both* forms of argument, I will not distinguish Recanati's position in what follows.

12 In a helpful discussion of the issues involved here, Rob Stainton has tried to convince me that I'm overstating the case here — that processes like free-enrichment are not in tension with the core values of truth-conditional semantics. While it is true that truth-conditional pragmatists and what I'm calling 'standard truth-conditional semanticists' go a long way down the same road together, there do remain some pretty radical differences. For advocates of free enrichment (i.e. the existence of UCs) really do claim that pragmatic enrichment is a necessary precursor not merely of determining a *truth-value* for a token utterance but for delivering the *truth-conditional content* of a sentence token, whereas, apart from a quite constrained set of cases (e.g. delivering a referent for an indexical or settling ambiguity), truth-conditional semanticists simply deny that such a process is necessary. Top-down processing, from pragmatics to semantics, is extremely restricted for the advocate of standard truth-conditional semantics, yet it is a ubiquitous part of linguistic understanding for the truth-conditional pragmatist. Thus if UCs really do exist — if free enrichment plays the role the truth-conditional pragmatist envisages — the standard model of truth-conditional semantics must be mistaken.

13 (1) and (2) correspond to Bach's distinction between *completion* and *expansion* (see Bach 1994a); where completion occurs if "something must be added for the sentence to express a complete and determinate proposition (something capable of being true or false)" (p. 127), and thus corresponds to our first argument for UCs above. While expansion is the process of what Bach calls 'conceptual strengthening', which is not mandatory (unlike completion), and thus corresponds to our second argument above.

14 Carston 1988, pp. 33–4.

15 Bach 1994a, pp. 268–269.

16 Crimmins and Perry 1989 seem to envisage an argument of this form for UCs representing mode-of-presentation-like entities for belief reports.

17 This example is from Neale 1990 (*Descriptions*, Cambridge, Mass: MIT).

18 A third set of cases which may prove relevant here are Travis-type examples (see, for example, Travis 1985; 1996), where judgements of the truth of type-identical sentences seem to depend crucially on some kind of contextual sharpening, e.g. 'John's book weighs 8lbs', where we need to know if it's the book John wrote, the book he owns, the book he's carrying, etc.

19 Clearly, there are two different ways to argue against syntactically unrepresented but semantically relevant elements: one may argue that, contra first impressions, such elements *are syntactically represented* (see Stanley 2000 for an argument to this effect), or one may argue that, contra first impressions, such elements *are not semantically relevant*. This paper pursues the second strategy.

20 The following simplified truth-sentences would, of course, need relativisation to speakers and times (perhaps in the form of Higginbotham's 1995 'conditionalised' truth-sentences) in order to handle overt indexicality; see fn. 9.

21 If we embrace, as I'm inclined to, the earlier specification of 'sub-syntactic' material as influencing the syntactic characterisation of the sentence, then the right-hand side of (b) should in fact take notice of the status of 'continue' as a transitive verb, yielding:

(b*) 'Jane can't continue___' is true (in L) iff Jane can't continue something.

The advocate of UCs here would still claim that contextual features have a role to play in determining the correct truth-conditions for a token of 'Jane can't continue', for these must specify *what* she can't continue; but the current line of argument, that this sentence is not truth-evaluable as it stands, would no longer hold. That is to say, to borrow Bach's terminology (see fn. 13), the argument for UCs would now be one concerning *expansion* and not *completion*. Whether or not (a) should be rendered in this fuller form (i.e. whether the lexical entry for 'rain' is akin to 'raineth' or more akin to 'rain somewhere') is a moot point, to be settled by empirical study of our language and its lexicon.

22 It is sometimes suggested that, if a sentence allows a range of more specific conditions, then it itself must be providing only a truth-conditional schema, or propositional radical. Yet this claim seems far too strong, for no (contingent) proposition graspable by the human mind could be *maximally* specific about the world, thus every proposition will allow *some* more specific conditions to be provided.

23 It has been suggested to me that an advocate of UCs might respond in the following way: there *is* a relevant difference between 'Jane can't continue' and 'Jane is happy' (assuming for argument's sake that the latter does not require UCs); namely, though both sentences express propositions which do not uniquely constrain the situations which satisfy them, only the former sentence requires contextual supplementation to get a proposition in the first place. But such a response simply seems to me to beg the question: to assert that the difference is that, in the former case you don't, but in the latter case you do, get a proposition, seems to me little more of a statement of faith. We were looking for an *argument* as to why a putative truth-condition like (a) was unacceptable, while (c) was not, and the fact that (a) is not fully determinate about the precise condition which may satisfy it was adduced as a reason. Now however we have seen that this fact holds just as much for (c). If it turns out that very few, if any, sentences actually express fully determinate propositions (in the sense of *fully* describing how the world must be to satisfy them), then the fact that sentences like 'It's raining' don't do this provides *no* evidence that contextual supplementation is required to take us from sentence to proposition.

24 Here we have a major point of disagreement with Bach, who claims that, for many sentences, the propositions they literally express are incomplete and thus non-truth-evaluable; they are propositional radicals rather than complete propositions. However, at this juncture, I fail to see exactly what the argument is supposed to be. Considering the sentence 'Steel isn't strong enough', Bach asserts 'Notice that [this sentence] does not express the weak proposition that steel isn't strong enough for something or other' (1994b, p. 127), but the argument behind this intuition is unclear.

25 Perry 1986, p. 138.

26 A similar thought might seem to be behind Taylor's comment on the same sentence: 'The semantic incompleteness is manifest to us as a felt inability to evaluate the truth value of an utterance of ["It's raining"] in the absence of a contextually provided location (or range of locations)' (2001, p. 53).

27 Similarly, for the sentence 'It is not raining' to be true, there must be no instance of rainfall anywhere in the world at the current time (so it is not the case that 'It is raining' and 'It is not raining' may both be true at the same time). Advocates of UCs might think it is dishonest to smuggle in reference to the time in these examples, however, I would suggest that this is admissible given the present tense of the sentences.

28 Recanati 2002 cites this kind of example as well.

29 Notice, however, that despite the confirming situation containing elements like *being by a lake* or *ten minutes ago*, there is, I would suggest, no temptation to see the literal meaning of the sentence produced as making implicit appeal to these further elements.

30 See Grice 1967; also Sperber and Wilson 1986.

31 Bach 1981, p. 238. See also the discussion of 'S-(sentence)-non-literality' in Bach 1994b.

32 Furthermore, we should note that this point is already endorsed by anyone who accepts a pragmatic, speaker-meaning analysis of so-called 'referential' definite descriptions, where it is rarely the case that the speaker will have explicitly non-literal intentions.

33 Returning to Perry's case, imagine that you are confused about the current conversational setting and think your son wants to say something about Palo Alto, when in fact he is continuing a conversation about how things stand with your other son in LA. Here the intended proposition is not that it is raining in Palo Alto but that it is raining in LA. Something has gone wrong here, but is it really a semantic failure? Have you failed to understand what your child's words, in that particular concatenation, meant? The suggestion I want to make is that you have not — though there has undoubtedly been a breakdown in communication, this isn't due to your inability to understand English, i.e. to grasp the literal meaning of the sentence, but because you've failed in some other respect, such as keeping up-to-date on which are the relevant objects in the current context.

34 Cf. Bertolet 1990, and Cappelen and Lepore 1997.

35 We should also note that facts about admissible reportings vary not only with the context of utterance of the original sentence, but also with the current audience to which the report is being made. For instance, a report of 'Blue is my favourite colour' with 'A said that that is her favourite colour' is clearly acceptable only in a quite specific range of contexts, viz. those that have a sample of blue available for demonstrative indication.

36 For responses of this kind, though not in the context of the UC debate, see Richard 1998 and Reimer 1998.

37 Bertolet 1990 allows exchange of co-referring terms but not co-extensive predicates, however little argument over and above the intuition that exchange is permitted in the former but not the latter case, is offered.

38 See Cappelen and Lepore's 1998 reply to Richard and Reimer. The argument surrounding the semantic irrelevance of judgments of 'what is said' is explored at greater length in Borg 2002.

[39] By ‘semantic innocence’ I mean some quite general principle requiring the elements we posit within a semantic analysis for a given sentence to be constrained by the syntactic elements we can find in that sentence.

[40] To return to the distinction made in §1, the claim is that we should endorse the first definition of UCs, allowing that there may be elements required to grasp the thought communicated by a speaker which have no immediate counterpart in the proposition literally expressed by the sentence they produce. Some readers have suggested this position tacitly grants all that theorists such as Sperber and Wilson demand, since they are concerned to offer a theory of cognitive content per se (not merely that restricted to linguistic understanding); however, I would disagree (see fn. 41).

[41] In Recanati’s 2002 terminology, I wish to defend ‘radical literalism’. It is worth being clear, however, exactly where I see the disagreement between my position and that of, say, the Relevance Theorists. For whereas the latter kind of approach seeks some general principle of human cognition, seeing no special boundary between understanding a language and understanding non-linguistic communicative acts, I wish to maintain a clear division, treating linguistic understanding as autonomous from other bodies of knowledge (i.e. pragmatic processes) yet still dealing with fully propositional knowledge (i.e. able to yield determinate truth-conditions for sentences). This fundamental difference in outlook impacts elsewhere, e.g. on questions of the semantic relevance of ‘what is said’, or analyses of non-literal uses of language.

[42] Notable exceptions here include Bach and Harnish 1979, and Levinson 2000.

[43] See Borg 2000b for further discussion of such putative functional definitions.

[44] It also perhaps yields an initial understanding of non-sentential speech, e.g. holding up an object and saying ‘From France’ or pointing and saying ‘New dress?’. On the current view, though these speech acts would fail to reach the standards of linguistic communication (since the speaker does not produce something which expresses a complete proposition), the speaker might nevertheless ‘get her message across’ due to the public accessibility of the linguistically elided material. The complete proposition ([This is from France] or [That is a new dress?]) would have the status of a pragmatically conveyed proposition, which interlocutors could recover, despite the linguistic infelicity. For much further discussion of these issues, see Stanley and Szabo 2000, who adopt a treatment sympathetic to the suggestion here, or Elugardo and Stainton 2003 who argue for an alternative view.

[45] Some theorists might object that *all* this information should be construed as genuinely semantic, since the concepts deployed in semantic theorizing are to be individuated by their inferential role, and thus all such inferential relations should be located within the domain of the semantic theory. However, as is well known, such theories face a serious problem with differentiating the essential, meaning-constituting inferences from the (social or idiosyncratic) inferences people are inclined to draw on the basis of past experience, etc. So, to borrow a favourite example of Fodor’s 1998, because I am inclined to infer ‘x is dangerous’ from ‘x is a brown cow’, because all brown cows I have run into up till now have been dangerous, this of course doesn’t mean that this inferential move should be taken to be constitutive of the meaning of the expression ‘brown cow’. The suggestion above, then, is that instead we take *no* such inferences as constitutive of meaning; agents make conceptual connections, but these connections come into play as part of the wider, non-linguistic cognitive architecture of the agent and they hold between independently individuated concepts. The meaning of the word ‘rain’ is just the concept *rain*; what inferences someone is willing to draw on the basis of a deployment of this concept is a function of their experience of the world, not a function of their knowledge of language.

[46] Examination of certain cases of deficit is perhaps relevant here, such as sufferers of Williams syndrome, who have advanced linguistic skills despite being significantly retarded, or those who suffer other impairments of cognitive function which leave language skills untouched. For instance, Pinker 1994, pp. 50–53, describes a case from the psychologist Richard Cromer, where a girl called ‘Denyse’ talks in detail about the problems with her joint bank account, despite the fact that cognitive disability, as a result of being born with spina bifida, means that she has never had a bank account, cannot read or write, or handle money, and clearly lacks most of the knowledge usually associated with possession of the concept ‘joint bank account’.

[47] Recall the quote from Carston 1988, in §2, where she suggested that, given an utterance of ‘She didn’t get enough units and can’t continue’, the disambiguation of ‘get’ and ‘units’, and the referent assignment to ‘she’ are “surely part of the explicature”, while the assumption that ‘she is not happy about this’ is “surely part of the implicature”. What I want to suggest is that this kind of carving up of semantic and non-semantic understanding is *only* possible if we *don’t* start from a characterization of what counts as semantic drawn from considerations about what is required for understanding the communicative act per se.

[48] Thanks are due to Kent Bach, Eros Corazza, Ray Elugardo, Ernie Lepore, Mark Sainsbury, Rob Stainton, and audiences at the Nottingham 'On Referring' conference, and the London Language Reading Group, for helpful comments and discussion. Also to François Recanati for making available draft work on this topic.

## REFERENCES

Bach, K., "Referential/Attributive." *Synthese* 49 (1981): 219–44.

Bach, K., "Semantic Slack: what is said and more." In *Foundations of Speech Act Theory: philosophical and linguistic perspectives*, ed. S. Tsohatzidis. London: Routledge. 1994a: 267–291.

Bach, K., "Conversational Impliciture." *Mind and Language* 9 (1994b): 124–162.

Bach, K., and Harnish, R., *Linguistic Communication and Speech Acts* Cambridge, Mass.: MIT. 1979.

Bertolet, R., *What is Said: A theory of indirect speech acts*. London: Kluwer. 1990.

Bezuidenhout, A., "Pragmatics, Semantic Underdetermination and the Referential/Attributive Distinction." *Mind* 106 (1997): 375–410.

Borg, E., "An Expedition Abroad: metaphor, thought and reporting." In *Midwest Studies in Philosophy.* XXV, P. French and H. Wettgtein (eds.). Oxford: Blackwell. 2001: 227–248.

Borg, E., "The Semantic Relevance of What is Said." *Protosociology* 17 (2002): 6–24.

Cappelen, H., and Lepore, E. "On an Alleged Connection Between Indirect Speech and the Theory of Meaning." *Mind and Language* 12 (1997): 278–296.

Cappelen, H. and Lepore, E. "Reply to Richard and Reimer." *Mind and Language* 13 (1998): 617–621.

Cappelen, H., and Lepore, E., "Radical and Moderate Pragmatics: Does meaning determine truth-conditions?" In *Semantics vs. Pragmatics*, ed. Z. Gendler Szabo. Oxford: OUP. forthcoming.

Carston, R., "Implicature, Explicature, and Truth-Theoretic Semantics." In *Mental Representations*, R. Kempson (ed.) Cambridge: Cambridge University Press. 1988: 155–81.

Carston, R., "Explicature and Semantics." UCL Working Papers in Linguistics, 2001.

Crimmins, M., *Talk About Beliefs*. Cambridge, Mass: MIT. 1992.

Crimmins, M., and Perry, J., "The Prince and the Phone-Booth." *Journal of Philosophy* 86 (1989): 685–711.

Dalrymple, M., "Against Reconstruction in Ellipsis." This volume.

Fodor, J., *Concepts: Where Cognitive Science Went Wrong*. Oxford: OUP. 1998.

Elugardo, R., and Stainton, R. "Grasping Objects and Contents." In *The Epistemology of Language*, A. Barber (ed.) Oxford: Blackwell. 2003: 257–302.

Grice, P., "Logic and Conversation (William James Lectures)." In *Syntax and Semantics*, Vol. 3, P. Cole and J. Morgan (ed.) New York: New York Academic Press. 1967: 41–48.

Higginbotham, J. "Tensed Thoughts." *Mind and Language* 10 (1995): 226–249.

Levinson, S., *Presumptive Meanings: The Theory of Generalized Conversational Implicature*. Cambridge, Mass.: MIT. 2000.

Perry, J. "Thought Without Representation." *Proceedings of the Aristotelian Society Supplementary Volume* LX (1986): 263–283.

Pinker, S., *The Language Instinct*. London: Penguin. 1994.

Recanati, F., "Unarticulated Constituents." *Linguistics and Philosophy* 25 (2002): 299–345.

Reimer, M., "What is Meant by 'What is Said'? A Reply to Cappelen and Lepore." *Mind and Language* 13 (1998): 598–604.

Richard, M., "Semantic Theory and Indirect Speech." *Mind and Language* 13 (1998): 605–616.

Sperber, D., and Wilson, D., *Relevance: Communication and Cognition*. Oxford: Blackwell. 1986.

Stanley, J., "Context and Logical Form." *Linguistics and Philosophy* 23 (2000): 391–434.
Stanley, J., and Szabo, Z., "On Quantifier Domain Restriction." *Mind and Language* 15 (2000): 219–261
Taylor, K., "Sex, Breakfast, and Descriptus Interruptus." *Synthese* 128 (2001): 45–61.
Travis, C., "On what is strictly speaking true." *Canadian Journal of Philosophy* 15 (1985): 187–229.
Travis, C., "Meaning's role in truth." *Mind* 105 (1996): 451–466.

# Studies in Linguistics and Philosophy

1. H. Hiż (ed.): *Questions*. 1978 ISBN 90-277-0813-4; Pb: 90-277-1035-X
2. W. S. Cooper: *Foundations of Logico-Linguistics*. A Unified Theory of Information, Language, and Logic. 1978 ISBN 90-277-0864-9; Pb: 90-277-0876-2
3. A. Margalit (ed.): *Meaning and Use*. 1979 ISBN 90-277-0888-6
4. F. Guenthner and S.J. Schmidt (eds.): *Formal Semantics and Pragmatics for Natural Languages*. 1979 ISBN 90-277-0778-2; Pb: 90-277-0930-0
5. E. Saarinen (ed.): *Game-Theoretical Semantics*. Essays on Semantics by Hintikka, Carlson, Peacocke, Rantala, and Saarinen. 1979 ISBN 90-277-0918-1
6. F.J. Pelletier (ed.): *Mass Terms: Some Philosophical Problems*. 1979 ISBN 90-277-0931-9
7. D. R. Dowty: *Word Meaning and Montague Grammar*. The Semantics of Verbs and Times in Generative Semantics and in Montague's PTQ. 1979 ISBN 90-277-1008-2; Pb: 90-277-1009-0
8. A. F. Freed: *The Semantics of English Aspectual Complementation*. 1979 ISBN 90-277-1010-4; Pb: 90-277-1011-2
9. J. McCloskey: *Transformational Syntax and Model Theoretic Semantics*. A Case Study in Modern Irish. 1979 ISBN 90-277-1025-2; Pb: 90-277-1026-0
10. J. R. Searle, F. Kiefer and M. Bierwisch (eds.): *Speech Act Theory and Pragmatics*. 1980 ISBN 90-277-1043-0; Pb: 90-277-1045-7
11. D. R. Dowty, R. E. Wall and S. Peters: *Introduction to Montague Semantics*. 1981; 5th printing 1987 ISBN 90-277-1141-0; Pb: 90-277-1142-9
12. F. Heny (ed.): *Ambiguities in Intensional Contexts*. 1981 ISBN 90-277-1167-4; Pb: 90-277-1168-2
13. W. Klein and W. Levelt (eds.): *Crossing the Boundaries in Linguistics*. Studies Presented to Manfred Bierwisch. 1981 ISBN 90-277-1259-X
14. Z. S. Harris: *Papers on Syntax*. Edited by H. Hiż. 1981 ISBN 90-277-1266-0; Pb: 90-277-1267-0
15. P. Jacobson and G. K. Pullum (eds.): *The Nature of Syntactic Representation*. 1982 ISBN 90-277-1289-1; Pb: 90-277-1290-5
16. S. Peters and E. Saarinen (eds.): *Processes, Beliefs, and Questions*. Essays on Formal Semantics of Natural Language and Natural Language Processing. 1982 ISBN 90-277-1314-6
17. L. Carlson: *Dialogue Games*. An Approach to Discourse Analysis. 1983; 2nd printing 1985 ISBN 90-277-1455-X; Pb: 90-277-1951-9
18. L. Vaina and J. Hintikka (eds.): *Cognitive Constraints on Communication*. Representation and Processes. 1984; 2nd printing 1985 ISBN 90-277-1456-8; Pb: 90-277-1949-7
19. F. Heny and B. Richards (eds.): *Linguistic Categories: Auxiliaries and Related Puzzles*. Volume I: Categories. 1983 ISBN 90-277-1478-9
20. F. Heny and B. Richards (eds.): *Linguistic Categories: Auxiliaries and Related Puzzles*. Volume II: The Scope, Order, and Distribution of English Auxiliary Verbs. 1983 ISBN 90-277-1479-7
21. R. Cooper: *Quantification and Syntactic Theory*. 1983 ISBN 90-277-1484-3
22. J. Hintikka (in collaboration with J. Kulas): *The Game of Language*. Studies in Game-Theoretical Semantics and Its Applications. 1983; 2nd printing 1985 ISBN 90-277-1687-0; Pb: 90-277-1950-0
23. E. L. Keenan and L. M. Faltz: *Boolean Semantics for Natural Language*. 1985 ISBN 90-277-1768-0; Pb: 90-277-1842-3

*Volumes 1–26 formerly published under the Series Title: Synthese Language Library.*

# Studies in Linguistics and Philosophy

24. V. Raskin: *Semantic Mechanisms of Humor*. 1985
ISBN 90-277-1821-0; Pb: 90-277-1891-1
25. G. T. Stump: *The Semantic Variability of Absolute Constructions*. 1985
ISBN 90-277-1895-4; Pb: 90-277-1896-2
26. J. Hintikka and J. Kulas: *Anaphora and Definite Descriptions*. Two Applications of Game-Theoretical Semantics. 1985 ISBN 90-277-2055-X; Pb: 90-277-2056-8
27. E. Engdahl: *Constituent Questions*. The Syntax and Semantics of Questions with Special Reference to Swedish. 1986 ISBN 90-277-1954-3; Pb: 90-277-1955-1
28. M. J. Cresswell: *Adverbial Modification*. Interval Semantics and Its Rivals. 1985
ISBN 90-277-2059-2; Pb: 90-277-2060-6
29. J. van Benthem: *Essays in Logical Semantics*. 1986
ISBN 90-277-2091-6; Pb: 90-277-2092-4
30. B. H. Partee, A. ter Meulen and R. E. Wall: *Mathematical Methods in Linguistics*. 1990; Corrected second printing of the first edition 1993
ISBN 90-277-2244-7; Pb: 90-277-2245-5
31. P. Gärdenfors (ed.): *Generalized Quantifiers*. Linguistic and Logical Approaches. 1987
ISBN 1-55608-017-4
32. R. T. Oehrle, E. Bach and D. Wheeler (eds.): *Categorial Grammars and Natural Language Structures*. 1988 ISBN 1-55608-030-1; Pb: 1-55608-031-X
33. W. J. Savitch, E. Bach, W. Marsh and G. Safran-Naveh (eds.): *The Formal Complexity of Natural Language*. 1987 ISBN 1-55608-046-8; Pb: 1-55608-047-6
34. J. E. Fenstad, P.-K. Halvorsen, T. Langholm and J. van Benthem: *Situations, Language and Logic*. 1987 ISBN 1-55608-048-4; Pb: 1-55608-049-2
35. U. Reyle and C. Rohrer (eds.): *Natural Language Parsing and Linguistic Theories*. 1988
ISBN 1-55608-055-7; Pb: 1-55608-056-5
36. M. J. Cresswell: *Semantical Essays*. Possible Worlds and Their Rivals. 1988
ISBN 1-55608-061-1
37. T. Nishigauchi: *Quantification in the Theory of Grammar*. 1990
ISBN 0-7923-0643-0; Pb: 0-7923-0644-9
38. G. Chierchia, B. H. Partee and R. Turner (eds.): *Properties, Types and Meaning*. Volume I: Foundational Issues. 1989 ISBN 1-55608-067-0; Pb: 1-55608-068-9
39. G. Chierchia, B. H. Partee and R. Turner (eds.): *Properties, Types and Meaning*. Volume II: Semantic Issues. 1989 ISBN 1-55608-069-7; Pb: 1-55608-070-0
Set ISBN (Vol. I + II) 1-55608-088-3; Pb: 1-55608-089-1
40. C. T. J. Huang and R. May (eds.): *Logical Structure and Linguistic Structure*. Cross-Linguistic Perspectives. 1991 ISBN 0-7923-0914-6; Pb: 0-7923-1636-3
41. M. J. Cresswell: *Entities and Indices*. 1990 ISBN 0-7923-0966-9; Pb: 0-7923-0967-7
42. H. Kamp and U. Reyle: *From Discourse to Logic*. Introduction to Modeltheoretic Semantics of Natural Language, Formal Logic and Discourse Representation Theory. 1993
ISBN 0-7923-2403-X; Student edition: 0-7923-1028-4
43. C. S. Smith: *The Parameter of Aspect*. (Second Edition). 1997
ISBN 0-7923-4657-2; Pb 0-7923-4659-9
44. R. C. Berwick (ed.): *Principle-Based Parsing*. Computation and Psycholinguistics. 1991
ISBN 0-7923-1173-6; Pb: 0-7923-1637-1
45. F. Landman: *Structures for Semantics*. 1991 ISBN 0-7923-1239-2; Pb: 0-7923-1240-6
46. M. Siderits: *Indian Philosophy of Language*. 1991 ISBN 0-7923-1262-7
47. C. Jones: *Purpose Clauses*. 1991 ISBN 0-7923-1400-X

# Studies in Linguistics and Philosophy

48. R. K. Larson, S. Iatridou, U. Lahiri and J. Higginbotham (eds.): *Control and Grammar*. 1992 ISBN 0-7923-1692-4
49. J. Pustejovsky (ed.): *Semantics and the Lexicon*. 1993 ISBN 0-7923-1963-X; Pb: 0-7923-2386-6
50. N. Asher: *Reference to Abstract Objects in Discourse*. 1993 ISBN 0-7923-2242-8
51. A. Zucchi: *The Language of Propositions and Events*. Issues in the Syntax and the Semantics of Nominalization. 1993 ISBN 0-7923-2437-4
52. C. L. Tenny: *Aspectual Roles and the Syntax-Semantics Interface*. 1994. ISBN 0-7923-2863-9; Pb: 0-7923-2907-4
53. W. G. Lycan: *Modality and Meaning*. 1994 ISBN 0-7923-3006-4; Pb: 0-7923-3007-2
54. E. Bach, E. Jelinek, A. Kratzer and B. H. Partee (eds.): *Quantification in Natural Languages*. 1995 ISBN Vol. I: 0-7923-3128-1; Vol. II: 0-7923-3351-9; set: 0-7923-3352-7; Student edition: 0-7923-3129-X
55. P. Lasersohn: *Plurality, Conjunction and Events*. 1995 ISBN 0-7923-3238-5
56. M. Pinkal: *Logic and Lexicon*. The Semantics of the Indefinite. 1995 ISBN 0-7923-3387-X
57. P. Øhrstrøm and P. F. V. Hasle: *Temporal Logic*. From Ancient Ideas to Artificial Intelligence. 1995 ISBN 0-7923-3586-4
58. T. Ogihara: *Tense, Attitudes, and Scope*. 1996 ISBN 0-7923-3801-4
59. I. Comorovski: *Interrogative Phrases and the Syntax-Semantics Interface*. 1996 ISBN 0-7923-3804-9
60. M. J. Cresswell: *Semantic Indexicality*. 1996 ISBN 0-7923-3914-2
61. R. Schwarzschild: *Pluralities*. 1996 ISBN 0-7923-4007-8
62. V. Dayal: *Locality in WH Quantification*. Questions and Relative Clauses in Hindi. 1996 ISBN 0-7923-4099-X
63. P. Merlo: *Parsing with Principles and Classes of Information*. 1996 ISBN 0-7923-4103-1
64. J. Ross: *The Semantics of Media*. 1997 ISBN 0-7923-4389-1
65. A. Szabolcsi (ed.): *Ways of Scope Taking*. 1997 ISBN 0-7923-4446-4; Pb: 0-7923-4451-0
66. P. L. Peterson: *Fact Proposition Event*. 1997 ISBN 0-7923-4568-1
67. G. Păaun: *Marcus Contextual Grammars*. 1997 ISBN 0-7923-4783-8
68. T. Gunji and K. Hasida (eds.): *Topics in Constraint-Based Grammar of Japanese*. 1998 ISBN 0-7923-4836-2
69. F. Hamm and E. Hinrichs (eds.): *Plurality and Quantification*. 1998 ISBN 0-7923-4841-9
70. S. Rothstein (ed.): *Events and Grammar*. 1998 ISBN 0-7923-4940-7
71. E. Hajičová, B. H. Partee and P. Sgall: *Topic-Focus Articulation, Tripartite Structures, and Semantic Content*. 1998 ISBN 0-7923-5289-0
72. K. von Heusinger and U. Egli (Eds.): *Reference and Anaphoric Relations*. 1999 ISBN 0-7923-6070-2
73. H. Bunt and R. Muskens (eds.): *Computing Meaning*. Volume 1. 2000 ISBN 0-7923-6108-3; Pb: ISBN 1-4020-0290-4
74. S. Rothstein (ed.): *Predicates and their Subjects*. 2000 ISBN 0-7923-6409-0
75. K. Kabakčiev: *Aspect in English*. A "Common-Sense" View of the Interplay between Verbal and Nominal Referents. 2000 ISBN 0-7923-6538-0
76. F. Landman: *Events and Plurality*. The Jerusalem Lectures. 2000 ISBN 0-7923-6568-2; Pb: 0-7923-6569-0
77. H. Bunt, R. Muskens and E. Thijsse: *Computing Meaning*. Volume 2. 2001 ISBN 0-7923-0175-4; Pb: 1-4020-0451-6

## Studies in Linguistics and Philosophy

78. R. Musan: *The German Perfect.* Its Semantic Composition and Its Interactions with Temporal Adverbials. 2002 ISBN 1-4020-0719-1
79. G. Grevendorf and G. Meggle (eds.): *Speech. Acts, Mind, and Social Reality.* Discussions with R. Searle. 2002 ISBN 1-4020-0853-8; Pb: 1-4020-0861-9
80. G.-J.M. Kruijff and R. T. Oehrle (eds.): *Resource-Sensitivity, Binding and Anaphora.* 2003 ISBN 1-4020-1691-3; Pb: 1-4020-1692-1
81. R. Elugardo and R. J. Stainton (eds.): *Ellipsis and Nonsentential Speech.* 2005 ISBN 1-4020-2299-9; Pb: 1-4020-2300-6

Further information about our publications on *Linguistics* is available on request.

springeronline.com